Minerals Warfare Redux

Minerals Warfare Redux

Securing America's Strategic Metals And Minerals Supply Chains

Eric Lyon

GW Strategies LLC
Tucson

Foreword

As I write this book, the U.S. is involved in an intensifying trade war with China. Part of this conflict involves the export and import of minerals, many of which have been identified as "critical" by American geologists. While the U.S. has moved forward with a concerted campaign to limit China's access to sophisticated semiconductor technology, Beijing has responded by restricting the very elements this technology is based on. Amazingly, U.S. leaders appear oblivious to the reality that China controls half of America's critical minerals supply chains. Equally perplexing is that Washington appears unprepared for Beijing's use of minerals warfare as a political and economic tool to advance their national interests.

At one time, the U.S. had a sense of its own critical minerals security and implemented an effective strategy to mitigate its supply chain weaknesses. However, this understanding has long been eroded and now the U.S. has a vulnerable critical minerals position while its chief competitor in the international system, China, has a much stronger one. The U.S. has seemingly forgotten that every aspect of its society is built on the mining of metals and minerals. And the more one examines the American military and economic colossus, the more one sees its clay feet.

This work looks at the U.S.' critical minerals history and how it went from a raw materials superpower to a minor player in a global game it became disinterested in. It also examines the evolution of the U.S.' critical minerals strategy and the ideas underpinning it, from the strong policies during WWII to the ineffective half measures that we see today. Integral to this examination is understanding the U.S.' perception of its mineral security, what China's view is of its own, and how the two compete in the same space. It is obvious that China has implemented a disciplined, whole-of-government critical minerals strategy while the U.S. is just realizing that it should have one.

As mentioned, we must look at the U.S.' critical minerals strategy in the context of China's since they are intertwined. As an indication of this, the U.S. majority-sources twenty-five of its fifty identified critical minerals from China itself. A significant reason for this enmeshed and vulnerable position is that the U.S.' political-economic system doesn't understand how to compete with the Chinese one. This is because Beijing has implemented a long-term strategy based on a Geopolitical Return on Investment that short-circuits America's own short-term, profit-based thinking.

To highlight the gulf between these ideologies, I'll mention a recent conversation I had with a colleague. We were discussing the recent Chinese export controls placed on various critical minerals in response to President Trump's April 2025 "Liberation Day" tariff increases. My colleague said we should respond by placing a Marine Corps division in Taiwan. I said, what does that have to do with China producing 99% of the world's gallium? That's like bringing a knife to a spelling bee - it has nothing to do with the contest at hand. But our conversation highlighted exactly how the U.S. has failed to grasp the nature of the match it must play.

This book goes beyond merely observing the U.S.' minerals security problem but also offers solutions. The metals and minerals environment is a complex one with many stakeholders, competing ideas, and external influences. If the U.S.' minerals insecurity problems were easy, they would have already been solved. However, ignoring the scope of the challenge and looking for superficial fixes won't put the U.S. in the much stronger position it needs. Only a comprehensive plan executed consistently over time and across administrations will bear fruit. This requires intelligent and tough choices based on expert understanding of the global flow of metals and minerals. Anything less is a hallucination.

This book is divided into two sections. I wrote the last part first which consists of fifty mini-chapters, each one providing an overview of a critical mineral identified by U.S. Geological Survey. Many of my observations in the first part are based on the many months of research conducted for these individual minerals. These individual overviews are meant to act as a reference for the reader while they bravely advance through the book and encounter the scores of different minerals discussed.

Now let's address the cover. The main picture is AI generated and shows a sword cutting through a rare earth deposit. The sword represents steel made from iron ore which is the foundational metal of every society. Although no less important today, this "old" metal is often overshadowed by specialty minerals like those used in batteries, magnets, and electronics. However, it's important not to forget what our current world was built from.

The sword also represents how an effective critical minerals strategy cuts through global uncertainty and a legion of obstacles to provide a country with the resource security it needs. To be successful, a strong strategy must be forged from the external pressures of international competition and then wielded expertly by wise leaders. Let this book contribute to the process of forging a much better critical minerals strategy.

Eric.

Table of Contents

Introduction

Hungry is the Beast

The *Shanghai Star*, a seventy-foot, dark blue and white trawler sat listlessly in the international waters of the Yellow Sea, rocking peacefully in the calm morning waters as the sun began to rise. The boat was positioned precisely thirty-six miles east of Hengsha Island at the mouth of Changjing River Estuary which formed the northern part of the Port of Shanghai, the busiest shipping center in the world. Two slender women in bright yellow bikinis, cherry red lipstick, and black sunglasses lay motionless in white lounge chairs on the deck, increasingly bathed in the comforting rays beaming earthward.

Suddenly, a deep roar began somewhere in the hull of the boat which quickly grew in intensity as the vessel shuddered from a violent explosion within. The roof of the bridge disintegrated as a projectile was hurled skywards, then another, and another. Although engulfed in flames, thick smoke, and burning debris, the two women remained motionless. If one were to look closer, they would see that the lounge chairs were welded to the surface of the deck and the women were actually mannequins, secured to the chairs with clear plastic zip-ties.

But let's rewind. The *Shanghai Star* began its final journey three days earlier from the eastern coast of Mindanao, the Philippines' large and southernmost island. Mindanao had been a hotbed of revolutionary activity for decades with a Maoist guerrilla movement beginning in 1969 and an Islamist rebellion in 1970. Both the New People's Army (Maoist) and Abu Sayyaf (Islamist) continued to wage their insurgencies and control turf as they ran shadow governments challenging the legitimacy of Manilla. Consequently, certain areas of Mindanao were ungoverned space where criminal activity was rampant and the government's reach was absent.

A week before, the trawler was moored at an isolated location where the local warlord was paid to keep people away and not ask questions. Work began quickly. The floors within the bridge of the ship were torn up and three silos were installed so that they were hidden from outside observation. The original bridge roof was removed and replaced with a thin plastic sheet and painted white to match the upper structure. Two well-maintained 400-hp diesel engines powered the trawler which had a six-thousand-mile range, although it would only be 1,500 miles to its ultimate destination.

The most difficult part of modifying the vessel was setting up the gear to remotely control the ship since there would be no one on it. This was a one-way operation with such geopolitical consequences that no human could be on the ship to be taken alive and questioned. No matter how tough and committed you were, over time and under pressure, everybody talked, especially when they started cutting off fingers. Automation would require the bare minimum of rudder and throttle control, 360-degree cameras, accurate global positioning, and remote missile launch initiation.

The remote-control system replicated human interaction with the ship's controls and was securely bolted in place and hard-wired into the onboard power system and backed up with a dozen daisy-chained lead-acid car batteries. Command and control of the remote system would be done via satellite communications (SATCOM) using Elon Musk's SpaceX Starlink system. Because Starlink was designed to provide SATCOM service to remote locations, it was perfect for connectivity during long-distance ocean travel.

The Iranian-made Fath 360 missiles were transferred on board during darkness which took several hours as they weighed almost a ton apiece and were seventeen feet long. Each one had a 330-lb high-explosives warhead and a 75-mile maximum range. The missile was medium-size, easily acquired on the Russian black market, and technologically simple. Once emplaced by crane in the three silos, they were wired for future remote ignition. The bridge easily concealed the three projectiles and the plastic roof was meant only to keep out sea spray and look authentic. During launch, the missiles would drive right through the flimsy roof.

The team would have to maneuver the ship for a 72-hour period of time. They conducted backwards planning where the ship would arrive at the chosen position after traveling the last 12-hour period of darkness. The first 24-hour block of travel put the trawler parallel to Luzon, the Philippines' northernmost island. The second leg put it east of Taiwan, while the third put it off the coast of Shanghai. An important question was how to travel from Mindanao to Shanghai without disruption, but this was much easier than one might think.

Tens of thousands of ships transited the South China Sea annually with 99% of them never being stopped, inspected, or boarded by anyone. A ship was almost always only placed under scrutiny when its cargo entered customs at port and then maybe. There was so much maritime traffic in the South China Sea that it was unmanageable by any one country. Therefore, the best tactic was to simply look and act like a normal ship and blend into the surrounding traffic. The *Shanghai Star* was originally a fishing trawler that had been converted to a pleasure yacht, a common and boring combination. The team would turn on the trawler's AIS (automatic identification system) twelve hours after it left Mindanao and then turn it off for the last twelve-hour leg.

Target Identification

After reaching its position off the coast, the team waited until 0900 hours when the Shanghai Stock Exchange officially opened for the day. No need to wait any longer than necessary. The distance from the trawler to the Stock Exchange was 72 miles, which would take the Fath 360 less than a minute to cover since its terminal velocity reached Mach 4 speeds. After the three missiles were launched and visually confirmed by the ship's cameras, the team detonated two separate 250-pound explosive charges, one positioned in the bow and one in the stern. With two massive holes blown in its hull, the *Shanghai Star* quickly took on water and sank. This would make it difficult but not impossible to locate and recover the boat.

The Fath 360s were solid fuel rockets guided by GLONASS (Global'naya Navigatsionnaya Sputnikovaya Sistema) backed up with an INS (inertial navigation system) which provided accuracy within 30 meters of the programmed target. While this was reasonable accuracy for a battlefield, it also meant one could miss a rather small hard target like an individual building. Consequently, there was a need for redundancy. The team considered using Shahed drones which were even easier to get and had considerably further range at 1,000 kilometers. But these were less accurate over distance and their largest warhead was smaller at 200 lbs.

The Shanghai Securities Exchange Building at 528 Pudhong Road was a beautiful structure built by the Canadian company WZMH Architects and completed in 1997. It proudly stood twenty-six floors tall with a square opening in the middle, giving it a distinctive design, much different than any of the other skyscrapers next to it. More importantly, the exchange was the third largest in the world with a $5.9 trillion market cap. According to Google Earth's imagery which uses the World Geodetic System WGS84 maintained by the National Geospatial Intelligence Agency, its coordinates were: 31°14'17"N latitude, 121°30'24"E longitude.

The first missile was off slightly, striking the ground near the southeast corner of the building, in between the Exchange and the adjacent skyscraper. The blast sent shrapnel, chunks of concrete, and shattered glass flying in all directions. Windows shattered on the ground level and second floors of both buildings, wounding or killing everyone within 25 meters of the point of impact. Several people walking outside were knocked over by the explosion, suffering shrapnel wounds and concussive brain injuries from the blast waves.

The next projectile hit seconds later and this one was dead on target, meaning it flew through the large square opening in the middle of the Exchange, striking the ground behind it, between the intended target and the building directly to the west. As with the first rocket, shrapnel burst in all directions shattering windows at different levels and injuring office workers who happened to be in the path of hot flying metal. Multiple pedestrians were injured and several cars on the adjacent street were struck with shrapnel.

The third and final missile struck the upper northern corner of the Exchange, ten windows over from the end of the building on the 19th floor. The blast blew the front of the structure off, one level above and below the point of impact and twenty feet on either side. The thirty or so employees in the immediate blast range died instantly, while another 100 received a range of injuries, from minor shrapnel wounds to traumatic brain injuries and various limbs torn off. Because of the relatively small size of the warhead and the fact that it struck so high on the building, there was no danger of a larger structural collapse beyond the several floors that absorbed the direct impact of the blast.

At exactly 0902 hours, the Shanghai Stock Exchange ceased all trading activity. Thousands of office workers poured out of the Exchange and adjacent buildings in fear of another strike. Scores of people were pushed down stairwells, trampled, crushed, and suffocated by the stampede in the frenzy to get outside. Overall, the combined missile attack killed about fifty people immediately, wounded another two hundred, and scores more would later succumb to their injuries. It was several minutes before emergency service personnel arrived onsite to assist the wounded and to control traffic.

At 0905 hours, 660 miles away in Beijing, Paramount Leader Xi Jinping was notified of the attack, causing him to immediately cancel the New Energy Vehicle roundtable strategy meeting he was sitting in so he could focus on the information that arrived in bits and pieces. Little was known other than that it appeared to be an intentional attack and not an accident like a gas pipe explosion. His instincts told him to wait and gather more information, balanced by the reality that the eventual response should be significant. His reputation as a competent leader would be on the line as would that of the entire Chinese Communist Party (CCP).

Meanwhile, the Exchange was cordoned off, people continued to be evacuated, and security personnel began investigating what caused the damage. It was obvious that three large projectiles hit the building and the immediate area in rapid succession, indicating some kind of missile volley. Forensic teams would later recover pieces of the projectiles that identified them as Iranian. The probable trajectory led investigators to look eastward, toward the coast. All resources were activated to determine the sequence of events including local police, the navy, closed circuit security cameras, and eyewitnesses. All security services were put on heightened alert.

The Response

At noon, Paramount Leader Xi addressed the Chinese nation on state television, providing an overview of what happened, asking the populace to remain calm, and assuring them that everything was being done that could be to help the unfortunate victims. He also began conditioning the populace for future action, stating that China's response would be resolute, and at a scale that the perpetrators of this crime could never imagine. The foundation for war had to be laid publicly. In the background, the search for what must have been a ship-launched missile attack began in earnest.

The People's Liberation Army Navy (PLAN) was put on immediate alert with three missions: increase protection of the Chinese coast, find the ship that probably launched the missiles, and prepare to forcibly secure the South China Sea in preparation for follow-on operations. No expense would be spared in locating the vessel responsible for the attack and all national security and government services would support the PLAN in doing so. Senior PLAN leaders were instructed to begin immediate preparations for a naval blockade and a maritime invasion of an unnamed country.

Xi Jinping and the Central Committee were under pressure to show a strong response, especially from the Shanghai political faction, not just because of the location of the attack, but because they wanted to move Xi out and get one of their own in power. Regardless of the attack's ultimate origination, this was the provocation Beijing needed to move on Taiwan. Chinese intelligence surmised this could have been an attack from Taiwanese hardliners to provoke a war between China and the U.S. which would ultimately weaken the CCP. Xi understood that the national response had to be significant but also not play into a global war with Washington.

The PLAN eventually found the location of the *Shanghai Star* and through a combination of trajectory analysis, satellite imagery, AIS data sifting, customs and sales records, were able to determine the identity of the vessel. The ship was at one time owned by a Taiwanese businessman and then sold successively to a Japanese, South Korean, and finally a Chinese owner. However, the last three owners did not appear to ever exist, merely being fake personas to launder possession of the boat. So, who was actually behind the attack? It was either a nation's intelligence service or a nonstate actor, probably the latter. Regardless, action had to be taken and the gears of revenge were already in motion.

Xi Jinping addressed the Chinese nation and the international community on state television. He placed the blame squarely on Taiwan as an intentional provocation and announced Beijing would take immediate unilateral action which included a complete naval blockade of the island nation. All goods from South Korea and Japan would also be intercepted and turned back. The Chinese North Sea Fleet stationed in Qingdao was already moving in position to form a naval picket line to block trade from Tokyo and Seoul. The East Sea Fleet in Dinghai was ordered to enact a total blockade of Taiwan.

The PLAN was also given orders to conduct a series of covert operations to cut the undersea communication cables connecting Taiwan to the mainland. They were put on standby to conduct the same follow-on missions against Japan, the Philippines, Guam, and Hawaii. The PLAN would use an unmanned mini-submarine equipped with a diamond-coated grinding wheel operating at 1,600 rpm. The cutting device had already been successfully tested at depths of 4,000 meters and could cut through the armored deep-sea cables used by countries for their communications and data transfer needs. The West had already proven incapable of responding to previous "grayzone" attacks on European undersea cables by Russia and this would be no different.

The U.S. filed a resolution in protest through the United Nations security council which was promptly blocked by both China and Russia as Washington knew it would. The U.N. structure rarely allowed for collective or even just action as competing interests ensured bureaucratic paralysis. This time was no different. The BRICS countries (Brazil, Russia, India, China, South Africa) voiced support for Beijing's blockade while the U.S. and G7 opposed it. The western countries in the G20 opposed China's unilateral action but this was irrelevant as the BRICS countries were all G20 members and supported Beijing's aggressive moves.

The U.S. 7th Fleet stationed in Yokosuka, Japan was brought to full alert as were the Japanese, South Korean, and Taiwanese navies which, combined, surpassed the size of the PLAN. China rapidly moved its East Sea Fleet around Taiwan, creating a 50-ship ring with orders to fire on and destroy any vessel attempting to breach the blockade. The Taiwanese navy and land forces remained on 100% alert, in defensive positions, with orders not to breach the blockade or to open fire unless fired upon first.

The U.S. Secretary of Defense called his Chinese counterpart and stated that U.S. naval vessels would not recognize China's naval pickets of South Korea and Japan and would ensure free passage of commerce. Simultaneously, the President of the U.S. opened discussions with the Chinese Premier reference the Taiwan blockade. The U.S. made the decision that it would not attempt to breach the Chinese blockade but would shadow the Chinese navy until further decisions were made by the National Command Authority. In other words, China's blockade would remain in place while the U.S. and China pursued diplomatic avenues to avoid an all-out war.

Critical Minerals Warfare

While the two opposing groups faced off against each other in the South China Sea, Beijing made the decision to squeeze its opponents' economic, industrial, and military foundations using a more subtle tool - critical minerals. Specifically, the Ministry of Commerce (MOFCOM) added all fifty of the U.S.' critical minerals to its list of materials requiring an export license. MOFCOM received direction from the Central Committee not to approve any of these exports for the U.S., Taiwan, South Korea, or Japan until further notice.

Sixteen of these critical minerals included the group called Rare Earth Elements (REE). China domestically mined most REE in the world by volume

(68%) and imported even more for midstream processing, establishing a global monopoly where 95% of REE passed through the country. In fact, up until the end of 2023, the U.S.' only REE mining operation in California sent 100% of its mined material to China for processing and reimport. The halt of all REE to America and its Asian intermediaries that would resell them to the U.S. had significant economic repercussions.

Most American's didn't realize that eight of the seventeen REE were required for their technology dependent society for items that included cell phones, hard drives, industrial robots, speakers, electric motors, and wind turbines. These minerals included cerium, dysprosium, gadolinium, lanthanum, neodymium, praseodymium, samarium, and terbium. The U.S. imported directly from China 91% of its Neodymium-Iron-Boron (NdFeB) magnets and 73% of its samarium-cobalt (SmCo) magnets used in EV motors, wind turbines, and guided missile systems. The U.S. national stockpile held four months of reserves for NdFeB magnet production and six months of SmCo magnet production. For the other REE elements used to enhance these magnets' performance, the U.S. held no reserves at all.

All battery minerals were also cut off to the U.S. and its Asian allies which included lithium, nickel, cobalt, manganese, and graphite which were needed in all kinds of batteries to include EVs and residential and utility energy storage systems. Although the U.S. imported most of its lithium, nickel, manganese, and cobalt needs, less than 1% came from China. However, graphite was a different story with the U.S. importing 64% of its synthetic needs directly from China and almost half of its natural graphite needs. For these five battery minerals, the U.S. held virtually no reserves in its national stockpile.

More importantly, China also banned the export of all lithium-ion batteries (LIB) which had significantly more impact because they had developed a LIB production monopoly. The U.S. imported 91% of its LIBs from China, Taiwan, South Korea, and Japan, with most coming directly from Beijing. Beijing's LIB policy meant Taiwan, South Korea, and Japan's battery plants located in China were all frozen and could only supply the China market – all exports to their home markets were banned.

Because almost 100% of the world's graphite anode material (the negative terminal of the battery) was made in China, this effectively shut down global LIB production outside China. China didn't have to control the world's battery mineral supply chains, they just needed a stranglehold on midstream LIB production. While some American's thought they "made" batteries in their country, all they really did was assemble the component parts.

Of the fifty critical minerals the U.S. had identified as crucial to its national economy and defense industrial base, half of them were majority imported from China, either directly or indirectly. Of these twenty-five, the U.S. had six-month reserves in the national defense stockpile for just two of them and a one-year reserve for another two. Despite the many years of warnings, the U.S. had never taken its critical minerals security seriously and was now confronted with a catastrophic disruption of its supply chains. Along with the magnet and battery vulnerability, the U.S. would soon experience shortages in specialty alloys for its aerospace industry, materials for the medical sector, and many key components for laptops, cellphones, and semiconductors.

The President of the United States immediately convened an emergency meeting of the principal members of the Strategic and Critical Materials Board comprised of the Secretary of State, Secretary of Commerce, Secretary of Energy, Secretary of the Interior, and the Assistant Secretary of Defense for Industrial Base Policy, who was the board chairman. While no one had any detailed knowledge of critical minerals, they knew it was a topic of concern and had advanced different projects under their purview.

Although the SECDEF was the presidentially designated National Defense Stockpile Manager, he was not a member of the board and was thus absent. The most knowledgeable person in the room should have been the Secretary of the Interior because U.S. Geological Survey was one of their offices. However, neither the Secretary nor any of the officials responsible for the country's national minerals security had read any of the scores of annual reports highlighting the U.S.' growing critical minerals dependence on China.

It didn't take long for the Board to realize that their complex bureaucracy had failed them and in fact provided no critical minerals security for the country at all. The national defense stockpile existed in name only and the government agencies responsible for its maintenance had failed to do their jobs. In just one example, the country had less than one week's supply of dysprosium which was used in nuclear control rods and permanent magnets.

Clearly, no one on the board understood how the critical minerals acquisition system worked. How could this have happened? They agreed to reconvene in three days and come back with better answers as to how they got in such a predicament and what they should do moving forward. Meanwhile, China's critical minerals export ban remained in place as the U.S.' strategic commodities continued to dwindle. Beijing had consistently played a strong minerals hand, providing them global political leverage while the U.S. leadership had stumbled its way into potential economic disaster.

This is a fictional story based on real circumstances.

Chapter 1

Minerals Warfare Redux

"No single thing better measures the industrial standing of a nation than its use of metal."

– Victor S. Clark, American Economist

Introduction

All modern industrial states are mineral dependent societies as everything humankind makes is either mined or grown. Every building, every car, every cell phone, and every computer is a product of mining. Anything made from metal, like trains, boats, and planes, come from minerals extracted from our Earth. The most mundane things that we take for granted in everyday life, from pens and paperclips to soda cans and zippers, come from a mine. And any natural product we use, like wood and clothing, was made from tools as the result of mining. In fact, every manufacturing process used today only exists because of mining.

From early on, organized societies recognized the importance of minerals critical to their development, economy, and military capability. The Roman Empire capitalized on the Iron Age to ruthlessly exploit metal to carve out their Mediterranean kingdom.[1] Minerals were crucial for driving civilization forward and thus more had to be discovered, safeguarded, and acquired from abroad, either through trade or conquest. Importantly, the inability to harness minerals to advance a society could prove devastating as seen by the European invasion, conquest, and subjugation of the Western hemisphere societies beginning around the year 1500.

Although harnessing minerals has been crucial to a society's success or failure, modern governments often put little thought into developing a com-

1 The European Iron Age was from approximately 1300 BC to 100 BC and was preceded by the Bronze Age – bronze is made from copper and tin.

prehensive strategy to ensure their own minerals security. Some nations took ad hoc measures to secure access to mineral resources, like the British Empire 1600-1960, but rarely did they develop a wholistic approach. Serious thought about the development of a critical minerals strategy emerged only after World War I when the major industrialized powers began to understand the importance of minerals necessary for their increasingly mechanized economies and war machines. However, by the time World War II began in 1939, no single developed country had achieved absolute minerals security.

The U.S. provides an example of how typical modern nation states have lurched forward haphazardly in an attempt to secure their critical minerals supply chains. Since the end of World War II, the U.S. has shown periodic fits of increasing its mineral security and then much longer periods of apathy. Curiously, the U.S. has recognized its increasing mineral insecurity over time while simultaneously standing on the sidelines allowing it to happen. The primary reason for this absurd reality has been the U.S.' own economic process running separate from and parallel to its attempts at developing a national mineral strategy. In other words, profits prevailed over security.

Because the two are disconnected, the dominant economic process has undercut minerals security. In this case, the U.S. has mostly accepted the idea of free market economic principles and global efficiencies (i.e. allowing other countries to produce minerals at a lower price and then purchasing them through trade.) Consequently, the U.S. has progressively closed its own domestic mining industry as it imports cheaper mineral products abroad. Over time, these domestic mining assets have deteriorated or been sold off to the point that the U.S. has lost the ability to use many of its own minerals.

Over the past two millennia, human society has become more complex with advances in both knowledge and technology allowing humankind to extract more minerals to create increasingly sophisticated products. To put this in perspective, the Roman Empire ran mostly on just seven metals: iron, tin, lead, zinc and precious metals (gold, silver, copper). Rome had no need for battery minerals, magnet metals, catalytics for cars or Rare Earth Elements used in cell phones. Our modern societies have evolved very complex manufacturing processes which correspondingly require an increasing variety of minerals to feed them.

Because these mineral needs are so diverse, no single country has the needed materials within their own geographic boundaries to be self-sufficient. For example, the U.S. has no tantalum deposits which is used in electronics and superalloys. Thus, the more complex the minerals needs of a country, the more minerals insecure they become. Countries must either acquire new territory to secure these minerals or more realistically, today, they trade for them. And if one country in the world can extract a mineral cheaper than anyone else, this makes all other competing efforts uneconomic in comparison. Although the U.S. has a diverse mineralogy, most are uneconomic to extract such as cesium, vanadium, and tungsten.

Since the U.S. as a society has experienced increasing levels of national wealth, it has suffered from accompanying inflation. This wealth/inflation trap means poorer countries in the international system with lower inflation and costs outcompete the U.S. in the mineral production space. The combination of the U.S.' increased wealth and adherence to free market principles has contributed the most to its own mineral insecurity. The U.S., in pursuit of economic growth, has offshored much of its underperforming mining capability which necessarily creates foreign mineral dependencies.

This reality must be balanced with the understanding that all minerals are finite resources and become scarcer over time with continued extraction. Overall, humanity does a poor job moderating its consumption of minerals. This is because it functions with the mentality that if we need more we will get more. However, this is not true and the result of our boundless consumption over time, mathematically speaking, is minerals extinction. Hence, every year we increase our collective mineral insecurity through resource depletion with some countries running out before others.

Recently, the U.S. has found itself increasingly locked into a minerals resource battle with China. This began in earnest in 2001 when China joined the World Trade Organization and began growing its economy at a rapid pace. Hand in hand with this increasing economic power, China has sought to challenge the U.S.' own leading position in the international system. An integral part of China's strategy is securing the minerals needed to grow its economy while challenging the U.S.' own critical minerals supply chains. Consequently, Beijing constructed critical minerals monopolies in several sectors while the U.S. remained seemingly oblivious to the growing imbalance of relative global minerals power.

While China pursued an obvious and comprehensive critical minerals strategy, the U.S. did not even know a contest for limited resources had begun. Only in 2017, beginning with the first Trump administration, did Washington display a gradual interest in its own critical minerals insecurity in relation to China's much stronger position. Although the Trump administration began conditioning its own apathetic bureaucracy for possible future action, it did nothing to change the critical minerals power imbalance with China. It was only under the Biden Administration, beginning in 2021, that the U.S. began the necessary action to address its critical minerals insecurity. Even then, it would take years to develop any tangible impacts.

However, securing a nation's critical minerals supply chains to an acceptable level is at least a decade-long endeavor. This effort requires strong national leadership, a coherent strategy, government subsidization of the domestic mining industry, the creation of a national stockpile, mandatory recycling, and technological innovation and investment in the mineral extraction space. While the Biden administration made huge strides in some areas of critical minerals security, other areas remained starkly unaddressed. At the conclusion of 2024, the U.S. had started firmly down the path to improved critical minerals security but was still much closer to the beginning of its journey than the end. An important question for the 2025 Trump Administration was how they would improve on the initial critical minerals security momentum they started in 2017.

Lex Metallis Dicta: Lessons from the Roman Empire

To them I set neither goals for their fortunes nor seasons, I granted rule without limit.

- Jupiter, on the boundless power he granted Rome (from the Aeneid)

One of the key elements of Roman power was its ability to effectively harness metals to grow and sustain its empire. Roman society required a wide variety of metal tools for constructing its cities, building ships, farming, and for everyday life. From the perspective of practical military conquest, a single Roman legion required an estimated 38 tons of iron to equip it with short swords, daggers, spear and arrowheads, shields, helmets, and body armor.[2] Especially important to an empire built on commerce was the acquisition of valuable metals to produce coins used as established currency for domestic and international trade.

2 Lang, Janet. "Roman iron and steel: A review, Materials and Manufacturing Processes." 2017.

From early on, the growing Roman state found a source of iron on the small island of Elba which produced metal for Etruscan society as early as the 6th Century BC.[3] The Romans exploited the iron deposits there to such an extent that they denuded the island of all tree life to make charcoal for blast furnaces, requiring them to import wood from the Italian peninsula. Specifically, Rome ran the Rio Marina iron smelting operation on the eastern end of the island as well as the nearby Populonia and Follonica smelting operations across the Baratti Bay in Italy that were fed iron ore imported from the island.[4] In total, an estimated two million tons of iron were extracted from Elba.[5] Early access to large quantities of iron allowed Rome to build its society, equip its armies, and seize more territories and resources through conquest.

This expansion included the Alps, Spain, Gaul, Dalmatia, and Britain which enabled the Empire to acquire higher quality steels used in tools, mining, and warfare. Additionally, Rome imported high-quality steel products (including unworked ingots in bulk) from India which had an established iron and steel industry. India was not only blessed with iron ideal for making steel, but it could also ship its product rather cheaply to the Persian Empire. Although ancient trade between the Roman Empire and China is well established, Rome most likely did not import iron products from there as their average quality did not justify the expense of overland transportation.[6]

Because Roman currency consisted primarily of metal coins with gold and silver content, the conquest of new territories with these deposits was important. Rome began the conquest of the Piedmont Alps in northwestern Italy during the 3rd Century BC which brought existing gold mines under its control. From 26-25 BC, Augustus conquered northwest Spain that allowed for the exploitation of additional gold and silver mines, providing a continuing source of coinage through at least the 3rd Century AD. Similarly, the conquest of Arabia Petraea by Emperor Trajan in 106 AD brought copper production from the Phaeno mines (modern day Jordan) under Roman control through the 6th century AD.[7]

3 Greek peoples lived on the island and extracted iron as early as the 10th Century BC and named it *Aethalia*, meaning "smoky" from the fumes of the many iron ore smelting furnaces that operated even then.

4 Benvenuit, M., et al. "Experimental smelting of iron ores from Elba Island (Tuscany, Italy)." Journal of Archaeological Science, April 6, 2016.

5 Healy. "Mining and Metallurgy in the Greek and Roman World."

6 Schoff, Wilfred H. "The Eastern Iron trade of the Roman Empire." Journal of the American Oriental Society, pp. 224-239, 1915.

7 Wilson, Andrew Ian. "The metal supply of the Roman empire." Journal of Roman

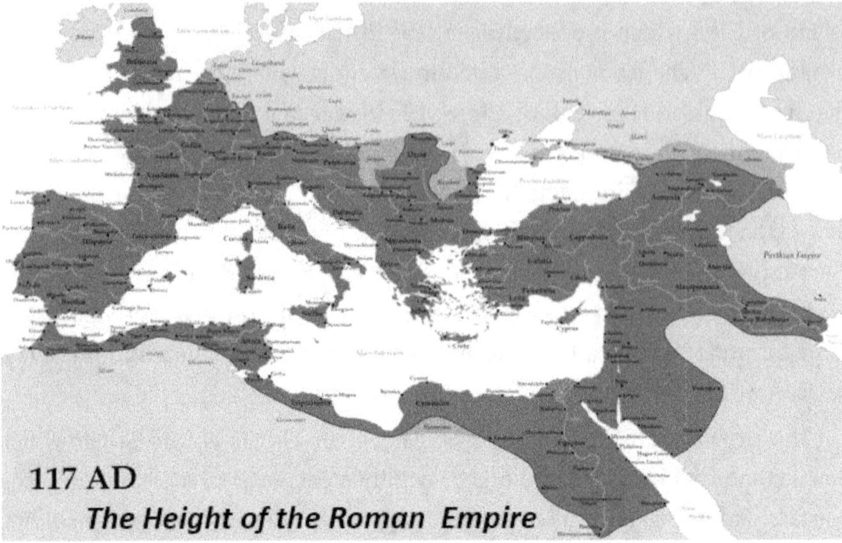

117 AD
The Height of the Roman Empire

The Roman Empire was a consumer society which required more and more resources to sustain itself. This meant the Empire had to continue to expand and bring new resources under its control if it wanted mineral security. Once this expansion ceased, the Empire relied more and more on trade to secure its critical minerals as its own finite resources became diminished through continuing consumption. By 117 AD, under the reign of Emperor Trajan, the Roman Empire reached its geographical zenith. The Empire circled the entire Mediterranean Sea, occupying most of Europe, the coastal regions of North Africa, and Asia Minor (consisting of modern-day Türkiye and parts of the former Persian Empire).

In 395 AD, in a sign of its internal fragmentation and decline, the Roman Empire formally split into Eastern and Western Empires with the Western Empire being the weaker of the two. While the Roman Empire could provide itself with mineral security through conquest, a superior enemy could take it away. In 410 AD, Rome permanently abandoned Britain as it focused on fighting the Visigoths, losing its sources of gold, silver, copper, iron, lead, and tin. This led to cascading events where the Western Roman Empire began to cede territories in Gaul and Hispania to invading Germanic tribes and then collapsed as a coherent political entity in 476 AD. Lost with this were the hundreds of mines that had produced valuable metals for coinage and durable goods.

Archaeology, 2007.

The Eastern Roman Empire, also referred to as the Byzantine Empire, continued in various forms until the final fall of Constantinople in 1453. Since the Empire lost its direct control of, and thus the profits from, the mines in Western Europe, it required a strong trade balance to buy the minerals it needed. This geographic reality also placed more importance on the eastern mines it still controlled in modern-day Cyprus, Jordan, Bosnia, and Türkiye. Particularly valuable were the gold and silver mines in the border state of Armenia which Constantinople fought several wars over to secure. However, just as the expanding Roman Empire provided it with increased mineral wealth and power, the declining Byzantine Empire became increasingly weaker as is it lost its remaining mines to competing powers.

At its height, Rome grappled with the challenge of managing a vast, diverse mining enterprise to support a society that demanded more metal resources. Most mining operations were owned by the State (i.e. the Emperor) although Rome frequently contracted private companies to run them.[8] Rome also allowed provincial governments to operate state mines to reduce administrative costs of the central government. Wholly owned private mining operations were allowed and taxed accordingly. Often, Roman military units ran mining operations because they provided needed security, could organize and control workers which included slave labor, and their blacksmiths had technical know-how from crafting their own armor and weapons.[9]

Rome published and refined its mining laws over time as required to meet the needs of the Empire, including the *Lex Metalli Dicta (*the Law of Metal).[10] From an overarching perspective, Rome regulated production across the enterprise in different provinces to prevent one operation from pricing out another. In an example of this, Rome limited how much lead Britain produced because it put pressure on Spain's own production, which was much harder, and thus more expensive, to extract. While this was undoubtably a political decision to mollify wealthy Spanish-Roman elites, it discouraged lead "dumping" in Britain and ensured continuous production from multiple regions, thus providing resource security.

8 Privately owned mines were often seized by the state to harness the resources for the Empire and became *metalla publica.*

9 Edmondson, J. C. "Mining in the Later Roman Empire and beyond: Continuity or Disruption?" Journal of Roman Studies, Vol. 79, 1989.

10 Various Roman leaders published mining laws at different times in history with some regionally focused. There was also a *lex ferrariarum* that may have regulated the Empire's overall iron mining industry but a comprehensive reference has yet to be recovered.

Mining operations themselves were organized endeavors with direct oversight from Rome. As mentioned, mines were often owned by the state but then leased to wealthy businessmen (Equestrians) who paid a tax to cover Imperial administrative costs. Regardless of who owned or operated a mine, a senior Imperial official (*Procurator Metallorum*), oversaw the operations and ensured 50% of paid duties were sent to the Imperial treasury (*fiscus*).[11] The Procurator oversaw engineers that monitored day-to-day operations and an administrative staff that inspected provincial mines to ensure they followed published mining regulations. Imperial labor laws allowed slaves, convicted criminals, and free contracted laborers to work in the mines, although their numbers were regulated by the Procurator.[12]

Rome also experienced the problem of growing metals consumption from dwindling resources, requiring the Empire to make difficult decisions. For example, the gold content by weight in the Empire's minted coins dropped from 7.3 grams in 200 AD, to 4.79 grams in 250 AD, and then just 1 gram in 265 AD. This devaluation of Rome's currency was likely due to declining production from Spain's gold mines. To reverse this trend and increase the flow of precious metals for minted coinage, Constantine I and subsequent rulers began closing pagan temples in the 4th Century AD, seizing their gold and silver ornaments. However, looting the temples and melting down their metals was obviously only a temporary solution for Rome's currency problems.[13]

By fully embracing the Iron Age, the Roman Empire became the most sophisticated and powerful society of its era. The Empire understood the value of mining early on and subsequently organized, regulated, and protected it. For Rome, iron was its most critical mineral which enabled it to maximize its acquisition and exploitation of other metals like lead, gold, silver, and copper. The Empire's annual consumption of iron products at its peak was estimated at 82,500 tons.[14] Samples from the Greenland ice core indicate Rome ran a massive mining enterprise, the largest since the beginning of the Iron Age.[15] One

11 The Procurator Metallorum worked for the provincial Procurator and was responsible for collecting taxes from all mining operations.

12 Elkington, David. "Roman Mining Law." Mining History: Peak District Mines Historical Society, Volume 10, Number 4, 1988.

13 Wilson, Andrew. "The Metal Supply of the Roman Empire." Journal of Roman Archeology, 2007.

14 Sim, David and Isabel Ridge. "Iron for the Eagles: The Iron Industry of Roman Britain." The History Press, 2002.

15 McConnel, Joseph R., et al. "Lead pollution recorded in Greenland ice indicates Eu-

cannot overstate the importance and impact of metal on Rome's everyday life and its trajectory as a cohesive geopolitical force.

Although the Empire understood how important minerals were to its economy and war machine, it periodically suffered incredible lapses of complacency and insecurity. For example, in 175 AD, a Moorish force invaded Spain from North Africa, crossing the Gibraltar Strait. While the Empire had thirty legions under arms at that time, only one was stationed in Numidia (now coastal Algeria) with the next two closest units 1,600 miles marching distance away in Alexandria. Spain itself only had one legion because it was a pacified province firmly under Roman control. Particularly vulnerable were the lucrative Rio Tinto mining operations in Huelva, only 120 miles from the strait. The raid disrupted mining operations for several years and interrupted the Empire's downstream flow of precious metals used for its imperial currency.

The Roman Empire thrived mainly on the exploitation of just seven metals with the most important being iron. Rome conquered new lands to grow its mineral wealth and equip and maintain its legions. The army often managed mining operations because it could keep slave laborers in line.

Rome was also a victim of its own greed, spurred on by wealthy elites who benefited disproportionately by exploiting the Empire's uneven social and political structure. Thus, there was constant pressure on the mining system to produce more gold and silver for jewelry and ornamental products. Also, as the Empire became weaker and its people no longer valued service in its own armed forces, Rome spent large sums to pay foreign armies not to attack it, instead of destroying them in combat. Over time, Roman elites developed the

ropean emissions tracked plagues, wars, and imperial expansion during antiquity." PNAS, May 14, 2018.

self-serving groupthink that the Empire existed for their narrow interests and that it could always get more resources. Reality showed that resources were limited and required conservation was shown by the need to seize and melt down pagan religious ornaments. Also, coinage in circulation was sequestered, melted down and reissued.

While the Roman Empire published mining policies, it never developed a comprehensive critical minerals strategy. Many policies were instituted to regulate mining labor because the industry suffered from high turnover rates due to the inherently brutal nature of the work. Also, Rome intentionally exploited resources in its provinces while prohibiting mining on the Italian peninsula to keep large numbers of potentially rebellious slaves from the capital. Generally, Rome allowed the free market to guide the mining enterprise where operations had to prove economic to keep running. However, Rome was also known to regulate mining production if special interest groups pressured it to do so.

While professional government staffs oversaw mining in the provinces, there was no central office in Rome to coordinate mining across the Empire. Also, there was no published guidance to mitigate the regional deforestation that occurred to supply the charcoal to run smelters. This was a growing problem since it took 1.7 million tons of charcoal a year just to support the Empire's annual iron production.[16] Rome supported supply-side economics as opposed to a demand-side approach, in that the Empire was expected to always provide more mineral resources as opposed to moderating consumption behavior. Because the Empire did not recognize the need for a strategic minerals stockpile to insulate itself from disruption, it periodically suffered from supply-side shocks.

While just one of many forces impacting the Roman Empire's rise and fall, metals and minerals were critical to its trajectory as a political entity. Rome's rise went hand in hand with gaining access to new critical minerals as did its decline as it lost control of the same. The Empire simultaneously understood the importance of its mineral resources while regularly forfeiting productive mines to its enemies and never regaining them. Rome adopted the mentality that they could always secure more minerals through trade even if this meant reducing their own wealth and undermining their fiscal system. Because the Empire never adopted a comprehensive critical minerals security strategy, they grew accustomed to living with minerals insecurity and the resulting crisis management when forced to by circumstances.

16 Sim and Ridge. "Iron for the Eagles." The History Press, 2002.

The Iron Age in North America

While Europe experienced the Iron Age as early 1,000 BC, North American natives were only introduced to iron and steel around the year 1500 AD when the European countries began their colonial invasions. The native societies mainly used stone and some copper for their tools. While they worked with hematite, an iron oxide mineral, they never learned the crucial step of smelting it into iron. Because they lacked the necessary iron technology, native Americans never developed large-scale farming, or built cities, and had no industrial military capability. They were ripe for exploitation by the highly developed European countries whose societies were built on the exploitation of metals from organized mining.

Over the centuries of colonization, native Americans were introduced to metal goods through trade with different European settlers. Natives acquired metal arrowheads, fishhooks, knives, axes, other tools of all kinds, and eventually rifles. The introduction of metals to North America was uneven and depended on what European country sent an expedition and to where. The eastern seaboard of what is now the United States was first to be exposed to metals through trade. Because these native societies were relatively isolated, metal products often remained local, explaining why other native groups never acquired them. This explains why European traders pushing into California in the 1840s found little evidence of metal use among the regional natives.[17]

It is crucial to understand that although natives were able to obtain finished metal products, they never learned how to mine or manufacture them at scale themselves. Because Europeans controlled the means of metal production, both from a practical physical and a knowledge aspect, natives never developed a mining and metals capability. Natives remained wholly dependent on their European conquerors who would never provide them the metals technology or resulting products at scale to effectively challenge their expansion into the "New World". Native American societies were gradually immersed in metal products which changed every aspect of their lives but they were merely end-users, not masters, of their Iron Age.

Until the United States' independence from Great Britian in 1783, the original thirteen colonies provided their mother country very little in the form of metallic wealth. It is true that early English explorers and colonists traveling

17 Mason, Otis T. "Introduction of the Iron Age into America." American Anthropologist, Vol. 9, No. 6, June 1896.

to the eastern United States in the 1500s and afterward were interested in discovering valuable mineral deposits and actively searched for them. However, the U.S. eastern seaboard simply did not hold the gold and silver deposits to exploit, so England never replicated the success Portugal and Spain had in their plundering of the native South American societies.

Industrial metals like iron ore were not found in economically viable deposits. Early Virginia settlers discovered bog iron and even shipped one hundred tons of this to England by 1612 for smelting into usable iron. Since the iron extraction was done by human labor from shallow open pits and the intermediate product then had to be shipped across the Atlantic for refining, it was not deemed worth continuing. In 1622, in another setback, an iron blast furnace operation in the Jamestown settlement was attacked and destroyed by Powhatan natives.[18]

After the colonies defeated England in the American Revolution, the newly established United States of America found itself with limited deposits of useful minerals and a rudimentary mining industry focused primarily on pig iron production.[19] Required metals were imported from established European companies which necessarily meant the U.S. experienced extreme foreign minerals dependency. The U.S.' position only improved with the nation's expansion westward to the Pacific coast, the introduction of the American Industrial Revolution in the 1790s, and advances in both mining and manufacturing technology.

The U.S.' continued westward expansion was the chief reason for its access to materials required to meet its growing industrial demands and its accompanying increased minerals security. Just like the Roman Empire two millennia before, the U.S. conquered new territories, increasing its minerals wealth. The single largest acquisition was the Louisiana Purchase of 1803 where the U.S. bought the middle third of the country from France, doubling its existing territory. This freed the U.S. from foreign competition, allowing the U.S. to continue moving west as it subjugated the native American tribes.

Napolean's sale of this territory much larger than France itself was just the start. In 1818, Britain ceded to the U.S. portions of North Dakota and Minnesota along the Canadian border. Then, Spain ceded Florida and the panhandle

18 Heuvel. *Early Attempts of English Mineral Exploration in North America.*

19 Pig iron is a crude product and considered an intermediate step in the process of making steel.

in 1819. In rapid order, the U.S. annexed Texas in 1845, secured the Oregon Territory from Britain in 1846, bought most of the Southwest from Mexico in 1848, and then more with the Gadsden Purchase in 1854. The massive purchase of Alaska from Russia came in 1867 and Hawaii came under U.S. control in 1898. By 1900, a surging U.S. had greatly increased its geographic size and the minerals under its control by ruthlessly exploiting both European and native weakness.

The water-powered Saugus Iron Works in Massachusetts, several miles north of Boston. This was the colonies' first integrated iron operation but was only in business from 1646-1670 because it could not return a profit.

Iron Age 2.0: The American Industrial Revolution

By the middle of the 19th century the political consequences of the industrial revolution were manifest. They indicated that the economic control of the earth's resources would fall to the great manufacturing nations.

– Victor S. Clark

The American Industrial Revolution was a period from 1793 until the end of World War II in 1945. The first date marks the year Samuel Slater's first water-powered textile mill came online in Pawtucket, RI. The second date is when the U.S. ended its massive wartime armaments production, although U.S. manufacturing continued to grow aggressively into the 1950s. Midway through this economic explosion, in 1890, the U.S. became the world's biggest economy. Integral to the Revolution and U.S. wealth accumulation was its domestic supply of and ready access to large amounts of iron ore.[20] No other mineral was singularly so important to the nation's growth and a secure supply chain ensured uninterrupted growth.

20 U.S. Geological Survey estimates U.S. iron ore resources at 110 billion tons.

Like the Roman Empire, the U.S. was blessed with large deposits of iron ore, the most critical metal for growing and modernizing its society. As mentioned, small-scale iron ore production was distributed amongst the original colonies and remained an eastern seaboard industry until the late 1840s. This was due to established supply chain dependencies, the U.S.' relatively low level of manufacturing, and the ability to import cheap metals from European countries (like England) with mature export systems. However, these dynamics changed with the discovery of significant iron ore deposits in the Lake Superior region and subsequent mass production.

Early on, the U.S. produced low volumes of iron with an estimated 30,000 tons a year before the American Revolution.[21] In 1810, this increased modestly to 54,000 tons and then shot up six-fold to 300,000 tons in 1840. The first iron ore mining in the Lake Superior region came from the Marquette Iron Range in Michigan which began in 1846. The U.S. required ever growing amounts of iron and steel to match its industrial revolution, with iron production in 1847 exploding to 800,000 tons.[22] For the one hundred years from 1855-1955, the Michigan mining enterprise produced 2.7 million tons of iron ore annually.[23]

In neighboring Wisconsin, iron ore was extracted from the Gogebic Iron Range at scale beginning in 1884 but in much lower volumes than neighboring Michigan, averaging just 845,000 tons annually from 1884-1955.[24] (Michigan's last iron operation closed in 1982). But the largest iron ore find was in Minnesota's Mesabi Iron Range which began extraction operations in 1892. While other regions in the U.S. produced iron ore, the Superior Lake region provided 84% of total production through the year 1955 with three billion tons.[25] Because of these large deposits positioned within its territory, the U.S. achieved iron ore self-sufficiency throughout its industrial revolution.

The biggest test for U.S. manufacturing and steel consumption came during World War II when American defense production surpassed any other country, allied or enemy. At the height of U.S. wartime production in 1942, the U.S. produced 105 million tons of iron ore while consuming just 102 million tons, providing a surplus. In 1945, the U.S. produced 80 million tons of steel which was more than 60% of world production. This trend continued through

21 Temin, Peter. "Iron and Steel in Nineteenth Century America." Cambridge, 1964.

22 Skaggs. *Lukens 1850-1870.*

23 Reed, Robert C. "Michigan Iron Mines." State of Michigan, 1957.

24 Carr & Dalton. *Iron-Ore Resources of the United States.*

25 Carr & Dalton. *Iron-Ore Resources of the United States.*

the 1950s where the U.S. consumed an average of 110 million tons of iron ore annually from 1950-1955, double that of its World War I-era consumption.[26]

After the U.S. Industrial Revolution ended and peak manufacturing stabilized and then declined, the U.S. no longer met its iron ore needs from domestic production. The U.S. went from importing just 4.7% of its steel needs in 1960 (3.3 million tons) to 26.4% in 1984 (26.2 million tons).[27] During this period, the U.S. reached peak steel production in 1974 with 145 million tons. This shift was due largely to an increase of cheaper European and Japanese steel production enabled by improved smelting technology. Heading into the 1990s, as U.S. iron ore and steel needs declined in a post-industrial America, the steel industry lost the political power it had once used to successfully extract protective trade measures from successive administrations.

In 2000, the U.S. produced 63 million tons of iron ore with most coming from Minnesota and Michigan, requiring it to important another six million tons to meet its needs. Most of these imports came from neighboring Canada (51%) and Brazil (35%). The world produced over one billion tons of iron ore that year with China leading with 224 million tons, then Brazil with 195 million tons and Australia with 168 million tons. In addition to its own production, Beijing imported another 70 million tons with most coming from Australia, India, Brazil, and South Africa. China was entering an accelerated stage of its own Iron Age 2.0 just as the U.S. had done sixty years prior.[28]

For steel, the U.S. produced 102 million tons in 2000, requiring it to import another 16 million tons to meet annual consumption needs. Of this, most came from the European Union (19%), Canada (14%), and Japan (10%). Of the 845 million tons of steel produced worldwide in 2000, 158 million came from the European Union (19%), 127 million from China (15%), and 106 million from Japan (12%). Beijing also imported $11 billion of iron and steel products with much coming from Japan, Taiwan, and South Korea. China required more steel to feed its growing economy that was based largely on manufacturing, especially their burgeoning automobile industry, and unrestrained residential and commercial construction.[29]

---

26 Ibid.

27 Moore, Michael O. "The Rise and Fall of Big Steel Influence on U.S. Trade Policy." National Bureau of Economic Research, 1996.

28 USGS and UN Comtrade data.

29 USGS and UN Comtrade data.

By 2024, U.S. iron ore production was just 48 million tons, a drop of 25% from the year 2000. In fact, the U.S. was a net exporter of iron ore, shipping almost 10 million tons overseas. That year, the world produced an astounding 2.5 billion tons of iron ore led by Australia with 930 million tons (37%), Brazil with 440 million tons (17%), and then China with a big increase to 270 million tons (11%). China was the world's largest importer of iron ores by far, taking in 733 million tons from Australia, 246 million tons from Brazil, and 35 million tons from South Africa.

The U.S. produced considerably less steel in 2024 with just 81 million tons, a drop of 21% from 2000. The U.S. imported 26 million tons of steel products or 28% of its total consumption, up 62% from 2000. More than a third of these imports came from neighboring Canada and Mexico. In 2024, the world produced 1.9 billion tons of raw steel with China producing 990 million tons (52%) and the next closest country being India with 150 million tons (8%).

Above, the Carnegie Steel Company in Pittsburgh (1892-1901) was part of the U.S.' massive overlapping coal, iron ore, and steel enterprise that enabled its modern Iron Age and accompanying Industrial Revolution.

The iron ore industry is instructive because it shows the supply chain security lifecycle of what was once the U.S.' most important mineral. Colonial America initially lived with extreme iron insecurity until they constructed a widespread domestic pig iron industry. As the U.S. grew and experienced its Industrial Revolution, it achieved minerals security by expanding its national borders and exploiting its rich iron ore deposits. However, after reaching peak production, its aging steel industry became less competitive with foreign producers benefitting from new technology and lower operating costs. The U.S. only increased its steel security as its domestic consumption declined.

World War I and the Idea of Minerals Security

Going into World War I, the U.S. government did not have a national minerals strategy. Washington operated with the idea that the U.S. was a leading producer of critical minerals, as were key allies like Great Britain, and they only needed to maintain business as usual practices. There were good reasons for this with the U.S. producing 60% of the world's copper, 35% of its zinc, and being the largest producer of iron ore and steel in the world.[30] What the U.S. lacked in domestic mineral production, it could acquire from allied countries.

For instance, the U.S. produced little chromite but was able to import sufficient quantities from French-controlled New Caledonia and British-run Rhodesia. The U.S. also required manganese for steel alloys and historically sourced this from India, Brazil, and Russia (all future BRICS countries). Because Türkiye closed the Dardanelles to Russian shipping, the U.S. had to quadruple its imports from nearby Brazil, bringing in just 114,000 tons of manganese in 1914 to over 513,000 tons in 1917.[31] While it is true unrestricted German submarine warfare had the potential to disrupt the maritime transportation of minerals critical to the U.S. war economy, the Allied tactic of convoys solved this problem.

The chief topic concerning the U.S.' mineral supplies was the debate over increasing imports to meet growing wartime manufacturing demands or expanding domestic extraction. The minerals of concern were high-grade manganese, chrome, and pyrites. Based on advice from the Committee on Mineral Imports, it was agreed that imports of these three minerals would be restricted so as not to create oversupply. Ultimately, B. M. Baruch who was chairman of the powerful War Industries Board allowed for the additional importation of chrome which put the U.S. domestic market in a state of oversupply after the war.

In recognition of the U.S. reliance on critical minerals for its war effort, the U.S. Congress passed the *Minerals Control Act of 1918*. The Act addressed forty different metals and minerals that the U.S. relied on for its war economy (of note, 18 of these were listed on the USGS critical minerals list over a hundred years later in 2020). The President was authorized $50 million to purchase any of these minerals as required for government use, to apply tariffs as needed to protect domestic production, and to seize mines and smelters as necessary to

30 Eckes, *The United States and the Global Struggle for Minerals.*

31 Ibid.

support the war effort. By law, the Act was rendered null and void two years after the declaration of peace on November 10, 1920.

Members of the War Industries Board (1917-1918) responsible for coordinating the purchase of war supplies to include raw materials. The board was criticized for being unable to effectively harness the U.S. economy to support the war effort in a timely or efficient manner.

After the end of the Great War, much effort was put towards regulating the destructive behavior of nations through the creation of the League of Nations in 1920. The central goal of the League was the attainment of universal peace which would be achieved through collective security, disarmament, and settling conflicts by negotiations. One aspect of defusing conflict was recognizing that the competition between countries for limited resources, to include critical minerals, could lead to war. President Woodrow Wilson's principal minerals advisor, Dr. Charles K. Leith, contributed to a League framework for minerals and national security.[32]

Ideas for a post-WWI peace included the need to centrally manage minerals to ensure their equitable distribution. It was recognized that some countries, including the U.S., had achieved near-monopoly status on certain minerals. Also, a centrally managed global minerals regime would ensure the European countries devastated by the war would receive the raw materials necessary to rebuild their societies. Importantly, a centrally controlled minerals regime would enable the League to discipline other members by withholding raw materials as necessary to achieve compliance with established League rules. Ultimately, the League never established a minerals regime and the existing global status quo of unequal distribution of minerals by geographic chance continued.

32 Professor Charles K. Leith taught Geology at the University of Wisconsin and became the foremost U.S. expert in the field of minerals. During WWI he was the mineral adviser to the War Industries and Shipping boards.

The U.S. never joined the League of Nations despite President Wilson's support because of a lack of domestic political support - the U.S. Senate would not ratify membership. Subsequent administrations would surely have balked at an international minerals regime as the U.S. had the most to lose. In 1913, the U.S. produced 36% of world minerals output and was considered to have the most mineral security of any major industrial nation. Any equitable distribution of world minerals would have negatively impacted the U.S.' ability to export its minerals at profit and would erode its commanding raw materials position.[33]

In 1933, the Mineral Inquiry chaired by Professor Leith published *Elements of a National Mineral Policy*, an overview of findings from a conference held to determine the way ahead for the U.S. as the world marched towards another devastating war. The report suggested that the U.S. should conserve the minerals it had in limited quantities (manganese, tungsten) and not mine them to exhaustion. It was also necessary to create a stockpile of key minerals required for national defense as insurance from getting cut off by foreign powers during the time of war. Additionally, the U.S. should avoid economic nationalism and pursue the free trade and flow of minerals as this would encourage international cooperation and discourage preparations for war.[34]

Between the World Wars, Professor Leith chaired the Planning Committee for Mineral Policy and published a report on the state of U.S. mineral extraction and production capacity in 1936.[35] Similar to the Roman Empire, the report revealed that the U.S. was a world leader in major industrial minerals like iron ore, copper, lead, and zinc. Although the report made no policy suggestions, it noted that of the 31 major minerals addressed, the U.S. was deficient in nine of them and reliant on China for antimony and tungsten.

When the U.S. first began looking critically at its own mineral security after World War I, its bureaucracy remained unconvinced that it needed to do anything other than to maintain the status quo. After all, from 1900-1929, the country extracted 96% of the minerals it consumed.[36] The U.S. was largely self-sufficient and it was the world's leader of iron and steel which was the stuff modern nations were made of. Securing the minerals its economy depended on

33 *Mineral Resources of the United States 1917.*

34 The Inquiry made a total of nine recommendations for both foreign and domestic mining markets.

35 This was done through the National Resources Board.

36 Eckes, *The United States and the Global Struggle for Minerals,* p 49.

was merely a theoretical exercise by academics who didn't understand U.S. power and the dynamics of global shipping.

World War II: The Allies' Mineral Dominance

To permit Japanese domination and control of major sources of world supplies of tin and rubber and tungsten would jeopardize our safety in a manner and to an extent that cannot be tolerated.

- U.S. State Department Draft Document, November 29, 1941

From a minerals perspective, the U.S. entered WWII much as it had WWI, with an overall belief that it had the resources to effectively fight a protracted war. It became increasingly clear that Italy, Germany, and Japan would be on the opposing side and the British Empire, the French Empire and the Soviet Union would be allied with the U.S. The Axis forces controlled few important minerals while the Allies, with their colonies, had a clear raw materials superiority. The Allies controlled the resources of North America, the African continent, Australia, and the Russian land mass.

The Axis powers promoted the idea that a coming war was necessary over this very resource disparity because it limited their growth as great nations. In reality, the resource issue was used to disguise their need for raw materials to prosecute their wars of conquest. For example, Italy invaded Ethiopia in 1935 even though it had no raw materials of significance, holding only small reserves of manganese and scrap iron. Rome's invasion is best explained as an expression of Mussolini's desire to build an Italian East Africa as part of a growing colonial empire.

In Germany, the Nazi bureaucracy argued that they should be ceded its previous African colonies and provided unspecified access to raw materials necessary for the country's unhindered economic growth. German Reichsminister Hjalmar Schacht argued this very point in 1937 stating that, "So long, then, as the problem of colonial raw materials is not solved for Germany, so long will she remain a source of unrest despite all her love of peace."[37] However, this was a ploy to secure resources for Germany's war machine. Hitler did not begin his war to obtain metals, he did so to destroy an imaginary Judeo-Bolshevik conspiracy to ensure the survival of the Aryan people through a contrived war of annihilation.

37 Schacht, Hjalmar. "Germany's Colonial Demands." Foreign Affairs, January 1937.

Japan, as a relatively small island nation, relied almost entirely on international trade to secure its own resources critical to its rapidly industrializing economy. Their invasion of China in 1931 and later expansion in Southeast Asia to create the Greater East Asia Co-Prosperity Sphere was an expression of Japanese imperialism and colonialism. This subjugation of Asia was not to secure resources denied to them by free trade. Instead, raw materials were needed to build a Japanese Empire that satisfied the nexus of militant nationalism and racial ideology based on the inherent superiority of the Yamato race.[38]

Japan and the U.S. both valued the resources of China (tungsten, antimony) and Southeast Asia which included the Philippines (chromium), Dutch East Indies (rubber, oil, tin), and British Malaya (rubber, tin). Accordingly, the U.S. and England supplied China with material and arms that bogged Tokyo down in a seemingly endless war that absorbed more and more resources. The U.S. limited sales of oil to Japan in 1940 and then cut them off altogether in 1941.[39] This was due to many reasons including Japan's occupation of French Indonesia and their continued military build-up which threatened Singapore and other Western colonies in Southeast Asia.

As a result of Japan's subsequent conquest of Southeast Asia in 1942, the U.S. and its allies were cut off from its resources. The U.S. adapted to these circumstances through a variety of measures. On the topic of rubber, the U.S. enforced conservation measures at home, developed synthetic products, and invested in new projects in Latin America. For tin, lower-grade material was shipped in from Bolivia and refined into usable material. The U.S. had delayed military conflict with Japan as long as possible in part because of their dependence on these materials and the fact that Washington had insufficient stockpiles.

Another critical war mineral was tungsten, a metal used in armor-piercing projectiles, gun manufacturing, and armor plating.[40] Tungsten was so closely associated with military manufacturing that the volume and price of tungsten sold on the international market was considered a barometer of either impending war or likely peace. All warring nations needed it in large quantities and at the start of the war, most flowed from China. In 1939, the world produced an

38 In 1943, Japan's Ministry of Health and Welfare published a 3,127 page report *An Investigation of Global Policy with the Yamato Race as Nucleus.*

39 Before Japan's conquest of the Netherland's colony in 1942, it imported 80% of its oil from the U.S. and 14% from the Dutch East Indies.

40 Tungsten has the highest melting point of any metal.

estimated 36,400 tons of tungsten with 10,900 tons (30%) coming from China followed by British-controlled Burma with 4,300 tons (12%).[41]

A U.S. aircraft flies "The Hump" over the Himalayan Mountains after Japan cut the Allies' Burma Road in 1942. Due to Japan's successful ground operations, the U.S. was forced to fly tungsten out of China.

The U.S. was initially concerned with its tungsten supply because it had not stockpiled enough in preparation for war and feared Japan would seize the key Asian production centers. China, under the leadership of Chiang Kai-Sheck, saw tungsten as a commodity to be sold to all sides for profit and not a raw material used strictly for political leverage. Nazi Germany bought stocks of tungsten from 1936-1941 until they invaded Russia and China, who in turn, declared war on Germany. Japan also purchased Chinese tungsten through British controlled Hong Kong until 1941. Importantly, as much as 30% of Chinese tungsten was extracted illegally meaning it continued to be sold on the black market to the Axis powers.[42]

China also sold minerals to the U.S. who provided them with a series of loans in return for critical war metals like tin, antimony and tungsten. From 1942-1945, the U.S. was the single largest purchaser of Chinese tungsten, using it for its own production needs and shipping the excess to Britain and the Soviet Union. The Chinese tungsten supply chain became more tenuous as Japan occupied Burma in 1942, cutting off the road connecting British controlled India with China. This forced the U.S. to fly over the Himalayas to ship the minerals by air. In 1944, tungsten production was cut by two-thirds after Japanese forces conducted a devastating ground operation towards Indochina.

41 Rockoff, Hugh & Leonard Caruana. "A Wolfram in Sheep's Clothing: Economic Warfare in Spain and Portugal, 1940-1944." Rutgers University, June 2000.

42 Thomas, Joan. "Tungsten in the Second World War: China, Japan, Germany, the Allies and Iberia." Comillas Journal of International Relations, 2017.

The U.S. was not solely dependent on China as it increased its own domestic tungsten production. The U.S. went from producing just 3,200 tons in 1939, which was 9% of world production, to being the largest producer with 10,700 tons in 1943, which was 20% of world production. The U.S. also imported tungsten from Latin America (Bolivia, Argentina) and participated in a preventive purchasing effort with Portugal and Spain to limit German access which reduced Berlin's own acquisition by an estimated 30%.[43] Germany lost direct access to the remaining tungsten on the Iberian Peninsula when the Allies invaded France in June 1944.

By 1943, the U.S. had more tungsten than it could consume, importing 13,575 tons while only needing 11,000 tons. The next year was even more of an imbalance with the U.S. importing 23,500 tons and only consuming 12,000 tons. This meant the U.S. had the luxury of shipping its excess tungsten to its allies while Japan had to increasingly rely on its Korean colony. Germany had to ration its own tungsten consumption for priority use categories while increasingly relying on black market smuggling.[44]

As the case of tungsten shows, from a minerals perspective, almost everything went the U.S. and the Allies' way. This was due to the reality that the territory controlled by the Allies accounted for an estimated 75% of world mineral production. Also, because the combined Allied navies were so powerful, the Axis powers were never able to disrupt the Allies' strategic mineral supply chains to any extent that made a difference towards the outcome of the war. Italy conquered no territories of mineral significance and Germany did only marginally better.[45] In Asia, Japan acquired the most significant mineral resources of the war but did not achieve a monopoly status and Allied adaptations proved effective.

As the war went on, Italy and Germany were increasingly isolated and cut off from raw materials controlled by Allied forces. However, Germany developed an effective critical metals strategy which included rationing, stockpiling, recycling, domestic production, black market importation, and substitution. Germany was not defeated due to a raw materials shortage and had budgeted its metals reserves through 1948. Japan's fate was different in that it suffered from increasing raw materials restrictions as the U.S. recaptured key islands,

43 Ibid.

44 Ibid.

45 France held bauxite resources and Ukraine held manganese.

mined its harbors, and sunk its merchant marine shipping.[46] Japan's war industry eventually used up its pre-war stockpiles and became starved of iron ore, steel, nickel, tin, and copper, resulting in an overall manufacturing collapse in 1945. In just one example, Tokyo went from producing a high of 318,500 tons of alumina in 1943 to eking out a mere 16,200 tons in 1945.[47]

Despite the U.S. victory in the critical minerals wartime battle, the environment had changed. The American economy had become more technologically advanced and required an increasingly complex supply chain to build products like aircraft, radios, and radar systems. During the war, over sixty minerals were imported from fifty-three different countries from across the globe: Asia, Latin America, Africa, and Europe. Of these, twenty-seven minerals were provided exclusively by foreign suppliers.[48] Long gone were the days where the U.S. dominated its Iron Age and this was enough.

To meet its wartime needs, the U.S. consumed large amounts of its own domestic mineral reserves. For example, the U.S. extracted 500 million tons of iron ore, 2.2 million tons of lead, 3.5 million tons of zinc, 5 million tons of copper, and 14 million tons of bauxite.[49] Although these numbers were impressive, the U.S. also had to import 23% of its copper needs, 35% of its lead, and 35% of its zinc.[50] There were fears that the U.S. could not replicate this same level of production in a future war of the same length and intensity. This domestic resource exhaustion combined with import reliance created a strategic minerals security dilemma for the U.S.

As the U.S. moved forward into a new and uncertain post-WWII security paradigm largely of its own making, it faced fundamental questions about the future of its own minerals security. Should it increase its domestic minerals production or conserve them for future use in crisis? Should the U.S. establish tariffs to protect non-competitive domestic mining or trade freely? How much and what kind of minerals should the U.S. buy from foreign countries? How should the national defense stockpile be managed? Could the U.S. rely on fu-

46 Japan built 9.4 million tons of merchant shipping during the war – the U.S. sunk 2.2 million tons (23%) by mines alone. Source: Lott, Arnold. "Japan's Nightmare – Mine Blockade." U.S. Naval Institute, November 1959.

47 Cohen, Jerome. "The Japanese War Economy: 1940-1945." Far Eastern Survey, Vol. 15, No. 24, December 4, 1946.

48 Bateman, Alan. "Wartime Dependence on Foreign Minerals." Economic Geology, Vol. 41. 1946.

49 Cates, L.S. "Clouds Over Mining." Mining and Metallurgy 27, December 1946.

50 Eckes, *The United States and the Global Struggle for Minerals,* p.122.

ture, unproven technology to improve mineral extraction? A post-war world with much different power dynamics would require an evolving approach to minerals security.

A German heavy anti-tank destroyer is stuck on a collapsed bridge near Nikopol, Ukraine in 1943. General von Manstein wanted to withdraw from the area to shorten German lines. However, Hitler and Albert Speer insisted holding the city and its nearby manganese mines due to their importance to the German steel industry. Russia recaptured Nikopol in February 1944.

The Cold War: Parts of a Strategy

Good mineral policy should not be a policy of reaction, but rather the product of a steady commitment that recognizes the indispensability of minerals to the Nation's industrial base and its national security.

- Subcommittee on Mines and Mining, 1980

With World War II successfully concluded for the U.S. and its allies, a new global security challenge arose. It immediately became clear to the U.S. that the Soviet Union had been a partner of convenience meant to balance the more pressing threat of Nazi Germany. The U.S. found itself at economic, political, and military odds with Moscow, an authoritarian regime determined to keep its wartime spoils which included half of Europe. Importantly, the Soviet Union's immense land mass contained vast amounts of minerals which had been employed against the Axis powers. In a future East-West conflict, these resources would be denied to the U.S. and its allies.

Since WWII, U.S. strategic planners anticipated a future war with the Soviet Union lasting an estimated five years. This was based primarily on the experiences derived from both world wars and the U.S.' and Russia's existing alliance system. If there were ever a war, it would in fact be global in nature. However, with Russia's development of nuclear ICBMs (Intercontinental Ballistic Missiles) in the late 1950s, military strategists anticipated a nuclear war would be much shorter, perhaps only 30 or 60 days. This drove critical material planners from pursuing a five-year stockpile of minerals to one of just three years.

Associated with this idea of a global thermonuclear exchange was that a stockpile of minerals used as basic inputs to manufacturing would not be the most useful materials needed. Immediate lifesaving goods would be more important like food stocks, clothing, medical supplies, and shelter. An undue amount of government funds shouldn't be spent on critical minerals which wouldn't be useful for a short-term apocalyptic recovery scenario. It was important to note if the U.S.' major population and manufacturing centers were hit with nuclear missiles, there would remain neither the work force nor equipment required to put mineral feedstocks to use.

Over the course of the five decades that encompassed the Cold War (1945-1991), the geopolitical landscape in relation to minerals ownership and security changed greatly. The most profound shift was the decolonization of territories controlled by the European powers. The great British Empire was broken up with India becoming independent in 1945, followed by their holdings in the Middle East, Asia, and Africa. In Asia, colonial holdings disintegrated rapidly with the Dutch East Indies gaining independence in 1945, the Philippines in 1946, French Indochina by 1954, and British Malaya in 1957. The African continent which had been a European colonial preserve, was largely independent by 1975.

Consequently, the U.S. equation changed dramatically when planning for its mineral needs in case of international conflict. The U.S. could no longer ally itself with just a handful of Western European countries to secure its mineral needs. Now, it had to increasingly maintain positive relations with scores of countries who previously were dominions of just a few empires. Importantly, the U.S. had to reckon with the influence of Russia and China who intentionally engaged the newly independent countries to their own advantage.

Under the Truman Administration (1945-1952), the U.S. saw the start of the Korean War in 1950 as an attempt by the world's communist forces, led by Moscow and supported by China, to expand their influence in Southeast Asia. This necessarily meant a threat to the same regional resources that were so important during WWII. However, the threat was no longer Japan but a global communist movement that used revolution and conquest to threaten the U.S.-led Western critical minerals supply. The invasion led to passage of the Defense Production Act which gave the president broad authorities to purchase critical and strategic metals and minerals for the national defense industrial base.

In 1951, Truman established the International Materials Policy Commission chaired by William Paley to assess the U.S.' raw material supply chains as they related to national security. The Paley Commission published an extensive 900-page document the following year entitled *Resources for Freedom*. Key concepts included that the U.S. had a strategic imperative to grow its economy and society and that the minerals to support this should be provided at the least possible cost. The key to achieving this was mainly through private industry and with help from the government only as needed. Importantly, the U.S. quest for materials security could only be done in concert with its allies to strengthen the free world in its struggle against the communist bloc.

The incoming Eisenhower administration (1953-1960) continued to feel the Cold War threat. In the first year, the U.S National Security Council issued guidance to support and improve the security of a variety of critical mineral production facilities worldwide. Foreign owned companies included cobalt operations in the Belgian Congo, Canadian nickel production, and Dutch-owned Bauxite operations in Surinam. U.S. owned companies included nickel operations in Cuba, bauxite extraction in Surinam, and copper production in Chile. While the Office of Defense Mobilization would manage the program, the CIA would determine these operations' vulnerability to sabotage and communist infiltration of labor unions.[51]

In 1953, Eisenhower appointed a Cabinet Committee on Minerals Policy which issued a report the following year with eleven recommendations for a national minerals strategy. Key ideas included that the U.S. should expand its strategic materials stockpile to avoid future disruptions as experienced during both

51 *Security of Strategically Importantly Industrial Operations in Foreign Countries*, National Security Council, October 24, 1953. Based on the amount allocated to this program for Fiscal Year 1954, just $100,000.00, this was not a serious initiative.

WWII and the Korean War. Domestic mining production was a key component and should be closely monitored and receive government assistance when required. Also, the Office of Defense Mobilization should have the authority to coordinate the interagency activity necessary to implement the strategy.

Above, Fidel Castro at a guerrilla camp in the Sierra Maestra Mountains. In 1959, the Cuban Revolution brought to power a new communist government close to U.S. shores. Castro subsequently seized the Nicaro nickel plant owned by the U.S. government - its labor force was previously placed under surveillance by the CIA to warn of communist infiltration.

The administrations that led the U.S. for the rest of the Cold War represented a period that was a critical minerals dead zone where no presidency pursued a comprehensive minerals strategy. The Kennedy and Johnson Administrations (1961-1968) were consumed by a variety of crises and initiatives such as the Cuban Missile Crisis, Kennedy's own assassination, the Great Society programs, and the Vietnam War. Other than Kennedy publicly recognizing that the National Defense Stockpile was grossly mismanaged due to excessive secrecy, he and Johnson never organized a critical minerals strategy.[52] [53]

While the Nixon/Ford administrations (1969-1976) were also devoured by the U.S. debacle in Vietnam and later President Nixon's resignation in 1973 for criminal activity, they managed to pass the Mining and Minerals Policy Act of 1970. However, this one-half page document was largely an admission that the U.S. did not have a critical minerals strategy and had no time to put any thought into the subject. The overly vague act directed the Department of the Interior to run the country's minerals strategy which rested on encouraging private enterprise to invest in domestic mining and recycling efforts. Nixon's most

52 https://www.jfklibrary.org/archives/other-resources/john-f-kennedy-press-conferences/news-conference-22

53 Draft legislation written in 1962 to repeal the Domestic Minerals Act of 1958 revealed that the Kennedy administration opposed government subsidizing of domestic mining and preferred free market principles to determine supply and demand.

important minerals legacy was that he gutted the National Defense Stockpile, reducing it by 85% and using the profits to balance the budget.

Separately, the National Materials Policy Act of 1970 passed with the purpose of developing U.S. natural resources efficiently while recognizing environmental protections. The act established the National Commission on Materials Policy which published a 305-page report on the state of the U.S. materials system.[54] The commission made twelve recommendations for a national materials policy. Salient ones included the need for market forces to drive domestic mining and imports except when the U.S. became overly dependent on foreign sources, then the government must intervene. Second, a comprehensive national recycling program should be instituted. Finally, a single agency overseen by a joint congressional committee should be established to coordinate the necessary integrated federal activities.[55]

Two years into the Carter presidency (1977-1980), the administration stood up the Non-Fuel Mineral Policy Coordinating Committee chaired by the Secretary of the Interior. The committee's mission was yet again to conduct a study resulting in recommendations for a domestic minerals policy. However, the draft report released in 1979 was deemed inadequate by critics because it failed to grasp the necessary elements of an overall minerals strategy. Because of this, the congressional Subcommittee on Mines and Mining held a series of hearings as part of a minerals policy review that resulted in a 432-page transcript.

These scathing proceedings highlighted the U.S.' systemic bureaucratic incompetence and inability to execute a coherent critical minerals strategy. The reality was that a national strategy had to be driven at the presidential level; individual cabinets such as the Department of the Interior were incapable of it. The subcommittee published a final report the next year entitled *U.S. Minerals Vulnerability*. The most damning conclusion was that the government's policies undermined the country's minerals security by increasing its dependence on foreign sources.

The Reagan Administration (1981-1988) and the U.S. Congress recognized that the U.S. had increasingly fallen into minerals insecurity over the previous years. They also understood that the Soviet Union was pursuing relations with various mineral producing countries (such as in Africa) to deny the U.S. access

54 "Material Needs and the Environment Today and Tomorrow." National Commission on Materials Policy, June 27, 1973.

55 None of these were instituted by the administration.

to these raw materials as part of the continuing Cold War. In response, the Reagan administration developed their National Materials and Minerals Program Plan and passed the National Materials and Minerals Policy, Research and Development Act of 1980. However, the administration's plan was an unimaginative effort that provided no real solutions.

To start, in an unsuccessful attempt to cut through the bureaucracy of the more than twenty agencies involved in critical minerals management, Reagan appointed a Cabinet Council on Natural Resources and Environment. One goal was to open more federal land to private mining operations although the reality was that most domestic mining operations were already priced out of the market. Another ill-defined goal was the exploration of seabed minerals although this was uneconomic and infeasible. And although the administration recognized a $12.5 billion shortfall in the National Defense Stockpile of sixty-one different minerals, they requested only $100 million for 1981, meaning it would take 125 years to fill the stockpile.[56]

While the Act of 1980 recognized that the U.S. lacked a coherent national policy up until that point, the Act itself was nothing more than a bureaucratic world salad. For example, the main substance of the six-page document directed agencies to improve on their existing critical mineral duties – something they were already empowered to do. Further highlighting the Act's policy emptiness were the last two pages devoted to a revision of the Act of 1970 which addressed geothermal rights in Boise, Idaho.

Congress subsequently passed the National Critical Materials Act of 1984 which established the National Critical Materials Council that, would report directly to the President. The Council was created specifically to enforce the provisions of the 1980 Act which were never implemented. However, the Council failed to craft a cohesive minerals strategy and was later disbanded in 1993. While the Reagan administration talked tough on critical minerals, this was mostly political camouflage meant to mollify domestic critics while continuing business as usual.

The Collapse of the Soviet Union, 1989-1991

With the dissolution of the Soviet Union as a coherent political entity in 1991, the U.S.' main threat and competitor in the international system disap-

56 National Materials and Minerals Program Plan and Report to Congress, April 1982.

peared. No longer did an opposing political block control territory in Eastern Europe or support political entities hostile to the U.S. in Africa, Asia, and Latin America. By 1992, Russia was a financial weakling with a GDP of just $460 billion USD while the U.S. GDP was fourteen times larger at $6.5 trillion. The only other major communist power in the world was China with an even smaller economy at $426 billion. The U.S.' global position was so dominant, the only possible threat political theorists could conjure up was Japan who wielded a mighty $3.9 trillion GDP.[57]

With the U.S. now holding the single most powerful economic and military position in the world while simultaneously maintaining the largest alliance system, it had few existential security concerns. The Bush Administration's (1989-1992) minerals policy reflected this heightened sense of security, passing the Strategic and Critical Minerals Act of 1990. However, this anemic single-page act had the sole purpose of directing the Minister of the Interior to establish a Strategic Resources Mineral Technology Center at a university "west of the 100th meridian." The center was never built and the Bush administration continued the U.S.' business as usual approach to its minerals insecurity.

The subsequent Clinton Administration (1993-2000) inherited the U.S.' dominant political, economic, and military position and the accompanying complacency. In 1994, Clinton issued Executive Order 12929 which merely told the Departments of Interior and Defense to continue their already established critical mineral responsibilities. Otherwise, the U.S. passed no legislation relating to its minerals security. By the administration's end, U.S. GDP had grown to $10.2 trillion while Russia's had shrunk to just $260 billion while China's was now a respectable $1.2 trillion.

For perspective, in 2000, the U.S. mined $40 billion worth of non-fuel mineral products, processed $429 billion worth, and contributed $1.8 trillion to the GDP by major mineral consuming industries. Of note, the U.S. imported many key products including graphite (100%), manganese (100%), cobalt (74%), rare earths (72%), and tungsten (68%). The U.S. also sold off $668 million worth of minerals from its stockpile or 18% of its total holdings.[58] Overall, the U.S. felt secure in the idea that it could trade for whatever minerals it needed on the open market and no exceptional actions were required. This coexisted with

57 George Friedman, former CEO of STRATFOR, published a book in 1991 predicting that the U.S. would fight another future war against Japan over trade imbalances and raw materials.

58 USGS Mineral Commodity Summaries, January 25, 2001.

the reality that the U.S. continued to become increasingly dependent on foreign sources of minerals.[59]

The Rise of China

The George Bush presidency (2001-2008) was dominated by Al-Qaeda's attack on September 11, 2001, which resulted in a Global War on Terror (GWOT) that consumed U.S. politics for the next twenty years. Other than rolling back environmental regulations that allowed for increased mining on federal lands, the Bush administration did little to develop a critical minerals strategy. The most important event impacting critical mineral supply chains during this period, although the U.S. missed it, was China joining the World Trade Organization (WTO) on December 11, 2001.

By joining the WTO, China gained access to new markets by agreeing to reduce tariffs, protect intellectual property (IP), and to follow WTO rules. Since joining, China lifted 400 million of its citizens out of poverty, became the largest exporter of goods in 2009, and developed the second largest economy in 2010. Although the U.S. believed China's membership in the WTO would moderate its international behavior and encourage democratic reforms, it served to legitimize the Chinese Communist Party (CCP). Overall, China used the WTO to catapult its economy forward while becoming a world power second only to the U.S. But unlike the U.S., Beijing implemented a disciplined strategy to secure its critical minerals supply chains underpinning its economy.

The Obama administration (2009-2016) inherited the GWOT and was also consumed by it. The administration did establish a subcommittee on Critical and Strategic Minerals Supply Chains, funded the Critical Materials Institute, and improved trade surveillance data on rare earths.[60] However, it never developed an overarching critical mineral strategy and spent much effort collecting information on the topic while pretending that the U.S. Geological Survey (USGS) did not exist which already had all the relevant data. Meanwhile, China continued to grow its own critical minerals supply chains by becoming a midstream processing powerhouse and cementing monopolies on rare earth magnets and EV batteries.

It was under the first Trump administration (2017-2020) that the U.S. identified the strategic need to divest itself of the GWOT and refocus on great

59 USGS 2001 Minerals Summary.

60 CMI evolved into the Critical Materials Innovation Hub.

power competition with China and Russia. The U.S. began winding down its global counterterrorism efforts while becoming more concerned with China's minerals strength. During this term, USGS identified a list of 35 critical minerals while Trump declared a critical minerals emergency. In 2018, the administration published *A Federal Strategy to Ensure Secure and Reliable Supplies of Critical Minerals.* This 50-page document offered six main elements to include increased technological advances such as recycling, downstream manufacturing, trade, and domestic mining. However, this strategy was never paired with legislation or funding and thus did not have the power to shift global supply chains.

In the last month of the term, Congress passed the 533-page Energy Act of 2020 which devoted 46 pages to critical minerals security. The Act provided the Department of Energy (DOE) with $127 million over five years to execute a rare earths (REE) coal recovery R&D program.[61] The Act also briefly amended the National Materials and Minerals Policy, Research, and Development Act of 1980 with no substantive changes. DOE was provided with a further $600 million over five years to create a much needed critical materials research, development, demonstration, and commercialization program. In a separate effort, DOE was provided with $75 million over three years to stand up a Critical Materials Supply Chain Research facility.[62] Finally, $12.7 million was put towards three separate REE projects using the authorities of the Defense Production Act (DPA).

Of interest, the Act required the Director of National Intelligence (DNI) to report on China's minerals investments through their Belt and Road Initiative. This continued the government's official amnesia that the U.S. taxpayer already funded U.S. Geological Survey and their National Minerals Information Center. Instead of wasting the intelligence community's finite resources on collecting information that was already publicly available, DNI could also just get a subscription with Benchmark Mineral Intelligence or Fastmarkets, two private sector companies who collect minerals intelligence for a living.

Despite the U.S.' delayed interest in securing its critical minerals supply chains, the overall domestic mining industry continued to grow. In 2020, the

61 By the end of 2024, the program had still not produced an economic process for extracting rare earths from coal or coal byproducts.

62 By the end of 2024, this facility was still not built. The Office of Fossil Energy and Carbon Management was responsible for what was now called project METALLIC.

U.S. mined $82 billion worth of non-mineral fuel products, processed $710 billion worth, and contributed $3 trillion to the GDP by major mineral consuming industries. However, the U.S. remained import dependent on key minerals like graphite, gallium and manganese (100%), battery minerals like cobalt (76%) and lithium (+50%), and rare earths (100%). Also, the U.S. inexplicably sold off another $56 million from its stockpile despite being chronically under-sourced. Although mining value had increased significantly since 2000, this was counterbalanced by the U.S.' considerable foreign dependencies.[63]

Final Thoughts

Until WWII, the U.S. never had to develop a national critical minerals strategy because, like the Roman Empire, it was largely self-sufficient in raw materials. However, WWII placed the U.S. under supply chain stress which forced it to develop and execute an effective strategy – but only temporarily. Due to the U.S.' extensive alliance system with the European colonial empires who controlled 75% of the world's raw materials, the U.S. knew it could ultimately navigate any minerals disruption through crisis management. But, with the progressive collapse of the European colonial system and a complex economy requiring a diverse minerals base, the U.S. experienced increasing insecurity.

Despite repeated calls by mineral experts for a coherent policy during the Cold War, the U.S. political system was only able to institute parts of a strategy. U.S. critical mineral policy dysfunction was characterized by a lack of leadership at the presidential level, an inability for interagency cooperation, and infighting by self-interested groups. An underlying reason for the lack of a coherent minerals vision was the revolving door of administrations who developed the pattern of establishing mineral strategy panels who took years to produce redundant reports. Successive presidencies suffered from critical minerals amnesia, pretending the relevant information they sought did not already exist in abundance. This paralyzing bureaucratic process enabled administrations to kick difficult mineral strategy decisions much further down the road as they embraced the status quo.

With the collapse of the Soviet Union, the U.S. became the world's uncontested leading power which served to fuel its own critical minerals complacency. In the 1990s, the U.S. suffered a lack of geopolitical focus while China

63 USGS 2021 Minerals Summary.

accelerated its economy and simultaneously developed a disciplined strategic minerals plan. After the U.S. became consumed with its Global War on Terror, Beijing steadily grew into an international power while developing key critical mineral monopolies which the U.S. became dependent on. As the year 2020 neared, the U.S. became aware of its own ongoing critical minerals vulnerability. However, this awareness only developed because of the perceived threat from China, exposing the U.S.' reactionary mindset.

The next chapter examines the Biden administration's (2021-2024) critical minerals policy and if it moved beyond merely producing parts of a strategy. Just like Rome two thousand years before, the U.S. public and political leadership had a store-shelf mentality where they expected their mineral needs to always be met regardless of their own actions and inactions. However, this apathetic groupthink undermined U.S. national security as the U.S.' and China's increasingly heated trade war illustrated Beijing's willingness to use its superior minerals position for political and economic retaliation. For the U.S. to compete effectively with China and secure its own economic and industrial needs, something much different needed to be done.

Sources

Carr, Martha S. and Carl E. Dalton. "Iron-Ore Resources of the United States." Geological Survey Bulletin 1082-C, 1959.

Clark, Victor S. "History of Manufactures in the United States, Volumes I -III." New York: Carnegie Institution of Washington, 1929.

Eckes, Alfred E. "The United States and the Global Struggle for Minerals." Austin: The University of Texas Press, 1979.

"Elements of a National Mineral Policy." The Mineral Inquiry, New York: 1933.

Emeny, Brooks. "The Strategy of Raw Materials: A Study of America in Peace and War." New York: The Macmillan Company, 1937.

Gini, Corrado. "Problem of Raw Materials and Foodstuffs." League of Nations, 1922.

Healy, John F. "Mining and Metallurgy in the Greek and Roman World." London: Thames and Hudson, 1978.

Heuvel, Lisa L. "Early Attempts of English Mineral Exploration in North America: The Jamestown Colony." Virginia Division of Mineral Resources Publication 176, 2007.

Leith, C. K. "The Political Control of Mineral Resources." Foreign affairs, July 1, 1925.

Leith, C.K. & Donald M. Liddell. "The Minerals Reserves of the U.S. and its Capacity for Production." National Resources Committee, March 1936.

Leith, C. K. "World Minerals and World Politics." Kennikat Press, 1931.

"Raw Materials in War and Peace." United States Military Academy, 1947.

Skaggs, Julian C. "Lukens 1850-1870: A Case Study in the Mid-Nineteenth Century American Iron Industry." University of Delaware, 1975.

2020 U.S. Mineral Dependencies			
Mineral	**Percentage**	**Countries**	**#1 Exporter**
Arsenic	100%	China, Morocco, Belgium	China
Asbestos	100%	Brazil, Russia	BRICS
Cesium	100%	Canada	
Fluorspar	100%	Mexico, Vietnam, China	
Gallium	100%	China, U.K., Germany	China
Graphite	100%	China, Mexico, Canada	China
Indium	100%	China, Canada, S. Korea	China
Manganese	100%	Gabon, South Africa, Australia	
Mica	100%	China, Brazil, Belgium	China
Nepheline	100%	Canada	
Niobium	100%	Brazil, Canada, Germany	BRICS
Rare Earths	100%	China, Estonia, Japan	China
Rubidium	100%	Canada	
Scandium	100%	Europe, China, Japan	
Strontium	100%	Mexico, Germany, China	
Tantalum	100%	China, Germany, Australia	China
Yttrium	100%	China, S. Korea, Japan	China
Gemstones	99%	India, Israel, Belgium	BRICS
Vanadium	96%	Brazil, South Africa, Austria	BRICS
Tellurium	95%	Canada, China, Germany	
Bismuth	94%	China, S. Korea, Mexico	China
Potash	90%	Canada, Belarus, Russia	
Titanium	88%	South Africa, Australia	BRICS
Diamonds	84%	South Africa, India, Botswana	BRICS
Zinc	83%	Canada, Mexico, Peru	
Antimony	81%	China, Belgium, Thailand	China
Silver	80%	Mexico, Canada, Peru	

Above is a list published by U.S. Geological Survey of the 27 minerals that the U.S. relied on for imports from foreign sources for 80% or more of its needs in 2020. China is the #1 exporter for ten of these and the Beijing led BRICS (Brazil Russia India China South Africa) coalition is #1 for another six. Successive administrations have pretended that they didn't have the data revealing the country's growing foreign minerals dependence. USGS publishes detailed annual reports of the U.S.' mineral supply chains and is always aware of the country's mineral vulnerabilities.

Chapter 2

U.S. Critical Minerals Strategy

"The Energy Act of 2020 defined critical minerals as those that are essential to the economic or national security of the United States; have a supply chain that is vulnerable to disruption; and serve an essential function in the manufacturing of a product, the absence of which would have significant consequences for the economic or national security of the U.S."

"Mineral criticality is not static, but changes over time as supply and demand dynamics evolve, import reliance changes, and new technologies are developed."

- U.S. Geological Survey

2021-2024: A Sense of Urgency?

The first Trump administration, while failing to construct a cohesive critical minerals strategy, created momentum which conditioned the U.S. bureaucracy for future action. The incoming Biden Administration had a chance to develop a real strategy backed by legislation since it had a majority in the House and a tie in the Senate where the Vice President would cast the majority vote. The new administration didn't need to commission more studies and create more expert panels, but it did need to secure its twenty-five critical minerals that were majority sourced from China.

In March of 2021, Biden issued Executive Order 14017 entitled *America's Supply Chains*. Its intent was to make the U.S.' supply chains more resilient by increasing domestic production, developing diverse supply chains, establishing stockpiles, and cooperating with allies. The major agencies were given 100 days to provide supply chain risk analysis for semiconductors, EV batteries, critical minerals (including rare earth elements), and pharmaceuticals. Furthermore, within one year, specific agencies would provide supply chain risk analysis of major industrial sectors to include defense, public health, information and communications technology, energy, transportation, food products, and manufacturing.

It is interesting to note that EO 14017 directed the administration to update work started by Executive Order 13953 *Addressing the Threat to the Domestic Supply Chain From Reliance on Critical Minerals From Foreign Adversaries and Supporting the Domestic Mining and Processing Industries* issued by Trump 1.0 on September 30, 2020. Biden's order also directed a follow up of Executive Order 13806 *Assessing and Strengthening the Manufacturing and Defense Industrial Base and Supply Chain Resiliency of the United States* also issued by Trump 1.0 on July 21, 2017. Although this did show continuity across administrations to improve critical mineral supply chain security, Washington was littered with the bones of presidential orders that went nowhere and accomplished nothing.

Infrastructure Investment and Jobs Act (IIJA) of 2021

The first major flexing of the Biden administration's political muscle was the passing of the Infrastructure Investment and Jobs Act of 2021 (IIJA), a massive $1.2 trillion far-reaching bill 1,039 pages long.[64] Included in the Act was *Title II - Supply Chains for Clean Energy Technologies* whose eleven different sections addressed critical minerals, REE, geological mapping, and battery minerals. This was the first legislation passed by an administration that recognized the importance of low carbon energy production and sought to reorder associated global value chains at scale. However, due to the large scope of the act, it was possible the administration would not be able to focus on and move forward many aspects of the legislation.

(Section 40201) The Earth Mapping Resources Initiative (MRI) authorized $320 million over five years to accelerate U.S. Geological Survey's existing Earth MRI program. The program was needed to conduct high-quality mapping of the continental U.S. to discover new potential critical mineral resources. While comprehensive effective mapping has always been needed - only 18% of the U.S. has been adequately covered – U.S. Geological Survey (USGS) was never provided the resources to accomplish the mission.

64 This act is more commonly referred to as the Bipartisan Infrastructure Law (BIL) of 2021.

(Section 40202) The National Cooperative Geologic Mapping Program amended the National Geologic Mapping Act of 1992 to focus on the mapping of abandoned mines and their remaining waste products. Specifically, USGS would work with state geologic survey offices to focus on mines that contained multiple critical minerals and not just a single source. Both the Act of 1992 and the new initiative were admissions that the U.S. had not effectively surveyed its own territory. This section authorized $64 million a year for the program, extending it from 2023 through 2031.

(Section 40203) The National Geological and Geophysical Preservation Data Program amended the previous Act of 2005 with the same name. The amendment directs the Department of the Interior through USGS to preserve samples of critical minerals so they can be tracked in an associated database. While this relatively minor change authorized no additional funds for the effort, it provided additional emphasis on critical minerals as defined by the Energy Act of 2020.

(Section 40204) USGS was directed to stand up an Energy and Minerals Research Facility in partnership with an academic entity although USGS would retain ownership of the structure. USGS received $167 million to create the facility, after which additional funds would have to be appropriated. This project moved slowly with USGS choosing to partner with the Colorado School of Mines in Golden, CO. With construction scheduled from 2023 to 2026, this was a questionable choice given that USGS already had a facility located six miles away in Lakewood.

(Section 40205) The Energy Act of 2020 was further amended to authorize Department of Energy (DOE) to establish a REE demonstration facility by partnering with an academic institution. The facility was required to separate REO (rare earth oxides) from historic mining waste streams into individual elements and produce rare earth metals. The facility was authorized $140 million in 2022 which would be used until expended, an increase of $36 million as compared to the 2020 Act. In 2023, DOE selected both the University of North Dakota and West Virginia University to build the described REE facilities.

(Section 40206) Critical minerals supply chains and reliability were addressed by an attempt to improve waiting times for the mining permitting process. For decades, the U.S.' collective paralyzing federal bureaucracy had delayed mine permitting with companies waiting up to five years before their initial submissions were reviewed. However, this section did nothing but direct the responsible government offices to do their jobs in a timely manner which they should have been doing anyway. There was nothing here indicating the Biden administration had a solution to this continuing problem.

(Section 40207) This was the first law that recognized the U.S. was a battery-dependent nation and offered real incentives for battery minerals processing and manufacturing. The act supported eligible entities through the Battery Material Processing Grants program with $3 billion authorized from 2022-2026.[65] Eligible battery manufacturers and recyclers were also authorized grants totaling $3 billion from 2022-2026. Battery recycling R&D efforts were authorized $60 million for 2022-2026. Overall, $6.06 billion was authorized in an attempt to reorder global battery supply chains to the U.S.

(Section 40208) The Energy Independence and Security Act of 2007 was amended to address electric vehicle (EV) battery reuse and recycling and authorized $200 million in grants from 2022-2026. This was far more than the $50 million originally authorized over the span of ten years in the Act of 2007. It was also an effort to develop urban mining where battery metals are continuously recycled which obviates the need for traditional earth mining operations and their associated problems.

(Section 40209) An Advanced Energy Manufacturing and Recycling Grant program focused on fuel cells, carbon capture, energy conservation and grid modernization was authorized $750 million to be spent from 2022-2026. This section was intended to reduce greenhouse gas emissions and assist low-income communities and minority-owned businesses.

(Section 40210) A Critical Minerals Mining and Recycling Research Program was established in partnership with eligible universities, national laboratories, and nonprofit organizations. Focus areas included advanced mineral extraction technology, geologic mapping technology, and critical minerals recycling. The Critical Minerals Subcommittee of the National Science and Technology Council was directed to manage this program and provide expert advice to other concerned agencies. Although this program was authorized $400 million to be spent over the course of four years from 2022-2026, the funds were never appropriated by Congress.

(Section 40211) Finally, the Department of Energy (DOE) was directed to create a 21st Century Energy Workforce Advisory Board to train the workforce

65 Designated Foreign Entities of Concern (FEOC) were ineligible for incentives.

for the future energy sector. The intent was to find, educate, and employ the workforce who would be working in the clean energy industry. The Board was given a single five-year term that ended in 2026 which could be renewed by the Secretary of Energy. The board wasn't authorized funding and any expenses would come from DOE's existing budget.

In total, the IIJA authorized at least $8.6 billion in funds to improve different aspects of various critical minerals supply chains. But was it worth it? The American taxpayer had to wonder if this considerable investment actually reordered global supply chains in a manner more favorable to the U.S. By the end of 2024, what did the Biden Administration have to show for it?

Infrastructure Investment and Jobs Act of 2021 Supply Chains for Clean Energy Technologies		
Section	**Initiative**	**Funding authorized**
40201	Earth Mapping Resources Initiative	$320 million
40202	National Cooperative Geologic Mapping Program	$64 million annually (2023-2031)
40203	National Geological and Geophysical Preservation Program	N/A
40204	Energy and Minerals Research Facility	$167 million
40205	Rare Earth Demonstration Facilities	$140 million
40206	Critical Minerals Supply Chains	N/A
40207	Battery Processing and Manufacturing	$6.06 billion
40208	EV Battery Reycling Program	$200 million
40209	Advanced Energy Manufacturing	$750 million
40210	~~Critical Minerals Mining and Recycling~~	~~$400 million~~
40211	Energy Workforce Advisory Board	N/A
	Total Funds Authorized: $8.6 billion	

(Section 40201 & Section 40202) U.S. Geological Survey distributed competitive grants for the Earth MRI program through its National Cooperative Geologic Mapping Program (NCGMP). In 2022, the program provided $64 million in IIJA grants for projects in 30 different states which included lidar mapping by low flying aircraft. Another $51 million was expended in 2023 for mapping projects in 35 states. Through 2024, $198 million had been obligated to Earth MRI projects with more than 10% of the U.S. being mapped. USGS clearly put their IIJA funding to use as intended, although it will be years before mapping leads to actual mineral discovery and extraction operations.

(Section 40205) As mentioned, DOE partnered with two different universities for the rare earth demonstration initiative. In 2023, both the University of Noth Dakota (UND) and West Virginia University (WVU) received $8 million grants from DOE for initial Phase I funding for a 21-month period. These amounts were DOE's 80% commitment to the project while the universities fronted the other 20% or $2 million apiece. In 2025, DOE would select one of the schools to move forward with the remaining $124 million grant of which the university will cost share 50%. At the end of Phase II, which is three years in length, the selected facility is expected to produce useable REE.

(Section 40207) DOE's $6 billion battery processing and manufacturing program was by far the single largest initiative of the IIJA. In 2022, DOE's Office of Manufacturing and Energy Supply Chains announced the award of $1.8 billion to 14 separate projects. In 2024, the office announced another $3 billion awarded to 25 different projects. The next round of project awards were scheduled for 2025. In one example, Albemarle Corporation was awarded a $149 million grant with Albemarle cost sharing another $225 million to construct a new lithium processing plant in North Carolina. Although Albemarle submitted initial plans for the project in 2024, they have delayed moving forward due to declining profits from the drop in prices for battery- grade lithium products.

(Section 40208) For the EV battery recycling and second use program that amended the Energy Act of 2007, an initial $74 million for Phase I testing was granted to ten separate entities for 34% of the total fund. $37 million for Phase II advancement was announced in 2023 although no entity had been selected by 2024. American Battery Technology Company (ABTC) was one of the Phase I companies who received a $10 million grant and in turn put up $10 million of their own. As of 2024, their 137,000 square foot recycling plant in Reno, Nevada was not yet operational.

(Section 40209) Of the $750 million authorized for the Advanced Energy Manufacturing and Recycling Program, $275 million was deployed to seven different companies for Phase I operations by 2023. By far the biggest operation was with Microporous (formerly MP Assets Corporation) who received a $100 million grant while cost sharing $424 million to build a new battery separator plant in Virginia. Construction was forecasted to begin in 2025 and production in 2026. Phase II opportunities with $425 million available were opened in 2024 with no announcements yet made of awardees.

We can conclude from this overview of the IIJA critical mineral supply chain provisions did not restructure the associated global supply chains. The minerals in question were largely battery minerals (lithium, nickel, cobalt, manganese, graphite) and REE although all critical minerals were addressed with improved mapping operations by USGS and the research facility collocated with Colorado School of Mines. On average, it took five years or more to get a new operation off the ground with most funding only going through 2026. Clearly, more would have to be done to improve the U.S.' critical minerals security.

Inflation Reduction Act of 2022

The Inflation Reduction Act (IRA) of 2022 was the most significant legislation passed in U.S. history to lower industrial carbon emissions, to advance electrification, and to restructure global critical mineral supply chains. Although the 725-page bill's funding authorization was much smaller than the previous one at just $433 billion, it focused squarely on incentivizing critical mineral extraction and manufacturing. This was the last large bill the Biden administration could get through as it lost control of the House of Representatives in 2023.

Title I – Committee on Finance, Subtitle D Energy Security, Part 4 – Clean Vehicles, Section 13401. Clean vehicle credit.

This provided a $7,500.00 federal tax credit for eligible EVs which depended on the price of the vehicle and the income of the buyer.[66] To qualify for the federal 45X tax credits the critical minerals used in the batteries of an EV manufactured in the U.S. must be extracted or processed in a country in which the U.S. has a free trade agreement or were recycled in North America. Specifically, to be eligible, from the date of the initial passing of the bill, 40% of the value of the critical minerals had to meet the above requirements. In 2024, the amount rose to 50%, then 60% in 2025, 70% in 2026, and 80% in 2027 and after.

For the components of the battery (other than critical minerals) from the date of the passing of the law, the requirement was 50%. From 2024-2025 it increased to 60%, then 70% in 2026, and 80% in 2027 and after. Countries listed

66 $3,750.00 each for the minerals and the battery components.

as a Foreign Entity of Concern (FEOC) were ineligible for the incentives which included Chinese companies "significantly influenced by their government."[67] Obviously, this included state-owned entities (SOEs) but it could also mean companies with high levels of government subsidies or other assistance.

Part 5—Investment in Clean Energy Manufacturing and Energy Security, Section 13501. Extension of the Advanced Energy Project Credit.

This section provided $10 billion for Section 45X Advanced Manufacturing Production Credits which were federal tax credits recognized by the Internal Revenue Service. The 45X credits were meant to promote increased domestic green energy, critical mineral, and low-carbon emission vehicle production. The Joint Committee on Taxation estimated that the 45X credits from 2023-2027 would be valued at $72.7 billion. The 45X tax credits expire for all programs in 2033 except for critical minerals which will retain the tax credit in perpetuity.[68]

Tax credits were provided for the solar manufacturing industry to include components such as photovoltaic wafers (silicon/quartz, gallium arsenide-GaAs), solar grade polysilicon (silicon, cadmium, tellurium), polymeric backsheet (polyester), and solar modules (silver, aluminum). Offshore wind turbines' individual components also received credits to include torque tubes (steel, aluminum), structural fasteners (steel), inverters, and electrode active material used in batteries. For battery manufacturing, tax credits for battery cells were $35 per kWh, battery modules were $10 per kWh, and associated critical minerals were 10% of production costs.

Most importantly, the act provided a 10% annual federal tax credit for the manufacturing and processing of the fifty critical minerals identified by U.S. Geological Survey. Each mineral had its own specification depending on its own characteristic. For instance, cobalt could be converted to cobalt sulfate or purified to a minimum purity of 99.6% cobalt by mass. However, the critical mineral production had to take place inside the U.S. This law stacked manufacturing incentives on top of existing 14%/22% depletion allowances for mining operations that were authorized by the IRS before WWI.[69]

67 The FEOC battery ban took effect in 2024 while the critical minerals ban took effect in 2025.

68 "The Section 45X Advanced Manufacturing Production Credit." Congressional Research Service, November 7, 2024.

69 A mining company received either a 14% or 22% tax write-off depending on the mineral. Foreign companies were also allowed the depletion allowance at the lower 14% rate.

Wind Turbine Raw Material Requirements		
Raw & processed Materials	Sub-components	Components
Fiberglass		Blades
Carbon fiber		
Resins, foams, paints		
Balsa		
Iron	Large castings	Hub
Specialized steels	Gear boxes	Nacelle
Copper,Bronze		
Rare Earth Elements*	Generators	
Specialized steels		
Copper		
Specialized steels	Bearings	
Platinum group metals	Semiconductors	
Steel		Tower
Concrete		Foundation
Steel		
Specialized steels, zinc		Substructure
Aluminum, copper		Grid Connection

**REE permanent magnets with neodymium and praseodymium*

Title V—Committee on Energy and Natural Resources, Subtitle A—Energy,

Part 4—DOE Loan and Grant Programs.

Under Section 50141, DOE could issue $43.6 billion in loans and grants available through 2026 to support projects under Section 1703 of the Energy Policy Act of 2020. These projects included energy storage solutions (ESS) which would in turn require associated battery minerals like lithium, nickel, cobalt, manganese, iron, phosphate, graphite, and vanadium. An additional $5 billion in funding was offered for low-carbon emitting and EV manufacturing under Section 50142 Advanced Technology Vehicle Manufacturing ($3 billion) and under Section 50143 Domestic Manufacturing Conversion Grants ($2 billion).

The IIJA of 2021 and IRA of 2022 were the two most significant legislative measures in U.S. history to improve its critical minerals security and restructure associated global supply chains towards North America. Between the two laws, depending on how you counted the programs, an estimated $129 billion was authorized for the effort. However, it takes many years to get new mining and manufacturing projects off the ground and there is no easy or quick fix. Most likely, the three-year period that this legislation impacted was not enough for the desired results although it created momentum. But was this momentum irreversible?

Did the U.S. Restructure Its Mineral Supply Chains?

Solar Production 2020-2024

By 2020, over 760 GW of solar power was deployed worldwide. That year, China deployed an additional 48 GW, Europe over 19 GW and the U.S. also 19 GW.[70] Of the 139 GW deployed in 2020, the Asia market accounted for 61% (China accounted for 35%), North and South America 18%, and Europe 16%.[71] China was the world leader of solar panel manufacturing which fed the larger Asia market. Because Beijing dominated world solar panel pricing, they delivered the majority of Europe's and North America's solar panels. Consequently, supply chains (silicon, aluminum, gallium, GaAs wafers) largely lead to China/Asia.

At the end of the Biden administration in 2024, the world added 550 GW of solar installation bringing the global total to 2.2 TW.[72] Once again, China led with 340 GW of solar expansion, Europe installed 60 GW (Germany led with 18 GW), the U.S. was close behind with 50 GW, and India over 30 GW. China led with 62% of all installations while Europe accounted for 11%, and the U.S. just 9%. Not only did the U.S. fail to restructure solar-related critical mineral supply chains, but China increased its market share. This meant Beijing retained its dominance of solar cell manufacturing, putting the U.S. further away from chipping away at its first mover position.[73]

70 GW = 1 Gigawatt of power or 1 billion watts.

71 International Energy Agency (IEA) Snapshot of Global PV Markets 2021.

72 TW=Terawatt of power or 1 trillion watts.

73 International Energy Agency, Global Energy Review 2025.

Wind Production 2020-2024

In 2020, wind power generation reached 733 GW deployed globally, slightly less than solar. The majority of this was onshore 699 GW (95%) with offshore trailing with 34 GW (5%). Of this total amount, China accounted for 281 GW (38%), Europe had 207 GW (28%), while the U.S. came in a distant third with 118 GW (16%). Importantly, China dominated wind turbine and blade manufacturing with six companies in the top ten. GE Vernova was the only U.S. company on that list. Also, China produced 90% of the world's permanent magnets for wind turbines, so the associated critical mineral supply chains flowed through China (rare earths).[74]

In 2024, the world added a modest 123 GW of wind capacity, bringing the total to 1.1 TW. Asia led by adding 86 GW of which almost all came from China with 80 GW. This gave the region 52% of all wind production with China responsible for most of it. Europe added just 11 GW of wind capacity which gave them 268 GW total (24%). The U.S. added very little wind power, just 5 GW, bringing them to 153 GW total (14%). In summary, China improved its market share from 38% of all wind capacity in 2020 to 46% in 2024. Far from gaining ground during Biden's tenure, the U.S. fell further behind.[75]

EV Production 2020-2024

In 2020, the world sold 3.2 million BEVs (Battery Electric Vehicles) with 1.4 million sold in the China market for a 44% share.[76] Of this, 245,000 BEVs were sold in the U.S. (7.6%) with Tesla dominating by making 204,000 of these for 83% of U.S. market share.[77] Other U.S. manufacturers like Ford and GM sold statistically insignificant volumes. Because of this market dominance, most battery manufacturing took place in Asia to feed the China market with the associated battery mineral supply chains following suit (lithium, nickel, manganese, cobalt, iron, phosphate, graphite). This also meant that the rare earth permanent magnet supply chain supporting electric motor production led to Aisa/China.

By 2024, world BEV sales skyrocketed to over 10.8 million annually with China leading with 6.3 million for a 58% share, increasing its lead greatly from just four years prior. Europe sold 1.99 million BEVs for an 18% market share

74 IRENA 2024 Annual Report

75 IRENA 2024 Annual Report.

76 https://ev-volumes.com/news/ev/global-ev-sales-for-2021/

77 https://cleantechnica.com/2023/02/25/us-electric-car-sales-increased-65-in-2022/

and the U.S was last with 1.3 million for a 12% market share. The rest of the world bought the remaining 11% of EV production.[78] In the U.S., Tesla increased its sales to 633,000 which resulted in a significant drop of market share to just 48%. Other market leaders in the U.S. included Hyundai/Kia with 117,700 BEVS sold (9%), Ford with 97,800 sold (7.5%), Chevrolet with 68,000 sold (5.2%), and Rivian with 51,400 (4%). With China increasing its relative market lead in the BEV space, the associated critical minerals pathways to remained unchanged.[79]

Under the IRA's Advanced Technology Vehicles Manufacturing (ATVM) Loan Program, American BEV manufacturer Rivian received a $6.57 billion loan from the DOE in 2025 to build a production plant in Georgia. American BEV manufacturer Lucid Motors did not get a DOE loan and is largely funded by Saudi Arabia's Public Investment Fund. Because Lucid had such low sales, just 10,000 BEVs in 2024, they most likely did not meet DOE's requirement of having a reasonable expectation to repay the loan.

Also, under the IRA's Domestic Manufacturing Conversion Grant Program, DOE provided $1.8 billion in 2024 for internal combustion engine (ICE) manufacturers to convert production plants they were unwilling or unable to do themselves. Stellantis (Chrysler) received by far the largest grant at $584 million, followed by General Motors with $500 million, and then Mercedes-Benz $284 million. These grants were an admission that traditional U.S. and European ICE manufacturers were non-competitive with the Chinese BEV industry and were unable to make the conversion to BEVs without government subsidies.

Battery Production 2020-2024

In 2020, global EV battery production was centered in Asia and specifically in China. The top ten battery manufacturers in the world accounted for over 92% of production with seven of the companies being Chinese (taking 54% of total market share), two were South Korean, and one Japanese. While South Korea and Japan produced EV batteries, much of their manufacturing capacity was positioned in China to feed what was the single largest BEV market in the world. In the U.S., EV battery manufacturing was dominated by just three foreign companies: Panasonic (Japan), LG Chem (South Korea), and AESC (China).

78 www.evuniverse.io

79 Kelly Blue Book 2024 EV Sales Report.

U.S. EV Battery Plants

Company	Plant Description	Status in 2025
SK On & Ford	43 GWh, Kentucky	Opens in 2025
~~SK On & Ford~~	~~43 GWh, Kentucky~~	~~Halted indefinitely~~
~~SK On & Ford~~	~~43 GWh plant in Tennessee~~	~~Halted until 2027~~
CATL & Ford	20 GWh, LFP, Michigan	Opens in 2026
LGES	5 GWh (25 GWh), Michigan	Opened in 2010
LGES	41 GWh, NCMA, Michigan	Under construction
LGES	36 GWh, Arizona	Under construction
LGES & GM	30 GWh, Ohio	Opened in 2022
LGES & GM	35 GWh, Tennessee	Opened in 2024
LGES & Honda	40 GWh, Ohio	Under construction
LGES	53 GWh, Arizona	Under construction
LGES & Hyundai	30 GWh, Georgia	Under construction
Samsung & Stellantis	33, GWh, Indiana	Opens in 2025
Samsung & Stellantis	33 GWh, Indiana	Opens in 2027
~~Samsung & GM~~	~~27 GWh, Indiana~~	~~Delayed until 2027~~
SK On	22 GWh, Georgia	Opened in 2022
SK On & Hyundai	35 GWh, Georgia	Opens in 2025
Panasonic & Tesla	38 GWh, NMC, Nevada	Opened in 2016
Panasonic & Tesla	30 GWh, NMC, Kansas	Opens in 2025
AESC	3 GWh, Tennessee	Opened in 2012
AESC	30 GWh, South Carolina	Under construction
AESC	30 GWh, Kentucky	Under construction
EVE Energy	21 GWH,Mississippi	Under construction
~~Kore Power~~	~~6 GWh, Arizona~~	~~Cancelled Feb 2025~~
~~Gotion~~	~~Michigan~~	~~In litigation~~
~~Gotion~~	~~50 GWh, Illinois~~	~~In litigation~~

** Out of 26 battery plants 6 were operational by 2024*
**A total of 133 GWh battery capacity operational in 2024*
**AESC is a Japanese company, but majority Chinese owned*
** KORE is an American owned company*

In 2024, the world produced more than 894 GW of battery capacity with Asia still dominating. This amount included batteries for both grid support and BEVs. Just ten companies accounted for almost 90% of production. Of this amount, six Chinese battery companies held 67.1% of production, South Korean companies 18.5%, and Japan just 3.3%. While this data showed a minor increased dispersion of battery production, the top six Chinese manufacturers significantly increased their market share[80]

In 2020, the U.S. had three operational battery plants run by AESC, LGES and Panasonic with a 46 GWh production capacity. In 2022, DOE loaned LG Energy Solutions and General Motors $2.5 billion to build three battery plants. In 2023, DOE announced plans to loan Ford Motor and SK On $9.2 billion to build their three battery plants. And in 2024, DOE announced more plans to loan Samsung SDI and Stellantis $7.5 billion to build two battery plants. At the end of 2024, the U.S. had tripled its battery capacity with six operational plants and a 133 GW capacity.

The IRA incentives drove this onshoring of battery plants in the U.S. and must be considered an effective policy measure. But 25 out of these 26 plants were foreign-owned: two were Japanese, five were Chinese, and eighteen were South Korean. This is important because in the short run, the critical mineral supply chains still flowed through the parent companies. For example, if 98% of the world's graphite anodes are made in China, then a key component of battery manufacturing still flows through Asia before getting to the U.S. Onshoring battery plants, although a necessary transitional step, didn't immediately restructure the associated global battery mineral supply chains.

The Minerals Security Partnership

The world has only one global metals and minerals system which does not recognize humankind's contrived geographic boundaries. Because of our cellphone syndrome (a cellphone requires thirty-five different minerals to make) our mineral needs are complex. Consequently, no single country has all the mineral resources required to support their economy and society. Thus, increased domestic mining won't ensure a country's absolute mineral security (MINSEC). This reality means a country must develop international partnerships and resilient trade relationships to achieve a higher level of MINSEC. Or we can give up our cellphones.

In 2022, the Biden Administration established the Minerals Security Partnership (MSP) which now consists of fifteen countries and the European Union.[81] MSP was created specifically as a counterbalance to China's own worldwide minerals investments, especially in the energy minerals space. It

80 Cnevpost.com

81 All G7 countries are members.

was critical for the U.S. to have both Canada and Australia onboard since their territories covered large expanses with established mining industries. The goal of the organization was to direct investments towards critical minerals projects worldwide with a focus on those used for battery production, rare earths, and copper. Specifically, the objectives were:

- Diversifying and stabilizing global supply chains
- Investment in those supply chains
- Promoting high standards in the mining, processing, and recycling sectors that ensure companies compete on a level playing field
- Increasing recycling of critical minerals

In the fall of 2022, the U.S. convened the first MSP event in New York City with participation from major minerals producing countries like Brazil (nickel), Democratic Republic of the Congo (cobalt) and Mozambique (graphite). In the spring of 2023, MSP members met again in South Africa (manganese, PGM) with attendance by seven different African countries. It took the U.S. several years to grow its membership and figure out how it should operate, resulting in the establishment of the MSP Forum in 2024. The first forum included attendance by Kazakhstan (chromium), Namibia, Ukraine (graphite), and Uzbekistan.

In the waning months of the Biden administration in late 2024, the organization announced the establishment of the MSP Finance Network where members would contribute funds to pool resources and invest in mining projects of mutual interests. However, the MSP took years to organize due to its international nature, leading to political and bureaucratic complexities. As of early 2025, the MSP most likely had not invested in any mining projects.

For instance, on the State Department's website, the MSP's U.S. spokesperson "welcomed" a deal between Belgium's Umicore and the Democratic Republic of the Congo in 2024. In this arrangement, Umicore signed a long-term agreement with the DRC to provide them with germanium extraction technology in return for exclusive rights to the recovered material.[82] Although the State Department's posting led one to believe this was an MSP orchestrated deal, neither Belgium nor the DRC were members of the MSP. This was just hyping a program that still needed years to work out the mechanics. As soon

82 In their official company announcement, Umicore did not mention any involvement by the MSP.

as the Trump administration took over in 2025, they froze the previous MSP's website and critical minerals were no longer listed as a policy focus.

During this period, China moved out aggressively in the international battery minerals space. To start, six different Chinese companies inked agreements with Morocco to build LFP battery manufacturing plants in the country, essentially securing all available phosphate production. In Zimbabwe, three Chinese companies owned the only productive lithium operations, creating a monopoly. Also, several Chinese companies moved into Indonesia where they came to dominate its nickel extraction operations. By harnessing the global flow of battery minerals, China was able to retain its dominance in both the LFP and NMC battery space in contrast to the U.S.' own weak position.

Friendshoring

The objective of this Agreement is to strengthen and diversify critical minerals supply chains and promote the adoption of electric vehicle battery technologies by formalizing the shared commitment of the Parties to facilitate trade, promote fair competition and market-oriented conditions for trade in critical minerals, ensure robust labor and environmental standards, and cooperate in efforts to ensure secure, sustainable, and equitable critical minerals supply chains.

- U.S. – Japan Critical Minerals Agreement, 2023

In 2023, the Biden administration introduced another pillar of its critical mineral strategy called "friendshoring" where the U.S. sought to secure the flow of critical minerals from its allies. Specifically, the U.S. signed a bilateral Critical Minerals Agreement (CMA) with Japan concerning five minerals: cobalt, graphite, lithium, manganese, and nickel. The CMA was required for Japan to benefit from the Inflation Reduction Act incentives since the U.S. and Japan did not have a standing Free Trade Agreement (FTA). Only countries with an FTA were eligible to receive the incentives. For the purpose of receiving the incentives, the U.S. Department of the Treasury recognized the CMA as having the same designation as a FTA.

This CMA was important because Panasonic had partnered with Tesla to produce batteries for their BEVs and had been operational at their Nevada factory since 2016. At the time of signing, Panasonic was the single largest battery manufacturer in the country. If Japanese companies could not benefit from the

IRA incentives, they could choose to prioritize their operations elsewhere in Europe and Asia as opposed to North America. However, Japanese-based battery company AESC which already had one battery plant in the U.S. and was building two more, was majority Chinese owned. According to the DOE, AESC would be considered a Foreign Entity of Concern (FEOC) and not eligible to receive the incentives.

To be clear, the CMA was not a comprehensive critical minerals agreement and only addressed the five minerals already identified. Its sole purpose was to give Japan access to the IRA incentives for battery production in the U.S. There were only two "hard" provisions in the CMA: 1) both parties agreed not to restrict the import or export of critical minerals between the parties and 2) neither party would impose export tariffs on these minerals.[83] The rest of the CMA had "soft" language in that the two parties were not obligated to do anything concrete but would endeavor to work together to facilitate the trade of the five identified battery minerals.

The administration also entered CMA negotiations with the European Union (EU), the UK, and Indonesia, all of which did not have FTAs with the U.S. The CMAs discussed were like the one with Japan, focusing squarely on battery minerals for IRA tax incentives. Sticking points for the EU included the problem that the agreement could draw battery factories away from Europe, undermining their own minerals security. Issues with Indonesia included environmental protections and fair labor practices. By the start of 2025, CMA discussions had stalled and future agreements were in doubt.

The U.S. attempt to friendshore specific critical minerals through CMAs met with limited success just as the Minerals Security Partnership had. The biggest failing of the U.S. was not opening up 45X tax incentives for all countries with critical minerals, regardless of their trade status. The global flow of metals and minerals defied joint coordination just as it had during the period between WWI and WWII. Competing domestic stakeholders, such as mining companies and battery manufacturers, and divergent national interests between negotiating countries, ensured that larger critical mineral cooperation was politically unattainable. The fractured response by the U.S. and its allies on even relatively minor topics like battery minerals ensured China's continuing strong position in the space.

83 Japan and the U.S. were already obligated to do this under the 1994 General Agreement on Tariffs and Trade (GATT). GATT obligations are still in effect under the World Trade Organization founded in 1995.

The Growing Minerals Cold War: The U.S. & China

The concentration of production within China for certain critical global supply chains leaves the United States and other countries vulnerable to disruption and potential strategic trade interdictions by the Chinese Communist Party (CCP).

- U.S.-China Economic and Security Review Commission, 2023 Annual Report to Congress

The U.S.' recent efforts to improve its MINSEC through creation of a comprehensive critical minerals strategy must be seen in context of larger U.S.-China competition. One layer of this competition is ideological where Beijing's communist political system embodies values significantly different from Washington's democratic system. The Chinese system is considerably more authoritarian where individual liberties are less important than the collective accomplishments of society and the goals of the State. In comparison, the U.S. system disperses government power more widely and individualism is seen as a key pillar to the success of the State. Some have argued that the two systems are diametrically opposed, cannot coexist peacefully, and one will inevitably consume the other.

The second layer of this competitional foundation is China's stated goal to supplant the U.S. as the world's most powerful country. After WWII and the Allies' resounding victory, the U.S. found itself in a dominant position, having both the world's largest economy and military. The U.S. was subsequently instrumental in shaping an international system led by western liberal democracies. The U.S. benefitted greatly from the international mechanisms is helped to create and was contested only by a crumbling Soviet Union. With the total collapse of the Soviet Union in 1991, the U.S. truly had no peer. The U.S. recognized its relative dominance and was determined to retain its position in the international system, although it saw no challengers at the time.

In the mid-1990s, China gradually but relentlessly began to fill the space left in the international system by the Soviet Union's demise and Russia's own economic stagnation. Their growth was paired with the understanding that a global outlook was required to improve their own critical minerals security. In an early example of this, a Chinese consortium bought the U.S.' only rare earth magnet manufacturer in 1995 and in 1998 shipped all the equipment from one of the plants to China. In 2013, China formalized their Belt and Road Initiative (BRI), a global enterprise that provided partner countries loans for infrastructure development. Importantly, this provided Chinese companies with access to raw materials like minerals required for battery, wind, and solar manufacturing.

Beyond the competition for finite resources, there are many other friction points that keep U.S.-Chinese relations at a distance including continued U.S. support for Taiwan and recognition of its sovereignty. The U.S. and its Asian allies also oppose China's attempts to expand its influence in the South China Sea in violation of the United Nations Convention on the Law of the Sea (UNCLOS) and established Exclusive Economic Zones. China and the U.S. compete in Southeast Asia for political and economic primacy as Beijing's growth as a global power seeks to erode the U.S. position there.

On a larger scale, Beijing deliberately challenged the U.S.-led global status quo everywhere by creating its own competing political block in 2009, the BRICS (Brazil, Russia, India, China, South Africa) coalition. In 2014, the block created its own monetary mechanism, the New Development Bank, with authorized capital of $100 billion. The original BRICS has now expanded to included eleven members which China leads to counter the influence of the stablished and U.S.-led G7. These calculated moves are part of China's global geopolitical insurgency to overthrow U.S. power and place itself in the center of the international system. Existential questions remain: will China succeed in its quest and will a declining power allow a rising power to replace it without a fight?

Both the U.S. and China recognized that their economies were increasingly co-dependent, reaching a high of nearly $660 billion in combined trade in 2018. However, the U.S. had a $420 billion trade deficit, meaning they were more dependent on China while simultaneously and disproportionately feeding the economy of their chief competitor. That year, the Trump administration enacted a series of tariffs against Chinese imports ranging from 25% to 10%, depending on the category. The overarching intent was to reduce U.S. dependency on China through a strategic decoupling of their economies.

The subsequent Biden administration kept the tariffs on China, indicating the measures had bipartisan support and were in line with U.S. core national security interests. The new administration then went further and took measures to actively limit Chinese access to U.S. sourced advanced semiconductor technology. The continuation of the trade war to limit China's strategic technological capability resulted in retaliation by Beijing with its own restrictions on select critical minerals and related technology.

U.S.-China Trade War Timeline

2021: The U.S. Department of Defense puts Chinese battery manufacturer CATL on its Section 1260H list of Chinese military companies operating in the U.S. This is the first year DOD published this list in accordance with the National Defense Authorization Act of 2021. This is the only Chinese battery company selected and would remain on the list through 2025. CATL had no obvious connections to the Chinese military although their military most likely purchased CATL products.[84]

AUG 2022: The U.S. passes the CHIPS Act, a strategic investment in U.S. semiconductor capability to ensure long-term dominance in the space.

OCT 2022: The U.S. updates its Export Administration regulations that restrict the sales of advanced semiconductor manufacturing equipment to China. Restrictions were also placed on Foreign Direct Product (FDP) rules where foreign countries used U.S. technology to manufacture products that were then sold to China. The national security rational given was this restricted China's ability to develop Weapons of Mass Destruction (WMD) and conduct mass surveillance of its own citizens.

JAN 2023: The Netherlands and Japan implement export restrictions on Semiconductor Manufacturing Equipment (SME) in agreement with the U.S. While China is not mentioned, it is clearly the target of these actions.

MAR 2023: European Commission President Ursula von der Leyen calls for diplomatic and economic de-risking, making the EU less dependent on a rising China.

AUG 2023: In a move described as ensuring its national security, China institutes gallium and germanium export controls. Chinese manufacturers now had to apply for export licenses from the Ministry of Commerce (MOFCOM) and provide details of who they were selling their products to. While this enabled Beijing to deny sales, it also created another layer of bureaucracy which meant uncertainty, delays, and inflation for potential buyers.

OCT 2023: The U.S. places additional export restrictions on advanced computing and semiconductor manufacturing to China. The national se-

84 CATL = Contemporary Amperage Technology Limited

curity rational given was that this restricted Chinese development of advanced weaponry and the ability to violate human rights that are contrary to the interests of the U.S. and its allies.

OCT 2023: China's MOFCOM announces that battery-grade natural flake and synthetic graphite products now require export licenses and would take effect December 1st.

AUG 2024: China's MOFCOM announces antimony export restrictions with six different products, including separation technology, requiring an export license with enforcement beginning September 15.

OCT 2024: China issues comprehensive regulations on their domestic REE mining industry which included the implementation of quantitative controls. These regulations also crack down on illegal REE mining and sales. Overall, these new rules were expected to reduce REE exports for 2025 and increase prices.

DEC 2024: The U.S. restricts exports of additional American-made semiconductors, chipmaking tools, and software tools to 140 Chinese companies. Countries restricted from shipping their equipment to China include Israel, Malaysia, Singapore, South Korea, and Taiwan while the Netherlands and Japan were exempt.

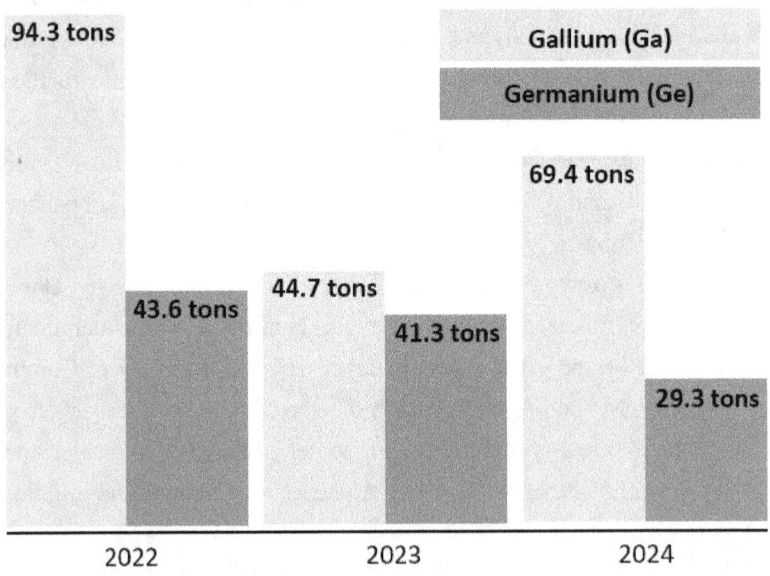

China's Gallium and Germanium Exports

DEC 2024: China's MOFCOM adds more export controls to gallium, germanium, antimony, and graphite that are considered dual-use by the U.S. military.

JAN 2025: China's MOFCOM updates its Catalogue of Technologies Prohibited and Restricted for Export. The list includes LFP (Lithium Iron Phosphate) cathode battery technology; LFMP (Lithium Iron Manganese Phosphate) battery technology; metallic gallium extraction technology; and lithium carbonate, lithium hydroxide, lithium metal, and direct lithium extraction (DLE) and processing technology.

FEB 2025: The Trump administration announced an across-the-board 10% tariff on all Chinese imports. Inexplicably, the tariffs did not include the Chinese Special Administrative Regions of Hong Kong and Macau. China responds by requiring export licenses for tungsten, indium, bismuth, tellurium, and molybdenum.

APR 2025: Trump issues sweeping tariffs against its trading partners, to include China.

APR 2025: China directs companies selling seven different REE to apply for export licenses with MOFCOM.

From a larger perspective, restricting battery technology meant China would better retain its existing global dominant position by denying the U.S. access to critical battery cathode and midstream processing technology. In turn, the U.S. would be locked into using technology through its existing relationships with South Korean and Japanese battery manufacturers. This also put in doubt Ford and CATL's plans to open their joint LFP battery plant located in Michigan, forecasted to open in 2026. Overall, the restrictions put pressure on the U.S. to develop an ex-China battery value chain, something they had been unable or unwilling to do.

What the long-term impact of China's mineral and related restrictions turns out to be will take several years to determine. In the short term, some buyers stockpiled minerals before the actual restrictions took place, raising prices. Exports from China slumped as sellers navigated the new bureaucratic requirements which delayed shipments for months. U.S. buyers had to find new sellers which meant higher prices as they had to pay intermediary service fees. It remained to be seen how strictly the Chinese bureaucracy would restrict sales to third-party sellers who ultimately sold their products to U.S. end-users.

Antimony: The initial announcement in August 2024 required an export license but not an outright ban, meaning there were no restrictions on its sale to the U.S. The December 2024 announcement may be more restrictive. Because of these relatively soft measures, there was no immediate negative impact felt and U.S. imports of antimony products actually increased from 21,000 tons in 2023 to 24,700 tons in 2024. However, China decreased its own production from 62,300 tons in 2023 to 60,000 tons in 2024. The price for antinomy metal increased significantly from \$10,980.00 a ton in 2023 to \$19,000.00 a ton in 2024.

Gallium: The first MOFCOM announcement in August 2023 required an export license for gallium products but was not a ban. The follow up restriction in December 2024 will likely have more impact. U.S. imports of gallium metal decreased slightly from 11.4 metric tons in 2023 to 11 tons in 2024 while GaAs wafers increased from 163 metric tons to 180 tons. Although China restricted its gallium exports, it increased production significantly from 621 tons in 2023 to 750 tons in 2024 which was almost 99% of global primary production. High-purity gallium prices increased from \$4,500.00 a metric ton in 2023 to \$5,000.00 a ton in 2024.

Germanium: The first MOFCOM announcement in August 2023 required an export license on germanium products but not a ban. The follow up restriction in December 2024 will likely have more impact. U.S. imports of germanium products fell slightly from 36 tons in 2023 to 33 tons in 2024. However, imported germanium metal prices increased drastically from \$1.39 million a metric ton in 2023 to \$2.1 million in 2024 while germanium dioxide also went up from \$880,000.00 a ton to \$1.4 million. While the U.S. does not know how much germanium the world collectively produces, China's is believed to be the single largest producer and exporter.

Natural Flake Graphite: This followed the same pattern with MOFCOM requiring an initial export license in 2023 and then stricter measures the following year. While the U.S. decreased its imports from 73,500 tons in 2023 to 60,000 tons in 2024, this was due mainly to its increased use of synthetic graphite sourced from China. Meanwhile, Beijing increased its natural graphite production slightly from 1.21 million metric tons in 2023 to 1.27 million tons in 2024. Average graphite flake prices decreased from $1,080.00 a metric ton in 2023 to $1,070.00 a ton the following year because of a continuing overproduction by China.

From these four examples we see that Beijing initiated soft restrictions as a form of strategic messaging that they had the ability to leverage mineral exports to the U.S. Subsequent stricter measures were easier to enact because Beijing had taken a year to condition their own bureaucratic system through export licensing. This also had the effect of acquiring market intelligence as China built an official database of who was importing minerals from their sellers. Although these soft measures did not negatively impact the volume of U.S. imports, they did contribute to considerable inflation in three of the four minerals restricted. Since harder restrictions were enacted only at the end of 2024, it remains to be seen what the effects will be for 2025.

Beijing took a relatively soft retaliatory approach considering that the U.S. sourced the majority of 25 different critical minerals from China. A complete ban of these minerals would put the U.S. in a short-term supply shock across many industries. The potential economic leverage Beijing wields is very real since the U.S. has studiously neglected its own National Defense Stockpile and has only 4% on hand (two weeks) of a one-year reserve. While the U.S. has recently made significant steps to improving the security of its critical minerals supply chains, it is unprepared for a critical minerals war with China.

Critical Mineral Supply Chains 2020-2024

Overall, the U.S. mining industry expanded significantly in value from the first year of the Trump administration in 2017 to the end of the Biden administration in 2024. To be specific, the net export value of raw minerals rose over 30%, net import value grew 16%, while overall domestic mining value increased 41%. For processed minerals, net export value grew only 12%, net imports rose 30%, and overall domestic value increased 24%. The U.S. exported more raw materials than it imported while the opposite was true for processed minerals.[85]

85 U.S. Geological Survey.

While the overall mining industry grew consistently over both administrations, we should focus on how the U.S.' fifty identified critical minerals and their associated supply chains responded to the Biden administration's efforts from 2021-2024. For this purpose, I compared the available data relating to domestic production and reliance on foreign imports for each mineral for the year 2020 and then compared this same data with the year 2024.[86] The results showed several improvements, increased insecurity for many, and little or no change for the bulk of the minerals.

To start, the U.S. reduced its reliance on foreign imports of four minerals (beryllium, tellurium, vanadium, tin) although some of the gains were modest.[87] The vulnerability of 27 minerals actually increased for a variety reasons. In one example, the U.S. increased arsenic imports with a higher reliance on direct sourcing from China.[88] For the remaining 19 minerals there was no significant change in their vulnerability. If we look at cobalt, a battery mineral, the U.S.' already limited domestic production decreased while our overall import reliance remained the same at 76%.

U.S. Non-Fuel Mineral Industry 2017-2024

Raw Materials	**2017**	**2021**	**2024**
Net Exports Value	$8.1 billion	$10.6 billion	$10.6 billion
Net Imports Value	$5 billion	$5.3 billion	$5.8 billion
Domestic Mining Value	$75.2 billion	$90 billion	$106 billion
Recycled Products Value	$22.9 billion	$43 billion	$48 billion
Processed Minerals			
Domestic Value	$727 billion	$820 billion	$900 billion
Net Imports Value	$137 billion	$192 billion	$178 billion
Net Exports Value	$90 billion	$102 billion	$101 billion
Value Added to GDP*	$2.9 trillion (15%)	$3.3 trillion (15%)	$4 trillion (14%)
National GDP	$19.38 trillion	$22.4 trillion	$29.1 trillion

**Value added to the gross domestic product by major industries that consume processed mineral materials.*

From this comparative data, it is clear that the 10% IRA Section 45X tax credits for critical minerals were not enough to restructure established supply

86 USGS provides an import average over four years so the 2020 data is an average over the course of the Trump administration and the 2024 data an average of the Biden administration.

87 For tin, the U.S. went from a 77% reliance to a 73% reliance.

88 The U.S. is 100% reliant on arsenic (As) imports. It increased As metal imports from 522 to 530 tons and As trioxide from 7,780 tons to 8,600 tons.

chains. If we look at graphite where Novonix is building a $1 billion synthetic manufacturing operation, a 10% tax credit, although helpful, is rather insignificant in comparison and not enough to move the market. A real shift requires other assistance like grants and guaranteed loans. Also, it was not realistic to think minerals that had become increasingly vulnerable over decades could be quickly secured in a span of just two to three years. It could take ten years for the gears of government assistance to get moving, approvals granted, manufacturing facilities built, and trial production tested. Critical minerals security had to be based on continuous effective policy and not crisis management.

It was also evident that blanket government policies, although helpful, were not enough to address the very specific needs of different minerals with unique industry characteristics. For instance, the U.S. has been losing primary aluminum smelter capacity over the previous decade due to high electricity costs as smelter operations are energy intensive. Also, the U.S. extracts no bauxite used for aluminum production and is primarily dependent on imports from Jamaica. If the U.S. were to increase its aluminum supply chain security, it would look a lot different than what it would do to secure its niobium supply chains, which is a very low volume product with a 100% import reliance.

What is The U.S.' Critical Minerals Strategy?

Despite the Biden administration doing more to secure the U.S. critical minerals enterprise than any other administration since the 1950s, it still had no published critical minerals strategy. There was no single document laying out in detail what the U.S. national plan was, although multiple federal agencies like DOE published their own critical mineral strategies. Despite this lack of official national guidance, Biden chose to coordinate his critical minerals agenda internally through his cabinet leaders, leaving us with a de facto critical minerals strategy.

The Eight Pillars of the Biden Strategy, listed in descending order by how much was invested in each one through both the Bipartisan Infrastructure Law of 2021, Inflation Reduction Act of 2022, and other identified sources:

- Restructuring Battery Minerals Supply Chains
- Restructuring Critical Minerals Supply Chains
- Restructuring Greentech Mineral Supply Chains
- Expanding Geological Mapping of the U.S.
- Improving Critical Minerals Research w/ Focus on REE

- Speeding up the Domestic Mining Permitting Process
- Training the Critical Minerals Workforce
- Developing International Mineral Partnerships

The strategy's focus was clearly on battery minerals to support the U.S.' underdeveloped BEV and associated battery manufacturing industries. Although it was too soon to tell, initial indications revealed that enough of the associated battery supply chains would eventually be restructured towards the U.S. to satisfy the American market. The same could be said for scores of domestic critical mineral projects, although it would take several more years for these to develop. Notably, REE were one area where significant progress was made. Most likely, there weren't enough incentives to significantly shift solar and wind supply chains toward the U.S. because of China's overwhelming dominance.

A glaring failure for the Biden administration (and every other prior administration) was its inability to harness a massive and apathetic federal bureaucracy that defied any attempt to increase its agility. There was no indication that the mining permitting process had been improved nor would it without significant structural change to the bureaucracy. Another shortcoming was the inability to develop effective mineral partnerships – this was clearly an area where the U.S. needed to act decisively but didn't. Two other areas that should have been made priorities were the recycling of all critical minerals and filling out the National Defense Stockpile (NDS). Recycling was not addressed adequately and the NDS was completely ignored.

For the U.S. critical minerals enterprise to thrive moving into 2025 and beyond, it is crucial that Trump 2.0 continue the previous programs and existing momentum. Much of the de facto Biden strategy overlapped with the Trump 1.0's policies except for the focus on low-carbon energy minerals. Because the Republican party is the political repository for climate change denial in America, it is likely that greentech mineral supply chains won't be supported under Trump 2.0. However, the 45X critical mineral tax credits will likely endure along with battery manufacturing efforts due to the economic momentum these programs have. Regardless, securing the critical minerals enterprise is a core national interest and thus a bipartisan issue. The U.S. must have continuity across administrations if it is going develop an overarching vision that achieves the minerals security it wants.

Sources

"A Critical Minerals Policy for the United States." The Aspen Institute, Energy and Environment Program, Spring 2023.

"Building Resilient Supply Chains, Revitalizing American Manufacturing, and Fostering Broad-Based Growth." The White House, June 2021.

"Critical Minerals and Materials, U.S. DOE's Strategy to Support Domestic Critical Mineral and Material Supply Chains, FY 2021 - FY2031.

"Critical Minerals Resources: National Policy and Critical Minerals List." Congressional Research Service, April 8, 2024.

"Fostering an Electric future: A Federal Perspective on the U.S. Critical Mineral Supply Chain." Zero Emissions Transportation Association, September 2023.

Kocakusak, Diren, et. al. "Wind and solar year in review 2024." Global Energy Monitor, February 2025.

Nassar, Nadal T., et al. "Evaluating the mineral commodity supply risk of the U.S. manufacturing sector." Science Advances, February 2020.

Nassar, Nedal and Steve Fortier. U.S. Geological Survey. " Methodology and Technical Input for the 2021 Review and Revision of the U.S. Critical Minerals List."

Nassar, Nedal T., et. al. "Quantifying Potential Effects of China's Gallium and Germanium Export Restrictions on the U.S. Economy." USGS, 2024.

"North American Industry Classification System." Office of Management and Budget, 2022.

"Renewable Capacity Statistics 2025." International Renewable Energy Agency, February 2025.

"The Quest for Growth, Critical Minerals & The Majors." Benchmark Minerals Intelligence, 2024.

"2025 Mining Facts." National Mining Association.

U.S. Geological Survey identified Critical Minerals			
Mineral	**Use**	**Mineral**	**Use**
Aluminum	alloys	Magnesium	alloys
Antimony	alloys	Manganese	alloys
Arsenic	semiconductors	Neodymium	magnets
Barite	weighting agent	Nickel	alloys
Beryllium	alloys, electronics	Niobium	alloys, electronics
Bismuth	alloys, electronics	Palladium	electronics, catalytics
Cerium	magnets, catalytics	Platinum	catalytics, alloys
Cesium	oil industry	Praseodymium	magnets
Chromium	steel, alloys	Rhodium	catalytic converters
Cobalt	batteries	Rubidium	photoelectric cells
Dysprosium	magnets	Ruthenium	electronics
Erbium	fiber optics	Samarium	magnets, optics
Europium	cathode ray tubes	Scandium	electronics, lasers
Fluorspar	steel, alloys	Tantalum	electronics
Gadolinium	magnets	Tellurium	alloys, electronics
Gallium	semiconductors	Terbium	magnets
Germanium	semiconductors	Thulium	x-rays, lasers
Graphite	batteries	Tin	electronics
Hafnium	semiconductors	Titanium	alloys
Holmium	magnets	Tungsten	alloys, steel
Indium	photovoltaics	Vanadium	alloys, steel
Iridium	semiconductors	Ytterbium	alloys, optics, lasers
Lanthanum	alloys	Yttrium	alloys, optics, lasers
Lithium	batteries	Zinc	steel, electronics
Lutetium	oil refining	Zirconium	alloys

Above are the fifty critical minerals identified by U.S. Geological survey. These were assessed as being vulnerable due to a variety of factors such as majority importation from overseas sources, single sourcing as opposed to multiple import streams, and sourcing from companies under financial distress and subject to future bankruptcy proceedings or being bought out by a foreign company.

Chapter 3

The Great Minerals Game

"It is imperative for our national security that the United States take immediate action to facilitate domestic mineral production to the maximum extent possible."

- White House Directive, March 20, 2025

Trump Administration 2.0

We know what Trump 1.0's critical minerals strategy was after observing it from 2017-2020. As a review, the administration declared a critical minerals emergency, announced its intent to "buy" Greenland, issued *A Federal Strategy To Ensure Secure and Reliable Supplies of Critical Minerals*, published a 50-page strategy, and passed the Energy Act of 2020 which authorized $127 million for REE recovery and $600 million for critical minerals research. Trump 1.0 raised awareness of the country's continuing minerals insecurity, socialized the government groupthink for future action, and took initial steps to improve the U.S.' minerals supply chains.

A central part of Trump 2.0's strategy was increased domestic mining as was published in the March 20, 2025, Executive Order *Immediate Measures to Increase American Mineral Production*. The EO addressed not just critical minerals but also uranium, potash, copper and gold. The NEDC (National Energy Dominance Council) was given responsibility for improving the federal mining permitting process.[89] The Secretaries of Defense, Interior, Energy, and Agriculture were tasked with identifying federal lands suitable for private mining operations to include midstream processing facilities. This guidance was clearly done to bypass restrictive environmental regulations and avoid litigation from private organizations.[90]

89 This would be done in consultation with the Permitting Council.

90 This would be done in consultation with the Assistant to the President for Economic

The relevant federal agencies and the Small Business Administration were further directed to provide access to federal funding to advance mineral production. The mechanisms directed to assist with access to capital included the National Security Capital Forum, the U.S. International Development Finance Corporation (DFC), the Office of Strategic Capital, authorities under the Defense Production Act, and the Export-Import Bank. The overarching intent was to make the necessary private-public capital available for mineral operations as identified by the EO.

The inclusion of copper in the directive must be taken in the context of the subsequent EO *Strengthening the Reliability and Security of the United States Electric Grid* published on April 8, 2025. Although the order did not address minerals specifically, a secure and reliable supply of copper was required to improve the national grid. Also, other critical minerals were required such as REE permanent magnets for wind turbine manufacturing, tellurium for solar panels, and a variety of battery minerals for ESS (Energy Storage Solutions).

However, the U.S.' minerals security was directly impacted by Trump 2.0's trade policies with just one being *Modifying Reciprocal Tariff Rates to Reflect Trading Partner Retaliation and Alignment* issued on April 9, 2025. The administration regularly shifted its tariff positions so often that it was uncertain what metals and minerals would receive tariffs, at what rate, and for what countries. In one instance, Trump 2.0 vowed to put 25% tariffs on all steel and aluminum imports, including from allies like Canada and Mexico. China received the highest tariff rates to address ongoing trade imbalances which triggered Beijing to start a series of critical minerals export restrictions against the U.S.

While these published policies indicated what a larger strategy may entail, the administration pursued other means to improve its critical minerals security. To start, Trump 2.0 made repeated overtures to "buy" Greenland from Denmark although the massive island was a sovereign country. The administration also made efforts to secure conflict minerals from Ukraine which quickly became a political bargaining chip for Kyiv in its efforts to defeat Russia.

Another piece of the Trump 2.0 strategy was growing the critical minerals workforce which required effort in both the federal and civilian space. However, this was easy to say but hard to do, especially with Trump 2.0's policy of cutting the federal work force. U.S. Geological Survey was already overworked and understaffed and couldn't accomplish all its tasks as was true of the federal

Policy and National Security Affairs.

permitting workforce – mining permits already took years just to be reviewed for initial processing. Also, the continually shifting tariff policies made it impossible to forecast manufacturing input costs, which in turn paralyzed the hiring process.

The published policies and other observed actions formed a de facto critical minerals strategy. The five pillars of this were: 1) increased domestic mining, 2) protectionist policies, 3) securing new territory with minerals, 4) securing conflict minerals, and 5) maintain existing Biden-era policies with Trump 2.0 characteristics. Combined, this strategy embraced both novel and old ideas, some that made sense and others that didn't. Since Trump proved himself to be transactional minded and able to quickly shift gears from what he stated publicly to what he eventually did, any strategy was best described as "fluid."

Greenland Syndrome

On the face of it, Trump's attempt to "buy" Greenland in 2019 and 2025 to acquire its minerals made little sense. After digging into the topic and understanding the country's mineral resources, history, economics, and political status, it might be slightly less unhinged. However, this was the start of Trump 2.0's critical minerals strategy, the initial piece of spaghetti thrown into a tornado, hoping it might stick somewhere. This was also typical of Trump 2.0's foreign policy: outrageous, unconventional, and confrontational. It's best to start at the beginning.

Greenland is the world's largest island and, geographically, is considered part of North America. Because of its location near the North Pole, the island resides in an arctic and subarctic climate which is why it has the world's second largest ice sheet. Greenland is cold, rugged, and makes living there difficult, which is why it is sparsely populated.[91] Because of rising average temperatures from manmade global warming from our carbon-fueled economies, the Greenland Ice Sheet is melting which will likely raise global sea levels by one foot or more.

Western Europeans first discovered Greenland in 982 AD when the famous Norwegian Erik the Red landed on its shores after traveling there on an expedition from neighboring Iceland. It has since been passed down through history that Erik the Red called it "the green land" because of the time of year that he landed in the southern part of the country. Erik the Red returned in 985 with

91 Approximately 56,000 people live in Greenland.

several hundred Norse men and women to form permanent settlements in their periodically lush green coastal lands. Later, more settlers came from Iceland, Norway, and Scandinavia, probably numbering several thousands. During the 1400s, for reasons that can only be guessed, this Norse presence disappeared, leaving Greenland alone to the Inuit people.[92]

Europe reengaged Greenland in 1721 when Hans Poulsen Egede, a Lutheran missionary, traveled there to connect with the lost Norse colonies and spread the Christian faith. While Egede only found the existing Inuit societies, his expedition began a second wave of European colonization which the underdeveloped Inuit had no chance of stopping. At the time, Egede was a citizen of the Dano-Norwegian Realm, a political union consisting of Denmark, Norway, Greenland, Iceland, the Faroe Islands, and two states that are now part of Germany. As part of the political fallout from the Napoleonic Wars, the Treaty of Kiel in 1814 ended the Denmark-Norway union and ceded Greenland to the Danish Kingdom.

A statue of Hans Egede stands watch over Greenland's capital of Nuuk, located in the southwest of the country.

At the end of World War I, the Danish Kingdom began losing control of its Norse island colonies, starting with the Danish-Icelandic Act of Union in 1918 which granted Iceland its independence.[93] In 1948, Denmark granted the Faroe Islands home rule although Copenhagen was responsible for their security. Because Greenland increasingly sought independence from Denmark, it was granted home rule in 1979 and then self-rule in 2009. Today, Copenhagen

92 The Inuit arrived in the 1200s when Norse settlements were still active.

93 In 1944, while Denmark was occupied by Germany, Iceland held a constitutional referendum declaring itself an independent republic.

still provides for the island's national defense because it is incapable of doing so itself as it has little industry with just a tiny GDP of $3.85 billion.

While Trump's offer to buy Greenland made his administration look like neocolonial bullies and quite possibly detached from political reality, this is not the first time the subject has been raised. In 1867, the U.S. increased the size of its territory by more than 660,000 square miles when the Andrew Johnson administration bought Alaska from the Russian Empire for a mere $7.2 million - the steal of the century. Secretary of State William Seward, fresh from orchestrating the deal, wanted to expand U.S. territory further and contemplated purchasing both Greenland and Iceland from Denmark. The U.S. State Department even published the Peirce Report in 1868 to influence public opinion to support the idea.[94]

The report emphasized that Denmark treated its Iceland colony poorly, its citizens were therefore disgruntled, and that it was ripe for acquisition by the U.S. Furthermore, the island could support a population of 1 million people (at the time they were estimated to have just 70,000) due to its vast agricultural, livestock, furs, and fishing resources. Iceland's "valuable mines" were also mentioned with a focus on sulfur and coal, although an attached appendix on Iceland's exports in 1806 revealed no mineral products at all.

Greenland, too, was described as being neglected by Denmark and with vast natural resources comprised of accessible farmland, animals, furs, and fishing. The country also contained "great mineral wealth" which mostly consisted of coal deposits located close to viable ports which could quite practically be shipped to Alaska in summer months. Furthermore, Greenland was identified as having vast cryolite resources which were used to process aluminum. The cryolite mines were described to the public as "inexhaustible" and the overall mineral potential of the island was considered "immense".

But how serious was this idea of acquiring two new colonies in the North Atlantic Ocean? According to reporting at the time, Secretary Seward had prepared an offer of $5.5 million in gold and would soon present the Pierce Report along with a draft of the treaty to the senate.[95] Simultaneously, Copenhagen was negotiating a sale of the Danish West Indies to the U.S. which was formally rejected by Congress in 1870. Since there was considerable criticism of the recent

94 *A Report on the Resources of Iceland and Greenland.* The author, Professor Benjamin Peirce, was a mining engineer.
95 Cleveland Daily Leader, July 2, 1868.

sale of Alaska and growing resistance to the pending purchase of the islands, Seward was forced to drop the idea of acquiring Greenland and Iceland.

The idea of gaining Danish territories came up again in 1910 when the U.S. representative to Denmark, Ambassador Maurice Egan, proposed a three-way land swap. The plan was for the U.S. to take Greenland and the West Indies from Denmark, who would in exchange receive the Island of Mindanao that was part of the Philippines which the U.S. had acquired during the Spanish-American War. In turn, Denmark would give Mindanao to Germany who needed a Far East naval base. Germany would in return give Denmark the European state of Northern Schleswig. The deal never went through.[96]

With the onset of World War I in 1914, buying Danish territory became fashionable again when the U.S. finally purchased the West Indies which became the U.S. Virgin Islands of St. Thomas, St. John, and St. Croix. The chief concern for the U.S. was preventing Germany from using the islands as U-boat bases to attack the U.S. east coast and shipping that traversed the strategically important Panama Canal. However, the price had gone up from the $7.5 million agreed to earlier to $25 million in gold with the Treaty of the Danish West Indies being ratified in 1917. The precedent of purchasing Danish territory had been set.

World War II set in motion subsequent efforts to secure Greenland, specifically, with Germany's invasion and occupation of Denmark in 1940. To prevent German claims to and military use of the island, the U.S. set in motion plans to occupy it. However, this required some political acrobatics because the U.S. was officially a neutral country and Denmark never agreed to their island's occupation. Citing the Monroe Doctrine, the U.S. signaled that any country's interference in Greenland would be taken as a direct threat. In 1941, the Danish ambassador to the U.S. signed the *Agreement Relating to the Defense of Greenland* which gave the U.S. the political cover it need to occupy the island.

After signing the treaty, the U.S. instituted its own wartime Belt and Road Initiative where it built out the necessary infrastructure to support a network of airfields, naval bases, barracks, radio stations, and other support sites. One of the U.S.' priorities was securing the Danish-owned cryolite mining operation at Ivigtut (aka Ivittuut) which supplied the Pennsylvania Salt Manufacturing Company.[97] Penn Salt then forwarded an agreed amount (20%) to the Alumi-

96 https://history.state.gov/historicaldocuments/frus1917/d759

97 The U.S. opposed Canada's own plans to occupy and secure Greenland's cryolite

num Company of Canada (ALCAN).[98] While the allies feared Germany could conduct a quick naval raid and destroy the mining operations in less than an hour, Berlin showed no understanding of the mine's importance to Allied aircraft manufacturing.[99]

After the end of WWII, during which the U.S. experienced de facto sovereignty over Greenland, the island remained important for strategic reasons to counter the Soviet Union during the Cold War. While Copenhagen wanted U.S. forces to depart the island, Washington made a counteroffer in 1946 with three options: 1) a base leasing agreement for 99 years, 2) a defense agreement allowing the U.S. to defend the island, or 3) sell the island to the U.S. for $100 million. Denmark refused to sell the island while noting the U.S.' own hypocrisy as it pushed for European decolonization.

Danish mining company Kryolitselskabet Oresund ran the cryolite mine in Ivigtut which was adjacent to the sea.

In 1951, the U.S. and Denmark who were both NATO members, finally signed a defense treaty that replaced the original one. The new treaty, which was explicitly an implementation of the existing North Atlantic Treaty, was an agreement by the two parties to share responsibilities for securing Greenland. As the U.S. was a military superpower and Denmark a small country recovering from five years of German occupation, the U.S. obviously provided the vast amount of the military resources on the island which led to commentary that the U.S. again had de facto sovereignty.

mines, a key mineral for refining aluminum.

98 In 1939, the Ivigtut mine sent 41,000 tons of cryolite to Denmark for refining and 15,500 tons to the U.S. who forwarded 2,900 tons to Canada.

99 Smith, Gordon. "Cryolite, Control, and Canada-US Relations over Greenland, 1940." The Northern Mariner, Autumn 2021.

At least twice during the Cold War, different elements of the U.S. bureaucracy made suggestions to purchase Greenland such as by the Joint Chiefs of Staff in 1955 which was based on military expediency. Then, Vice-President Rockefeller (1974-1977) mentioned purchasing the island after reading an article about the economic strain it placed on Denmark.[100] When the Soviet Union dissolved in 1991, the U.S. showed declining interest in Greenland as its obvious strategic value receded. The topic did not come up again until the U.S. elected a president interested in building an American empire.

Minerals Hallucinations

In 2018, Senator Tom Cotton (R-AR) presented the idea of purchasing Greenland to the ambassador of Denmark and later wrote an opinion piece in the New York Times outlining his logic. The first reason was to deny Chinese access to the island since Beijing had offered to buy a retired U.S. naval base there and wanted to build their own air bases. The Trump administration successfully pressured Denmark not to take these deals. Second, Cotton emphasized the U.S.' desire to access the island's mineral resources which included rare earth elements. While these reasons were in line with U.S. interests, Greenland was a sovereign country and thus Denmark could not sell it if it wanted to. Greenlanders would have to vote and agree to join the U.S. as a territory.

Trump later confirmed in 2019 that the U.S. was interested in purchasing Greenland stating that it was, "essentially a large real estate deal." Along with this, he provided a word salad of why he wanted to buy the island which did not mention countering China or securing minerals. Trump doubled down on the same blunder as Cotton did, insisting he could complete the transaction directly with Denmark, oblivious to the island's sovereignty. Denmark's prime minister was compelled to give Trump a history lesson: "Greenland is not for sale. Greenland is not Danish. Greenland belongs to Greenland. I strongly hope that this is not meant seriously."[101] A year later, the Trump administration established a U.S. consulate in Nuuk, the capital of Greenland.

If one thought the matter was dead, they would understandably be mistaken. In January 2025, Trump brought up the idea of buying Greenland again, "I think we're going to have it." Trump served up another cocktail of statements

100 Chapin, Catherine. "Did Rocky Want to Buy Greenland?" The Charlotte Observer, February 26, 1982.

101 Reed, Betsy. "Trump confirms he is considering attempt to buy Greenland." The Guardian, August 18, 2019.

showing he had no better understanding of Greenland's sovereignty, "I don't really know what claim Denmark has to it, but it would be a very unfriendly act if they didn't allow that to happen because it's for the protection of the free world."[102] Donald Trump, Jr. even made a trip to the island for a staged photo op where he got locals to wear MAGA hats in exchange for a free lunch.

As was characteristic with Trump's style of brute force diplomacy, in an interview, he refused to rule out using military force to secure both Greenland and the Panama Canal citing "economic security." Trump also stated that he would enact high-level tariffs against Denmark if they refused to "cede or sell" the island to the U.S. However, Greenland's Prime Minister Múte B. Egede made it clear that, "We don't want to be Danes. We don't want to be Americans. We want to be Greenlanders."[103]

On March 28, 2025, U.S. Vice President J.D. Vance visited the U.S.' Pituffik Space Base in Greenland which was seen as a continuing attempt by Trump 2.0 to annex the country. During the trip, Vladimir Putin made comments at a Russian arctic security forum supporting the U.S. moves, "As for Greenland this is an issue that concerns two specific states and has nothing to do with us."[104] This led to speculation of a quid pro quo: if Trump ceded Ukraine to the Russian sphere, Putin in turn would cede Greenland to the U.S. sphere. After Vance left, the U.S. commander of Pituffik base, Colonel Susan Meyers, sent a base-wide email supporting Denmark and Greenland's independence. This resulted in Trump relieving Meyers of her command.[105]

In May 2025, Trump ordered the Director of National Intelligence (DNI) to collect intelligence relating to the acquisition of Greenland. Specifically, the DNI published a "collection emphasis message" to gather intelligence about the Greenland independence movement and their attitudes about the U.S. taking their natural resources. The Greenland Order also directed the CIA, DIA, and NSA to identify people in Denmark who supported the Trump administration's political agenda. The DNI, Tulsi Gabbard, said, "The Wallstreet Journal should

102 Aikman, Ian. "Trump says he believes US will 'get Greenland'". BBC, January 25, 2025.

103 Weizman, Jakob. "Greenland's PM: We don't want to be Americans." January 10, 2025.

104 Roth, Andrew. "Putin's endorsement of Trump's Greenland takeover reflects their vision of a new world order." The Guardian, March 28, 2025.

105 Copp, Tara. "Head of US Space Force base in Greenland is fired after Vance visit." AP News, April 11, 2025.

be ashamed of aiding deep state actors who seek to undermine the President by politicizing and leaking classified information."[106]

"Make America Go Away" hats went viral in Greenland in March 2025, around the time JD Vance's wife, Usha, visited.

Let's momentarily suspend any disbelief we might have on the potential sale of Greenland and consider how much the deal could actually cost. Some have tried to compare the deal with what the U.S. bought Alaska for in 1867 which was $129 million in today's value. Another data point is the Truman offer in 1946 which was $1.6 billion in 2025 money. But if we use U.S. Geological Survey's valuation of the island's resources, it has $4.4 trillion worth of mineral reserves which includes $2.7 trillion of non-fuel minerals like gallium and niobium.

This of course excludes what one might hang as a price tag on the security gained from locking out China and its Polar Silk Road. The U.S. already blew the bargain basement deals it might have gotten twice before, could it afford to pay today's premium prices? The value of prime real estate never goes down, it only goes up, and Greenland is the Manhattan of the Arctic. Also, trying to get minerals from the island's barren wasteland could be a sucker's bet where the costs to develop its infrastructure to even get access to these resources would make them uneconomic.

106 Long, Katherine. "U.S. Orders Intelligence Agencies to Step Up Spying on Greenland." The Wall Street Journal, May 6, 2025.

Conventional wisdom says that as the Greenland Ice Sheet melts due to manmade global warming, new mining opportunities will become possible. However, we have already seen what mining operations look like on the island. As mentioned, the cryolite operations on the coast at Ivigtut closed in the 1980s. This did not deter Australian company Eclipse Metals Limited which bought the mothballed mine in 2021 for $20 million with plans to extract cryolite, quartz, gallium, and rare earth elements from historic mine tailings. Since the purchase, Eclipse has yet to commercialize any of these minerals and their stock has gone from $0.068 per share in 2021 to a low of just $0.0045 cents a share in 2025. Obviously, this market intelligence tells us that investors do not believe the company can extract a product economically.

The privately owned Norwegian company Greenland Ruby opened a ruby and sapphire operation on a small undeveloped island at the mouth of Tasiussarssuaq fjord in the southwest of the island in 2014. However, the company remained unprofitable due to high operating costs and was forced to put the mine in a care and maintenance mode in 2022. Two years later, the ownership filed for bankruptcy protection in both Greenland and Denmark, seeking a new owner. The island's inhospitable environment, lack of infrastructure, and isolated location all contributed to a non-competitive business model.

In another example, Lumina Sustainable Materials, a privately owned company, runs an anorthosite (aka feldspar) operation in Qaqortosuaq on the west coast of the island.[107] While Lumina bought the mine in 2020 and spent $90 million to get it production ready in 2022, two years later they still had not received approval to export its product. Because the Greenland government claims public ownership of all land and its resources, there are no privately owned mines and their mineral exports can be denied if they violate the Mineral Resources Act of 2009. Because of these permitting delays, Greenland's only export-ready mine has no revenue stream as its operational costs continue to rise.[108]

One of the reasons that Trump 1.0 became interested in Greenland was based on a presentation by Australian geologist and mining CEO Greg Barnes in 2019. During a closed meeting, Barnes sold the White House on the impor-

107 Anorthosite is composed mainly of feldspar with a high alumina and calcium content and is used in glass, ceramics, paint and concrete.

108 USGS estimates the mine has an annual capacity of 200,000 metric tons. The average sales price in the U.S. market in 2024 was $110.00 USD per ton. Türkiye produced 9.5 million tons of feldspar in 2024 at an average sales price of just $50.00 USD per metric ton. In 2019, the mine produced 17,000 tons which is $850,000.00 at $50.00 a ton.

tance of his own Tanbreez rare earths mining project on the island.[109] Was this the solution to Washington's rare earth insecurity or a clever pump and dump scheme? While we will never know, in 2024, Barnes sold the mining claim to another Australian company, Critical Metals Corporation, for just $5 million and stock compensation. Barnes had to sell because of financial stress since the mine remained unproductive. As of early 2025, the mine was still not operational.

These examples illustrate the difficulty of doing business in Greenland and should act as a break on the momentum for acquiring the island. The idea that the U.S. must buy Greenland to advance its own security interests is a false narrative. An alternative idea is that the U.S. can continue to enforce its existing NATO treaty with Denmark and even strengthen its provisions to block China's Polar Silk Road. However, this takes negotiating, diplomacy, and creating mutual benefits for the parties involved.

When it comes to critical minerals, the U.S. can simply operate like the rest of the world does and incentivize private mining companies to pursue extraction operations on the island. Trump 2.0 could also employ the Minerals Security Project already gifted to him by the Biden administration to harness joint investments. As the Roman Empire discovered a millennia ago, you don't have to conquer a territory to get its minerals wealth if you have the money to simply trade for it. Getting minerals out of Greenland is much harder than one might think and the concept of extracting them as an easy solution to the U.S.' own insecurity is riddled with challenges.

Through the Ukraine Looking Glass

As Trump 2.0 worked through its Greenland Syndrome, it saw opportunity in the conflict minerals offered by the ongoing war between Russia and Ukraine. Although the world thought it understood the basic premise of a U.S.-Ukraine minerals agreement to be signed in February 2025, it quickly realized the deal was stuck in a traveling carnival's hall of mirrors where everything was distorted and nothing was real. What ended up being drafted and leaked to the public was not a minerals deal at all. How was this possible?

To start, let's look at the Ukrainian minerals industry to determine its theoretical approximate value, production rates, and locations. As we saw with

109 Smith, Sean & Neale Prior. "Perth geologist who briefed White House welcomes Trump's renewed interest in Greenland." The West Australian, January 8, 2025.

Greenland, just because a country has raw materials does not necessarily mean they can be extracted economically. In 2025, the most important consideration for a successful mining industry in Ukraine was the war. The country's mining production plummeted after Russia's invasion in 2022 as enemy forces captured mining operations in the eastern Donbas region, mines near the battle lines were shuttered, and Ukrainian miners were recruited into the army.

In 2020, Ukraine's GDP was $156 billion, its industrial production was valued at $119 billion, and the total value of Ukrainian mining was $13.4 billion or 8.5% of its GDP. In comparison, the U.S.' mining value that year was much smaller at just 3.3% of its GDP. Ukraine was not a top producer of any single metal or industrial minerals. While Ukraine produced fuel minerals like coal, natural gas, and petroleum, compared to global production, the amounts were trivial.

For metals, Ukraine's biggest volume products by far were iron ore, pig iron, and steel. For other large volume critical metals that the U.S. needed (aluminum, copper, manganese, magnesium, nickel, titanium, zirconium) Ukraine produced very little. For smaller volume and specialty critical minerals that the U.S. majority-sourced from China (germanium, gallium), Ukraine produced insignificant amounts. While there was uninformed talk about the U.S. sourcing rare earth elements (REE) from Ukraine, the country has never produced REE and has no capacity to do so.

Russia's 2014 Invasion

The Ukraine war is the largest conflict in Europe since WWII, indeed the largest one in the world at the time of writing, that also has a significant minerals component. To be sure, Russia invaded Ukraine in 2014 and again in 2022 to expand the Russian Empire which was Putin's political agenda supported by his coopted oligarchs. These invasions were driven by the Russian desire to expand their national power, not to secure lithium deposits in Ukraine. Having said that, Moscow is aware of the mineral operations it has captured and seeks to maximize their own revenue while denying Ukraine from benefitting from theirs.

Russia's initial invasion of Ukraine in 2014 led to a downward trend in the country's minerals industry due to the overall negative political impact and to a lesser extent the physical loss of mining operations. In 2015, as compared to the previous year, mining and quarrying production declined 14.5%, metals manufacturing decreased 16.4%, and coke and refined petroleum production plummeted 21.9%.[110] While Crimea only had a minor minerals industry, Russia did capture a Titanium Dioxide (TiO2) plant there with a 80,000 tpa capacity. To feed the plant, the new owners had to import ilmenite from Sri Lanka as its historic Ukraine sourcing was now severed.

Also, Ukraine's entire minerals enterprise was under financial distress since it was still based on the old Soviet model with excessive state control that led to inefficiencies and corruption. In one example, most coal mines operated at a continuing loss which forced the government to subsidize them to the tune of $430 million in 2015. Kyiv recognized this was a drain on its national economy and advertised its intent to put 36 separate coal mines up for sale to private investors. Of these, 23 were in the Donbas which was the eastern part of the country and what would be on the front lines of the 2022 war.

Ukraine's minerals enterprise was further complicated by that reality that Russian companies still owned mining and metal operations in the country despite the limited ongoing war. In 2015, Kyiv took measures to change this and increase their domestic minerals security. Specifically, Kyiv nationalized the Zaporozhye Aluminum Complex (ZAlK), taking a majority ownership from the Russian aluminum company Rusal. As of 2025, ZAIK was no longer operational and Kyiv put it up for sale with an absurdly low $1.8 million price tag but still could not find a bidder. The Russian invasion ensured that investing in the Ukrainian minerals industry was a high-stakes gamble and few could stomach the risk.

The country's iron ore production was impacted just slightly with a 2.1% decrease in 2015 while exports increased 11.8% with the largest amount going to China (45%). In contrast, Kyiv's iron ore import volumes declined significantly (30%) with most of this coming directly from Russia. Even though the two countries were at war, they still traded with one another, if at reduced rates. Importantly, Ukraine's iron ore industry was in dire straits as Kyiv needed more capital to fight Russia and make up for lost revenue from captured territories. This led Kyiv to raise taxes on their iron ore industry from $1.00 per ton to $3.10 per ton while average global iron ore prices dropped to just $50.00 which was the industry's break-even point.[111]

110 *The Mineral Industry of Ukraine, 2015.* U.S. Geological Survey.

111 *The Mineral Industry of Ukraine, 2015.* U.S. Geological Survey.

Ukraine Minerals Production 2013-2015 (metric tons)			
Mineral	**2013**	**2015**	**Change**
Alumina	1.49 million	1.48 million	N/A
Iron Ore	38.7 million	36.8 million	(-5%)
Ferroalloys	1.1 million	991,000	(-10%)
Steel, crude	33.2 million	22.9 million	(-33%)
Nickel	24,300	18,000	(-26%)
Titanium, sponge	9,400	7,700	(-18%)

**U.S. Geological Survey Data*

Ukraine's steel industry declined across the board with a drop in pig iron, rolled steel, and crude steel production with an accompanying decrease in furnace activity. For instance, twenty-two blast furnaces were active out of thirty, seven open-hearth furnaces were active out of nine, and fifteen oxygen furnaces were running out of twenty-one.[112] In 2015, the Donetsk Metallurgical Plant (1 million ton capacity) and the Alchevsk Metallurgical Complex-AMC (5.2 million ton capacity) were both seized by Russian-backed separatists, bringing them under enemy control. This reduced Ukraine's own steel production capacity while potentially increasing Russia's. Beginning in December 2023, AMC produced armor plating for Russian tanks, shipping these urgently needed products to the Uralvagonzavod manufacturing plant for final vehicle assembly.[113]

The 2022 "Special Military Operation"

With Russia's second invasion in 2022, Ukraine's minerals enterprise rapidly declined in all aspects with production dropping across the entire industry. Problems included mining operations being captured by enemy forces, facilities coming under direct fire from artillery and airstrikes, and a general deterioration of the country's infrastructure necessary to support mining operations. If a mine ended up closing, the remaining ones had to pick up the slack, related exports were reduced or halted, and imports increased.

The Russian invasion was ambitious, based on the assumptions that their armed forces were much better than they were and that Ukraine's were much

112 Ibid.

113 "Russia Produces Armored Vehicles Using Steel From the Temporarily Occupied Territories of Ukraine." Defense Express, January 23, 2024.

worse than they were. This strategic miscalculation meant that the Russian pincers driving towards central Ukraine to slice the country into pieces were defeated in detail. The main Russian armored column moving south to seize Kyiv was eventually halted and then slaughtered. Also, the main thrust north from Crimea also suffered unsustainable casualties with Moscow threatening to use tactical nuclear weapons if Ukraine didn't let their forces retreat safely south of the Dnipro River.

In the east, Russian forces moved west to secure the Donetsk Oblast which included the need to capture the coastal city of Mariupol. Russian forces quickly invested the city at the end of February 2022, surrounding it a week later, and cutting off all outside access to the Ukrainian forces trapped there. By April, the remaining Ukrainian soldiers in the city fell back to the Illich Iron and Steel Works, which was captured on April 13th, and the Azovstal Iron and Steel Works. However, despite directing a constant bombardment against Azovstal, Russian forces couldn't take it by assault and decided to surround and starve the defenders out. The Ukrainians held out in the massive Azovstal industrial complex until May 16th, making valuable use of the many underground tunnels, raising comparisons to the Battle of Stalingrad.

Both the Illich and Azovstal complexes received such extensive damage from Russian airstrikes (bunker busting bombs) and artillery barrages (thermobaric warheads) that they were inoperable afterwards. Metinvest Group, Ukraine's largest private steel company, subsequently sued Russia for damages to their two facilities which included $10 billion for pre-war capitalization and another $1 billion for raw materials and finished steel products on site.[114] Metinvest also had 234,000 tons of steel products stored at the Mariupol port which Russia had not returned, spurring the company to advise its customers not purchase these products which were now considered illegal.[115] The Metinvest CEO, Yurii Ryzhenkov, estimated it would take 3-5 years to rebuild their facilities.

While the Russian army cemented its hold on Mariupol, taking out some 12.7 million tons of annual steel production capacity as it did so, other forces moved west from Luhansk. These were led by the Wagner mercenary group and their target was the town of Bakhmut. Wagner would ultimately achieve their

114 Kolisnichenko, Vadim. "Azovstal and Ilyich Iron and Steel Works damage cost $11 billion SCM says." GMK Center, May 18, 2022.

115 https://metinvestholding.com/en/media/news/metnvest-zasterga-spozhivachv-vd-kupvl-vikradenogo-rosyanami-ukransjkogo-metalu

objective but only after losing tens of thousands of casualties in "meat wave" assaults spearheaded by recruits released from Russian prisons. However, to get to Bakhmut, Wagner first had to secure the small town of Soledar, known primarily for its salt mines.

Yevgeny Prigozhin poses with his Wagner mercenaries in one of the underground tunnels of the Soledar salt mines. January 2023.

The Russians placed Soledar under fire beginning in May 2022 as they worked their way west. Early on, the mine's main administration building was damaged by a glide bomb and its rail lines were destroyed, making it impossible to ship out any salt.[116] In August, Wagner moved on Soledar, making continuing direct assaults to capture both the town and its mines. By mid-January 2023, Wagner had full control of the area and pushed out the last Ukrainian elements holding out at Mine #7. While the mines consisted of 200 km of tunnels, they weren't useful for military operations due to their deep and narrow shafts. Also, the Artemsil mining company turned off the ventilators that circulated oxygen underground, further complicating its use by soldiers.

In 2015, Moscow banned the import of salt from Ukraine which previously provided 24% of its market.[117] This forced Russia to increase imports from neighboring Belarus and Kazakhstan. Although Russia intended to restart salt production at the mine, Soledar was destroyed and its population had fled, so there was no infrastructure or people left to make the mine functional. Although Wagner left an estimated 25,000 corpses stacked in and around Soledar, the mine was still not productive. In 2024, a former employee of the mine helped

116 https://iwpr.net/global-voices/ukraine-battle-soledars-salt-mines

117 Ibid.

develop a *Minecraft* mod called *Minesalt* which allows video gamers to roam the mine's tunnels as they search for hidden crystals.[118] Yevgeny Prigozhin, the head of Wagner who was assassinated by Putin seven months after he conquered the Soledar salt mines, is not a character in the game.

While Mariupol and Soledar were some of the more prominent battles involving Ukraine's mineral resources, the daily grind of war took its toll on the entire industry. For example, the Nikolaev Alumina Refinery with a 1.6 million ton annual capacity closed in March 2022 because it was located north of the contested city of Kherson and couldn't export its products. Because the refinery also made gallium secondary to alumina, this critical mineral was zeroed out. Also, the Pobuzhsky Ferronickel Plant, which is 100 miles north of the Nikolaev facility, closed in the fall of 2022 due to Russian airstrikes to the electrical grid. Besides these issues, most if not all mineral operations suffered severe problems from systemic inflation, grid unreliability, and personnel shortages.

Another problem for the Ukrainian minerals enterprise is ongoing corruption which undermines the war effort and aids Russia. For instance, Ukraine's state-owned UMCC (United Mining and Chemical Company) exported 82,000 tons of ilmenite and rutile ores from 2022-2023. Much of the material was funneled through obvious front companies in Hungary and Poland to Russia. Zaporizhzhia Titanium-Magnesium Plant (ZTMC), previously owned by Russian oligarch Dmitry Firtash, did the same. In this case, ZTMC sold titanium products from Jan-October 2022 to more front companies in Montenegro, Austria, and Czechia which were clear pipelines to Russia.[119] Moscow, in turn, took this material and produced aircraft and bombs used to destroy Ukrainian towns.

Into the Hall of Mirrors

"No one is going to talk to you about critical minerals in Ukraine, it is very political. Only the highest levels of government in Kyiv are authorized to even discuss it. We would have to personally know you, know what agency you are with, and understand what you would do with the information we provided you. So, in reality, we can't talk to you."

- Author's contact in Ukraine

118 https://www.wired.com/story/ukraine-soledar-salt-mine-minecraft-rebuilding-fundraiser/

119 Kazanskyi, Denys & Daria Dmytriieva. "Ukraine sells titanium to Russia in wartime for airplane and missiles production." RBC-Ukraine, August 07, 2023.

As we saw with Greenland, it is hard to determine a country's overall theoretical minerals industry value as it often doesn't mesh with ground reality. The moon could have $10 trillion worth of cobalt on it, but we'll never see that value because we cannot get to it or transport it back to Earth. Forbes estimated that Ukraine held a theoretical value of $14.8 trillion in minerals – a very high number. But this must be balanced with the fact that the country's minerals industry contributed just $13.4 billion to its economy in 2020 and its production value for 2024 was well under $5 billion. For all practical purposes, war-torn Ukraine might as well be the face of the moon.

In the fall of 2024, President Zelensky publicly presented his "Victory Plan" to win the war consisting of five points and three secret annexes. Point four offered joint protection of Ukraine's natural resources with its strategic partners as well as joint investment opportunities. Minerals worth "trillions of dollars" included uranium, titanium, lithium and graphite. A secret annex was attached to this point of the victory plan and probably included exclusive minerals rights in exchange for security guarantees. While the Biden administration said they would discuss these points further with Kyiv, the minerals part went nowhere.

While Biden didn't seem interested in an immediate minerals deal, maybe the incoming administration would. Afterall, Trump fashioned himself a skilled negotiator and exhibited a transactional mindset, always looking to get something for giving something. All Zelensky had to do was convince the new administration that Ukraine's mineral resources were worth a binding deal and he might even be able to tack a security guarantee onto it. Judging from the subsequent statements made by Trump and his cabinet officials, they took the bait.

It is quite possible that one could predict how all of this would play out based on Trump 1.0's earlier affliction with Greenland. In that instance, the administration convinced itself that vast wealth awaited it on the frozen island and others must be fools for not previously recognizing and seizing this obvious opportunity. The way those events unfolded, it was as if the administration didn't have even a basic understanding of the island's geology and what it would take to exploit its minerals in an economic manner. Would history repeat itself?

In a softball interview with Fox News host Brit Hume on February 10, 2025, Trump said, "I want the equivalent of $500 billion worth of rare earth and they have essentially agreed to do that." Many interpreted this to mean that Ukraine would give the U.S. $500 billion worth of "rare earth" in exchange for continued U.S. military aid. The central problem with this line of thought was that Ukraine didn't mine rare earth elements (REE) and therefore had no capability to refine them into useable products. Clearly, Trump misused the term but the media didn't know any better and repeatedly quoted his "rare earth" comment, failing to do even basic fact checking. This was Greenland Syndrome all over again.

Two weeks later, the deal was made public but it didn't look like anything that had been discussed by the media. The title of the agreement was very different: *Bilateral Agreement Establishing Terms and Conditions For A Reconstruction Investment Fund.* The eleven-paragraph document revealed that the fund would be jointly managed by both parties which would consist of 50% of revenues from future monetization of Ukrainian government-owned fuel and non-fuel minerals. The fund would invest in reconstruction projects in Ukraine while any kind of security guarantee was conspicuously absent.

When you boiled this nothing burger down to its core, this was merely an agreement that Kyiv would use sales from its natural resources to fund its own reconstruction. However, since Ukraine had started privatizing its mining industry, the potential future 50% could amount to very little. And where was the $500 billion in "rare earth" for the U.S? Clearly, such language was struck out by Ukraine when the U.S. refused to include security guarantees as part of the agreement. Since the U.S. offered very little, they got the same in return.[120]

In a two-hour press conference on February 23, 2025, Zelensky revealed how and why the original minerals deal had collapsed: "I know we had 100 [billion dollars from the U.S.], and I'm not going to acknowledge U.S. $500 [billion of debt], no matter what anyone says." Under the original agreement drafted by the U.S., Ukraine would be required to pay back twice as much money as it had been lent. This prompted Zelensky to say, "I'm not going to sign something that ten generations of Ukrainians will be paying for." It is possible that Ukraine's advertisement of its mineral resources value resulted in the U.S. expecting a maximal payout.

By this time, the Trump administration knew this wasn't a minerals deal at all, exposing the truth that they weren't able to negotiate much of anything from a minerals perspective, never mind half a trillion dollars. As often happens

120 U.S. Treasury Secretary Bessent presented a proposal to Zelensky on February 13th, 2025, that allegedly would have given the U.S. ownership of half of Ukraine's "rare earths." If true, Zelensky removed this language.

in Washington, the process developed a momentum of its own and Zelensky flew into town on February 28, 2025, to sign what was essentially a worthless piece of paper. Both sides were going through the motions to save political face, neither getting what they wanted and tensions were sure to run high.

During a televised discussion between Zelensky, Trump, and Vice President J.D. Vance that took place before the signing of the agreement, all three got into a heated argument. The basis of the exchange was if Putin could be trusted to negotiate a lasting peace deal. With tempers flaring and all three talking over each other, the signing of the reconstruction fund was canceled on the spot. Zelensky unceremoniously departed for Ukraine. Importantly, due to the non-binding language in the much watered-down agreement, this failed PR event had no impact on the critical minerals security of either Ukraine or the U.S.

Part of the sensitivity of the minerals negotiations was that Ukraine had already signed a Critical Raw Materials deal with the European Union (EU) in 2021. Ukraine saw this EU deal as an important step in its future accession into the EU economic bloc. This was an incentive that Europe could offer Ukraine and the U.S. couldn't. Hence, Kyiv was careful to ensure that any deal with the U.S. wouldn't jeopardize its relationship with the EU. When questioned about the deal Zelensky responded, "Nothing that could endanger…Ukraine's accession to the EU can be accepted."[121] Ukraine subsequently hired the American-British law firm Hogan Lovells to help with the ongoing negotiations.[122]

Two months later, the "minerals deal" was finally signed on April 30, 2025. This version was similar to the previous in that it established a reconstruction investment fund. However, this one was much milder and was described in the document as a "Limited Partner Agreement (LPA)." Specifically, the LPA was flexible so Ukraine could meet future EU obligations, no third-party would get better terms than the partners, and U.S. companies had offtake rights based on going market rates. The LPA appendix listed fifty-four different minerals impacted by the deal including battery minerals and REE. Ultimately, the U.S. was granted no preferential access to or benefits from Ukrainian mineral operations. This final product looked nothing like what President Trump had initially advertised with the LPA providing no solutions to the U.S.' critical minerals insecurity.

121 Gus, Camille." Zelensky says no to any US minerals deal that might risk Ukraine's EU bid." Politico, March 29, 2025.

122 Shalal, Andrea. "US, Ukraine hold tense talks as mineral deal remains elusive, source say." Reuters, April 11, 2025.

Putin's Counteroffer

Moscow observed the ongoing minerals negotiations between Ukraine and U.S. without the advantage of having perfect knowledge about the parties' respective positions. Hence, Putin feared that the two may actually ink a meaningful deal. To counter this, during discussions in Saudi Arabia on February 18, 2025, Putin floated the idea of giving the U.S. access to minerals in the areas of Ukraine that it controlled. On this topic Trump stated, "We're trying to do some economic development deals. They have a lot of things that we want. You know they have massive rare earth."[123]

Moscow was capitalizing on Trump's transactional mindset by dangling the "rare earth" mantra that had now become an all-encompassing idea that the uninformed equated with national minerals security. A necessary question had to be asked at this juncture, did the Putin regime know what they were talking about? Did Putin consult with the All-Russian Geological Research Institute which was part of Rosnedra (Federal Agency for Mineral Resources) to get the details or was he shooting from the hip, hoping the Trump administration would take the bait? Most likely, it was the latter and Moscow didn't know any more about the mineral resources of the Donbas than did Washington. Also, since this was all about politics, ground reality didn't matter.

Senior Sergeant Dianov was injured while defending the Azovstal Iron and Steel Works in Mariupol. In May 2022, the Russians captured the factory which had a 6.2 million-ton annual production capacity.

The Russian occupied territories and their minerals enterprise suffered from the same problems as free Ukraine but even more so. To start, all the captured mineral facilities were considered stolen property and subject to legal

123 https://www.nbcnews.com/politics/national-security/russia-offered-us-deal-minerals-ukranian-territory-seized-rcna193700

liability. As mentioned previously, Metinvest filed a $11 billion lawsuit against Russia for damages incurred by its two steel factories in Mariupol. Also, Russia's unconstrained, destructive method of warfare ensured that the mines it did capture were rendered inoperable such as the salt and gypsum operations in Soledar. Russia got no value from these destroyed facilities and incurred even more costs if they were to repair them.

Occupying Ukrainian territory caused other complex problems. When Russia invaded Crimea in 2014, it came into possession of the Crimean Titan titanium dioxide plant owned by Russian oligarch Dmitry Firtash. Ukraine subsequently cut water to the peninsula which disrupted the plant's operations and then they stopped supplying ilmenite, forcing it to import new feedstock from Sri Lanka. The plant's ownership entered bankruptcy proceedings in 2017 while plant production remained low. In 2022, the plant transitioned to producing fertilizer. In 2023, reporting indicated Russian forces had rigged the plant with explosives, either to prevent its capture by Ukraine or to create an improvised chemical attack.

Titanium dioxide was a minor effort compared to Ukraine's steel, manganese, and titanium industries which required iron ore (steel) and ilmenite & rutile (titanium). However, Russia's 2014 invasion didn't secure any of these resources as they were located in the central and western areas of the country. The subsequent invasion in 2022 resulted in the capture of just a single underground iron ore mine located south of Zaporizhzhia while Ukraine maintained control of nineteen others. And because Russian forces were stopped south of the Dnipro River, they were denied access to the manganese ore mines outside of Nikopol. The failure to secure any meaningful active ore sites meant Russia had to import these raw materials if they were to operate any metal refining factories in the occupied territories.

During Russia's two invasions, they captured eight steel production plants and a single ferroalloy one. In 2018, the Stakhanovskiy ferroalloy plant in Luhansk was reported to only have one of its eight furnaces operational for a 12% production rate.[124] The occupied iron and steel enterprise suffered from fundamental inefficiencies because they were originally established to use local feedstock. However, the Russian invasion severed this raw material-production supply chain and now the feedstock was in enemy territory.

124 https://globalenergymonitor.org/projects/global-steel-plant-tracker

The Yenakiieve Metallurgical Plant located in Donetsk was a typical example of the train wreck that was the occupied steel enterprise. The plant was captured in 2017 and was considered an illegal operation by the Metinvest Group. In 2020, reporting indicated 1,200 workers quit their jobs due to reduced production and no pay. Also, the plant halted operations periodically from 2020-2021 while the Russian owners prepared for bankruptcy and refused to pay for imported iron ore from Russia.[125] In 2022, because production was so low, 500 plant workers were called up for military service.[126]

Based on the reality of the occupied metals enterprise in Ukraine (Ti02, iron ore, steel, ferroalloys), one can only conclude Putin's offer was nothing but political fairy dust. Alternatively, if the U.S. did not bite, he might offer access to other undeveloped resources with no active mining operations which included iron ore, manganese, titanium, zirconium, lithium, and rare earths. But many of these resources were located on or near the FLOT (Forward Line of Troops) meaning no extraction could take place until the fighting stopped. There were other problems too.

Russian Controlled Steel Operations - Occupied Ukraine in 2024

Factory	Location	Production Rate
Avostal	Mariupol	0% (BD)
Ilyich Iron and Steel Works	Mariupol	0% (BD)
Azov Electrostal (Azovmash)	Mariupol	0%
Elektrostal	Kurakhove	0% (BD)
Yuzovsky Metallurgical Plan	Donetsk	0% (RM)
Donetskstal	Donetsk	0% (RM)
Yenakiieve Metallurgical Plant	Donetsk	25% (PD)
Alchevsk Metallurgical Complex	Donetsk	25% (PD)

BD = Battle Damage RM = Rolling Mill PD = Periodic Disruption

Future operational costs in the occupied territories were sure to be high based on the need for landmine removal and building out the energy infrastructure. Also, these projects would compete with ongoing domestic iron ore, lithium, manganese, and REE operations in the U.S. – how would Trump 2.0 tariffs affect this? Other questions remained. Would their hard rock lithium mining in Ukraine be priced out by the cheaper brine operations in South America? How could the Russians produce manganese competitive with Gabon's and South

125 Ibid.

126 Zubkova, Daria. "Occupiers Cancel Postponement of Mobilization of 500 Workers of Yenakiieve Metallurgical Plant." Ukrainian News, Sept. 20, 2022.

Africa's massive operations? How could Ukrainian REE operations survive when China controlled 95% of the market and were willing to operate below cost? Putin hoped the Trump administration didn't have the answers.

Tariffs and Protectionism

A salient feature of both Trump administrations was the implementation of sweeping tariffs directed at competitors, neighbors, and allies who he determined were treating the U.S. "unfairly." During Trump 1.0, tariffs were noticeably directed against China, which was the U.S.' single largest trading partner in 2018. From a strategic perspective, the administration wanted to decouple from China's economy because the U.S. was disproportionately fueling their growth. This was problematic because Beijing was working to supplant the U.S. as the most influential power in the international system. In other words, the U.S. trade imbalance with China served to fuel its own decline.

As part of Trump 1.0's growing concern with its own critical minerals and metals insecurity, the administration conducted a Section 232 investigation into foreign steel imports in 2018.[127] Upon conclusion, Trump 1.0 determined the U.S. would impose a 25% tariff on most steel imports to protect its domestic steel industry with exceptions that included among others Canada, Mexico, the EU, and Ukraine. However, Trump 2.0 determined that these exceptions allowed steel dumping by China which used countries like Mexico as an intermediary to funnel their much lower-priced products. As of March 12, 2025, these exceptions were replaced with a 25% ad valorem tariff. The only exceptions were provided to steel products with inputs that were originally "melted and poured" in the U.S.[128]

The reasoning for the tariffs was that lower priced steel was "a threat to the national security" which meant that a strong domestic steel industry was necessary for the country's economic security. Trump's goal was for the U.S. to produce 80% of its own finished steel products. In 2017, the year before the tariffs took place, the U.S. made 73% of its finished products and imported 17% of all steel products. In 2020, the U.S. made 86% of its own finished products which fell again to 77% in 2022 due to the exceptions noted above. However, in 2024, finished products were at 80% again and overall steel imports just 13% –

127 Section 232 of the Trade Expansion Act of 1962.

128 Presidential Proclamation, *Adjusting Imports of Steel into the United States*, February 10, 2025.

so what was the point of the new tariffs? Were self-interested domestic politics really driving the decision?[129]

As with steel, Trump 1.0 conducted a Section 232 investigation into aluminum imports which he determined "threatened to impair the national security of the U.S." This triggered a 10% ad valorem tariff on most countries beginning in 2018. As with steel, the administration provided exceptions to the same countries except Ukraine who was not an aluminum producer. Even with the tariffs, U.S. primary smelter production decreased 58% over the eight years from 2016-2024 with three aluminum smelters going out of active operation. Again, Trump 2.0 identified China as funneling cheap aluminum products through Mexico to take advantage of their tariff exception.

Consequently, Trump 2.0 initiated a 25% ad valorem tariff on aluminum products also commencing on March 12, 2025.[130] There were exceptions for aluminum products whose original inputs were "smelted and cast" in the U.S. However, the U.S. aluminum industry was different from the steel industry in that the U.S. imported far more if it, 47% of total production in 2024. But putting up a tariff wall around the aluminum industry wasn't necessarily going to save it. The industry suffered from expensive energy intensive smelting methods which the Trump and Biden administrations both failed to address. The new tariffs were a band-aid applied to a gaping wound that really required major reconstructive surgery.

While copper was not defined as a critical mineral, it most likely would be if current trends continued. U.S. copper mining declined 8.5% from 2020-2024 with primary and secondary refining also declining noticeably during the same period. However, demand for copper products increased with refined copper imports rising 20% from 2020-2024. Accordingly, overall U.S. import reliance on copper products of all kinds went up from 38% to 45% from 2020-2024. Once U.S. import reliance hits one-half or more, this will trigger copper's designation as a critical mineral as defined by U.S. Geological Survey.

Because of the U.S.' growing copper insecurity, Trump 2.0 directed the Secretary of Commerce to initiate a Section 232 investigation of the national security risks from the U.S.' growing import reliance.[131] This was in line with

129 Data from USGS.

130 Presidential Proclamation, *Adjusting Imports of Aluminum into the United States*, February 11, 2025.

131 White House announcement, February 25, 2025.

Trump 2.0's "America First Trade Policy" announced in January 2025 which sought to redress any and all unfair trade balances with other countries.[132] Specifically, the U.S. would scrutinize its existing trade agreement with China which should illuminate the fact that the U.S. majority-sourced twenty-five of its critical minerals from Beijing.

But applying tariffs wasn't always a straightforward process. In 2018, Trump 1.0 placed a 10% tariff on primary aluminum imports (and later derivative products) under Section 232 of the Trade Expansion Act of 1962, excluding Canada, Mexico, Australia, and Argentina.[133] The intent was to get existing aluminum smelter operations up to 80% of their maximum capacity. In 2023, the Biden administration added a 200% ad valorem tariff rate to Russian aluminum resulting in no imports of aluminum products through September 2024. In 2024, the Biden administration announced it would triple Section 301 tariffs on Chinese imported aluminum from 7.5% to 22.5% which, combined with the existing Section 232 tariffs, would increase the rate to 32.5%. In Jan-Feb 2024, Chinese aluminum imports were 30,000 tons or just 3% of the total.[134]

However, the tariffs were not effective in revitalizing the aluminum industry as seen by the closure of ALCOA's smelter and M7M's bankruptcy. There were many reasons why the tariff regime did not work. To start, businesses were allowed to request exclusions to the tariffs and by early 2021 the Department of Commerce had received over 27,000 submissions, approving 61% of them.[135] Also, U.S. customs were unable to provide the surveillance required to enforce the tariffs, allowing in 6-7% of aluminum imports without collecting the required fees.[136] Because Canada was tariff-exempt, they increased their sales to U.S. customers, accounting for 64% of imports in Q1 2024. While the EU initially received a TRQ (tariff-rate-quota) system, exempting the first 384,000 tons of aluminum annually, the Biden administration exempted the EU altogether in 2022. As a result of all these exceptions, only 10% of total aluminum imports were likely tariffed.

---

132 https://www.whitehouse.gov/presidential-actions/2025/01/america-first-trade-policy/

133 Historically, 52% of aluminum imports were from Canada.

134 U.S. Geological Survey, Mineral Industry Survey, May 2024.

135 "Section 232 Investigations: Overview and Issues for Congress." Congressional Research Service, May 18, 2021.

136 Barlas, Stephen. "Report cites U.S. failure to collect some steel tariffs." The Fabricator, September 8, 2023.

By April 2025, Trump 2.0 had placed tariff exemptions on critical minerals imported from China. Although the U.S. intended to decouple critical minerals from its overall tariffs regime, Beijing responded with emplacing export controls on seven different Heavy REE. The U.S. should have known that the Chinese leadership would respond to the larger trade war by using its critical minerals leverage like it had done previously. However, U.S. mineral importers could probably still secure limited volumes by using China's massive import-export grey market that evolved in response to Trump 1.0's initial trade war volley fired in 2018.[137]

Many thousands of Chinese logistics companies now exist that offer cheaply priced "double clearance and tax inclusive services" which works both ends of the export-import system. This grey market uses third-party services which obscure the origins of shipments and perform "importers of record" services. This enables shippers to sidestep export-import controls, mischaracterize goods shipped, and grossly undervalue tariffs paid. Because U.S. Customs and Border Patrol (CBP) inspect less than 1% of imports, Chinese sellers can get goods into the U.S. with only slightly higher costs. Goldman Sachs estimated that as much as $130 billion of Chinese goods evaded tariffs and entered the U.S. in 2023.[138]

U.S. mineral buyers could also use this grey market mechanism to buy low volume metals like gallium, germanium, and REE from China which avoids both Beijing's export and Washington's import controls. The buyer would do this by contracting with a grey market company to provide, let's say, a ton of gallium. The buyer would have no knowledge of the grey company's specific tactics and would just know it was receiving a hard to get product at only slightly higher prices. The buyer would have no incentive to look any deeper into the services rendered to legally maintain their plausible deniability.

Final Thoughts

The first Trump administration began the U.S.' awareness of its own critical minerals' insecurity but got little traction and implemented no significant legislation. The subsequent Biden administration provided more support to its critical minerals industry than any other one since the Eisenhower administration, instituting a blueprint for action. While the second Trump administration

137 The grey market is quasi-legal which integrates both legal and illegal aspects of trade to move products between sellers and buyers.

138 Xie, Stella Y. & Pak You. "China's formidable logistics sector challenges Trump tariff enforcers." Nikkei Asia, April 11, 2025.

showed a strong interest in critical minerals, its policy initiatives with Greenland and Ukraine were unrealistic. Furthermore, Trump 2.0 pursued an "America First" approach with its trade relations which wasn't nuanced enough to positively impact its own complex critical minerals enterprise.

Trump 2.0 had important decisions to make about the country's critical minerals future. First, the administration had to assess Biden's ongoing critical minerals plan and determine if they wanted to keep it, modify it, or add to it. Trump 2.0 also needed to decide if it would address the ongoing failure of the non-existent National Defense Stockpile, something he neglected the first time around. Another pressing problem was what would be done to secure the DOD's foreign-sourced supply chains. Finally, it was important to understand that these different critical minerals initiatives would have a much-reduced effect if they weren't coordinated at the national level. In mid-2025, the U.S. still hadn't developed an effective leadership and organizational construct to execute a whole of government approach. This absence goes far in explaining the U.S.' ongoing critical minerals insecurity.

Sources

"Critical Materials: Action Needed to Implement Requirements That Reduce Supply Chain Risks." GAO, September 10, 2024.

Donges, Alexander. "Import Dependence and Strategic War Planning – The German Iron and Steel Industry, 1933-1945." The International History Review, 2024, vol. 46, no. 4, 486–499.

Gissurarson, Hannes H. "Proposals to Sell, Anex or Evacuate Iceland, 1518-1868." 2015.

Gloclawska, Joanna A. "The Mineral Industries of Denmark, the Faroe Islands, and Greenland." U.S. Geological Survey, July 2022.

Gloclawska, Joanna A. "The Mineral Industry of Iceland." U.S. Geological Survey, January 2025.

Peirce, Benjamin. "A Report on the Resources of Iceland and Greenland." Department of State, 1868.

"Priemel, Kim C. "Occupying Ukraine: Great Expectations, Failed Opportunities, and the Spoils of War, 1941-1943." Central European History, March 2015, Vol. 48, No. 1.

"Possible Acquisition of Greenland by the United States." The Joint Chiefs of Staff, January 21, 1955.

Safirova, Elena. "The Mineral Industry of Ukraine 2015." U.S. Geological Survey, August 2019.

Safirova, Elena. "The Mineral Industry of Ukraine 2021-2021" U.S. Geological Survey, February 2025.

Smith, Gordon. "Cryolite, Control, and Canada-US Relations over Greenland, 1940." The Northern Mariner, Autumn 2021.

Unofficial Consolidation of the Mineral Resources Act through November 28, 2019.

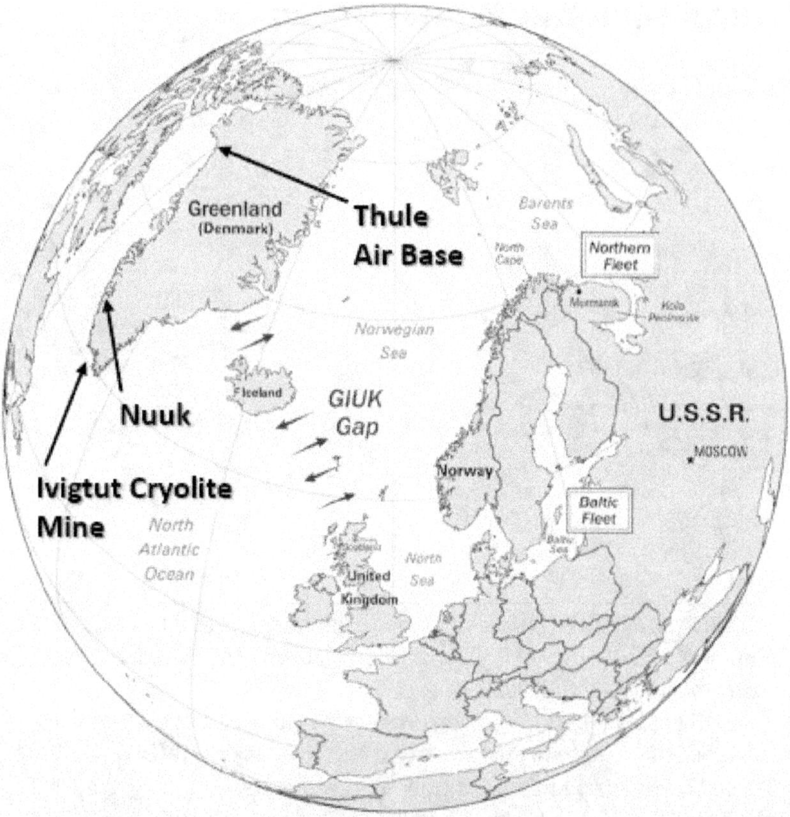

The strategic importance of Greenland for the U.S. and NATO is the Greenland-Iceland-UK (GIUK) gap used by Russian nuclear submarines. Thule Air Base (aka Pituffik), formerly a U.S. Strategic Air Command base during the Cold War, is now a U.S. Space Force site.

1 ALUMINA: (Mykolaiv) Nikolaev Alumina Refinery closed since March 2022.
2 FERRONICKEL: (Pobuzke) Pobuzhsky Ferronickel Plant closed in November 2022 from airstrikes on its electrical grid.
3 GRAPHITE: (Zavaliesky) Volt Resources closes its graphite operation in December 2024 due to high electricity prices and lack of staff.
4 GYPSUM: (Soledar) Knauf Gips Donbas gypsum plant was captured in September 2022 by the Wagner Group.
5 ILMENITE: Irshansk Mining and Processing Plant suspended operations from October 2022 – July 2023 due to financial problems.
6 IRON ORE: (Kryvyi Rih) Sukha Balka Mining and Processing Plant (GOK) has lower production due to wartime disruption of electricity and personnel.
7 MANGANESE: Marganets Mining and Processing Plant (MGOK) stops operations in October 2023 due to destruction of dam by Russian forces.
8 SALT: (Soledar) Artemsil's salt mines are captured in January 2023 by the Wagner Group.
9 STEEL: (Mariupol) Russia captures the Illich Steel & Iron Works, Azovstal Iron & Steel Works, and Azovelektrostal by May 2022; total annual steel capacity of 12.7 million tons.
10 TITANIUM: Zaporizhzhya Titanium-Magnesium Plant Combine (ZTMC) is closed since 2022; sole producer of titanium sponge and germanium.

Chapter 4
The Defense Production Act

"First, we should adopt such direct measures as are now necessary to assure prompt and adequate supplies of goods for military and essential civilian use. I therefore recommend that the Congress now enact legislation authorizing the Government to establish priorities and allocate materials as necessary to promote the national security; to limit the use of materials for nonessential purposes; to prevent inventory hoarding; and to requisition supplies and materials needed for the national defense, particularly excessive and unnecessary inventories."

- President Truman, July 19, 1950

The Defense Production Act of 1950

The Defense Production Act (DPA) is often discussed as a remedy for the U.S.' critical mineral insecurity, sometimes unrealistically as if invoking the act will immediately solve all its problems. While the act does provide the president broad authorities to purchase minerals as necessary to secure the national defense industrial base, it is subject to annual funding by Congress. The DPA has evolved over time, with each administration using the DPA differently, depending on their policy agenda, world events, and the authorities approved by Congress.

While the DPA was created to harness the economy to better equip and supply the U.S. military to fight the Korean War, it has been amended many times over. Until recently, the 81-page document was primarily used as a tool for national emergency preparedness. The DPA has always been limited in duration with "sunset rules" meaning congress had to regularly reapprove and update the act. From 1951-2025, the DPA has been reapproved fifty-three times with frequent gaps between approvals with the largest one being from October of 1990 to August of 1991. For the last four approvals, the average sunset period has been five years so that Congress doesn't have to renew it yearly like it did for early periods of its history.

The original act had seven different titles of authority:

- Priorities and Allocations
- Authority to Requisition and Condemn
- Expansion of Productive Capacity and Supply
- Price and Wage Stabilization
- Settlement of Labor Disputes
- Control of Real Estate Credit
- General Provisions

The DPA's roots lie with the First War Powers Act (FWPA) which was passed eleven days after the Japanese attack on Pearl Harbor. This was a short four-page document giving the sitting president unprecedented sweeping wartime powers by coordinating federal agencies, issuing government contracts, and regulating trade with enemy powers. While the act empowered the president to take decisive action across the federal government without prior congressional approval, its life was limited until six months after the end of hostilities which was February of 1946.

Three months later, the U.S. passed the *Second War Powers Act, 1942* which was a more detailed twelve-page document that further expanded and clarified the President's wartime powers. Some of the fifteen different provisions were rather mundane such as outlining auditing procedures for government contracts and setting the metallic content for five-cent pieces. Others had more impact such as the government's authority to seize land for military purposes and access confidential census information to identify Japanese-Americans for internment. Except for Title X, which authorized naturalization of citizens who served in the armed forces, the powers in the act remained in force only until the end of 1944.

Upon conclusion of WWII, the U.S. rapidly demobilized its standing military as the President's once powerful wartime powers expired and the Executive Branch lost its ability to leverage federal resources during time of conflict. When North Korea invaded South Korea in 1950, President Truman recognized the need for additional industrial and economic authorities to defend its allies in the new Cold War against the Soviet Union. Three weeks after the North

Korean invasion, Truman requested these authorities from Congress who later passed the DPA later that year.[139]

After China entered the war on the side of North Korea in November 1950, Truman created the Office of Defense Mobilization (ODM) which oversaw a host of subordinate agencies to coordinate economic support for the war. The ODM reintroduced the Controlled Material Plan (CMP) which was originally created in WWII to effectively distribute critical wartime materials like iron, steel, aluminum, and copper between civilian and military industries. ODM leveraged the presidential authorities of the DPA to enable the CMP by expanding minerals exploration in the U.S., increasing domestic mining production, and increasing the importation of minerals from abroad.

U.S. Marines fighting near the Chosin Reservoir watch an airstrike hit enemy positions ahead. Three weeks after the North Korean invasion, President Truman requested legislation leading to creation of the DPA.

During the initial two years of the Korean War, overall U.S. production was strained as it tried to maintain both regular civilian and increased military manufacturing. The CMP was used to regulate the flow of steel, aluminum, copper, and other materials like alloys between the two industries although there were difficulties. For example, Truman used the DPA to expand steel production, which grew by 4.8 million tons in 1950 and 4.3 million tons in 1951, with the industry reaching a new overall peak in early 1952 at 108 million tons. Even with these high production levels, it represented only 40% of the total increase the DPA had planned. In contrast, the steel industry worried they would overproduce in support of the war and be left with a surplus when the conflict ended.[140]

139 The law was passed on September 8, 1950.

140 Dawson, Sam. "Industry Nears Halfway Mark." The Spokesman Review, January 20,

Regarding aluminum, by early 1953, production still did not meet DPA expectations, resulting in them paying $70 million for The Wheland Company to build a primary aluminum manufacturing plant with a 50,000-ton annual capacity and an alumina ore concentration processing facility. In previous rounds of DPA financing, Olin Industries was contracted to build an additional 110,000 tons of annual aluminum smelter capacity. Likewise, the Harvey Machine Company agreed to produce 54,000 tons of aluminum annually. This increased capacity would give the U.S. an annual capacity of 1.7 million tons by 1955.[141]

To help manage challenges like these, the DPA created the Defense Minerals Administration (DMA) under the Department of the Interior. However, DMA was short lived with its functions transferred to the newly created Defense Materials Procurement Agency (DMPA) in 1951. To carry out the original minerals exploration mission of DMA, the Defense Minerals Exploration Agency (DMEA) was created. DMEA provided funds for the exploration of forty-one different critical and strategic minerals until it was discontinued in 1958.[142] Of these, the six Platinum Group Metals, the seventeen rare earths, and fourteen others that were listed are considered critical minerals today.

DMPA had responsibility for increasing and securing the supply of the minerals and metals required by the defense industrial base with this being done mainly through government contracts. DMPA purchasing activities addressed both domestic and foreign production by recognizing four different regions: North America, South America, Europe/Middle East/ Africa, and Asia. Through the summer of 1952, DMPA had secured contracts worth $4.6 billion with $792 million committed to aluminum purchases, $652 million to rubber, $363 million to manganese, and $330 million to copper.[143]

The DPA of 1950 also created the National Production Authority (NPA) which was originally placed under the Department of Commerce but then transferred under the Defense Production Administration in 1951.[144] The NPA mission was ensuring that civilian industry was represented and effectively supported defense mobilization. Created within the NPA was the Metals and

1952.

141 Schneider, Fred. "DPA Gives Wheland Authority to Build Big Aluminum Plant." Chattanooga Daily Times, January 31, 1953.

142 DMEA executed over 1,100 exploration contracts during its tenure and was replaced by the Office of Minerals Exploration (OME).

143 Joint Committee on Defense Production, Annual Report 1952.

144 The DPA was abolished by the Eisenhower administration in 1953 with its functions transferred to the Office of Defense Mobilization.

Minerals Bureau (MMB) with five divisions: 1) Iron and Steel, 2) Copper, 3) Aluminum and Magnesium, 4) Tin, Lead, and Zinc, and 5) Miscellaneous Metals and Minerals. While the MMB was ultimately abolished in 1953, it contributed significantly to the success of the Controlled Material Plan.

The Long Cold War

President Eisenhower inherited the Korean War, which ended during his first year in office, and a Cold War with the Soviet Union that continued the ongoing competition for global resources. With the war in Korea over, the administration reorganized parts of the defense minerals enterprise which included termination of the Controlled Material Plan. Also, the Defense Materials Procurement Agency was abolished in 1953 with its purchasing functions transferred to the General Services Administration (GSA).[145] With the previous administration's success in increasing critical mineral supply flows combined with the end of hostilities, the Eisenhower administration was able to decontrol major minerals like lead, zinc, iron ore, and tin that were previously managed through the DPA.

In 1953, Eisenhower created the Cabinet Minerals Policy Committee to better manage the minerals enterprise in concert with the provisions of the DPA. The policy body wrestled with difficult topics such as the need to disperse its minerals warehousing system in case of possible future nuclear attack by the Soviet Union. It also decided that the Department of Interior (DOI) would be responsible for determining the overall health of the U.S. domestic minerals capability even though they had no larger policy authority. To do this, DOI created the Office of Minerals Mobilization in 1955.

Importantly, since the Korean War had ended, Congress did not see the need for the President to wield as much power as they had during time of conflict. When Congress renewed the DPA in 1955, they stripped it of Title II (the authority to seize land), Title IV (price and wage stabilization), Title V (settling labor disputes), and Title VI (the control of real estate credit). The president retained the ability to prioritize and allocate defense related contracts, to promote ongoing minerals exploration, and purchase critical and strategic minerals for the DPA stockpile.

145 The DMPA was effective in its mission and processed $6.4 billion in various transactions that supported the DPA.

The administration so consistently pursued its mission to build a critical minerals stockpile that it developed oversupply problems and a growing domestic industry dependent on government contracts. For example, the President withheld support for a proposed bill in 1955 that would have committed $150 million to purchase additional minerals beyond what the U.S. already had stockpiled and could not justify. However, in 1956, Congress passed an act to purchase domestically produced tungsten, asbestos, fluorspar, and columbian-tantalum which were beyond what the government needed and had already acquired through the DPA.[146]

President Eisenhower carried forward the minerals momentum that Truman had developed. The new administration successfully increased the flow of critical minerals like nickel, chromium, and cobalt while decontrolling others like tungsten and molybdenum in 1958. By 1960, the only minerals that had not reached their designated goals set by ODM were beryl and mica. From 1950-1960, successive administrations successfully leveraged the DPA to reach their national security goals, spending more than $8 billion to secure necessary minerals, metals, and materials.[147]

Under President Kennedy's tenure(1961-1963), the Cold War continued to shape the U.S.' collective thinking with the Cuban Missile Crisis in 1962 being a salient example. In his first year, Kennedy issued Executive Order 10952 which delegated national emergency planning to the Secretary of Defense and created the Office of Emergency Planning (OEP). The OEP would leverage the DPA as necessary to accomplish its preparedness mission which included readying the minerals enterprise for potential wars, either conventional or nuclear.

War planners had gone from anticipating a five-year conflict where the U.S. could expect to have all foreign sources of minerals cut off, to a three-year plan.[148] This meant the U.S. mineral stockpiles immediately had a two-year surplus that had to be sold or offloaded as opportunities arose. Also, the U.S. did not have the need to purchase the same quantities of minerals from domestic and foreign providers. However, the General Services Administration (GSA) continued to purchase supplies of beryl and mica while Congress continued to fund the DPA at normal rates - $2.2 billion annually.

146 From 1956-1958, unobligated Treasury funds purchased $27.5 million of minerals.
147 Joint Committee on Defense Production, Annual Report 1961.
148 This shift occurred in 1958 as a compromise number between Army war planners who anticipated a long conventional war while Air Force planners predicted a much shorter one based on a thermonuclear exchange.

In preparation for a possible nuclear war, Kennedy issued Executive Order 10997 *Assigning Emergency Preparedness Functions to the Secretary of the Interior* on February 16, 1962.[149] The Interior's responsibilities included developing mineral resources for emergency purposes, stockpiling these minerals, preparing production facilities for overt and covert attacks, and salvaging these facilities after an attack. Specific responsibilities under Annex 33 guidance covered the mining and processing facilities for ninety-three separate minerals as well as their distribution.[150] To prepare the mining industry for such events, DOI published a 14-page pamphlet *An Alert to the Minerals Industry*.

A photograph released by the U.S. government in 1962 showing equipment for a surface-to-air missile facility in Cuba. These SAMs would be used to protect the ICBMs installed by the Soviet Union.

In 1963, the Joint Committee on Defense Production requested a study on U.S. foreign minerals dependence which was coordinated through the Office of Minerals and Solid Fuels and conducted by U.S. Geological Survey.[151] The report showed that the U.S. was majority dependent on eighteen separate minerals with 100% dependence on columbium, tantalum, and tin. And in line with planning for a shorter war requiring a smaller stockpile, the government sold $110 million of stored material which included almost $30 million of minerals purchased through the DPA.

The Johnson administration (1963-1968) was defined by the Vietnam War where the country's strategy of confronting communism everywhere was met

149 The other major agencies received similar orders.

150 National Plan for Civil Defense and Defense Mobilization, National Energy and Minerals Plan, Annex 33.

151 OMSF was formerly the Office of Minerals Mobilization.

by resistance from the American public. Consequently, Johnson was under pressure to make the war as palatable as possible to the average citizen, which meant keeping inflation under control. But the increasing need for metals for aircraft, ammunition, and electronics created inflationary pressures that were felt across the entire economy – it could not be walled off inside just the military industrial complex. Also, the administration grossly misjudged war expenditures by $14 billion in 1966 and $12 billion in 1967, putting them in a financial bind.[152] These pressures led the administration to increase imports and release metals from the national stockpile to feed military manufacturing to keep supply in line with demand.

For example, in 1967, the U.S. experienced a copper supply problem with a 187,000 ton deficit that was only made up by stockpile releases. The country's demand for rutile concentrates used to make titanium grew as well, with imports increasing from 110,000 tons in 1964 to 170,000 tons in 1966.[153] Just a single engine for a high-performance jet required 20 tons of titanium products. Also, the administration went head-to-head with the domestic aluminum industry in 1965 to keep prices down which was done through stockpile releases and political hardball tactics to keep companies from raising prices. Consequently, aluminum stabilized at $490.00 per ton.[154]

Throughout President Johnson's tenure, the U.S. continued its foreign dependence on minerals with the Department of the Interior reporting that the U.S. was majority dependent on 21 different minerals in 1966. In another indication of growing future minerals insecurity, a report from the Engineering Manpower Commission revealed that from 1955 to 1965, enrollment in college mineral-related technology fields dropped 47%.[155] And because the idea that the U.S. would only fight short conventional wars that it would ultimately win became the dominant bureaucratic groupthink, the U.S. was no longer investing in its national minerals stockpile. In fact, the war gave the administration an opportunity to offload its surpluses.

Since the DPA supported all aspects of the defense industry, the act was also used to compel nine different commercial companies to produce chemical

152 "Economic Effect of Vietnam Spending," Report of the Joint Economic Committee-Congress of the U.S., Report No. 394, July 7, 1967.

153 Joint Committee on Defense Production, Annual Report 1968.

154 Cuff, Robert. "Stockpiles and Defense Escalation, 1965-1968." The Public Historian, Autumn 1987.

155 Joint Committee on Defense Production, Annual Report 1968.

products for the military herbicide program in Vietnam with the most infamous being Agent Orange.[156] From 1962 to 1971, the U.S. Air Force sprayed almost 19 million gallons of herbicides as part of the military's defoliation program known as Operation Ranch Hand.[157] As of 1968, demand was so great that all commercial production of Agent Orange went to military use in Vietnam through government contracts authorized by the DPA.

During the Vietnam War, 1965-1972, successive administrations were under pressure to provide increased metals production for programs like the UH-1 helicopter while keeping resulting inflation under control.

The Nixon/Ford administration (1969-1976) inherited the losing war in Vietnam where the eventual withdraw of all U.S. forces greatly reduced the demand for minerals and metals for wartime manufacturing needs. However, the administration still used the DPA to provide "set-asides" for the defense industry as required. In 1973, this amounted to 250,000 tons of aluminum, 255,000 tons of copper, 2.4 million tons of steel, and 15% of overall commercial nickel production. Of note, the U.S. also set aside raw materials for the Canadian defense industry which included 770 tons of steel, 64 tons of copper, 1,000 tons of aluminum, and 100 tons of nickel alloys. Canada's atomic energy program also received support but in much smaller amounts with 235 tons of steel, 21.5 tons of copper, 7 tons of aluminum, and just 5 tons of nickel alloys.[158]

The DPA Atrophies

Under the Carter administration (1977-1980), the U.S. put the Vietnam War behind it and was consumed by a new challenge – the Energy Crisis. The

156 The U.S. military used different coded agents with different chemicals including Green, Pink, Blue, Purple, and White.

157 https://www.ncbi.nlm.nih.gov/books/NBK236347/

158 Joint Committee on Defense Production, Annual Report 1973.

crisis was caused by the OPEC oil embargo in 1973 and further disruption by the Iranian Revolution in 1979, causing increased fuel prices. As a result of these supply chain shocks, the U.S. government recognized energy as a national security concern requiring federal involvement. As part of the U.S. response, Carter was instrumental in passing *the Synthetic Fuels Corporation Act of 1980* which used amended authorities in the DPA to produce synthetic fuels.

With no active war to drive defense manufacturing supply chains and a greatly diminished stockpile to draw upon, the DPA was no longer used to shape minerals policy. In 1977, Carter abolished the Joint Committee on Defense Production and transferred its oversight responsibilities to the House Committee on Financial Services and the Senate Committee on Banking, Housing, and Urban Affairs. Starting with the Carter administration, the DPA received significantly decreased monies from congressional appropriations which would remain relatively low through the year 2000.

During the Reagan administration (1981-1988), DPA funding averaged around $30 million annually with no monies at all appropriated in 1984. The Bush administration (1989-1992) increased DPA funding slightly up to $50 million annually which then dropped to zero dollars in 1992. The subsequent Clinton administration (1993-2000) experienced a spike in DPA funding to $200 million in 1994 which then dropped to zero from 1996-1999.[159] This spending was indicative of the general critical minerals malaise where the overarching U.S. mentality assumed it could always get the raw materials it needed. It was during this period of growing U.S. critical minerals apathy that China took the opposite approach and took measures to improve its own minerals security.

After the 9/11 attacks, the Bush administration (2001-2008) funded the DPA at higher rates, going from just $3 million in 2001 to a high of $95 million in 2009. DPA projects included material used to fight in Afghanistan and Iraq such as Predator drones with Hellfire missiles, satellite communications to conduct joint operations with British forces, and improved ceramic plates for body armor. Other projects produced aluminum and titanium metal composites for the aerospace industry. However, these relatively small programs did not have the scale to move the underlying minerals and metals industries.[160]

159 The Clinton administration sold off large amounts of remaining material in the national stockpile.

160 Reauthorization of the Defense Production Act hearings, June 5, 2003.

Mine Resistant Ambush Protected Vehicles (MRAPs)

During the Bush and Obama tenures (2007-2009), DPA Title III authority wasn't required to compel manufacturing of MRAPs since private sector companies responded quickly to DOD contract needs. Also, Title III was irrelevant relating to increased steel production for armor because the U.S. simply did not have the domestic capability, hence increased imports were required. Title I authority was used to give the MRAP program a "DX" designation, prioritizing it in the acquisition system.

The DPA had fallen into such little use with a focus mainly on national emergency management that the Obama administration (2009-2016) took action and created the Defense Production Act Committee in 2009. While DPAC was supposed to provide interagency coordination, illuminate significant DPA policy issues, and expertly advise the President, they appeared to do little more than issue an annual report. Congress attempted to reform DPAC in 2014 to make it more effective but failed to do anything that changed its core reporting function. For example, DPA activity was coordinated by FEMA's DPA Program Division office which employed only four people as of 2021.[161]

From its inception, DPAC never reported on any minerals issues and its seventeen members making up the committee demonstrated no interest in or expertise on the topic. In one illustration of its impotence, DPAC's superficial reports averaged 25 pages in length compared to the ones by the former Joint Committee on Defense Production which ran as long as 500 pages. The committee stopped issuing annual reports after 2021 as it was sidelined by the Biden administration which moved forward with DPA funded mineral projects on its own. Ultimately, DPAC was swallowed up in the immense sea of bureaucratic apathy by a fragmented federal government who didn't understand its potential and didn't give it enough power to succeed.

Beyond establishing the ineffective DPAC, the administration delegated authorities of the DPA down to six different cabinet secretaries through Executive Order 13603 *National Defense Resources Preparedness* in 2012. The Secretaries of Defense and Interior were "to encourage the exploration, devel-

161 "The Defense Production Act Committee: A Primer." Congressional Research Service, February 23, 2021.

opment, and mining of strategic and critical materials and other materials." However, this was merely executive guidance that carried little weight since the administration had no critical minerals strategy. And Defense had no interest in managing its own national stockpile and was mostly unaware of its own critical mineral vulnerabilities. Thus, the DPA was never used by the Obama administration to restructure supply chains and improve minerals security.

The Trump administration (2017-2020) was hesitant to use the DPA because it violated free-market principles. The topic came to a decision point in March 2020 at the height of the COVID-19 pandemic when the administration was under pressure to use the DPA to secure medical equipment. Trump provided context: "We're a country not based on nationalizing our business. Call a person over in Venezuela. Ask them, how did nationalization of their businesses work out? Not too well. The concept of nationalizing our business is not a good concept."

He subsequently changed course and then used the DPA to compel companies like General Motors to manufacture ventilators. "We thought we had a deal with, as an example General Motors, and I guess they thought otherwise. They didn't agree, and now they do," Trump said. Along with this, the administration approved the release of thousands of ventilators from the national stockpile for distribution which numbered 18,000.[162]

Trump's use of the DPA for medical equipment set a precedent which subsequently impacted how his administration would address the U.S.' dependence on China for many of its critical minerals. On September 30, 2020, Trump issued an Executive Order which recognized the country's reliance on foreign sources of REE, gallium, and barite and directed the Department of Interior to coordinate increased domestic mining production.[163] Then, only six weeks later, he used the DPA to provide grants to three different REE companies: MP Materials, TDA Magnetics, and Noveon Magnetics (previously Urban Mining).

162 Dale, Daniel. "Fact check: Trump claimed he was left 'no ventilators.' His administration just confirmed he had more than 16,000." CNN, June 24, 2020.

163 EO 13953 *Addressing the Threat to the Domestic Supply Chain from Reliance on Critical Minerals from Foreign Adversaries.*

The DPA and Critical Minerals: 2021-2024

"I find that action to expand the domestic production capabilities for such strategic and critical materials is necessary to avert an industrial resource or critical technology item shortfall that would severely impair the national defense capability."

- President Biden, Presidential Determination 2022-11

As discussed in previously, the Biden administration took a variety of actions to improve the country's critical minerals supply chains and this included using the DPA. In early 2022, Biden issued Presidential Determination 2022-11 which invoked Title III, Section 303 of the DPA to increase domestic mining and minerals processing for the production of batteries. While the document listed five minerals (lithium, cobalt, nickel, graphite, manganese) others were eligible. This was the first time that batteries for EVs and energy storage were identified as a national security concern and critical to the defense industrial base.

The rational for using the DPA was its ability to cut through the bureaucracy to move the industry in a timely manner which was the original reason the Truman administration created it. The Secretary of Defense was given the responsibility to manage DPA funded projects which must have come as a shock as critical mineral mining had not been a priority for the Department of Defense since the 1950s. The projects would be executed in consultation with the Secretaries of the Interior, Agriculture, and Energy who were the actual repositories of minerals knowledge.

Another way to achieve improved minerals security was partnering with Canada and pooling their collective resources. In 2020, both countries signed the Canada-U.S. Joint Action Plan on Critical Minerals Collaboration with an agreement to pursue joint extraction initiatives. However, the Trump administration didn't move forward with any joint projects during its tenure. With the Biden administration's subsequent push for critical minerals production, the U.S. used the DPA to fund six different Canadian projects for $100 million (tungsten, bismuth, cobalt, graphite, LFP cathode material). Importantly, this signaled a much delayed recognition to both parties that Canada should be treated as part of a contiguous minerals industrial base.[164]

164 Although Canada was considered a "domestic source" for DPA sourcing in 1992, this was the first instance of it being applied for mining purposes.

The administration was also intent on using $500 million from the Inflation Reduction Act to fund green energy technology using DPA authorities. The DPA would focus on five areas: solar, transformers & grid components, heat pumps, insulation, and electrolyzers, fuel cells, and Platinum Group Metals (PGM).[165] While the money for these programs would push a low-carbon economy, it could also help to restructure critical mineral supply chains. The sectors that could have an impact on minerals were solar, grid components, and fuel cells. But this would have to be done at a scale that could shift existing global trade dynamics.

Because these were energy related industries, the Department of Energy (DOE) would manage their implementation through the DPA. In December of 2022, DOE put out an RFI (Request for Information) to the public which "... invites public comment on general use of Title III of the Defense Production Act as well as on transformers and critical electric grid components and three other technology areas announced by the President on June 6, 2022." While this crowdsourcing could generate new and useful ideas, it also slowed down the process and gave the impression that DOE didn't know exactly what it was doing.

Upon the conclusion of the Biden administration in 2024, it was clear that DOE's attempt to grow clean energy technology through the DPA was a failure. For example, the key component of transformers for the grid is electrical steel which is made by only one U.S. company (Cleveland Cliffs) with the rest being imported.[166] Most of the U.S.' electrical steel (85%) is first imported to Canada and Mexico, used to make transformers, and then shipped to the U.S. However, the DPA was not used to incentivize domestic production. While the Luxembourg steel company ArcellorMittal received $280 million in federal tax credits to build an electrical steel plant in Alabama, this was funded through the Inflation Reduction Act and their steel products were for EVs, not the grid .[167]

It was hard to see how the DPA could be used to significantly impact the solar panel market with China producing 97% of the world's solar wafers. Regardless, the DPA was used to provide a $14.4 million grant to Canadian com-

165 Heat pumps received by far the most support with $250 million.

166 Cleveland Cliffs owns AK Steel, the sole producer of electrical steel remaining in the country.

167 Scheduled for operation in 2027, this plant will produce NOES (Non-grain Oriented Electrical Steel) used in electric motors for BEVs as opposed to GOES (Grain Oriented Electrical Steel) which is used in transformers.

pany 5N+ Semiconductor to manufacture germanium substrates for solar cells used in commercial and defense satellites.[168] One assessment sized the global solar PV market at $170 billion, meaning the DPA's one lonely grant was a mere drop in a Chinese ocean already dominated by Asian producers led by Beijing.[169]

There is no evidence that the administration was able to use the DPA to move the PGM industry and its associated supply chains even a little. The South African company Sibanye-Stillwater runs a PGM operation in Montana and applied for assistance under the DPA through the Defense Industrial Base Consortium in 2024. While they were approved for the Section 45X IRS federal tax credits, they were still awaiting consideration for the DPA in 2025. The Canadian-based company Impala, which also produced PGM and could benefit from the Joint Action Plan, received no DPA assistance. The administration's aspirations to grow the hydrogen fuel cell market was most likely a bridge much too far. The U.S.' major producers like FuelCell Energy, Plug Power, and Bloom Energy either struggled or completely cratered from 2021-2024.

The administration's use of the DPA to support clean energy policies and critical minerals production was controversial and opposed by some lawmakers. Senator Joe Manchin (I-WV) did not believe the DPA should support green tech while he previously advocated its use to support a natural gas pipeline running through his state. Senator Dan Sullivan (R-AK) supported using the DPA to support domestic and not foreign mining operations, which was a regular U.S. mining industry talking point. And Representative Scott Perry (R-PA) introduced H.R.7601 to restrict the DPA from being used to support EVs and batteries.[170]

DPA Impact on Critical Minerals Security

It is necessary to assess what impact these DPA investments had on the U.S. critical minerals industry with the understanding that most of these projects are still in their infancy. Perhaps the salient lesson is that it takes many years to get a mining or midstream processing operation off the ground. The obvious conclusion should be that a country cannot produce a secure minerals

168 5N+ trades on the TSX as VNP.TO

169 https://www.grandviewresearch.com/horizon/outlook/solar-pv-panels-market-size/global

170 https://www.eenews.net/articles/the-next-big-energy-fight-defense-production-act-renewal/

supply chain quickly in time of emergency, which is exactly what the U.S. is trying to do. While the DPA is a tool that can cut through a certain amount of bureaucracy, it cannot automatically give the U.S. a superior position, say, in the cobalt space.

President Biden signs the Inflation Reduction Act on August 16, 2022. Through the Act, funds were transferred to the DPA that were then used to strengthen the U.S.' critical mineral supply chains.

Lithium Mining

Let's begin with the $212 million investment in battery minerals, which was less than half of the 25 separate projects sampled in this chapter. The biggest amount went to supporting lithium projects which included a hard rock extraction project with Albemarle ($90 million), another lithium mine with Lithium Americas Corporation ($11.8 million), and an LFP cathode operation with Nano One ($12.8 million). The reader must consider recent history where battery-grade lithium carbonate cost just $10,100.00 per metric ton in 2020 before skyrocketing to $80,000.00 a ton at the end of 2022 and then plummeting back down to $9,800.00 a ton in early 2025.

Albemarle, a U.S. mining company and major lithium producer, took the $90 million predicated on the fantasy that lithium prices would stay floating somewhere in the stratosphere. They planned to put the money towards purchasing mining equipment and opening their defunct hard rock lithium mine in Kings Mountain, North Carolina. However, Albemarle suffered from amnesia, forgetting that the Foote Mineral Company closed the King Mountain mine in 1996 after it became uneconomic. Albemarle misjudged the changing global lithium environment, failing to recognize that as they and other companies scrambled to expand production, they were driving lithium prices back down to earth.

Because the world's mining enterprise scrambled to grow lithium production in a desperate attempt to capture the insanely high yet fleeting prices, increased supply eventually met demand. This meant Albemarle went from net profits of $1.5 billion in 2023 to a net loss of $1.1 billion in 2024. Presently, Albemarle has a small lithium brine operation in Nevada, larger brine operations in Chile, and major hard rock operations in Western Australia. Albemarle says they will open the Kings Mountain mine anywhere between the years 2026-2030, depending on who you ask. However, it is far from certain whether Albemarle will be positioned to reopen the mine and if they can then run it in an economic manner.

The Biden administration made a much smaller investment in Lithium America's riskier open pit, hard rock lithium mine in Thacker Pass, Nevada. The DPA's paltry $11 million grant was insignificant compared to the $2.2 billion DOE loan the company received in 2024 which would also fund a 40,000 tpa capacity lithium carbonate facility. The operation eventually attracted interest from other major players in the industry with General Motors forming a JV with Lithium Americas in 2025 with a $625 million buy-in. As with the Albemarle operation, Thacker Pass may be operational by 2030. They too will have to prove that hard rock lithium mining operations in the U.S. can be economical.

Lithium Americas Corporation (LAC) is a Canadian company with existing lithium brine operations in Argentina. However, it is partially owned by the Chinese company Ganfeng Lithium. Obviously, this would have caused political problems for the company if China benefitted directly from lithium mining in the U.S. The company subsequently separated into two business with the Argentine operation named Lithium International and the U.S. operation Lithium Nevada. LAC's stock has fallen from a high of over $15.00 in 2022 to below $3.00 in early 2025.

Canadian company Nano One Materials received a relatively modest $12.8 million, which was matched by $20 million CAN from their government, to build an LFP cathode production facility. The company is currently in the laboratory and testing stage and is looking to partner with established companies to license their technology. Their current capacity is just 200 tpa and it remains to be seen if their lower energy and reduced water usage model can be scaled. For perspective, commercial scale LFP cathode plants cost in the range of $1 billion so the company will require much larger funding. If Nano One is successful, they will be the only functioning LFP cathode plant in North America and ex-Asia.

Graphite Extraction

The DPA used $49 million to invest in three separate natural flake graphite operations. The largest one is with Canadian company Graphite One ($37 million) that will extract graphite from an operation in Alaska and then process it at a future anode facility in Washington State. The Alaska production at Graphite Creek is still several years out with production forecasted to start in 2029. The company estimated they will produce 55,000 tons of finished graphite products annually with 41,850 tons for batteries and the remainder for industrial uses.

A much smaller investment ($8 million) went to Canadian company Lomiko Metals which is pursuing graphite, lithium, and antimony projects in Quebec. The Canadian government also awarded the company $6.6 million CAN as part of the Joint Action Plan. However, Lomiko is a mining start-up with no established operations and most likely would not produce a finished product until after 2030. One of their proposed graphite operations would produce 100,000 tons of graphite annually over a span of 15 years, indicating it is a short-term solution.

South Star Battery Metals Corporation received the smallest amount ($3 million) with natural flake graphite operations in Alabama and also Brazil. The company's BamaStar operation in Alabama has a projected capacity of 50,000 tpa of graphite concentrate by 2029 with a 19-year mine life, meaning it is a short-term solution. Their Santa Cruz operation in Brazil also has a projected 50,000 tpa capacity with a shorter 12-year mine life. South Star has plans to build a 60,000 tpa active anode material plant in the U.S. which would run upwards of $1 billion to construct.

If we add the numbers of up for these three operations, annual U.S. production would surpass 200,000 tons a year. However, we have a problem, because the U.S. only consumed 52,000 tons of natural flake graphite in 2024. This increased production is built on the assumption that the U.S. will onshore battery anode manufacturing which at present resides in Asia. Also, these numbers do not factor in Novonix's synthetic graphite operation in Tennessee with a 50,000 tpa capacity or Nouveau Monde's or Syrah Resources natural flake operations. Most likely, this overproduction will result in idled operations and bankruptcies as economic survival of the fittest regulates the space.

Cobalt Operations

The DPA put $48 million towards four separate cobalt operations which is an element of NMC (Nickel Manganese Cobalt) ternary batteries and compete with LFP (Lithium Iron Phosphate) batteries. The Canadian company Electra Battery Materials Corporation received the largest amount ($20 million) to advance cobalt sulfate production although they also pursue lithium-ion battery recycling and are exploring nickel sulfate refining. Electra's business model includes importing cobalt from the DRC to Canada for refinement which they will then sell to cathode precursor manufacturers. The company's initial projected capacity is 5,000 tpa with plans for an additional 1,500 tpa.

Australian company Jervois Mining Limited received $15 million for future cobalt production, although the company also has nickel operations. The company has active cobalt operations in Finland with a 5,100 tpa capacity. Jervois bought the Idaho Cobalt Operations in 2019 and improved the facilities although it has suspended operations there. The company also owns a nickel and cobalt operation in Brazil with a 2,000 tpa cobalt capacity. In 2025, Jervois declared bankruptcy in the U.S. and underwent restructuring and privatization.

The private Missouri based Doe Run Company received $7 million to construct a hydrometallurgical cobalt and nickel separation demonstration plant for future commercialization. Doe Run is an established mining company, extracting primarily lead, copper, and zinc from their Missouri mines but also lesser amounts of cobalt, nickel, tin, and antimony. They also have ongoing lead battery recycling operations, processing 8.5 million lead batteries annually which is 12% of the total U.S. industry.

Canadian company Fortune Minerals Limited received a $6 million award to develop cobalt products through the DPA with the Canadian government matching with $5.6 million CAN. Fortune is a long shot in that they are a start-up and their NICO critical minerals project (cobalt, copper, bismuth, gold) is not operational. Fortune estimates that they have 37,000 metric tons of cobalt as they pursue a 1,800 tpa capacity which equates to 8,780 tpa of battery-grade cobalt sulphate.

North America is in a tough position, producing just 4,800 metric tons of contained cobalt in 2024. The U.S. consumes 8,000 tons annually of cobalt which is used mainly for specialty alloys, chemicals, and none for battery manufacturing. This must be compared to the 290,000 tons produced worldwide with 220,000 alone (76%) coming from the Democratic Republic of the Congo (DRC). An increase in cobalt production from these various projects would fill the U.S.' current industrial needs for sure. However, they would in no way be able to fill future onshored NMC battery production needs which would still have to be imported from established Asian cathode producers.

Metals

While battery minerals received the most investment, a variety of companies received $112 million to pursue projects ranging from high-use metals like nickel and tin to low volume material like niobium. Two aluminum companies received $68 million from the DPA including Arconic Corporation which used a $45 million grant to upgrade its existing High Purity Aluminum (HPA) production capacity. Constellium Muscle Shoals received $28 million to enable an additional 150,000 tons of aluminum casting capability. Neither of these awards directly improved bauxite and alumina supply chains which the U.S. majority sourced from Jamaica and Brazil.

Global Advanced Metals USA received $26 million for a metal product most people have never heard of – niobium oxide – which is used in a wide variety of specialty metals and alloys, mainly in the aerospace industry. The U.S. lost its domestic niobium mining capability in 1959 and has since imported 100% of its needs with most coming from Australia and then Africa. The U.S. has not produced niobium oxide in the U.S. since the 1990s, importing most of it from Brazil (83%). Regaining this capability moves the U.S. up the niobium value chain.

The administration also moved $20 million to Canadian mining company Talon Nickel to develop their Tamarack Project (nickel, copper, cobalt) in Minnesota.[171] Talon's battery mineral processing facility in North Dakota also received $114 million through the Bipartisan Infrastructure Law. The U.S. imports half of its nickel needs with most coming from neighboring Canada. While Talon's nickel operation might become operational in 2027, it only has a ten-year life, so it is a temporary solution for the U.S.' relative nickel insecurity.

The manganese and magnesium metals industry received almost $40 million with half of this going to Australian mining company South32's open pit manganese project in Arizona. The U.S. has not mined manganese since 1970 and imports 100% of its needs with 85% coming from African suppliers. The

171 Talon is a joint venture with British-Australian mining company Rio Tinto.

rest of the DPA award went to U.S. company Magrathea Metals to build a demonstration plant that recovers magnesium metal from seawater. The U.S. has not produced primary magnesium metals since the 1980s and imports 75% of its need from a variety of regions to include the Middle East, North America, Europe, and Asia.

The tin and tungsten metal industry received more than $32 million with over half going to U.S. company Nathan Trotter & Company to develop a primary tin smelting, refining, and recycling capability. The U.S. has not mined nor primarily smelted tin since the early 1990s and imports 75% of its needs with most refined products coming from South America. Canadian company Fireweed Metals Corporation received the remainder of the funds and was matched with $12.9 million CAN from the Canadian government. However, the company's Mactung tungsten project is still in the pre-development stage and production likely will not start until after 2030. The U.S. does not mine tungsten and imports more than half of its needs with 27% of this coming directly from China.

Lastly, the DPA allocated $12.7 million to U.S. company IperionX to improve their demonstration plant and then scale up to 10,000 metric tons of titanium powder annually. This level of production would likely not occur before the year 2030. Key to IperionX's success will be their HAMR & HST processes with lower energy requirements and reduced costs combined with their Titan mining project (titanium, zirconium, rare earths) located in Tennessee.[172] Although it is critical for specialty alloys, the U.S. produces very little titanium, importing 95% of its needs with the vast majority coming from Japan.[173]

Overall, the Biden administration's use of the DPA to secure the country's critical mineral supply chains was a big step in the right direction for an industry that had been ignored and neglected for many decades. From briefly examining these separate cases, it is obvious that it will take a decade or more, from the start of the awards process to steady volume production, to make an impact. While U.S. politicians can argue over the details of the DPA and how it should be used, clearly, it can be used as a tool to strengthen the country's critical minerals enterprise.

172 Hydrogen-Assisted Metallothermic Reduction (HAMR) and Hydrogen Sintering and Phase Transformation (HSPT).

173 USGS data for titanium sponge metal.

Reauthorizing the DPA for 2025

The current DPA's authorities were set to expire on September 30, 2025, which meant Congress had to determine how competing ideas would impact and shape its reauthorization. On March 12, 2024, the House Financial Services committee held an initial hearing with four witnesses on reauthorizing the DPA. The hearing reflected an ongoing debate in U.S. policy circles as to what was the role of the DPA and how it should be used. One train of thought was that the DPA should only be used for clearly defined military readiness purposes. Other proponents have sought to widen the definition of national security. For example, in 2020, Trump 1.0 used the DPA to compel General Motors to produce ventilators in response to the COVID-19 pandemic. While this was clearly a national health priority, it certainly had no military connotation.

One witness from the Congressional Research Service (CRS) provided a history of the DPA and major trends in its evolution. CRS highlighted that the Defense Priorities and Allocations System (DPAS) was the most frequently used tool under Title I authorities. Each year, an average of 300,000 orders were prioritized with DOD being the most active DPAS user.[174] Also, DPA use had recently increased with Congress appropriating $932 million from 2010-2019, which grew significantly to $3.1 billion from 2020-2023. Differing opinions on DPA use included if the act provided the President too much authority and if the Congress should provide additional restrictions and reporting requirements.

A former Assistant Secretary of Defense for Industrial Policy testified that the DPA process lacked, among other things, critical minerals processing expertise and that subject matter experts (SME) should be hired to inform DPA decision making.[175] This highlighted the fact that the U.S. government continually failed to access the minerals knowledge that it already had and paid for with its own U.S. Geological Survey. The witness recognized that the U.S. had to use the DPA to acquire critical minerals from foreign suppliers, a step that should only be taken when absolutely necessary so as not to subsidize foreign defense programs.

Finally, the Director of Industrial Policy and Trade at the Roosevelt Institute reminded the committee that the DPA has always been used to support

174 DPAS is administered by the Department of Commerce's Bureau of Industry and Security.

175 Jeffrey Jeb Nadaner, Senior Vice President, Govini – a private company that sells software to the Defense Acquisition industry.

the health of both the defense industrial base and the national economy.[176] The witness recognized that China had secured large market shares in the steel, solar panel, and electric vehicle sectors. Beijing had also achieved supply chain monopolies in specific sectors like green energy, with upwards of 90% control. The DPA could be used to support other policies to address market imbalances, increase U.S. competitiveness, and erode China's dominant positions.

The Committee held a follow-up hearing on May 8, 2024, with additional testimony from three witnesses. The Assistant Secretary of Defense for Industrial Policy recommended that the annual DPA Fund balance be increased so that unspent funds aren't automatically returned to Treasury at the end of the year. Also, there should be more than one Executive Agent to execute the DPA's Title III program so DOD can use more contracting mechanisms. Third, DPA appropriated funds would be better served as non-expiring as opposed to having a five-year limit to give DOD more flexibility such as issuing loans.[177]

The Department of Commerce's (DOC) Assistant Secretary of Export Administration strongly supported continued use of DPAS under Title I of the DPA which was fundamental to prioritizing DOD supply chains and other national security needs. The same was said for Title VII authorities enabling supply chain security investigations to include implementation of CFIUS (Committee on Foreign Investments in the U.S.) DPA authorities were crucial for DOC to conduct Section 232 investigations with one example being an assessment of DOD's reliance on imported titanium sponge.[178]

Finally, a representative from FEMA (Federal Emergency Management Agency) spoke to the importance of DPA authorities for non-DOD responses like COVID-19, wildfire protection, and biodefense programs. Beyond this, the definition of "national defense" should be expanded to include homeland security threats such as public health risks. Lastly, the U.S. would benefit from a well-managed national stockpile and streamlined government responses to DPA priorities.[179]

---

176 Todd N. Tucker. The Roosevelt Institute is a non-profit economic policy think-tank.
177 Dr. Laura Taylor-Lake. For some bizarre reason, the Secretary of the Air Force is the President's delegated sole Executive Agent.
178 Thea D. Rozman-Kendler, Bureau of Industry and Security. The Titanium Sponge Working Group (TSWG) was created in 2020. It's hard to imagine exactly what the TSWG's purpose was other than admiring the problem since U.S. dependence on Ti Sponge imports went from 68% to 100%.
179 Cynthia Spishak, Associate Administrator, Office of Policy and Program Analysis. FEMA chairs the Defense Production Act Committee (DPAC) created by the Obama ad-

Beyond the testimony at these hearings, there were several proposed bills published in Congress that indicated some of the competing interests relating to the DPA. Two were from Representative Scott Perry (R-PA) who wanted to restrict the use of the DPA for non-military purposes which meant cancelling the provisions authorized by Biden to manufacture solar panels and batteries.[180] Another was a bill requiring the President to submit an annual report to Congress detailing their use of the DPA.

While these hearings indicated what some of the issues were involving the DPA moving into 2025, Trump 2.0 changed several aspects of the Act on March 14, 2025, with a blanket revocation of many of Biden's previous executive orders. These included the cancellation of DPA support for buying infant formula, solar modules and components, insulation, fuel cells and PGM, electric heat pumps, and DPA statutory waiver requirements on DOD supply chain resiliency. While these were in part a general revocation of previous Biden policies, they also narrowed the definition of national security.

One could easily argue that using the DPA for long-term purchasing of these products was not an appropriate use of the Act such as for green energy technology. Certainly, the money spent on the sectors with related critical mineral supply chains (solar panels: tellurium, aluminum; fuel cells: PGM) was not enough to change their supply vulnerability. There were other ways that the government could advance these sectors if it wanted to or it could leave it to private industry altogether.

On March 20, 2025, Trump 2.0 issued an Executive Order intended to boost domestic critical minerals production which included using tools from the DPA.[181] Specifically, Trump authorized DOD to use the DPA "for the domestic production and facilitation of strategic resources the SECDEF deems necessary or appropriate to advance domestic mineral production in the United States." Furthermore, the CEO of the U.S. International Development Finance Corporation (DFC) was given DPA authorities "for the domestic production and facilitation of strategic resources the CEO deems necessary or appropriate to advance mineral production."

ministration.

180 H.R. 7500 the Bullets not Batteries Act, H.R. 7602 Planes not Panels Act.

181 EO 14241 *Immediate Measures to Increase American Mineral Production.*

Looking Ahead

Clearly, the mentality of the U.S. federal government has evolved from that of the 1990s and the collapse of the Soviet Union where the country thought that everything in the world would go its way. The DPA can be a powerful tool that the President uses to assist the national military industrial base and respond to national emergencies. In fact, the U.S. has no other mechanism to compel private industry in such a way to support these needs in time of emergency. Most likely, Congress will reauthorize the DPA and continue to support rather broad definitions of national security in relation to emergency preparedness.

Trump 2.0 has already shown a willingness to restrict use of the DPA to be more security focused and not to advance manufacturing that can be accomplished through private industry. While Trump 1.0 was clearly hesitant to use the DPA during his first administration, Trump 2.0 has already issued directives to employ its authorities for the critical minerals space. In this we find continuity as Trump 1.0 was the first president to use the DPA to fund REE projects and that is likely to continue during his second term.

With these dynamics in mind, one must be realistic as to what the DPA can contribute to U.S. critical minerals security. A significant departure from previous DPA implementation would be to use Title III authority to compel mining companies to extract critical minerals. Although this would be unprecedented and unlikely, it is within the realm of legal possibility and would require a huge conceptual leap. However, Title III authority won't make nickel deposits appear within the U.S.' borders nor will it make Direct Lithium Extraction technology viable. While the DPA can slice through some bureaucratic barriers to advance a minerals project, it is just another funding mechanism that could be done through other means. Overall, the DPA is a helpful mechanism but not the final answer to the U.S.' critical minerals problems.

Sources

AK Steel Corporation Comments to the Department of Commerce Regarding the Section 232 National Security Investigation. July 2, 2020.

Bell, Douglas. "A Little-known Bill of Great National Significance: The Uses and Evolution of the DPA, 1950-2020." U.S. Army War College.

Cuff, Robert. "Stockpiles and Defense Escalation, 1965-1968." The Public Historian, Vol.9, No. 4, (Fall 1987).

"Defense Production Act of 1950, As Amended." August 13, 2018.

Hart, David M. "The DPA: National Security as a Potential Driver of Domestic Manufacturing Investment." Bipartisan Policy Center, 2024.

"Rapid Acquisition of Mine Resistant Ambush Protected Vehicles." Government Accountability Office, July 15, 2008.

King, Alwyn. "The Impact of the Vietnam Conflict on the Economy of the United States." Army War College, 1980.

"The Defense Production Act of 1950: History, Authorities, and Considerations for Congress." Congressional Research Service, Oct 6, 2023.

"Managing Materials for a 21st Century Military." National Research Council, 2007.

"Mission Critical: Restoring National Security as the Focus of Defense Production Act Reauthorization." CRS, March 12, 2024.

Nicastro, Luke A. Statement before the Committee on Financial Services hearings on the Defense Production Act. March 12, 2024.

"Reauthorizing the Defense Production Act." Congressional Research Service, January 14, 2025.

"2022 Invocation of the DPA for Large-Capacity Batteries: In Brief." Congressional Research Service, May 27, 2022.

Defense Production Act

Title I

- Prioritizes federal contracts over all other orders with either "DO" or "DX" designations
- Controls distribution of scarce materials within the civilian economy
- Allocates scarce materials against federal or private contracts
- Prevents hoarding of scarce materials
- Is used on average 300,000 times a year

Title III

- Offers incentives to develop, maintain, modernize and expand production capacity or critical technologies
- Section 301 offers loan guarantees & Section 302 offers loans to private companies
- Section 303 provides purchasing commitments which creates guaranteed demand and subsidies to companies that enables the purchase of equipment
- Section 303 investments require a Presidential Determination (PD) which are non-expiring and require Congressional notification if over $50 million

Title VII

- Mandatory survey authority of any U.S. registered businesses entity to collect data and information
- Provides anti-trust immunity for industry to develop and implement national emergency preparedness plans
- Provides authorities to the Committee on Foreign Investment (CFIUS) to investigate the impact of foreign company purchases on U.S. national security

DPA Critical Minerals Contracts Through 2024		
Company	**Project**	**Amount Awarded**
Albemarle	Lithium	$90 million
Arconic Corp.	High Purity Aluminum	$45.5 million
Graphite One*	Graphite	$37.5 million
MP Materials	Rare Earth Elements	$35 million
Lynas Rare Earths	Rare Earth Elements	$30.4 million
Noveon Magnetics	Rare Earth Elements	$28.8 million
Global Advanced Metals	Niobium Oxide	$26.4 million
Talon Nickel	Nickel	$20.6 million
Constellium Muscle Sh.	Aluminum	$23 million
Electra Battery*	Cobalt Sulfate	$20 million
South 32	Manganese	$20 million
Magrathea	Magnesium	$19.6 million
Nathan Trotter Co.	Tin	$19 million
Fireweed Metals Corp*	Tungsten	$15.8 million
Jervois Mining	Cobalt	$15 million
Nano One Materials*	LFP Cathode	$12.88
IperionX	Titanium powder	$12.7 million
Lithium Nevada Corp	Lithium	$11.81 million
Lomiko Metals Inc.*	Graphite	$8.35 million
Doe Run Resources	Cobalt, Nickel	$7 million
Fortune Minerals *	Cobalt, Bismuth	$6.4 million
Montana Tech	Minerals Education	$6.56 million
Rare Earth Salts	REE Lamp Recycing	$4.2 million
South Star Battery	Graphite	$3.18 million
TDA Magnetics	Rare Earth Elements	$2.3 million
	Total:	**$436.8 Million**

**U.S.-Canadian Joint Action Plan on Critical Minerals*

The largest investment of DPA funds was directed toward battery minerals which the Biden administration recognized as a strategic economic priority. Beijing has already expanded into the battery space to control as much of it as it can, giving it global leverage over the fasting growing sector of energy storage. The next largest investment was in the U.S.' declining metals enterprise which has largely been priced out due to cheaper global competition. Rare Earths received $101 million of support which had a noticeable positive impact in onshoring U.S. production.

Chapter 5

The National Defense Stockpile

"The Congress finds that the natural resources of the United States in certain strategic and critical materials are deficient or insufficiently developed to supply the military, industrial, and essential civilian needs of the United States for national defense."

– Strategic and Critical Minerals Stock Piling Act of 1939

Introduction

Although the *Strategic and Critical Minerals Stock Piling Act* provided the blueprint for an effective critical minerals strategic reserve program, today it is a decided failure. There are many factors contributing to this, including a lack of presidential interest, the creation of a byzantine acquisition process that is unable to fulfill its stated mission, and failed oversight mechanisms. The government stockpile management system has proven to be both fundamentally incompetent and apathetic towards acquiring and storing its own critical minerals. This chapter examines how this came to be and what the U.S. can do to fix it.

World War II and the National Defense Stockpile

The idea that the U.S. should have a stockpile of raw materials as an insurance policy for supply chain disruptions that could impact the national industrial defense base began to form after World War I. The first work to address the subject was the *International Control of Minerals* published in 1925 by two separate mining societies and ran 173 pages in length.[182] While they had not

182 Committee of the Mining an Metallurgical Society of America on Foreign and Domestic Mining Policy and the Committee of the American Institute of Mining and Metallurgical Engineers on Industrial Preparedness.

yet developed the concept for a centralized national stockpile managed by the federal government, they did conclude that some decentralized stocking should take place on a case by case basis.

For example, the report recognized the government should purchase and store at least 600,000 tons of manganese which could then be supplemented during wartime by domestic mining and private company stocks.[183] However, they applied this logic unevenly. Their assessment of tungsten revealed the same supply chain vulnerabilities as manganese but concluded the U.S. needed to maintain open seas to ensure its import. There was no mention of stockpiling as a strategy against disruption. Clearly, the authors held differing understandings of what critical minerals security entailed.

President Roosevelt (FDR) established the Natural Resources Board (NRB) in 1934 as an advisory committee to conduct studies and publish subsequent reports on how to best use the nation's resources.[184] Underneath the NRB was the Planning Committee for Mineral Policy which published a report in 1936 highlighting U.S. mineral deficiencies in tungsten, zinc, manganese, vanadium, nickel and tin.[185] Noticeably, the report described the nation's production capacity for thirty-two separate minerals but stopped short of offering policy advice. However, it was clear that some sort of action was required to secure the minerals identified as being deficient.

Interest in an undefined stockpile in preparation for the impending war continued with FDR requesting the War Department for a study of its stockpiling requirements. In 1936, Congress requested a similar study from the Navy Department. This was unfamiliar territory for the U.S. government and these initial efforts educated the bureaucracy and conditioned it for future action.

The idea for a stockpile gained traction in the bureaucracy with the *Navy Appropriations Bill for 1938* which requested $5 million for "strategic war minerals." The Navy identified seven minerals (antimony, chromium, ferromanganese, nickel, tin, tungsten, ferrovanadaium) which it wanted to stock to sustain its needs for a two-year period of conflict. Beyond this, the Navy also studied the need for a larger stockpile to support all U.S. industrial needs for a two-year period with an estimated cost of $95.8 million.[186]

183 The U.S. later developed an open air manganese stockpile in Wenden, AZ.

184 Executive Order 6777 June 30, 1934.

185 *The Mineral Reserves of the United States and its Capacity for Production.*

186 The Navy study went through their Fleet Maintenance Division, Procurement of War

The Navy requested the $5 million sum in both 1935 and 1936. While the House approved these requests each year, the Senate refused to appropriate the money. It was only in 1937, as the coming war became inevitable, that both chambers of Congress appropriated $3.5 million for the 1938 fiscal year. The recognition that the Navy needed raw material stocks continued for the years 1939 and 1940 with $500,000 appropriated for each.

As World War II consumed Europe, the U.S. Army continued to highlight the importance of raw materials and the need to stockpile them. In the magazine *Army Ordnance*, Captain G. K. Heiss from the Army-Navy Munitions Board (ANMB) published the article, "Why a Raw Materials Reserve? Our Stock Pile Shortages are Strategic and Critical."[187] Heiss argued that only through stocking could the country guarantee its material needs that couldn't otherwise be met through domestic production or substitution.

Enough momentum developed across the government bureaucracy with the threat of war so obvious that Congress passed the *Strategic and Critical Minerals Stock Piling Act of 1939*. The two-page act directed the Secretaries of War, Navy, and the Interior in conjunction with the ANMB to determine what was a strategic and critical material. These entities would further cooperate with the Secretaries of State, Treasury, and Commerce in the actual acquisition of these identified materials. The Treasury Department's Procurement Division would be responsible for purchasing, storing, and rotating the materials as needed.[188]

Importantly, these materials could only be released by order of the President. The government was also instructed to purchase materials in accordance with the *Buy American Act of 1933* which was meant to drive domestic mineral production.[189] The Act authorized $100 million in funds to be spent over five years (1939-1943), with Congress later appropriating 70% of this through 1940. Furthermore, the Secretary of the Interior was authorized $2 million to be spent over four years (1940-1943) for the exploration and development of mineral resources in the U.S.

When the act was signed, the ANMB had already developed a list of materials divided into three categories: strategic, critical, and essential. Strategic

Materials office which collaborated with the Army-Navy Munitions Board.

187 Heiss was assigned to the Office of the Assistant Secretary of War, Planning Branch with further duties with the Army-Navy Munitions Board.

188 The Procurement Division, the Army, and the Navy would store the material.

189 Treasury was to give domestic producers one year to deliver an ordered product before looking elsewhere.

materials were defined as those that were wholly or mostly obtained from foreign sources. Critical materials were those that were easier to obtain and could most likely be sourced domestically. Essential materials were those that were considered sufficiently secure but required continuing surveillance. The list was based on the Board's understanding of what the Army, Navy and the country required to function in consultation with private industry.[190]

Two months after the Stockpiling Act was passed, Congress enacted the *Exchange for Critical and Strategic Materials Act of 1939*. With this, the U.S. Commodity Credit Corporation (CCC) was authorized to exchange surplus agricultural goods with foreign countries for designated strategic and critical materials. The CCC, in consultation with the Department of Agriculture, would transfer their excess agriculture commodities and then store the incoming minerals in consultation with the Army and Navy. This created a CCC supplemental stockpile that would become separate from and augment the National Stockpile.

However, filling out the stockpile for critical minerals was difficult due to the complexities of the war and competing priorities. Passage of the *Neutrality Act of 1939* enabled U.S. allies to use American ships to transport goods on a "cash and carry" basis. The act greatly facilitated the export of material, supplies, munitions, and weapons from the U.S. to western European countries as intended. The U.S. subsequently instituted its "Arsenal of Diplomacy" policy at the end of 1940 and the *Lend-Lease Act* in early 1941. This meant limited resources were sent overseas to frontline countries as opposed to the U.S.' own stockpile.

Also, the U.S. was unable to meet most of its stockpile objectives, not only because of exports to allies but because the U.S. consumed more than it could store. For example, the U.S.' stockpile goal in 1941 for manganese ore was 3.7 million tons while at the beginning of 1942 it had only met 15% of this requirement. The goal for chromite was 1.9 million tons but fell short with only 17% of this requirement being met. In a final example, the goal for copper of 500,000 tons was only filled to 14%. Something more had to be done.[191]

190 During hearings for the Stockpile Act, congress questioned the ANMB's expertise in determining the importance of these materials which in turn revealed their own lack of knowledge.

191 Morgan, *Strategic Materials in World War II.*

To redress the problems with filling the stockpile which included limited funding, Congress amended the *Reconstruction Finance Corporation (RFC) Act* in the summer of 1940. The RFC could now be used to invest in companies producing "strategic and critical materials" and to even create corporations to do the same. The RFC received robust funding to the tune of $500 million which could be used to purchase agricultural commodities to support the CCC's barter program used to secure critical minerals.

As the U.S. progressively became more involved in the war and prepared for major combat operations, the idea of stockpiling its materials strictly on military bases evolved. Critical minerals were now stored according to different criteria such as transportation efficiencies and locations near end-using industries. The RFC and the Director of Stockpiling and Transportation (under the War Production Board) made the decisions on how and where material was stockpiled. Thus, stockpiling was increasingly managed by civilian organizations as the military focused on warfighting.

To develop the flow of minerals required to fill the stockpile, the RCF created an impressive bureaucratic architecture to create these pathways. This consisted of the creation of the Metals Reserve Company (MRC), Rubber Reserve Company, Defense Supplies Corporation, and the Defense Plant Corporation. Of these, the MRC was the most important which purchased large stocks of minerals from Latin America (tin, zinc, antimony, tungsten) and China (tin, antimony, tungsten).[192]

Towards the end of 1944, it was clear that both Germany and Japan had lost the war and it was just a matter of time before the Allied forces defeated their

192 For example, the MRC purchased all of Bolivia's exportable surpluses of tin, antimony, zinc, and tungsten.

forces in the field and forced unconditional surrenders. In preparation for this impending victory, Congress passed the *Surplus Property Act of 1944*. The act's intent was to dispose of the multitude of government-produced surplus items in a way that was beneficial to the U.S. economy and did not harm private industry. First, it relieved various government agencies of storing large amounts of unused material. Second, it helped to build the nascent and rather modest stockpile. Lastly, it prevented volumes of surplus material from being dumped into the national economy which could undercut existing industries.

The U.S. entered World War II with no centralized stockpile with individual agencies grappling with how to ensure raw materials security so as not to repeat the supply chain mistakes of WWI. The idea of a national stockpile evolved over the course of the war where its advocates continued pressuring the government to take action. Although a national stockpile was signed into the law, the U.S. was unable to fill it due to the demands of immediate consumption for wartime production needs. With the end of the war, the U.S. had the chance to fill a stockpile to ensure its future needs in time of emergency.

Into The Cold War

A year after the end of WWII, President Truman signed the *Strategic and Critical Materials Stockpiling Act of 1946*. The five-page document reflected the lessons learned during the war years. It was not only an acceptance of the need for a national stockpile, but it fine-tuned the mechanisms in which it would be implemented. The act, which amended the original signed in 1939, was the primary guide for U.S. stockpiling strategy through much of the Cold War.

The stockpile's primary goal was to prevent a "dangerous and costly dependence" on foreign countries during time of emergency. As had already been established, the Secretaries of War, Navy, and the Interior would work with the ANMB to determine what materials were consider "strategic and critical." These offices in turn would continue to coordinate with the Secretaries of State, Treasury, Agriculture, and Commerce for the acquisition of these materials. These offices were to appoint industry advisory committees with members knowledgeable of the materials being stockpiled.[193]

193 These members were allowed no more than $10.00 per diem for each day in conference as part of these committees.

For actual purchasing of materials, the Secretaries of War and Navy would direct the Treasury as what to secure while accounting for provisions of the *Buy American Act*. Treasury was responsible for storing the materials either on military bases or through civilian means. Conceptually, this meant the stockpile was not in a single location but dispersed geographically as needed. Treasury would also conduct refining and processing of acquired materials as well as rotating and replacing them as necessary to prevent deterioration.

In order to maintain accountability and oversight, the Secretaries of War and Navy would provide reports of the stockpile's status to Congress every six months. As with the original act, the President remained the only authority who could release material from the stockpile in time of national emergency. And if stockpile materials were to be disposed of (i.e., sold) as there was a surplus beyond published needs or they were no longer required, this could only be approved by Congress.

Upon signing the 1946 act, Truman made an official statement regarding the purchasing of critical materials as it related to the Buy American Act. Truman warned of buying critical minerals solely from domestic producers as this would serve to subsidize noncompetitive companies and inflate prices if the materials could be acquired more cheaply abroad. This cautionary warning was in line with Truman's economic philosophy that open and free trade would make the U.S. more prosperous than if it pursued protectionist policies. Truman correctly identified that domestic mining companies were self-interested and their actions weren't always aligned with the strategic logic of the stockpile.

To understand the politics of stockpiling, one had to understand the changes in the bureaucratic landscape. In 1947, the ANMB was renamed simply the "Munitions Board" and eventually grew to over 400 people consisting of both civilians and military personnel. The same year, the National Security Resources Board (NSRB) was created which now made stockpile policy and coordinated input from the various agencies jockeying to influence stockpiling decisions. And in 1949, the procurement function of the Treasury was transferred to the Federal Supply Service of the General Services Administration (GSA).

A 1949 amendment to the Commodity Credit Corporation Charter Act stated that the organization could purchase and stockpile agricultural products for future use. It could also acquire strategic and critical minerals from abroad in exchange for agricultural products. Minerals acquired by the Corporation would then be transferred to the stockpile in accordance with Munitions Board guidance. The amendment gave the CCC the authority to manage its mineral acquisitions as it saw fit, meaning it would hold a mineral reserve outside of the already established National Stockpile. By the summer of 1953, the CCC held $56 million of material acquired through its agricultural barter program.[194]

As the stockpile began to grow, managing it became no easy feat. In 1948, the stockpile was dispersed among 70 different military depots, 9 GSA depots, and 3 defense plants (used for temporary storage).[195] By 1953, the system was much larger and complex. The stockpile enterprise was now spread over 318 locations: 71 military depots, 9 GSA depots, 4 government vaults, 6 commercial vaults, 165 commercial warehouses, 34 commercial tank-farms, 7 open-air commercial sites, 4 open-air government sites, and 18 industrial plants. That year, it cost $210 million for maintenance and administrative costs.[196]

At this juncture it is important to discuss how the size of the stockpile was calculated. Originally, it was based on the assumption of a five-year global war (just like WWII) as determined by the Joint Chiefs of Staff (JCS). In 1950, the JCS adopted a new "factoring system" which accounted for the potential denial of access to foreign countries and their supply chains. Importantly, the new assessment was made during the start of the Korean War and after the issuance of National Security Council Report 68 which injected pessimism into the calculations.[197] As a result of using the new risk system, the estimated size of the needed stockpile increased 70% to $8.8 billion.[198]

Also in 1950, the bureaucracy governing the stockpile changed. After the start of the Korean War, Truman created the Office of Defense Mobilization (ODM) and the Defense Production Administration (DPA). ODM was given broad authorities to "direct, control, and coordinate all mobilization activities of the Executive Branch of the Government, including but not limited to production, procurement, manpower, stabilization, and transport activities."[199] From an organizational perspective, DPA worked directly for ODM and the two, combined, took over NSRB's previous stockpile policy responsibilities.[200]

194 Munitions Board, *Stockpile Report to Congress*, August 15, 1953.

195 Munitions Board, *Stockpile Report to the Congress*, January 23, 1950

196 Munitions Board, *Stockpile Report to Congress*, August 15, 1953.

197 NSC-68 was a classified report highlighting the potential for thermonuclear war with the Soviet Union and the fundamental clash of values between it and the U.S.

198 Snyder, *Stockpiling Strategic Materials*.

199 Executive Order 10193 *Providing for the Conduct of the Mobilization Effort of the Government*.

200 Executive Order 10200 *Establishing the Defense Production Administration*.

The Defense Production Act of 1950 also created a separate stockpile. This was done to support the expanded production of government sponsored programs by providing a guaranteed market for their products. The logic was that the second stockpile helped provide for increased defense industrial production and was thus essential for national security. This DPA stockpile ran in parallel to the national stockpile but was funded at much lower levels and thus contained less material by volume. The Defense Materials Procurement Agency (DMPA) was created specifically to manage the purchases for the DPA stockpile.

At the end of the Truman administration, the stockpile sat at a healthy $4.2 billion in value with another $879 million contracted for future delivery. This reflected 39 different stockpile objectives being completely satisfied, 13 objectives being above 80% of their intended goals, and 24 other objectives below 80% of fulfillment. With that said, 75% of the total stockpile objective was either in inventory or under contract. Additionally, the CCC's agriculture-for-minerals barter program held another $74 million worth of strategic and critical minerals.[201] Importantly, the military no longer controlled U.S. stockpiling strategy as it was now managed by civilian agencies who took a wider view on stockpiling policy and strategy.

Furthermore, to ensure that the necessary stockpiles are accumulated as rapidly as deemed advisable and with a minimum cost to the public, this Act should not be used as a device to give domestic interests an advantage over foreign producers of strategic materials greater than that provided by the tariff laws. – **President Truman, July 23, 1946.**

The Eisenhower Stockpile Expansion

With the new Republican administration came organizational change with both the Defense Production Administration and the NSRB being abolished and replaced by a revamped ODM. More importantly, the Munitions Board, which had fought for a "pure" defense stockpiling program free from political influence, was deleted and replaced by the Assistant Secretary of Defense for Supply and Logistics. These moves simplified the previously divided process by placing most responsibilities for stockpile management under ODM while the Department of Defense still provided input for their requirements.

201 *Stockpile Report to the Congress, July-December 1953.*

As the defunct military-run Munition Board predicted, the stockpile became a cash cow, manipulated for domestic politics by the self-interested mining industry, their allies in the Department of Interior, and the President himself. In 1953, Eisenhower appointed a Cabinet Committee on Minerals Policy chaired by Secretary of the Interior Douglas McKay. The committee recommended that the President pursue a new stockpile strategy which raised the previous minimum objectives.[202]

In 1954, Eisenhower directed ODM to purchase an additional "35 to 40" metals and minerals from domestic producers above the previous minimums predicated on the idea that the U.S. would not be able to access any minerals in a future war other than from North America. Hence, the new stockpile strategy consisted of two components: increased objectives based on domestic production. A large part of this market manipulation was driven by Felix Wormser who had ties to the zinc and lead mining industries.[203] Eisenhower appointed him as Assistant Secretary of the Interior where he could drive a larger stockpile acquisition process to provide cover for the very specific increase in lead and zinc production.

As an example of this stockpile expansion, there was a little-known effort to stock REO (Rare Earth Oxides). At the time, there was little use for REO which were known primarily for their use in lamps and being removed from uranium as impurities during nuclear weapons production. Regardless, the Molycorp Corporation signed a contract with GSA to deliver 7,200 tons of REO concentrate from their Mountain Pass mine in California to the national stockpile in 1954.

The same year, Congress passed the *Agricultural Trade Development and Assistance Act of 1954*. Its intended purpose was to "increase the consumption of U.S. agricultural commodities in foreign countries, to improve the foreign relations of the U.S., and for other purposes." These transactions would take place through the CCC with Section 104 of the act authorizing the purchase of strategic and critical minerals to be kept in a "supplemental stockpile." However, the supplemental stockpile would be governed by the same rules as the national stockpile.

The primary goal of the act was to dispose of large surpluses of agricultural goods and trading them for critical minerals was a means to do so. Also, storing

202 Snyder, *Stockpiling Strategic Materials*.

203 Wormser's company, St. Joseph Lead, sold $54 million worth of lead to the U.S. government for the stockpile.

minerals was much cheaper than storing food so it was a cost saving measure for the Department of Agriculture. For domestic mining companies, the CCC barter and acquisition of foreign minerals served the purpose of absorbing them before they could be imported into the U.S. at lower prices. At the end of the Eisenhower administration, the supplemental stockpile contained $1.1 billion worth of minerals with another $223 million having been transferred to the strategic stockpile.[204]

Major conceptual changes blew up the existing stockpile strategy in 1958 when the Joint Chiefs of Staff (JCS) changed their assessment of what a future war might look like. The new thinking was that the U.S. should prepare for a three-year conflict.[205] This meant that the metals and minerals in the stockpile which had met their maximum objectives automatically had a two-year surplus. At this time, 63 of the 75 stockpiled materials were in excess of their authorized levels based on the five-year war assumption.[206] Now, the administration had to either justify keeping this surplus to continue supporting the domestic mining industry or it had to come up with a plan to sell it off. Although each decision had political winners and losers, the long-term decision was to sell off the surplus.

The Downward Spiral

"The U.S. Government does not have an effective planning, policy analysis, and policy formulation system for basic commodities."

- GAO Report, 1974

When President John F. Kennedy (JFK) came into office, he authorized Senator Stuart Symington to conduct a congressional investigation into the state of the stockpile.[207] JFK was interested in exposing any irregularities of how the stockpile was managed and to determine a way ahead reference the surplus. Of course, there was political hypocrisy at play since Symington represented Missouri and had previously supported the over-stockpiling of lead and

204 Symington Hearings 1962.

205 This middle position was a tradeoff between a five-year conventional war and a nuclear war that could be so destructive that it rendered traditional ideas of minerals security obsolete.

206 Snyder, *Stockpiling Strategic Materials*.

207 Symington headed the National Stockpile and Naval Petroleum Reserves Subcommittee of the Senate Armed Services Committee.

zinc. Symington held hearings on the topic over the course of ten months, from March 1962 to January 1963.

Soon after these hearings concluded, JFK appointed an Executive Stockpile Committee to review the stockpiling program while considering Symington's findings. The committee made seven recommendations which reinforced the hearings' own conclusions. These were:

- The stockpile objectives should reflect a limited war.
- Material in the stockpile should have a single objective.
- The stockpile should reflect the possibility of multiple small wars.
- The idea of a three-year war should be reassessed.
- U.S. stockpiling should consider the needs of its allies.
- The U.S. should develop a long-range disposal program.
- Current maximum stockpile objectives should be used when considering how much excess will be disposed of.

Although JFK was murdered in 1963, the Johnson administration continued the decision to dispose of excess material from the stockpile. By 1965, the Office of Emergency Planning (EOP) began the consistent disposal of excess minerals worth about $300 million a year. At this point, the entire stockpile was valued at $8.5 billion while $5.1 billion of this was considered surplus and targeted for disposal. It is important to note that holding the stockpile in storage only cost $4 million annually, which was less than one-half of a single percentage point of the overall stockpile value.[208]

From the initial establishment of a stockpile program in 1939 through the end of Johnson administration in 1968, stockpile strategy evolved in several ways. First, the conceptual framework went from providing essential military raw materials based on wartime needs to being infiltrated by domestic mining interests who manipulated the system to profit from government purchases. As a reflection of this, the stockpile changed from military to civilian control. Also, the stockpile came to consist of four separate holdings due to various congressional actions. Clearly, successive administrations no longer valued the stockpile as a national security asset and thus failed to integrate it into an overarching security framework.

By the time President Nixon took office in 1969, the idea that the stockpile should be largely sold off was already established. In 1973, Nixon restructured

208 Symington hearings.

the bureaucracy that previously managed the stockpile. That year, the Office of Emergency Preparedness was abolished and the General Services Administration (GSA) took responsibility for managing the stockpile.[209] Also, the Interdepartmental Materials Advisory Committee (IMAC) was dissolved. The agencies that previously composed the IMAC and provided expertise to stockpile objectives would now coordinate with GSA's Office of Preparedness (OP). It appeared that Nixon was burying the stockpile in the bureaucracy so it had no powerful advocates and could be easily carved up and sold off.

By 1973, the administration had convinced the country and the government bureaucracy that they no longer needed much of a national stockpile at all and that they should sell off $4.1 billion worth of minerals. Publicly, this was based on input from a subjective study made by the Joint Chiefs of Staff. The reduction was predicated on the ideas that a conflict would only last one year ($1.5 billion reduction), mineral imports during a conflict would be possible ($500 million reduction), the country did not have to prepare for an initial first-year minerals disruption scenario ($1.2 billion reduction), and the U.S. would institute austerity measures ($900 million reduction).[210]

However, this very optimistic assessment of the U.S.' ability to secure its critical minerals in wartime and peace was questioned by other public entities like the National Commission on Materials Policy (NCMP).[211] In 1972, the NCMP published a report highlighting the U.S.' growing minerals insecurity and many possibilities for disruption. The General Accounting Office (GAO) published a report in 1974 illustrating the risks of increasing commodities disruption and the lack of policy to manage this.[212] Then, GAO followed up with another report in 1975 which questioned the wisdom of the Ford administration's $4.1 billion sell-off.

The collective responses to the 1975 GAO report by the White House, GSA, and the Departments of the Interior, Commerce, and Defense showed a total unwillingness to maintain a minerals stockpile as a national economic and industrial insurance policy. It was as if the administration didn't want to hear anything other than that they needed to sell off the stockpile. Journalists believed the administration was colluding with mining companies to sell them

209 Executive Order 11725, June 27, 1973.

210 GAO Report to Congress, March 11, 1975.

211 National Commission on Materials Policy, April 1972.

212 GAO Report to Congress, April 29, 1974.

minerals from the stockpile below market prices for political favoritism.[213] While Nixon was a corrupt individual and removed from office for criminal activity, was there any truth to this?

As part of the Nixon sell-off, GSA's Office of Stockpile Disposal (OSD) was to sell lithium to the Lithium Corporation of America and Foote Mineral Company for $45 million below fair market value.[214] OSD also planned to sell titanium to the U.S.' only two titanium companies, RMI and Titanium Metals Corporation (TMC), for $90 million under fair market value. RMI was later charged with conspiracy to fix titanium prices and TMC as an unindicted co-conspirator.[215] The Department of Justice investigated GSA from 1977-1979 for corruption, resulting in 117 criminal indictments and 89 convictions.[216]

By this point, the U.S.' critical minerals stockpile had become an afterthought, caught in a web of criminal activity, crony capitalism, and political corruption. The stockpile no longer had anything to do with national security as the President saw it merely as a means to pay off his political supporters. This dark phase in the stockpile history did irreparable damage to the integrity of the minerals acquisition process and the conceptual reasoning that underpinned it. Compare this outcome with the previous criticism of the military-run Munitions Board for being too rigid and only taking into consideration national security considerations.

Under the Carter administration, Congress revised the Strategic and Critical Minerals Stock Piling Act in 1979 to update and modernize the law in the aftermath of the Nixon debacle. In writing the act, Congress found the national stockpile to be inadequate with the U.S. having a "dangerous and costly dependence" on foreign sources. The act stated that the stockpile should "serve the interest of national defense only" and would not be used for "economic or budgetary purposes." Importantly, the act stated that the stockpile should sustain the U.S. for a three-year time of emergency.

---

213 Anderson, Jack & Les Whitten. "Nixon's Mineral Sale." The Washington Post, April 15, 1976.

214 These responsibilities were taken over by the Federal Property Resources Service in 1978.

215 Thomas, Jo. "Auditors allege mismanagement of defense stockpile." Minneapolis Tribune, July 22, 1979.

216 Goldenberg, Gene. "White House aid linked to 'bootleg investigations'." El Paso Herald-Post, September 27, 1979.

Accounting for President Nixon's, GSA's, and the mining industry's recent corruption, the act stated that materials could only be acquired or disposed of through a "formal advertising or competitive negotiation" process. Equally important was the guidance that material could only be sold at fair market value. Furthermore, the acquisition and disposal of material would be done in a way to "protect the U.S. against avoidable loss." This reinforced the idea that the government would not buy above market value and would not sell below it.

However, the act still had significant weaknesses in that the stockpile program was managed at the presidential level, meaning it was subject to presidential corruption and apathy. The President was responsible for defining what was a critical mineral, how to acquire materials, and when and how the stockpile would be disposed. The President was also empowered to buy materials outside of market value if they notified the Congressional Armed Services committees in writing thirty days prior to the transaction. The only accountability of the President's stockpiling authority was providing a written biannual report to Congress. Otherwise, the only check on Presidential stockpile power was the congressional ability to limit or deny appropriations to fund the stockpile.

Senator Stuart Symington represented the state of Missouri from 1953-1976 and served under the Truman administration as the first Secretary of the Air Force from 1947 to 1950. As chairman of the National Stockpile and Naval Petroleum Reserves Subcommittee, Symington swung the ax the Kennedy administration needed in 1962 to correct the Eisenhower administration's perceived mismanagement of the national stockpile.

The act created the National Defense Stockpile Transaction (NDST) Fund where all sales of material would be placed in the fund. Monies appropriated for the fund by Congress would remain in the fund for five years. The fund manager was responsible for providing biannual reports to Congress as a means of transparency and accountability. However, ten years into the fund's life, it was managed ineptly with the Defense Logistics Agency (DLA) unable to provide accurate reporting about the fund. For instance, in 1989, the fund balance was understated by $86 million and by $131 million in 1990. If not for audits by the Inspector General, both the Department of Defense and Congress thought they had much less funds to secure minerals with – if they were even inclined to do so.[217]

The End of the Cold War

At the start of the Reagan administration (1981-1988), the U.S. consumed approximately 25% of the world's non-fuel minerals while sustaining a $2 billion deficit in its minerals trade. To improve minerals security, the Congressional Budget Office (CBO) believed the U.S. should run a more intelligent critical minerals strategy. For example, CBO did not see the U.S. fighting a three-year protracted war and found the proposed purchase of $3.2 billion in common metals for the stockpile unwarranted. Instead, CBO thought a one-year stockpile goal was more reasonable and the U.S. should focus on stockpiling minerals that were imported from unstable sources such as Zaire and South Africa.[218]

The National Security Council (NSC) held other ideas and established an interagency working group to relook the nation's critical minerals security strategy. In 1984, the NSC conducted a stockpile study and published its recommendations. These were based on the idea that the U.S. stockpile must meet the country's "military, industrial, and essential civilian material requirements" in case of a protracted conventional war. The NSC found that the U.S. stockpile had shortages in various minerals that were critical for defense manufacturing.

The NSC proposed that they lead an interagency stockpile management group that would manage both the acquisition and disposal of critical materials.[219] The NSC identified the need to dispose of $2.5 billion in surplus material which they would do at a rate of $500 million annually over five years. An increase in nine minerals worth $700 million was identified which included metals like cobalt and titanium as well as minerals like mica and quartz. Additionally, a supplemental reserve worth $6 billion was identified as requiring 19 different materials such as rubber, silver, and tungsten. However, the NSC's attempt to gain control of the country's critical minerals stockpile policy failed as the other elements of the vested bureaucracy resisted.[220] Change would have to wait several more years until the end of the administration.

217 Audit Report of the Inspector General, DOD, September 30, 1992.
218 Congressional Budget Office report, 1983.
219 National Security Decision Directive #174, June 10, 1984.
220 DOD actively resisted the NSC's move.

In 1988, the President issued Executive order 12626 which transferred stockpile manager duties from GSA and FEMA to the Secretary of Defense. Stockpile management authorities were transferred down to the Assistant Secretary of Defense (Production and Logistics) and then the Defense Logistics Agency (DLA). The NDST fund was now managed by the Defense Finance and Accounting Service (DFAS) and their General Funds Division and Resource Finance Special Projects Division. This buried the stockpile deep enough in the bureaucracy to accurately reflect its overall irrelevance and DOD's own apathy towards it.[221]

U.S. and Soviet tanks confront each other at Checkpoint Charlie in Berlin, 1961. The eventual collapse of the Soviet Union convinced the U.S. that it no longer required a robust national stockpile.

The final collapse of the Soviet Union in 1991 convinced the Clinton administration (1993-2001) that the U.S. no longer needed a critical mineral stockpile. Consequently, based on a no-chance-of-war scenario, the DOD determined that the stockpile now had a 99% surplus. Over this period, the administration purchased only $32 million worth of material while selling off $3.6 billion, leaving the stockpile with $2.5 billion worth of material with 96% consisting of metals, ores, and minerals. This left the stockpile with almost no germanium (8 tons), beryllium metal (40 tons), or chromium (500 tons). Because the administration was only selling, not buying, minerals, the stockpile fund sat at a healthy $1.1 billion in fiscal year 2000.[222]

President Clinton's Executive Order 12919 *National Defense Industrial Resources Preparedness* issued in 1994 reflected a distinct lack of interest in maintaining the stockpile. This meant the Department of Defense, as the delegated stockpile manager, would manage it according to the President's guid-

221 DOD was also responsible for the CCC stockpile.
222 Strategic and Critical Materials Report, 2001.

ance to downsize the country's metals and minerals holdings. The executive order, which can only be described as a generalized form of bureaucratic housekeeping, provided no critical minerals guidance. It was during Clinton's tenure that China began securing its own critical minerals supply chains while the U.S. increasingly disengaged from the space.

The Great Distraction

"The hindrance was the availability of ingot steel to be rolled and tempered and quenched in the appropriate manner to make the steel we required, the thin-gauged armor plate. The problem was no one could melt enough steel of the type we needed in this country. And, therefore, we had the capability at Oregon Steel to roll and quench and temper that ingot, but they could not get steel to roll."

- Congressional hearings in 2009 about the U.S. inability to produce the steel required for armored vehicles used in Iraq and Afghanistan

As discussed earlier, the Global War on Terror (GWOT) was the most significant and consuming topic for every administration from 2001-2020. While the Clinton administration began a consistent and significant drawdown of the stockpile, the Bush administration (2001-2008) continued this. Importantly, Bush displayed no interest in nor an understanding of the critical minerals space and his administration issued no associated strategy. It made sense then that the administration would simply continue the Clinton-era policy of downsizing the stockpile.

During its tenure, the administration sold off $3.5 billion worth of material averaging $437 million a year which was a slightly lower rate than the Clinton administration which sold off an average of $450 million annually.[223] At the end of this period, the national stockpile was down to a market value of $1.2 billion with 100% of this residing in metals (76%) and ores (24%). The stockpile was so small at this point that the Defense National Stockpile Center consisted of only three storage locations and 89 employees. With this continuing sell-off, the stockpile had zeroed out its previous holdings of fluorspar, graphite, lead, chromium, and tantalum with just four metric tons of germanium remaining. The stockpile fund sat at $323 million.[224]

223 There had been no purchasing of minerals since 1997.
224 Strategic and Critical Materials Report, 2008-2009.

After sixteen years of selling off the country's critical minerals security, Congress meekly directed the DOD to review its stockpile disposal policy, forgetting that this was a presidentially directed program. However, the White House was detached from the entire process as it was mired in the two guerrilla wars raging in Iraq and Afghanistan with no end in sight. Only now did Congress think, perhaps, that it was not a good idea to sell off 99% of its critical minerals stockpile. DOD conducted a review of their stockpile policy in 2006, and again in 2008, issuing their findings in 2009. They were in no rush.

In July 2009, Congress held hearings on the report with witnesses called from the DNSC, Office of the Deputy Under Secretary of Defense (Industrial Policy), and the Institute for Defense Analyses (IDA). While DOD recommended the creation of a Strategic Material Security Program (SMSP), Congress believed it would take legislation to make any substantial changes. The hearings revealed a stockpiling system that was broken at every level. In just one example, the Army couldn't get tungsten released from the stockpile to manufacture MRAPs to protect its soldiers from IED attacks in Iraq and Afghanistan – they had to buy it on the open market with most imports coming from China.[225]

While the hearings did not result in any legislation or creation of the SMSP, the increased awareness of the U.S.' declining critical minerals security resulted in stabilization of the stockpile inventory. Over the course of the Obama administration (2009-2016) the U.S. sold off $704 million worth of materials. However, new material was acquired at the same rate as disposals and in 2017 the stockpile was valued at $1.15 billion - roughly the same as it was in 2008. In 2016, the stockpile fund stood at $191 million.

While the first Trump administration (2017-2020) began exiting from the GWOT wars and taking action to secure its critical mineral supply chains, it ignored the national stockpile. For example, in 2018, the stockpile manager purchased 4,800 tons of various minerals and 2,700 tons of explosives. That same year, in stark contrast, it sold 406,000 tons of minerals as well as quantities of very expensive platinum and iridium. Importantly, Congress did not appropriate any funds for stockpile material acquisitions in 2019-2021. It is not surprising that at the end of the Trump 1.0 tenure, the stockpile dropped 20% in value to $903 million.[226] While the administration talked about the importance of critical minerals security, it did the opposite of what it should have

225 USGS Tungsten Report, 2010.

226 Annual National Defense Stockpile and Planning Report, 2021.

with the stockpile. The U.S.' policy failure was truly bipartisan with Congress diverting 89% of all funds designated for the stockpile to other projects from 2003-2018.[227]

U.S. troops hump their rucks aboard a CH-47 helicopter in Afghanistan. The DOD was consumed by the GWOT from 2001-2020 and the National Defense Stockpile was not a priority

A Chance for Recovery

In 2024, the General Accounting Office (GAO) published a report to the Committee on Armed Services, House of Representatives on the state of the National Defense Stockpile. The detailed report revealed a stockpiling system that was embarrassingly dysfunctional with plenty of culpability to go around at the presidential and congressional levels. Most importantly, the Department of Defense appeared incapable of and uninterested in managing the stockpile with their ineptness spanning both the Trump and Biden administrations. All the above was possible due to the lack of a cohesive critical minerals strategy by either the Trump or Biden administrations. As mentioned before, the stockpile is a presidential responsibility and their vision and direction is instrumental to either its success or failure.

When it came to DOD determining what materials were required for the stockpile and in what quantities, it was paralyzed with a dearth of information resulting in poor decisions. From the years 2019-2023, of the 263 materials designated for the stockpile, DOD did not have enough data for 115 (44%) of them to make an effective stockpiling decision. Also, the number of materials

227 "Building Resilient Supply Chains, Revitalizing American Manufacturing, and Fostering Broad-Based Growth." The White House, June 2021.

that were considered in shortfall skyrocketed from just 37 to 99. Importantly, more than 90% of these materials identified in shortfall only had one domestic supplier or none at all.[228] Most likely, if they were identified by U.S. Geological Survey as a critical mineral, they were majority-sourced from China.[229]

When it came to running their material shortfall modeling process, DOD became tech stupid. For instance, they claimed they were unable to get the information required to make an effective stockpiling decision about titanium. How was this possible when there were commodities intelligence platforms available like the Shanghai Metals Market and the London Metals Exchange which specialize in this information? Part of the problem was that DOD looked to the intelligence community (IC) for commodities decisions. However, I worked in the IC for twenty years and never heard of any office ever looking into the supply and demand patterns of metals. Although this information was publicly available, DOD thought it was top-secret information that only a trained spy could retrieve.[230]

Another problem was that the DOD bureaucracy buried itself under such a mountain of confusing paperwork that it was unable to make simple and obvious decisions which the stockpile was created for. For example, the National Reconnaissance Office requested access to carbon fibers from the stockpile due to difficulties securing it from its only source in Japan. However, DLA refused to release the material because they had no idea if they were authorized to do so, despite having over thirty documents that were supposed to tell them what to do.[231]

It was around the year 2022 that DOD finally woke up from its 30-year dreamworld thinking it should sell off 99% of the stockpile because nothing could possibly threaten U.S. supply chains.[232] Suddenly, it now recognized that the country was facing a $18.5 billion materials shortfall for 2023. The Stockpiling Act was also amended in 2022, requiring DOD to brief Congress annually on its material shortfalls - because they needed to be compelled by law to do

228 The 2013 National Defense Authorization Act amended the Stockpile Act of 1939 so that stockpile supply chains did not rely on a "single point of failure." However, this was just more published guidance for DOD to ignore.

229 GAO Report, 2024.

230 In a shocking example of how apathetic the DOD enterprise is to its own supply chains, DLA stopped sending out surveys after 2019 when only 1% of the offices polled responded.

231 GAO Report, 2024.

232 DoD based this on "revised planning assumptions."

so. Additionally, in an effort to redress its previous critical minerals negligence, Congress appropriated $125 million for stockpile purchases in 2022 and $93.5 million in 2023.[233]

In 2023, the DOD published their first ever *National Defense Industrial Strategy.* The 60-page document had a section entitled "Resilient Supply Chains" with a small part addressing their stockpiling efforts. While this was no blueprint for a revitalized and intelligently managed stockpile, it did show a minimal awareness that they had a critical minerals supply chain problem. The document was revealing in that it said DOD would identify stockpiling requirements based on "international conflict or crisis" which obviously left out the current threat by China which carefully captured half of the U.S.' critical mineral supply chains without firing a shot.

In a leisurely attempt to fix the stockpile problem way down the road, Congress passed the 2024 National Defense Authorization Act (NDAA) which required DOD to develop a strategy by 2035 that ensures its supply chains don't rely on adversarial countries like China or Russia. To be clear, the NDAA did not direct DOD to actually secure its supply chains by then, but merely to have something written down on paper. In the meantime, this ensured Beijing had another decade to expand its critical mineral supply chain efforts while DOD contemplated what it should have been doing for the last thirty years.

A Stockpile Strategy That Makes Sense

From a critical minerals perspective, understanding that there are many other materials the U.S. holds in its national stockpile, we should start off with a straightforward solution. To begin, the U.S. should hold in the stockpile a one-year supply of each critical mineral as defined by U.S. Geological Survey (USGS). The one-year amount would be based on the U.S.' annual consumption of that mineral averaged over the last five years as provided by USGS. This would require information sharing between DOD and USGS as this annual consumption is sometimes masked to hide proprietary production data by domestic mining companies.

Because the U.S. is so far behind in its minerals security, it would realistically take ten years to reach what DOD has identified as its shortfall. With an $18 billion shortfall, it would take Congress appropriating $1.8 billion a year for the next decade to reach the published goals. It would make sense to first fill

233 Ibid.

out the minerals shortfalls that the U.S. majority-imports from foreign sources with a focus on those from adversarial and unstable countries. For example, the U.S. should fill out its cobalt stockpile from the Congo before it fills out its nickel needs from Canada.

Specifically, the U.S. must address the 25 critical minerals that it majority-sources from its chief rival in the international system which is China. With these minerals, the U.S. should stockpile more than just one-years' worth, based on its level of dependence. To illustrate this point, China produced 99% of the world's gallium in 2024, giving them an absolute monopoly. For this mineral, the U.S. should stockpile five-years' worth or more based on the potential catastrophic results if China shut this off completely and enforced a rigid gallium export restriction regime.

From a conceptual perspective, the Stockpile Act should be updated to allow the use of the stockpile for more than strictly national security concerns and as a means to help the national economy when required. It should only be used in this manner sparingly but it could be key to helping fight national inflation as we see today with the national electric grid from the rising price of copper. True, this would more readily introduce domestic politics into the equation as we saw with the Eisenhower administration and it would have to be tightly managed to stave off corrupting forces. One way to address this is to have one portion of the stockpile designated for economic purposes and another for military use only.[234]

No matter what the country decides, the three key elements of the national stockpile management system must be actively engaged in the process. The failures of the stockpile system are primarily a result of the executive branch being disengaged from the topic, even though the Stockpile Act makes it a presidential program. Not only must the President be engaged, but they must delegate stockpile responsibilities to an office that can manage it effectively, something DOD has failed spectacularly at. DOD is so large and concerned primarily with its warfighting duties that it has proven utterly uninterested in its assigned stockpile duties.

To effectively manage the stockpile process, something different must be done like the President assigning a critical minerals czar to coordinate the overarching minerals security enterprise to include the stockpile. The minerals czar

234 This would require identification of inflation as a national security threat which weakens the U.S. economy in relation to China's already superior Purchasing Power Parity.

could build their own office and staff (The Office of Minerals Security) or they could assign an existing entity to manage these minerals functions like the National Security Council which was once proposed during the Reagan administration. The minerals czar would have to be a cabinet level position and backed energetically by the President or it will fail like all the other dead-end boards and committees which are now piled up in the dustbin of U.S. minerals history.

Equally important is the Congress becoming engaged in the minerals security process and actually providing effective oversight of the stockpile, something it has failed at. For decades, Congress has been as apathetic to the country's stockpile insecurity as DOD and has repeatedly refused to hold them accountable for their gross mismanagement. The presidency-congress-managing agency triangle only works if each leg is fully engaged, works together for the same mission, and holds each other to the standards published by the Stockpile Act.

Another important problem that must be addressed, which the U.S. has the resources to solve, is the lack of even basic minerals knowledge by the managing bureaucracy. The minerals czar, the relevant congressional committees, and the agency managing the stockpile must all be infused with experienced officers from U.S. Geological Survey to expertly advise them on all minerals security matters. Because of this knowledge deficit, the managing bureaucracy has consistently made bad decisions relating to stockpile management which undermines the very foundations of U.S. national economic and industrial security.

The inability of the U.S. to view its stockpile as a form of national insurance reflects its adoption of two self-serving strategic assumptions: Mutually Assured Minerals (MAM) and Just in Time Minerals (JITM). With these, the U.S. assumes it will always get minerals in needs (MAM) and they will arrive exactly when they need them (JITM). These assumptions work until they don't. China's capture of 25 of the U.S.' identified critical minerals since the 1990s, the COVID-19 pandemic of 2020-2022, and the U.S.' trade war with Beijing from 2018-2025 should have provided enough evidence to shatter these assumptions. However, the U.S.' collective groupthink continues to persist.

While the U.S. remains confused as to what its critical minerals strategy should be and how the national stockpile contributes to this, China is on the move. In March 2025, Beijing announced that it was buying more cobalt, copper, nickel, and lithium for their strategic metal reserves – all minerals directly supporting the electrification of their vehicle industry. In contrast, the U.S. has no copper or lithium reserves in its national stockpile, just two-days' worth of cobalt (348 tons), and 1.5 days' worth of nickel (800 ton of nickel alloys). If we look at the U.S.' own published acquisitions for 2025, none of these metals are on its list. From this, we see that Beijing continues to prepare for extended minerals warfare while the U.S. remains badly unprepared.[235]

For sure, having an effective national critical minerals stockpile is just one part of a comprehensive minerals security program involving recycling, conservation, varied and redundant sources of importation, substitution, domestic production, and technological innovation. However, the U.S. is increasingly in conflict with the world's second largest economy which has a much stronger raw materials position and controls half of the U.S.' own identified critical minerals. Developing a robust critical minerals stockpile is crucial for the U.S. to improve its minerals security, to insure its economy and defense industrial base from supply chain shocks, and to break China of its relative critical minerals dominance.

235 https://www.energyconnects.com/news/oil/2025/march/china-to-add-cobalt-copper-in-boost-to-state-metal-reserves/

Sources

"A Report to the National Security Council." The Executive Secretary, April 14, 1950."

"Stockpile Objectives of Strategic and Critical Materials Should be Reconsidered Because of Shortages." Government Accountability Office March 11, 1975.

"International Control of Minerals." Mining and Metallurgical Society of America, American Institute of Mining & Metallurgical Engineers. NY: 1925.

Mikesell, Raymond F. "Stockpiling Strategic Materials: An Evaluation of the National Program." American Enterprise Institute, 1986.

Morgan, J.D. "Strategic Materials in World War II." Bureau of Mines, December 1, 1983.

National Defense Industrial Strategy, 2023.

"National Defense Stockpile: Actions Needed to Improve DOD's Efforts to Prepare for Emergencies." Government Accountability Office, September 2024.

"Proposed Reconfiguration of the National Defense Stockpile." July 23, 2009.

Snyder, Glenn H. "Stockpiling Strategic Materials: Politics and National Defense." Chandler Publishing Company, 1966.

"Strategic and Critical Nonfuel Minerals: Problems and Policy Alternatives." Congressional Budget office, August 1983.

"Towards a National Materials Policy." The National Commission on Materials Policy, April 1972.

"U.S. Actions Needed to Cope with Commodity Shortages." General Accounting Office, April 29, 1974.

A German King Tiger tank undergoes armor penetration testing in Sweden after the war. By 1944, Germany found it more difficult to get tungsten which was mixed with steel to harden armor. *(by S. Ericssson)*

The U.S. MRAP (Mine-Resistant Ambush Protected) vehicle program was delayed in 2007 because the U.S. didn't have the steel it needed to produce the vehicles at scale. Also, the stockpile manager refused to release tungsten for use in the vehicle's armor production.

Annual Materials Plan for FY 2025 (Potential Acquisitions)

Material	Unit	Ceiling Quantity
Aluminum (High Purity)	MT	1,700
Aluminum Alloys	MT	1,500
Antimony	MT	700
Cadmium Zinc Telluride	EA	2,800
Electrolytic Manganese Metal	MT	5,000
Energetics	LBS	20,000,000
Ferroniobium	LBS Nb	300,000
Grain Oriented Electrical Steel	MT	3,200
Hafnium	MT	2,300
Iso-Molded Graphite	MT	1,700
Lanthanum	MT	1,100
Magnesium	MT	3,500
Neodymium-Praseodymium Oxide	MT	300
NdFeB Magnet Block	MT	450
Rayon	MT	200
Samarium-Cobalt Alloy	MT	60
Tantalum	LBS Ta	64,500
Tire Cord Steel	MT	2,370
Titanium	MT	15,000
Tungsten	LBS W	4,500,500
Zirconium	MT	2,300

Above, we see DLA's acquisitions plan for additions to the National Defense Stockpile for Fiscal Year 2025. Notice that these additions are in very low quantities relative to U.S. annual consumption and doesn't come close to fixing DOD's enormous material shortfalls. A few other things instantly stand out to the informed reader. Antimony, lanthanum, NdPr Oxide, NdFeB Magnet Block, Samarium-Cobalt Alloy, and tungsten are all either directly or indirectly majority-sourced from China. Also, the single largest acquisition was 10,000 tons of "energetics" which is military-speak for explosives. These are needed for a variety of purposes such as increased 155 mm artillery shell and HIMARS rocket production for Ukraine. The U.S. imports a third of its energetics needs, including from China.

Chapter 6

Rare Earth Elements

"China's rare earth resources can be likened in importance to the Middle East's oil. They have immense strategic significance and we must certainly deal with rare earths issues with care, unleashing the advantages they bring."

– Deng Xiaoping, 1992

Introduction

Rare Earth Elements (REE) are one subset of minerals that modern industrial societies use for a variety of everyday applications from cellphones and catalytic converters to magnets and LED screens. However, the subject of REE provides us an example of how the U.S. once pioneered and dominated a mineral sector, gave it up completely to China, and is just now struggling to regain security of its REE supply chains. In this chapter we will see how the U.S. pioneered important technologies like REE permanent magnets and then offshored them completely in the 1990s.

The U.S. lost control of its REE supply chains due to its own predatory capitalism, an exuberant groupthink fostered by the collapse of the Soviet Union, and a belief in Mutually Assured Minerals (MAM) – that it could always get the materials it needed on the open market. It is equally important to understand that the U.S. government had no concept of minerals security and therefore had no mechanisms in place to prevent its erosion. China didn't have to work hard to conquer the U.S.' REE technology and supply chains – the U.S. simply gave it to them.

The Early REE Industry

The first REE were discovered by chemists in Sweden during the late 1780s followed by additional discoveries in Germany in the early 1800s.[236] Renown Austrian scientist Carl Auer von Welsbach discovered neodymium and praseodymium in 1885 and was the first to commercialize sales of a REE product, the Welsbach Light. His cotton mantle lamp used lanthanum, cerium, and yttrium oxides to produce an incandescent light when heated by a flame.[237] Welsbach then created a successful international company with a U.S. branch in Philadelphia that competed with electric and other gas fueled lights.

Welsbach also developed ferrocerium (aka flint or *mischmetal*), a mixture of iron and the REE cerium called *Auermetall* in Europe. In 1907, he created the Austrian company which would become Treibacher Industrie AG to manufacture flint products for use in devices like cigarette lighters. Today, Treibacher is a privately owned international company with a plant in Minneapolis and multiple product lines which still include flint. With these enterprises, Welsbach created the first global REE supply chains with monazite ores coming from Germany, Brazil, and India (Ceylon).

The U.S. found itself thrust into the REE space as part of the Manhattan Project and the pursuit of the atomic bomb. During the process of refining uranium during WWII, U.S. scientists found that REE impurities had to be removed to produce a viable product. To do this, the U.S. government enlisted the help of Dr. Frank Spedding, an experienced chemist from Iowa State University (ISU) who was the nation's leading expert in REE. Spedding was able to successfully achieve this by using ion-exchange resins. After the war, Spedding continued his work in this space at the Ames Laboratory, developing a process that created 99.99% purity REE metals in 1945. Ames became the center of REE innovation in the U.S. for many years after with the Atomic Energy Commission establishing the Rare-Earth Information Center at the lab in 1966.[238]

In 1949, prospectors searched for uranium in a remote desert area near Mountain Pass, California, close to the border with Nevada. While they found some radioactive material, they also found a mineral that was later identified by

236 REE consist of 17 different elements, divided into two groups, light and heavy.

237 The Journal of the Franklin Institute, 1900. Welsbach eventually used a cerium-thorium mixture. Thorium was considered a REE at the time.

238 Goldman. Under the Clinton administration, the U.S. closed the REE information center as part of the larger transfer of REE technology to China.

the U.S. Bureau of Mines as bastnaesite which contained rare earth oxides.[239] In both 1950 and 1951, the Molybdenum Corporation of America (MCA) purchased several REE claims in the Mountain Pass area and began drilling holes to determine its minerals composition. Production began soon after in 1952, becoming the first commercial scale REE operation in the U.S.

Carl Auer von Welsbach (1858-1929) was the first scientist to separate the rare earth didymium into neodymium and praseodymium. He invented the use of REE in lighting systems (cerium) and flint (ferrocerium) and thus created the first associated global supply chains for these commercially successful products. Welsbach imported most of his REE needs from India/Ceylon and Brazil.

Mountain Pass and the U.S. REE Industry

As background, MCA began as a subsidiary of the Electric Reduction Company in 1919 to mine molybdenum in Questa, New Mexico near the famous ski resort of Taos. By 1954, they were selling their RareMeT line of products from Mountain Pass which were refined without requiring a chemical process and subsequently used in the steel industry. In 1965, the company spent $2.7 million on expanding its York, PA operations to handle the processing of neodymium and praseodymium oxides to serve the ceramic and glass industries.[240] The plant would grow from 30,000 sq ft to 37,500 sq ft with a 10 tpa praseodymium oxide and a 30 tpa neodymium oxide capacity. In 1965, the company shipped 7,000 tons of rare earth oxides to feed the color television and oil processing industries, up from just 1,500 tons in 1964.[241]

MCA accurately judged the growing market for REE as supported by a 1967 report published by the management consulting firm Arthur D. Little (ADL) based out of Cambridge, MA. The report illustrated how the color TV sector was driving increased rare earth production with the REE market reaching $20.5 million that year. Even though the europium-yttrium oxide that re-

239 Bastnaesite consists of seven metals: cerium (50%), lanthanum (34%), neodymium, praseodymium, samarium, gadolinium, and europium.

240 Until then, the York facility processed rare earth chlorides, molybdenum and tungsten products.

241 "Industry to Expand, Add Two New Lines." The York Dispatch, November 6, 1965.

placed the previous phosphors cost $104 a pound as opposed to $22 a pound, the color quality was so superior that customers were willing to pay the extra price. MCA's europium-yttrium oxide sales in 1966 were estimated at $14 million.[242]

During the 1970s, MCA's molybdenum operations in New Mexico suffered from continuing environmental pollution problems from its tailings storage. The company was cited for scores of tailing pipeline breaks which spilled into the nearby Red River that was eventually declared an ecological dead zone. The periodic drop in global molybdenum prices caused a reduction in operations with almost half of its New Mexico mine workforce laid off by 1973. The company was able to remain profitable due to its REE sales and investment in a Brazilian columbium operation. In 1974, MCA shortened its name to Molycorp and in 1977 was acquired by the Union Oil Company of California (Unocal) for $240 million.[243]

Above, the entrance to Molycorp at Mountain Pass. In 1974, the company produced 60% of the world's REE and was the single largest exporter.

Into the late 1970s, the demand for REE products remained strong with Molycorp investing in a multi-million project to increase its separation capability. Six different solvent extraction circuits were built specifically to increase samarium, cerium, lanthanum, neodymium, gadolinium, and praseodymium production. The additional extraction circuit for samarium was to meet increased demand for high-strength magnets, jewelry, and electronics. The circuit for gadolinium was required to meet demand for computer memory systems.[244]

242 "Requirements of Color TV Spur Market for Rare Earths." The Idaho Statesman, November 05, 1967.

243 Molycorp operated as a wholly owned subsidiary of Unocal.

244 "Molycorp to raise output of rare earths." The Reporter Dispatch, July 03, 1978.

The increased demand was also for exports with 40% of production going to Europe and Japan.[245]

Molycorp's Mountain Pass operations experienced large swings in profits, making $110 million in 1981, which dropped to $60 million in 1982.[246] By the mid-1980s, the company faced financial pressures with the U.S. moving away from leaded to unleaded gasoline, reducing demand for lanthanum that accounted for 40% of its sales. In 1986, Molycorp forced their Mountain Pass mining workforce to leave their homes located on company property. The company paid $600,000 a year to subsidize the small town but now needed to cut these costs. This created considerable resentment with their workforce who had to move to other towns and incur higher living expenses.[247] Beyond these problems, China began producing and refining lanthanum by the end of the decade, undercutting Molycorp's prices.

After an almost 50-year run, Molycorp's Mountain Pass operations came to an end in the 1990s. In 1991, the company was charged by the State of California with illegally storing hazardous waste in 55-gallon metal drums that were disintegrating.[248] In 1996, Molycorp's wastewater pipeline ruptured, leaking 350,000 gallons containing heavy metals and radioactive material which resulted in $3.6 million in fines. In 1998, they closed the pipeline altogether, forcing Molycorp to reduce its operations and lay off part of their workforce. This resulted in a 50% decline in lanthanide production to 7,500 tons annually.[249] In 1999, Molycorp ceased all operations as U.S. and European companies now imported their REE needs primarily from China.

Molycorp: A New Beginning?

Heading into the 2000s, Molycorp was a zombie company, crushed by the weight of its legal liabilities and lower cost Chinese competition. In 2007, the company refined a small amount of rare earth ores which were previously extracted and stored on site, but this was a temporary and limited effort. That year Chevron saw an opportunity to revive the ailing company, purchasing Moly-

245 Johnson, Roger. "Rare earths helpful to industry." The Arizona Republic, June 25, 1979.

246 "Mining in San Bernardino." The San Bernardino County Sun, November 13, 1983.

247 Cooper, Steve. "Company tells a whole town to leave." The San Bernardino County Sun, June 08, 1986.

248 Molycorp was fined $400,000.00 – this was the largest fine ever.

249 Harris, Greg. "Molycorp temporarily suspends wastewater pipeline usage." Desert Dispatch, March 25, 1998.

corp and merging it with Pittsburg & Midway Coal Company to form Chevron Mining Inc. However, Chevron quickly sold off the Mountain Pass mine and rights to the name the next year to Molycorp Minerals LLC and its parent company Molycorp Inc. which traded on the NYSE as MCP as of 2010.[250]

The new Molycorp had an aggressive mindset and in 2011 bought the Phoenix-based Santoku America, Inc. (Molycorp Metals and Alloys) for $17.5 million. The same year, the company bought the REE processing company Silmet in Estonia for $89 million (Molycorp Silmet). Molycorp also formed a joint venture with Mitusbishi and Daido Electronics to sell NdFeB (Neodymium Iron Boron) magnets in the China/Asia market. The following year, Molycorp bought the Canadian company Neo Material Technologies Inc. (Molycorp Canada) which was created in 2006 by the merger of Magnequench, an REE magnet company, and the Canadian REE company AMR Technologies, Inc.

As a harbinger of things to come, Molycorp's CEO Mark Smith participated in House Hearings concerning China's monopoly of REE in 2011. During the hearings Smith showed no understanding of China's pricing power and went so far as to claim that Molycorp's twenty-five research scientists were more capable than China's 6,000 REE scientists. Smith also claimed his company could produce REE products at half the cost that China did. Neither of these were true and Molycorp would be out of business four years later, steamrolled by China's relentless REE machine.

How did all these acquisitions work out for Molycorp? In 2012, the company had $529 million in revenues based on sales of 9,233 metric tons of REO (Rare Earth Oxides) for an average of $57,356 per ton. However, the company suffered net losses of $460 million due to expenses from their various acquisitions, soft REE prices, and the loss of some markets due to high REE prices the previous year. Molycorp anticipated a stronger showing in 2013 based on their Mountain Pass mine reaching a 19,000 tpa capacity and stronger sales from its MQ2 magnetic materials product line.[251]

However, revenues in 2013 were up only slightly at $554 million with 61% of sales in Asia, 20% in Europe, and 16% in North America. Net losses were less but still significant at $374 million with the company selling its rhenium recycling operation in Canada and realizing disappointing market penetration

250 Chevron retained ownership of the other Molycorp assets such as the molybdenum operations in New Mexico.
251 Molycorp 2012 Financial Results.

for its cerium based SorbX water purification product. Because REO prices were dropping due to increased Chinese production, customers bought less in anticipation of securing cheaper products in the future. Consequently, due to this and operational disruptions at Mountain Pass, Molycorp produced much less REO, just 3,800 metric tons.[252]

The year 2014 brought more difficulties with REO production at the Mountain Pass mine reaching just 5,800 metric tons, causing the company's manufacturing divisions to buy from third-parties. Revenues dropped significantly to $475 million with losses skyrocketing to $604 million, meaning the company lost $1.4 billion over the previous three years. Loss of revenues was tied directly to average lanthanum and cerium prices falling to seven-year lows as China continued to produce these in high volumes. Also, a previous $20 million investment in Boulder Wind Power Inc. (permanent magnet generator technology) was a total loss as the company went bankrupt.[253]

Molycorp's Q1 2015 results were a bloodbath and the final nail in the company's coffin. The company reported revenues of $106 million on sales of 3,149 metric tons of REO at only $30,970 per ton, a drop in price of 46% a ton from 2012. This resulted in a net loss of $102 million for the quarter with its stock prices falling so low that they were delisted from the New York Stock Exchange. There was no Q2 report because the company declared bankruptcy in June 2015. China produced so much REO at such low prices they put Molycorp out of business – as intended. In 2016, the U.S. did not produce any REO.[254]

Rare Earth Permanent Magnets (REPM)

The first rare earth permanent magnets (REPM) were discovered by Dr. Karl Strnat and Dr. Alden Ray while working at Wright Patterson Air Force Base Materials Laboratory. Importantly, their work was greatly facilitated by the previous research done by Dr. Spedding and his separation of rare earths from uranium as part of the Manhattan Project. In 1965, Dr. Strnat discovered positive magnetic properties with yttrium-cobalt chemistry (YCo5) and then the next year with samarium-cobalt (SmCo5) chemistry. In 1968, Dr. Strnat went to work at the University of Dayton Research Institute (UDRI) to continue his research.[255]

252 Molycorp 2013 Annual Report.
253 Molycorp 2014 Annual Report.
254 Molycorp Q1 2015 report.
255 Phelps, Julia. "Dayton Contributes to the History of Magnetic Materials." University

Dr. Strnat and Dr. Ray collaborated through the 1970s and developed second generation REPM which improved on the original SmCo chemistry. These magnets were primarily used in military and space applications due to their superior anti-corrosive qualities and the ability to operate at high temperatures. SmCo magnets found uses in many other applications such as gyroscopes, magnetrons, electric motors, and microwave energy devices. As the U.S. pursued its own REPM research, similar work was being conducted in Japan. In the early 1980s, a third generation of REPM were discovered with higher energy densities, made from elements that were more readily available, and thus cheaper to produce.

Dr. Karl Strnat introduces Dr. Masato Sagawa, a founder of the NdFeB REPM, at the Magnet Conference in Pittsburgh, 1983.

Both U.S. and Japanese scientists worked simultaneously to develop an improved but less expensive REPM which could be used more widely and did not need to meet the high-performance qualities of SmCo magnets. In the U.S., Dr. John Croat graduated from Ames Laboratory and was hired by GM's Magnetic Materials Group Physics Department to develop REPMs for small electric motors used in GM's cars. While Dr. Croat worked for GM, half way across the planet Masato Sagawa worked for Sumitomo in Japan.[256] Both developed NdFeB permanent magnets and presented their new inventions at the Magnetism and Magnetic Material Conference in Pittsburgh on the same day in 1983.[257]

This was a significant discovery because magnets were increasingly used in cars, speakers, microphones, computers and were so ubiquitous that modern

of Dayton Research Institute, 1998.

256 Dr. Croat previously worked at Ames Laboratory under Dr. Spedding and was his last PhD student before Spedding retired.

257 Zorpette, Glenn. "The Magnet That Made the Modern World." IEEE Spectrum, June 21, 2022.

societies became magnet dependent. SmCo REPM were relatively expensive so NdFeB magnets facilitated a much larger use case and enabled miniaturization. For GM, NdFeB magnets were needed to replace existing SmCo magnets to miniaturize cars' motors to reduce the overall weight of the car to improve fuel efficiency. From a market perspective, the two different REPM worked together with SmCo magnets filling the more limited high-performance segment and NdFeB addressing the every day use segment like electric motors.

Magnequench: Everything is for Sale

In 1986, GM founded the company Magnequench located in Indiana to produce and sell NdFeB magnets to domestic and international markets. In 1992, as a cost-saving measure, GM announced they would sell off fourteen different operations that were not part of its core automotive business, including Magnequench. In 1995, GM finally sold the company for only $70 million to the Sextant Group which was really a front for the Chinese SOEs (State Owned Enterprises) San Huan New Materials and High-Tech Inc. and China National Nonferrous Metals Import and Export Corporation.[258] Under the sales agreement, the Indiana manufacturing plants would remain open until 2005.

However, the sales tag didn't make any sense as it greatly undervalued the company and its future potential based on very obvious market trends at the time. In 1993, the company earned $42 million in sales which jumped to $75 million in 1994. The global magnets market at the time was valued at $3.2 billion with REPM accounting for 23% or $736 million. Forecasts at the time predicted the market would reach $10 billion only six years later in 2000. GM clearly bungled this deal as it was focused solely on selling off its non-core assets and failed to exhibit the strategic economic vision one would expect of an established company.[259]

Beyond the economic argument for not selling a successful REPM company whose sales were about to explode, Magnequench provided the majority of its products to the Pentagon. The military combined the REPM with servo motors for precision guidance in its ballistic missiles and JDAMs (Joint Direct Attack Munition). With China's purchase of the company, they acquired all of its REPM technology for its own civilian and defense industry uses. In 2003, China closed Magnequench's Indiana plant and shipped all of its equipment to

258 The Chinese SOEs had majority ownership (62%).

259 The Indianapolis Star, December 17, 1995.

the mainland. After that, the DOD sourced its REPM products from China.[260] This was ironic in that DOD originally provided GM with a government grant to develop their magnets. In the final analysis, DOD had de facto funded China's REPM industry to produce precision guided weapons to potentially target the U.S. with.

An important reason why China was able to pull off the REPM heist of the century was because they had inside help. Archibald Cox, Jr., son of the former Watergate special prosecutor, was chairman of the privately owned Sextant Group who fronted for the Chinese SOEs.[261] Cox served as the CEO of Magnequench from 1995-2006 as he facilitated the transfer of the entire company and its technology to China. But it gets even better. In 2005, Magnequench merged with the Canadian REE company AMR Technologies to produce NEO products (neodymium, iron, boron) for magnet manufacturers. This was a logical choice since Magnequench had already given their IP to China and couldn't make magnets anymore. The newly merged company was called Neo Material Technologies Inc. (NMT) which was bought by Molycorp in 2012. After Molycorp's bankruptcy in 2015, NMT was rebranded as Neo Performance Materials.[262]

A necessary question that must be asked is how did the U.S. just give its REPM technology away – were there no mechanisms in place to prevent this? Actually, several were in place that were designed to stop economic and defense security defense breaches such as this. However, the collective U.S. bureaucracy didn't identify the Magnequench sale as a national security event requiring action. This reflected the failings of a complex bureaucracy as much as it did a conceptual deficit in the U.S.' understanding of its own critical minerals security.

In 1975, by Executive Order 11858, the Ford Administration created the Committee on Foreign Investment in the United States (CFIUS) which was chaired by the Department of the Treasury.[263] CFIUS had responsibility for monitoring the impact of foreign investment in the U.S. Specifically, CFIUS would "review investments in the United States which, in the judgment of the

260 Previously, DoD purchased 85% of its REPM needs from Magnequench.

261 https://www.heritage.org/asia/report/magnequench-cfius-and-chinas-thirst-us-defense-technology

262 NPM had a net loss of $13 million in 2024 and $8.3 million in 2023.

263 CFIUS dysfunction is based on a membership from 12 different offices. Not a single member had any obvious knowledge of critical minerals, their supply chains, and the impact on the U.S. economy or defense industrial base.

Committee, might have major implications for United States national interests." In 1988, the EO was amended by the Reagan Administration with Executive Order 12661 which added language that CFIUS would send a report to the President upon completion of any investigation.[264]

Additionally, Executive Order 12829 published in 1993 established a National Industrial Security Program (NISP).[265] However, from the start, NISP was overfocused on protecting the transfer of classified government information. NISP didn't grasp conceptually that there were equally significant unclassified threats, so the Magnequench deal failed to trigger a NISP response. After the 9/11 attacks, the *Homeland Security Act of 2002* led to the creation of 18 Critical Infrastructure and Key Resource sectors with critical minerals being noticeably absent. Who cared about magnets anyway? A real problem with these laws and regulations was that what looked good on paper didn't always work in the real world of a complex and disconnected bureaucracy.

In 2005, the senate held hearings to review the CFIUS process which revealed a broken system that was incapable of determining if the foreign acquisition of a U.S. company was a national security threat. The CFIUS members were confused as to what their own roles were which contributed to an absurdly low investigation rate of possible national security threats, just 1.5%.[266] In another example of CFIUS impotence, the committee failed to provide input for a study determining if foreign countries "are engaged in a coordinated strategy

264 The Exon-Florio Amendment to the Defense Production Act authorized the President to review CFIUS activity.

265 This was one of the final orders given by the Bush administration.

266 In one sampling, 24 transactions out of 1,540 were investigated with the President vetoing 1.

to acquire U.S. companies that develop or produce critical technology." This is exactly what China was doing.

Of interest, CFIUS did review the Chinese purchase of Magnequench and approved the transaction. The deal they cut was that the company would stay in the U.S. for ten years and retain all of its employees for that period. However, these restriction didn't thwart the Chinese who took the company's Intellectual Property (IP) and reconstructed its manufacturing process in China. Later, they physically took the company's equipment and shipped it to China. The CFIUS proved unable to detect the Chinese acquisition of U.S. critical minerals technology as a threat to national security. The U.S. quite literally let Beijing walk out the front door with the country's only REPM manufacturing company.

The fact that the Treasury Department was unable to provide fundamental minerals security for the U.S. is even more disturbing in light of outspoken resistance by members of the U.S. political establishment. Both Senator Evan Bayh (D-IN) and Representative Pete Voscloskly (D-IN) from Indiana were very public about their opposition to the sale to China based on national security and local economic considerations. The two asked Presdient Bush to kill the Magnequench deal based on the 1988 Exon-Florio provision under the Defense Production Act. He didn't.[267]

Both the Clinton and Bush administrations failed to appreciate the nation's minerals security and in doing so facilitated the Magnequench deal. This was initially due to the fact that during the Clinton era, China was not yet active in overtly acquiring U.S. technology. As a result, the U.S. was focused mainly on investments from Japan and Europe.[268] Both administrations failed to realize that the Magnequench deal was really a Chinese reconnaissance mission to see what economic and minerals defenses the U.S. had and what it was willing to give up for a price. For Beijing, this was a successful operation that revealed the U.S.' foreign direct investment (FDI) enterprise was vulnerable to exploitation. China understood that to get what it wanted, it simply needed to be a capitalist chameleon.

Afterwards, the U.S. struggled with the concepts of balancing transnational investments while protecting industries vital to its own economy and defense. In 2006, the National Defense Authorization Act (NDAA) created the Strategic

267 Official press release from Office of former Rep. Pete Visclosky (D-IN).

268 From 1988-1994, CFIUS reviewed 817 investments with 207 involving Japan, 184 with the U.K. but only five from China. (1995 GAO Report)

Materials Protection Board (SMPB) composed of six different DOD offices. One of the board's directives was to "Determine the need to provide a long-term domestic supply of materials designated as critical to national security to ensure that national defense needs are met." While the board broadly defined "critical materials," they specifically recognized metals like cobalt, copper, nickel, titanium, and zinc. There was no mention of the magnet minerals samarium or neodymium.

In 2007, the U.S. passed the *Foreign Investment and National Security Act* which enabled direct Congressional oversight and added language to the Defense Production Act, giving the President authority to cancel a foreign investment based on national security concerns.[269] The act assumed that Congress had better judgment than CFIUS and nowhere in the document were critical minerals and their associated supply chains addressed. Importantly, China contributed directly to this uncertainty by continuing to provide the U.S. all the REE it needed. It was unthinkable in Washington that China wouldn't provide the U.S. the critical minerals Beijing controlled and Washington depended on.[270]

REE Warfare: The Senkaku Incident

On September 7, 2010, the Chinese fishing trawler *Minjinyu 5179* collided with two Japanese Coast Guard patrol vessels in the historically contested waters of the Senkaku Islands. After the collision, Japan detained the Chinese captain, Zhan Qixiong, holding him for over two weeks despite protests from Beijing for his immediate release. Relations between the two countries soured to the point that U.S. Secretary of State Hillary Clinton confirmed that the Senkaku Islands were covered under the existing U.S.-Japan Security Treaty.

While the two countries worked out a diplomatic resolution to the temporary crisis, Beijing responded with the REE critical minerals leverage it had developed over the previous three decades for a situation just as this. China quickly enforced a REE embargo on Japan who imported 90% of these minerals from their Asian competitor. Tokyo found itself in the same situation as Washington, in that they had no understanding of their own critical minerals insecurity. The situation was far from 1978 when the Chinese government partnered with Japanese industry to share REE technology.[271] Tokyo wrongly assumed that no

269 The President was already empowered to reject foreign investments, so this was merely another means to do so.

270 A 2010 GAO report revealed DoD didn't know where it sourced its REE.

271 USGS Minerals Yearbook 1978/1979. China partnered with Inoue Japax Research

country would shatter the established global groupthink of Mutually Assured Minerals for purposes of strategic political-economic coercion.

In response to the embargo, Tokyo passed a $1.2 billion supplemental budget that October with five goals: 1) develop technologies that reduced REE use, 2) develop technologies using alternatives to REE, 3) invest in the recycling of REE, 4) invest in REE mines outside of China, and 5) stockpile REE reserves as a future insurance policy. In other words, Japan created a strategy for what it should have done for every critical mineral it majority-sourced from China. The U.S. was in the same vulnerable position as Japan and should have also pursued these very measures.[272]

After spending 15 years reducing its REE dependence on its main Asian rival, Japan still sourced 62% of its REE imports from Beijing in 2024. While one can classify this as a relatively a minor victory for Japan, it served to illustrate how much control China had over the global REE supply chain. As much as Tokyo tried, they still couldn't break Beijing's REE grip on their economy. One must understand that this unshakeable dependency was by design so Beijing could exert maximum leverage over Japan when required.

As part of its journey to achieve improved REE independence, Tokyo developed the Japan Australia Rare Earth (JARE) joint venture in 2011.[273] JARE invested $172 million AUS in the Australian company Lynas Rare Earths Limited with mining operations in Malaysia and Australia. In the deal, Japan would get 65% of the Heavy REE (HREE) produced from their Australian operations (dysprosium, terbium) and unspecified amounts of Light REE (LREE). In return, Japanese company Sojitz would be the sole distributor for Lynas' REE products for the Japan market.

Although Lynas was not yet a major producer compared to China, the company produced 10,900 metric tons of REO and 5,600 tons of NdPr (Neodymium, Praseodymium) in 2024. Lynas was profitable for the year with net profits of $84 million AUS which was a significant drop from the previous year of $310 million.[274] The primary reason for the difference was the drop in NdPr prices from a very high $60,400.00 a metric ton in 2023 to $44,000.00 in 2024

which was established in the REE space.

272 https://eneken.ieej.or.jp/en/chairmans-message/chairmans-message_202310.html

273 The Sojitz Corporation and Japan Oil, Gas and Metals National Corporation (JOGMEC).

274 Lynas' annual report ran from June 2023-June 2024.

and the temporary closure of its Malaysia operations. Importantly, Lynas had only one processing plant which was in Malaysia, meaning they shipped their REO 2,000 miles from Australia for refinement and subsequent forwarding to Japan (3,000 miles).[275]

Beyond this rather modest return from its investment in Lynas, Japan may have found an answer to its China-dependency on its own territory. Soon after Japan began investing in Lynas, geologists discovered REE rich deep-sea mud off the coast of the country's remote Minamitorishima Island in 2013. The mud contained an estimated 1.2 million metric tons of REO with the confirmed presence of yttrium, europium, terbium, and dysprosium.[276] Although Japanese geologists believed there were semi-infinite amounts of REE in the mud which was "easily recoverable," twelve years later it still remains on the bottom of the ocean. There are tentative plans of pumping it to the surface for processing somewhere around 2030. Scientific testing is relatively easy while commercial scale extraction can be very hard.

Minamitorishima Island burns after absorbing attacks by U.S. forces in 1943. This is Japan's easternmost island and is now an outpost for the Japan Meteorological Agency and Japan Coast Guard.

Another response to China's embargo was developing electric motors that didn't require REE. In 2010, the government-backed New Energy and Industrial Technology Development Organization (NEDO) announced the development of new REE-free magnets offering the same efficiency.[277] In 2018, Toyota revealed their own efforts to produce neodymium-reduced magnets, thrifting them with lanthanum and cerium, which were also also REE. Clearly, Japan

275 Lynas had yet to produce HREE which was projected for 2025.

276 "The tremendous potential of deep-sea mud as a source of rare-earth elements." Scientific Reports, April 10, 2018.

277 These never went into commercial scale production.

had much further to go before manufacturing REE-free magnets at commercial scale. Many other companies in Europe and the U.S. were also working to develop these types of magnets which Japan could simply purchase if and when they become available.

The most obvious measure Japan could take to insulate itself from REE supply chain shocks was establishing a national stockpile. As early as 2006, individual Japanese companies were doing just this as a hedge against potential Chinese leverage. While JOGMEC initiated a limited national stockpile in 1983, it included only two-months of stocks for just seven metals but no REE.[278] The Japan Rare Metals Stockpiling Association was responsible for coordinating rare metal stocks in the private sector. In 2020, Tokyo introduced its new International Resource Strategy with plans to stockpile 34 different metals, including REE, with up to six months for minerals "with a higher geopolitical risk," meaning China.

Japan also pursued recycling because it didn't matter if the country secured ex-China supply chains but then dumped their end-of-life REE products in a landfill or exported them back to China for recycling. Once REE entered the country, it needed to stay there. Recycling, aka "urban mining," could become its own domestic REE supply chain but this was difficult depending on how the REE was used. In one example, Dowa Holdings, which specializes in recycling various metals, tried and failed to establish an economic REE program. Most likely, they would have to focus on REPM recycling for the best chance of success.

A secondary effect of China's REE ban and Japan's response was skyrocketing prices from increased demand. Neodymium went from $42,000 a metric ton in 2010 to $283,000 the following year – an almost 700% increase. Samarium, the other most common REE used in magnets, went from $18,500 a metric ton to $146,000 a ton – an almost 800% increase. If Japan had stockpiled these REE beforehand, they could have released them to Japanese manufacturers as a deflationary mechanism. But they were caught unprepared.[279]

Like the U.S., Japan suffered from the national groupthink of Mutually Assured Minerals (MAM) where they thought the country could always get the raw materials it needed, regardless of geopolitical circumstances. In contrast,

278 JOGMEC presentation.

279 Bradsher, Keith. "Rare earth prices soaring as demand outstrips supply." The Plain Dealer, May 8, 2011.

Beijing did not develop this groupthink although they worked to instill this MAM mindset in their global competitors. In this instance, Japan learned what it should have already known, that it couldn't quickly develop secure critical minerals supply chains in a time of emergency. A country had to continuously work to secure its supply chains which could take many years. Securing national REE supply chains couldn't be a fad or an afterthought, it had to be ingrained in the government's daily lifestyle.

MP Materials

While Japan worked on improving its critical minerals strategy, the U.S. was ready for another try at fixing its own failed REE enterprise, starting with its shuttered mine in California. In 2017, MP Mine Operations bought the mine at an auction for the bargain basement price of just $20.5 million. After an internal reorganization, the purchasing entities formed the company MP Materials which began trading on the NYSE as MP in 2020. Importantly, the Chinese company Shenghe Resources held a 7.5% minority position which wouldn't trigger a national security investigation by CFIUS.[280]

Fortunately for MP Materials, their purchase coincided with the Trump 1.0 administration's renewed interest in critical minerals and especially REE. In early 2020, the company received a preliminary DOD contract for an HREE separation facility located at Mountain Pass. At the end of the year, the company was awarded $9.6 million through the Defense Production Act for their Stage II optimization project. This was a relatively small amount considering the project would require $220 million of capital investment.

From the start, MP was dependent on China which was the second best option for Beijing other than MP not going into business at all. Shenghe was a partner in the business because MP sold its REO to them where they then resold it to Chinese companies who processed and separated it into individual REE.[281] These companies then sold the separated REE to end-users in the Asia market. Importantly, these Chinese sales were giving MP the space and time that they needed to modernize their operations and stand on their own feet. Without Shenghe, MP couldn't survive.

280 Their parent company is Shenghe Resources Holding Company, a global REE production company, listed on the Shanghai Stock Exchange.

281 Shenghe Resources International Trading LTD is located in Singapore.

MP produced 38,500 tons of REO for the year, selling it at $3,311 a ton and a cost of $1,430 tons, indicating a profit of $1,881 a ton. Since they sold 38,367 tons, this resulted in $127 million in sales and gross profits of $72 million. However, this wasn't enough to cover MP's total costs so they ended the year $21 million in the red. If the company was going to keep the lights on, the next year had to improve.

In 2021, MP began working on their Stage III facility in Fort Worth, Texas to manufacture specialty metal alloys and REPM, something the U.S. had been missing since the GM/Magnequench sell-off. Related to this, and with much irony, the company negotiated a deal with GM for a long-term REPM contract. Although it wasn't the boost MP wanted, the COVID-19 pandemic's disruption of global supply chains contributed to a significant increase in REO prices that year.

Consequently, MP produced/sold 42,413/42,158 metric tons of REO at a realized price of $7,745 a ton, a 130% increase from the previous year. However, operational costs grew slightly to $1,493 a ton, indicating that work was still needed in this area. This resulted in a $6,252 profit per ton, $326 million in sales, and $263 million in gross profits. Finally, this put MP's bottom line in the black with net profits of $135 million which was badly needed to continue its Stage II and Stage III build-outs.[282]

One cannot ignore the reality that MP's relationship with Shenghe kept the company afloat. Importantly, Shenghe's location in Singapore helped it stay out of the crosshairs of the Washington-Beijing trade war. This was critical because MP sold 99% of its products through Shenghe. Also, Shenghe fronted MP tens of millions of dollars for future sales pursuant to its existing offtake agreement, giving MP needed liquidity. And for an unexpected windfall that year, China dropped their import tariffs on REO products, making MP's products more competitive in the China market.

MP carried this momentum into 2022 when they were awarded a $35 million contract from DOD's Office of Industrial Base Policy to build a facility to process HREE. The company also made real progress building out its Stage II REE separation circuit with an anticipated start date the following year. In Texas, MP completed the outer shell of its Stage III REPM manufacturing facility. Additionally, they formally inked the deal with GM to provide them with NdPr REPM for the company's electric motors used in their EV Ultium platform.

282 Shipping and freight costs were $8.9 million.

This was exactly what MP needed, domestic consumers at scale for their products so that they could claw their way out from under the smothering weight of China's massive REE enterprise.

While MP's REO production/sales for the year remained flat at 42,500/43,200 tons, prices increased dramatically from the previous year to $11,974 a ton while average operating costs continued creeping up to $1,728 a ton.[283] This profit margin of $10,246 per ton enabled $517 million in sales while their net income blew up to $289 million, more than double from the year before. Within this revenue was $10 million in sales of rare earth fluoride to Shenghe which had a growing use in the optics space.

In 2023, MP reached an important milestone with the company producing its first separated REE products. Previously, they shipped their REO to China for midstream processing which included separating the REO into different REE. MP also used VREX in Vietnam as a tolling partner to process its NdPr oxide into NdPr metal (NdPr alloys are used for high-performance applications).[284] In Q4, the company finished its REPM facility in Texas although it was not yet production-ready. Equally important, MP signed an agreement with Sumitomo where they would be the exclusive distributor of MP's NdPr oxide and NdPr metal to Japanese customers. These resulted in sales of $695,000.

MP's financial situation regressed with its production/sales reaching 41,500/36,800 tons, a significant decrease from the previous year. The realized price of REO was almost halved at $6,854 and production costs per ton continued to rise to $2,058. This resulted in sales of $252 million and gross profits of $176 million. The company produced 200 tons of separated NdPr products but only sold 10 tons for a realized price of $70,000 per metric ton. Overall, MP had an underwhelming year with the Stage II start-up process lowering total sales and a reduced global demand for REO/REE negatively impacting prices. Consequently, net income for the year was a mere $24.3 million.[285]

Moving into the next year, MP needed to further improve its Stage II separation operations to maximize sales of its separated REE products that brought 10 x more value compared to REO. Getting its REPM facility in Texas up and

283 This increase was due to higher personnel, material, energy, and shipping costs. MP trucked its REO an hour by road to the nearest rail head with follow-on travel to the Port of Long Beach in California. Shipping and freight costs were $13 million for the year.

284 The tolling partner, VREX Holdco, was a Shenghe subsidiary located in Vietnam. MP invested $9.7 million in VREX for a 49% equity stake.

285 Shipping and freight costs were a lower $7.4 million for the year.

running to realize income from these downstream finished products was critical. Lastly, it was important to see if its investment in VREX paid off and if they could grow distribution to the Asia market with its finished NdPr metals.

The Stage III facility in Texas was finally completed in Q4 2024 where the company could produce 1,000 metric tons annually of NdPr metal from NdPr oxide shipped from Mountain Pass for REPM production. This included the ability to make NdPr-Iron-Boron alloy flake, a precursor for magnet production. Also, the company began its trial production of automotive-grade sintered NdFeB magnets which was the step before commercial scale production.

Despite these strong milestones, MP's revenues declined to $203 million, a 20% drop from the previous year. REO concentrate accounted for $144 million of the total (71%) while NdPr oxide and metal accounted for $57.7 million (28%). This was a huge increase in value for its refined products as compared to the year before. However, the cost of sales grew dramatically to $192 million based on Stage II optimization and despite $12.2 million in 45X federal tax credits. Overall, this resulted in a disappointing net loss of $65 million.

While the company produced a record high of 45,400 tons of REO, it only sold 32,700 tons at a much reduced price of $4,414 per metric ton. This resulted in a growing stockpile of unsold REO which the company stored onsite. While this provided the company insurance against future increased demand and a hedge against inflation, it also reflected a loss of income. For its finished product line, MP realized much higher volumes of separated NdPr with 1,294 tons and sales of 1,142 which was 88% of production.[286]

Moving forward, MP had to get profitable which required their REPM facility in Texas coming online and producing at scale. This was underlined by the $100 million in prepayments from GM for magnetic precursor products that fell under their long-term supply contract. The company also needed to move its $31 million of stockpiled REO which it was unable to do in the previous two years. After observing China's increased REO production, this was unlikely. The other salient line of effort was maximizing their sales through VREX to Asian customers requiring finished NdPr products. (On April 17, 2025, MP Materials announced it had stopped shipping its REO to China for processing since they were subject to Beijing's 125% retaliatory tariffs. These tariffs made MP's product's economically non-viable in the China domestic market.)

286 Because MP sold less REO, its shipping costs were $4.8 million.

MP Materials 2020-2024 (Metric Tons)

Activity	2020	2021	2022	2023	2024
REO Production	38,500	42,400	42,500	41,500	45,400
REO Sales	38,300	42,100	43,200	36,800	32,700
NdPr Sales	None	None	None	200	1,100
Net Income	($21 mil)	$135 mil	$289 mil	$24.3 mil	($65 mil)

China's Rare Earth Empire

China first discovered REE resources in Byan Obo, Inner Mongolia in 1927 and began low-volume production thirty years later in 1957. China's initial REE exports were catalysts for petroleum and chemical products, similar to Molycorp's own efforts. Until Beijing saw a bigger role for the country's REE industry, exports averaged a modest 1,000 metric tons annually. An important reason why China was able to get their REE industry off the ground was the creation of research labs like the Baotou Research Institute for Rare Earths which opened in 1963. Then, Beijing stood up the Chinese Society of Rare Earths in 1979 and several years later the China Rare Earth Information Center. Advancing knowledge of REE and their associated technology was a crucial next-step for beginning large-scale commercialization.

It must be noted that the Chinese enterprise was helped immeasurably by the work of Dr. Xu Guangxian, a gifted chemist who studied at Columbia University in the U.S. from 1947-1951, earning both a Masters Degree and a PhD in chemistry. Xu later worked at Peking University's Rare Earth Laboratory where he discovered a new way to economically separate neodymium and praseodymium in 1972. This research led to the Chinese industry standard for separating NdPr at commercial scale. Xu became widely known as "The Father of Chinese Rare Earths Chemistry" and was personally recognized by Xi Jinping.[287]

China began showing real interest in the REE space in the early 1980s when Beijing made the decision to dominate the space. This required Chinese companies to increase their own domestic production, to acquire foreign REE technology, and to reestructure global REE supply chains to flow through China for midstream processing. Since the U.S. was the world's largest REE producer

287 Peking University article. Xu died in 2015 at age 95.

and the leader in REE intellectual capital, Beijing necessarily had to challenge and overthrow U.S. REE dominance. China proceeded in a methodical manner and even enlisted the U.S.' help in offshoring its own REE industry.

Above, Xu Guangxian was the Columbia University trained chemist known as the "Father of Chinese rare-earth metal." He taught at Peking University's Rare Earth Laboratory and created new NdPr separation techniques.

In 1983, the China Rare Earth Company (CREC) hired Texas-based Key Metals and Minerals Engineering Corporation (KMMEC) to provide technical advice for their REE operations in Baotou, Inner Mongolia.[288] The U.S.-owned Airtrust International Corporation also signed a joint venture with CREC to expand Chinese production and import these products into the U.S. Airtrust was the exclusive distributor of CREC's products. When CREC officials visited Texas for a business conference, local newspapers ran articles with pictures that showed their Chinese visitors enjoying the Galveston County Fair and Rodeo. The CREC leadership would gladly eat Texas BBQ if it helped them expand their REE operations and eventually put Molycorp out of business.[289] The first shipment of Chinese REE into the U.S. came in May 1983.[290]

A decade later, China broke into the Canadian market. Toronto-based Advanced Material Resources (AMR) signed a joint venture (JV) to form Jiangyin Jia Hua AMR (JAMR) with AMR holding 60% ownership in the JV as of 1993. AMR also formed the JV Zibo Jia Hua AMR (ZAMR) with 80% ownership. AMR was able to gain China REE industry access by hiring Michael Zeng, the former deputy general manager of the China Rare Earth Development Corpo-

288 "Mackey, China sign technical pact." The Galveston Daily News, February 17, 1983.
289 The Galveston Daily News, May 9, 1983. Dr. Tom Mackey was the CEO of both Airtrust and KMMEC. Airtrust also had an office in Singapore.
290 "China oil-gas field helped raise funds." The Odessa America, May 5, 1983.

ration. AMR would be the sole distributor of these REE products for their customers. AMR would later buy the U.S. REPM company Magnequench. AMR was subsequently bought by Molycorp, with the company evolving into its present form as Neo Performance Materials. While Neo continued to diversify its ex-China REE raw material inputs, the company was never able to break its original supply chain dependencies.[291] [292]

From 1985 to 1995, China's REO production increased dramatically from just 8,500 metric tons to 30,000 tons, 42% of world production.[293] China's growing REO production was done so rapidly, at such scale, with such incredibly low operating costs, that the U.S.' sole Mountain Pass operation was rendered non-competitive. It is also crucial to understand that the introduction of REE products at scale to the Western Hemisphere was directly facilitated by U.S. and Canadian companies who sought to profit from this influx. However, in doing so, they created their present REE supply chain dependencies which Beijing orchestrated but what North America failed to foresee.

The salient difference between the two parallel efforts was that Beijing recognized REE as a "protected and strategic mineral" in 1990 while the U.S. had no sense of its own minerals security and was selling off its national stockpile. While the U.S. closed its REE research effort at Ames Laboratory in 1998, the Chinese government stood up Program 863 (National High-Tech Research and Development) and Program 973 (National Basic Research). These research efforts were funded by the government and provided grants to research and advance REE technology.[294] Beijing took an active interest in advancing its REE security while Washington did the opposite and willingly sold off its technological advantage to China.

While China grew its REE enterprise into the world's biggest, it also had to conduct some industry housekeeping. For example, independent REE companies competed with one another, leading them to produce more than Beijing wanted. Also, illegal REE miners extracted and sold their products on the black

291 Nutt, Rod. "Toronto-based resource firm enters China's rare-earth industry." The Vancouver Sun, May 5, 1994.

292 In 2024, Neo sold 86% of its equity of the JAMR HREE separation facility and 88% of its LREE separation facility to Shenghe. They sold these assets because they were financially vulnerable and needed the money. 80% of Neo's NdFeB feedstock was from their China operations.

293 USGS Rare Earth Report 1996

294 Hurst, Cindy A. "China's Ace in the Hole; Rare Earth Elements." National Defense University Press, 2010.

market, raising the overall total in defiance of official guidance. Consequently, there were ongoing talks between mining companies and the government from the late 1990s-2000s to better regulate production and address issues like pollution control and resource preservation.

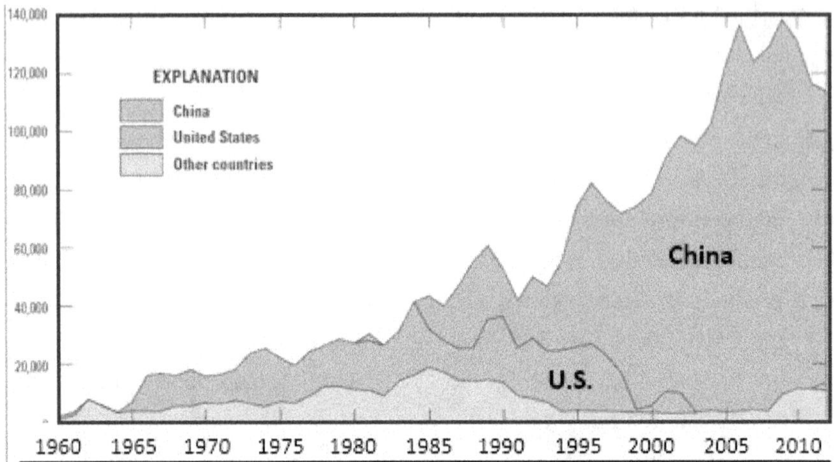

From 1965-1985 the U.S. dominated REE production. From 1985-2010 China grew its REE enterprise, producing as much as 130,000 tons of REO annually.

Beijing had instituted controls on the REE industry as early as 1990 when they designated it a critical mineral. From that time on, REE mining operations required approval from the State Development and Planning Commission (SDPC). While foreign companies could not mine for REE in China, they could form a JV with a domestic entity for refining work but had to be approved by SDPC and the Ministry of Commerce (MOFCOM). The Ministry of Land and Resources (MLR) instituted production quotas until 2008 when these responsibilities were given to the Ministry of Industry and Information Technology (MIIT).[295]

Beginning in 2006, China began exerting increasing control of its REE exports to limit the amount of raw materials that left the country and to increase the export of finished products. Subsequently, REO concentrate export quotas went from 48,000 metric tons in 2005, to 45,000 in 2006, 43,500 in 2007, 34,100 in 2008, 31,300 in 2009, 22,500 in 2010, and a steep drop to 14,400 in 2011. We must notice how these tighter export controls began well before the Senkaku incident with Japan in 2010. The biggest export drops were the year of the dispute and the year after. However, Beijing did cut its established REE

295 MIIT also now managed the Rare Earth Office which oversaw REE policy.

exports to Japan by 90% for the two months following the dispute. This is why Japan argued that Beijing was using minerals warfare for economic and political leverage.[296]

To comprehensively manage their REE industry, Beijing crafted a Rare-Earth Development Plan for 2009-2015. REO production would be limited to 130,000-140,000 tons annually, REO export quotas would be 35,000 tons, dysprosium and terbium exports would be restricted, and monazite mining containing radioactive elements would be banned. Minimum production capacity requirements were instituted to promote industry consolidation and squeeze out hundreds of small inefficient operations.

The strategy for getting control of the industry was placing 90% of all REE production under six SOEs: China Minmetals, Chinalco, Baotou Steel, Xiamen Tungsten, Ganzhou Rare Earths, and Guangdong Guangsheng Rare Earths.[297] These six companies would manage production of the existing 84 mines, spread over 18 provinces, which were organized into three newly designated rare earth mining districts (north, south, and west.) The six SOEs would absorb the hundreds of smaller operations and put the illegal mines out of business whose black market sales were 50% of official annual production.[298]

In response to external citicism and concerns by senior Chinese leaders (including Xi Jinping himself) REE producers who violated environmental standards would be shut down. Also, the China Rare Earth Industry Association was created in 2012 as a means for the REE enterprise to regulate itself in accordance with Beijing's guidance. The overall effect of the plan was to pressure advanced foreign REE manufacturers to move their businesses into China which provided Beijing with access to their technology.[299]

Because of China's increasing export restrictions, which included a 25% export tariff on 26 different REE products and prohibitions on another 41, the U.S., EU, and Japan initiated a dispute settlement with the World Trade Organization (WTO) in 2012.[300] The policies in dispute included China's use of quotas and export tariffs which lowered domestic REE prices while raising those of foreign purchasers. In 2014, the WTO ruled against China with Beijing filing

296 Sino-foreign JVs also have export quotas like AMR/Neo.

297 Inner Mongolia Baotou Steel Rare Earth is the single largest producer of REE as they are recovered secondary to their iron ore extraction operations.

298 Mancheri, Nabeel A. & T. Marukawa.

299 U.S. Geological Survey REE Report 2011.

300 The case also included tungsten and molybdenum. Metal Pages, 2014.

an appeal, but the next year China dropped their export quotas. In response, Beijing used the WTO ruling as a means to further leverage their domestic REE industry and get them in line with the national plan.

In 2016, MIIT issued the second Development Plan for Rare Earths Industry (2016-2020) which was a continuation and improvement of the previous one.[301] To start, the industry would pursue high-value downstream products based on improved extraction and refinement technology. The industry would be further consolidated, improved management and synchronization would occur across the enterprise, and environmental goals would be achieved. In just one example of the guidance given, the overall industry would achieve an industry profit margin of 12% by 2020 as opposed to just 5.8% achieved in 2015.

Perhaps the most striking aspect of the plan was that it was publicly available. No one could say they didn't know where China's REE industry was going or what regulations would be implemented. This allowed other countries like Japan to plan accordingly as they knew China's game plan – if they bothered to read it. Importantly, the plan distinguished itself from U.S. efforts in that it was a roadmap with clear milestones. In comparison, the U.S. was just throwing REE spaghetti at the wall, hoping it would stick somewhere at Mountain Pass. The plan also served to illustrate the contrast between a centralized economic process as opposed to a free market one.

After 2020, China lifted their previous production quotas and expanded their output greatly, almost doubling it from 2020 to 2024. During this period the U.S. maintained mostly flat production from its Mountain Pass operations. Production from the rest of the world also remained flat despite efforts from countries like Australia, Burma, and Thailand. Clearly, China had the technological ability to increase REE production where they extracted 70% of world REO in 2024. However, China imported another estimated 94,000 tons for midstream refinement, giving them control of 93% of the market.[302]

When 2024 came around, Beijing realized their REE enterprise still wasn't where they wanted it to be, prompting them to issue new *Rare Earth Management Regulations* with 32 separate articles. The law would be implemented at

301 This was 30 pages long and provided comprehensive guidance to improve every aspect of the REE industry.

302 31,000 tons from Burma, 22,000 tons from the U.S., 13,000 tons from Nigeria, 13,000 tons from Thailand, 13,000 tons from Australia, 2,000 tons from Madagascar, 300 tons from Vietnam, and 130 tons from Malaysia.

the national level by the Department of Industry and Information Technology (DIIT) of the State Council. A new initiative enforced by DIIT was a REE "product traceability information program" so Beijing could follow its REE products back to the source. The largest section of the law (11 articles) addressed illegal REE mining activity, indicating this was a widespread problem that had yet to be eliminated. Overall, the law meant to bring the industry under further government control to operate in a more efficient manner that supported national economic goals. This looked good on paper but was hard to enforce.

As seen with the data, the world overproduced REE products in 2024, causing prices to plummet to five-year lows, with China being the main culprit. Beijing proved it could not effectively manage the world REE supply chain with even its own REE manufacturers sustaining losses. For example, the SOE China Rare Earth Group formed in 2021, composed of three separate major REE mining companies, suffered over $100 million in losses in the first half of 2024. MP Material's partner Shenghe Resources also lost $8 million. The overproduction was a result of misjudging global demand, compounded by continued imports for midstream processing, and persistent black market REE sales.[303]

As discussed earlier, China's ability to produce REE products at volume and then refine them with their midstream processing has resulted in an entrenched monopoly. China operates at such scale that they control global pricing characteristics and undercut competition anywhere in the world. While some researchers used modeling that predicted China would reach peak REE/REO production in 2018 and then steadily decline, Beijing has defied these algorithms.[304] One can see how small REE operations like MP Material's Mountain Pass and Lynas' Mount Weld in Australia can be forced into bankruptcy. There is also undeniable evidence that Beijing is unable to control the REE beast it created with local mining districts defying the CCP to profit from illegal operations. This leaves the reader with the question: Is China seeking to achieve total rare earth dominance or merely increasing supply to meet growing global demand as Beijing claims?

303 Kawase, Kenji. "China's state rare-earth players bleed red ink as process fall." Nikkei Asia, July 16, 2024.
304 Wang, Xibo, et. al. "Production forecast of China's rare earths based on the Generalized Weng model and policy recommendations." Resources Policy, 2015.

Rare Earth Oxide Production MT 2020-2024					
	2020	2021	2022	2023	2024
China	140,000	168,000	210,000	255,000	270,000
U.S.	39,000	42,000	42,000	41,600	45,000
ROW	81,000	80,000	48,000	80,000	75,000
Total	240,000	290,000	300,000	376,000	390,000

**MT = Metric Tons, ROW: Rest of World*

Final Thoughts

The U.S. needs to recognize that it has been on the losing end of a 40-year rare earth war won decisively by the REE Death Star commanded by Xi Jinping. In response, the U.S. must wage a supply chain insurgency against Beijing's overwhelming forces arrayed in the field. The U.S. requires a comprehensive REE campaign strategy that addresses all aspects of the contest. At the very least, the U.S. should set the minimalist goal of sourcing less than half its REE needs from China. This effort requires harnessing both free-market and government forces.

To start, the U.S. must stockpile REO, finished REE material, and other downstream finished products like magnets. Presently, the U.S. stockpiles no REE material and only small amounts of finished products. The U.S. can use this stockpiling to drive domestic production as the Eisenhower administration did to meet national economic and security needs. This effort must be combined with the mandatory recycling of items made with REE where the recovered products are sent to the stockpile. The stockpile should be used to hedge against future market manipulation as seen by China from 2005-2012, leading to skyrocketing REE prices. Furthermore, a reserve is needed as insurance against a growing trade war where Beijing could use export controls to sever the U.S.' exposed REE supply chains.

The U.S. should double-down on its efforts to find alternative REE sources in the U.S. and to develop new extraction technology to make previously uneconomic sources viable. However, the U.S. must do more and export this process along with expeditionary geologic surveys to find REE sources elsewhere in the Western Hemisphere like Brazil. It makes sense for the U.S. to support all ongoing and future REE projects in Canada and Mexico to construct a North American supply chain. This means Washington must recognize one larger REE economic zone that includes our neighbors and its trade policies must reflect this special relationship.

While the U.S. should cooperate with Chinese REE companies in a commonsense way, the U.S. cannot afford another Magnequench debacle where it offshores REE industries to the obvious detriment of the defense industrial base. Since the global minerals and metals system does not recognize humanity's contrived geographic borders, the U.S. must cooperate with the Chinese REE enterprise in a manner that benefits both. MP's relationship with Shenghe shows that this is possible but the U.S. must do it in a way that does not disproportionately benefit China.

Another piece of the strategic puzzle is developing a REE coalition that includes the EU, Japan, South Korea, Taiwan, and Australia that combines their efforts to build non-coercive ex-China supply chains. This Rare Earth Free Trade Coalition (REFTC) should focus on developing their midstream refinement capabilities and pooling their collective resources, capital, and technology to create its own resilient REE ecosystem. This requires a common vision, diplomacy, and government-to-government engagement underpinned with a published agreement, signed by all parties. Finally, the U.S. and its allies need to recognize that minerals flow to where they are used. As we know, REPM go to wind turbine, EV motor, and other manufacturers for production. If the REFTC abandons their efforts to compete in the green energy and technology space, REE will continue to go to the end-user: China.

The U.S. has deluded itself for decades as to the extent of its own critical minerals insecurity with REE being the perfect example of this. Part of this delusion was refusing to see that China's REE calculations were based on a Geopolitical Return on Investment, something the U.S.' own 90-day profit driven thought process couldn't grasp. If the U.S. doesn't craft a wholistic plan that challenges and erodes China's REE dominance to meet its own supply chain security needs, it will continue to be vulnerable to Beijing's economic leverage. China has laid out all its cards - it is well past the time for the U.S. to ante up.

Sources

Bauk, George, et. al. "China's Rare Earth Subsidies and Structural Advantages." May 2, 2023.

"China's Rare Earth Industry & Export Regime: Economic and Trade Implications for the U.S." Congressional Research Service, April 30, 2012.

"China's Monopoly on Rare Earths: Implications for U.S. Foreign and Security Policy." House Hearing, September 21, 2011.

Jackson, James K. "Foreign Investment and National Security: Economic Considerations." Congressional Research Service, April 4, 2013.

Goldman, Joanne Abel. "Frank Spedding and the Ames Laboratory: The Development of a Science Manager. The University of Iowa, 2008.

"Foreign Investment. Implementation of Exon-Florio and Related Amendments." GAO Report, December 1995.

Johnstone, Sydney J. "The Rare Earth Industry." New York: D. Appleton and Company, 1915.

Mancheri, Nabeel A. & T. Marukawa. "Rare Earth Elements, China & Japan in Industry, Trade, and Value Chain." ISS, March 2016.

Park, Sulgiye, et. al. "Reimagining U.S. rare earth production." Resources Policy, 2023.

"Rare-Earth Mineral Deposits of the Mountain Pass District San Bernardino County California. U.S. Geological Survey, 1954.

"A Review of the CFIUS Process for Implementing the Exon-Florio Agreement." Senate Hearings, October 6 & 20, 2005.

Tse, Pui-Kwan. "China's Rare-Earth Industry." U.S. Geological Survey, 2011.

Zhou, Weihuan, et. al. "Demystifying China's Critical Minerals Strategies." Cambridge University Press, January 25, 2025.

One of the massive open pit mines of the Bayan Obo rare earth mining operation located in Baotou, Inner Mongolia. Most REE is extracted secondary to iron ore mining, meaning a decline in the steel industry would impact rare earth production. REE is commonly smuggled out as "iron ore" with the understanding that the receiving country will separate the ore and recover the rare earths.

Round Top Mountain in Texas is where the publicly traded company USA Rare Earth Inc. (USARE) plans to conduct extraction operations for both Light (neodymium, praseodymium) and Heavy (dysprosium, terbium) REE. The company also believes they can economically recover lithium, beryllium, and gallium; all three are identified critical minerals. USARE has proprietary L/HREE metal separation technology as confirmed with their patent published in 2024. The company anticipates their REE magnet facility being ready for commercial operations in 2026, although their mining operations most likely won't come online until 2030.

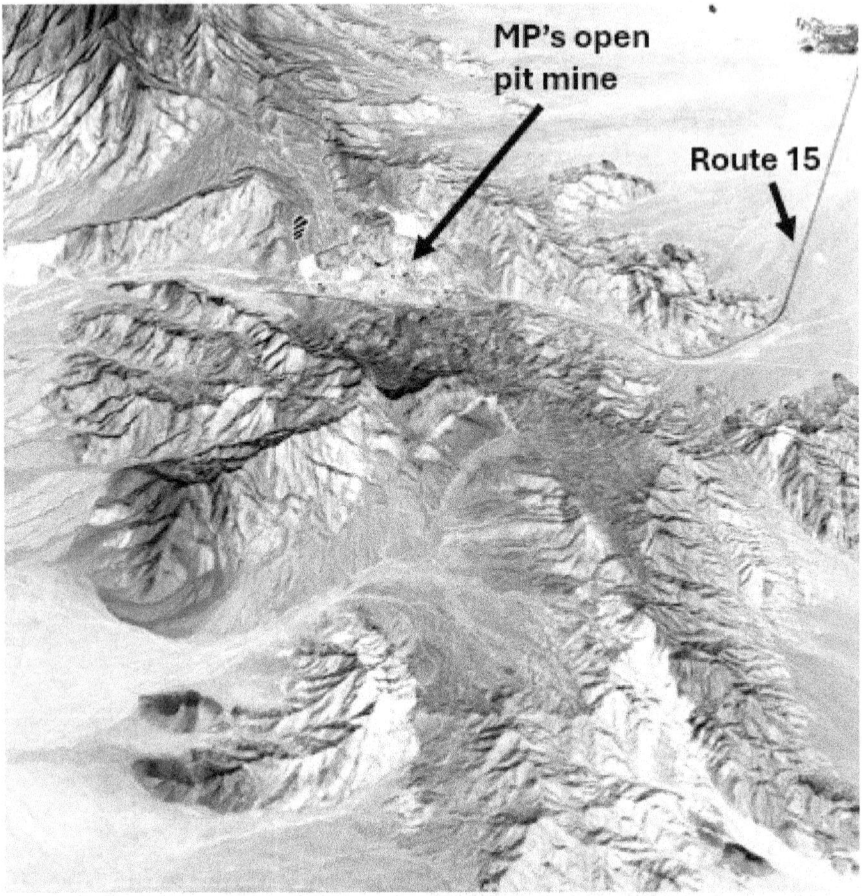

An aerial view of the terrain that is Mountain Pass, California. The picture was taken by NASA in March 2010, after the mine had been purchased by the newly reincarnated Molycorp. The company went bankrupt in 2015, and the mine was closed again until it was purchased by MP Materials in 2017. *Supply Chain:* The mine trucks its REO by road for an hour to the nearest railhead with four hours of subsequent travel by rail to the Port of Long Beach in California. MP uses Shenghe Resources in Singapore as its distributor for the Asian market which largely consists of Chinese buyers. With the creation of its own REO separation capability at the mine and its magnet production facility in Texas, the company has created its own vertically integrated domestic REE value chain.

Chapter 7

The Critical Minerals Index Fund

Introduction

This chapter is an exercise in constructing a Critical Minerals Index Fund (CMIF) that tracks different aspects of the U.S.' critical minerals industry. The fund is limited to ten publicly traded companies with each one contributing 10% to the overall fund. Also, the fund only includes companies that deal in a mineral that has been identified as "critical" by U.S. Geological Survey which gives us 50 different sectors to choose from. The fund strives to pick the best available option in a sector with the understanding that good offerings may be limited. While American companies are given priority, a foreign company operating on U.S. soil will be picked if they are the best or only option.

Companies were selected that we haven't already discussed in depth to broaden our understanding of the critical minerals space. For example, MP Materials wasn't chosen because it was covered in the previous chapter. Large volume metals such as aluminum were selected, non-metals were picked like graphite, and a recycling company was chosen to illuminate the black mass sector. Also, a downstream manufacturing company was identified to show how a polymetallic operation impacts the value chain. The overarching intent was to provide a variety of examples to better understand the larger critical minerals enterprise.

For the U.S. critical minerals industry to thrive it requires financial backing, both from the government and the private sector. In many cases, a critical mineral company may need initial government support to get it on its feet so that it can then grow in the construct of the existing capital markets. After we build the fund, we will compare its performance with that of the overall market to see how it stacks up. From this comparison we will take the lessons learned and see how this impacts the critical minerals investing space and what the supply chain security implications are.

Materion – Beryllium

Let's begin with Materion and the beryllium industry because this serves as an example of how the U.S. government can use its tools to help invigorate a floundering industry and put it on a path to success. Materion is a U.S. company headquartered in Ohio with an international footprint and over 3,000 employees. The company makes specialty alloys and materials with customers that include the defense industry. Founded in 1931 as the Brush Beryllium Company, this small start-up made beryllium-copper alloys which led to large military contracts for aviation products during WWII.

Fast forward to the year 1997 and what had evolved into Brush-Wellman Inc (BWI) was no longer a viable company.[305] Since BWI never updated its manufacturing equipment, it was rendered non-competitive over time compared to other companies located outside the U.S. Also, beryllium dust is highly toxic which opened the company to continuing legal liability and large payouts to its workforce. Subsequently, the company shut down its only beryllium manufacturing plant in Ohio and had to purchase beryllium ingots from the limited reserves of the National Defense Stockpile (NDS) to make its products.

Because the BWI plant was the only primary beryllium smelter in the country, the U.S. went from being a net exporter of primary beryllium products in 1996 to importing 48% of its needs in 1999. While BWI continued to extract beryllium from its mine in Utah, BWI paid for 76 tons of beryllium from the NDS in 1997 and 145 tons in 1999. Most of the beryllium products the U.S. imported were from Russia (31%), Canada (20%), Kazakhstan (12%), and then Germany (10%). Despite this, the U.S. remained the top producer of beryllium, extracting 231 tons in 1997 which was 70% of the world total (331 tons), followed by China with 55 tons (16%), and then Russia with 40 tons (12%). This meant the products imported from Canada and Germany were refined in Kazakhstan and originated from Russia.

In 2003, which was several years too late, Congress directed DOD (Department of Defense) to conduct a study on the impact of the loss of the country's only primary beryllium smelter.[306] In 2004, DOD determined that beryllium

305 BWI's parent company was Brush Engineered Materials Inc.
306 The company had a net loss of $12.7 million in 2003.

was critical to their production needs and agreed that the Defense Production Act (DPA) should be used to modernize BWI's capability. In 2005, DOD provided BWI an initial $9 million contract to construct a modern beryllium smelter. In 2010, the new facility came online with an 80 tpa capacity. $65 million more was provided through 2011 with another $11.8 million from 2021-2024. This government assistance through the DPA combined with investment from what was now called Materion turned the company around.[307]

In 2024, Materion had net sales of $1.68 billion while cost of sales were $1.35 billion, resulting in a net income of just $5.8 million for a margin of less than 1%.[308] The company suffered the biggest losses from its Precision Optics unit in Malaysia operations resulting in a $73.2 million impairment. The company also had losses in various other sectors that it serviced. This was concerning considering that beryllium-copper alloy was priced at a healthy $1.5 million per metric ton of contained content. The company's net profit was a razor thin margin, the equivalent of just 3.8 tons of beryllium. In the short term, Materion could benefit if the U.S. Government were to fill out the National Defense Stockpile which requires another 105 tons of beryllium for a one-year reserve.

For perspective, the world produced 360 tons of beryllium in 2024 with the U.S. producing 180 tons (50%), Brazil 80 tons (22%), China 77 tons (21%), and Mozambique 24 tons (6%). If we compare 2024 production with 1997, the U.S. has lost much of its market share although it still has a strong fundamental position, holding an estimated 60% of global beryllium reserves. Also, Materion had vertical integration in that it owns its one mine and a primary smelter located in the U.S. Both Kazakhstan and China have primary beryllium smelters and are the U.S.' main competitors.

Beryllium is a low volume, high margin market with little impact on the larger U.S. economy. If the U.S. sold its entire production at full market value, it would be $270 million (180 tons x $1.5 million per metric ton). Since the rest of the world now accounts for 50% of beryllium ore extraction, the U.S. no longer serves as a geographic chokepoint. Of the four beryllium smelter patents filed since 1984, three were Chinese with the fourth being German. In 2020, China formed a strategic beryllium alliance with its related companies to improve their beryllium technology. The U.S. could lose its export quality edge if China can produce superior products from advanced smelter technology.

307 The company changed its name to Materion in 2011.

308 Adjusted net income was $111 million.

5N+ - Germanium

5N is a mid-size Canadian Company with headquarters in Montreal with 790 employees and a worldwide footprint including the U.S., Germany, and China (Hong Kong). The company specializes in sophisticated downstream value chain products in the space, medical, pharmaceutical, solar power (terrestrial and space-based), and semiconductor sectors. While 5N deals in bismuth and tellurium, their germanium-based semiconductor business is their largest division, accounting for 70% of product sales in 2024 with the rest from their performance materials.

Germanium exists in a vague operating environment where the U.S. knows little about its global market. For example, U.S. Geological Survey has no reliable data on known germanium reserves or how much is produced in specific countries. Since germanium is most often recovered secondary to zinc and copper production, its sourcing follows these supply chains. Since zinc, also an identified critical mineral, is mined in over a dozen countries, there is no geographic choke point. However, China produced one-third of the world's zinc in 2024 with 4 million tons, followed by Peru with 1.3 million tons, and Australia with 1.1 million tons. The U.S. produced 750,000 tons.

Although the U.S. has several zinc operations, it imports more than 50% of its germanium needs with most coming from China (51%), then Belgium

(27%), and Germany (15%). The U.S. imports relatively low volumes of germanium products with just 33 metric tons in 2024, meaning overall consumption was about 50 tons after accounting for exports. While the U.S. produces germanium from a zinc smelter in Tennessee, it exports this for refinement. The U.S. has no primary germanium production capability while China produces an estimated 68% of refined products making them a production chokepoint.

Germanium metal is expensive, averaging $2.1 million per metric ton while germanium dioxide averages $1.4 million per ton. Although the U.S. has no primary germanium manufacturing capability, it does recover germanium scrap from various production and recycling efforts. This lack of primary production capability makes 5N vulnerable to China's germanium export restrictions. In 2024, DOD awarded 5N $14.4 million through the Defense Production Act (DPA) to expand their production capability of germanium substrates for use in solar cells for defense and commercial satellites. The money will be spent over the course of four years to upgrade 5N's St. George manufacturing facility.[309]

5N had revenue of $289 million in 2024 which was a modest increase from the previous year of $242 million. The cost of sales also increased to $211 million from $184 million the year before. However, net earnings dropped to $14.6 million from $15.4 million the prior period. Part of this loss was due to currency translation which cost them $4.9 million. 5N held $51 million in raw materials, which was up from $36 million the previous year, indicating they were stocking germanium products. This was a good idea considering the Trump-initiated tariff trade wars in 2025 and China's retaliatory export restrictions. Since $202 million of revenue was from their semiconductor sales, 5N is highly exposed and sensitive to the germanium market.

Like beryllium, germanium is a low volume, high margin specialty metal with high exposure to the China dominated market. The U.S. could establish domestic germanium refinement production and vertically integrate this effort with existing zinc mining operations but has not done so, primarily because it is such a low volume market. If we estimate an even 50/50 split of the two primary germanium products used in the U.S., this would be a $43 million value, much smaller than beryllium and with little overall economic impact on the U.S. However, we must realize that germanium and beryllium have a disproportionate impact on the U.S. defense industry that goes beyond the mere

309 5N has been awarded the contract to maintain germanium wafers for the National Defense Stockpile. This means 5N is both a producer for and a maintainer of the NDS.

monetary value of the products used. This is the exact space Beijing likes to get into and dominate, a scenario that is little understood with more impact than its price tag indicates.

Novonix - Graphite

Novonix is a small Australian battery technology company with just over 200 employees that was founded by students from Dalhousie University's chemistry program in Canada. The department is run by Dr. Jeffrey Dahn, an American, who specializes in battery chemistry and is one of the patent holders of the modern NMC 811 ternary battery used in BEVs today. Novonix has established a start-up synthetic graphite operation in Chattanooga, TN to make battery-grade products for the BEV sector.

Overall, natural flake graphite, which is mined, competes with artificial aka synthetic graphite which is made from discarded petroleum and coal tar products. Historically, the U.S. consumed synthetic graphite and natural flake at a ratio of 5:1 with most of this used in refractories and foundries as graphite electrodes.[310] Batteries only consumed 10% of synthetic and 5% of natural graphite use as one would expect since the U.S. was not in the EV battery manufacturing business.

310 Zhang, Jinrui. "Graphite Flows in the U.S.: Insights into a Key Ingredient of Energy Transition." Environmental Science & Technology, 2023.

Although China is the single largest producer of synthetic graphite anode material in the world (95%), they are neither a geographic nor production chokepoint. Any country with access to petroleum and coke byproducts has the feedstock for synthetic graphite production. Also, synthetic graphite production is widely dispersed with Japan, India, Spain, France, Mexico, and the U.S. all having domestic production capabilities. While the U.S. has several companies producing synthetic graphite material in the U.S, Novonix has a single competitor in the battery-grade space, private company Anovion Technologies.

Anovion is U.S.-owned which began initial production of their EV battery-grade synthetic grade products in 2021 with plans to expand beyond their current 5,000 tpa capacity. They received a $117 million grant from the Department of Energy (DOE) in 2022 to build a commercial-scale facility in Georgia with a production date of 2027 and a 40,000 tpa capacity.[311] In 2023, Anovion signed an offtake agreement for its products with Forge Nano Inc. who intends to enter the EV battery manufacturing space by 2026. This is a risky value chain since neither company has made their products on a commercial scale.[312]

Novonix is also an early stage company who is still fitting out their Riverside facility in TN with a 3,000 tpa initial capacity with production to begin in 2026. Expansion plans will take the facility to 20,000 tpa capacity in 2028. The company also intends to construct a separate facility with a 31,500 tpa capacity and will be production ready in 2028. Novonix has secured offtake agreements with VW-owned PowerCo SE, Stellantis, and Panasonic Energy with 157,000 tons of synthetic graphite committed through 2031. Additionally, LG Energy Solution has an option to purchase 50,000 tons of products.

Novonix operates in an established space with domestic and foreign companies offering competing products. The company's advantages include an integrated domestic production chain, strong intellectual property (13 battery-related patents) which includes proprietary high-performance anode technology, a $100 million grant from DOE in 2023, approval for a $754 million loan from DOE, and $103 million in 45C tax credits for 2024. Novonix has a deal with Harper International to provide custom graphite furnace technology. Having said this, the company accurately presumes that its product prices will still be above those offered by established Chinese companies operating at scale.

311 Total plant cost is $800 million.

312 Forge Nano has 22 battery-related patents.

Novonix has several other business lines to include a JV with Axon Graphite LTD in Australia which is pursuing natural flake graphite operations. The company also has proprietary all-dry, zero-waste cathode active material (CAM) technology and is working with Brazilian company CBBM to pursue commercialization. A third line of effort is its Battery Technology Solutions (BTS), something Novonix provides as a service to battery production companies.

Because the company does not yet sell its synthetic graphite or CAM products, its income is limited until it does. In 2024, Novonix earned $5.9 million in revenue, primarily from its BTS sales, with total comprehensive losses of $78.6 million. The company took a $15.3 million loss in 2024 on its investment in KORE Power which canceled its planned KorePlex battery plant in Arizona. Novonix will continue to operate at a loss until it can produce its synthetic graphite products profitably at scale.

Albemarle - Lithium

Albemarle Corporation is the only U.S.-owned lithium company with a global workforce of 8,300 people. The U.S.' other lithium company, Arcadium Lithium, was sold to English-Australian mining giant Rio Tinto in early 2025. In the U.S., the company owns the only operating lithium brine extraction operation in the country (Nevada), has processing facilities in North Carolina, and owns a decommissioned hard rock mine also in North Carolina. Albemarle is an international company with brine operations in Chile, hard rock and processing operations in Australia, and processing facilities in China.

Lithium is distributed among many countries so there is no geographic chokepoint. Chile has 9 million tons in reserves and Argentina 4 million tons which, along with Bolivia, combine to form what is known as the Lithium Triangle. While Bolivia only produces small amounts of lithium, they are believed to have large amounts of lithium resources equivalent to Chile. The lithium extracted from the Triangle is from underground salars and is recovered through evaporative brine pond operations. Overall, the lithium triangle is the largest producer of lithium from brine with the lowest costs in the industry. Australia has reserves of 7 million tons, China 3 million tons, the U.S. 1.8 million tons, and Canada 1.2 million tons. Outside of the Triangle, lithium is mostly extracted from hard rock open pit mining.

In 2024, lithium was sourced from ten different countries with a total production of almost 1.3 million metric tons of Lithium Carbonate Equivalent (LCE). The Lithium Triangle produced 356,000 tons of LCE from their brine operations, the U.S. a much smaller 8,500 tons of LCE, with China also extracting some lithium through their own brine operations. Australia produced the most lithium at 468,000 tons LCE followed by China with 218,000 tons. Zimbabwe (117,000 tons LCE) and Canada (53,000 tons LCE) were the only other significant producers of lithium. This is the landscape that Albemarle competes in.[313]

To understand where Albemarle fits into this picture, we must understand the global flow of lithium. First, the U.S. uses very little lithium, about 17,000 tons annually. Albemarle can easily fill these modest needs from both its domestic and foreign operations. While world production is dispersed, minerals flow to where they are used, with most going to Asia and China to satisfy growing lithium-ion battery (LIB) demand. Albemarle competes with several other major lithium producers which includes Arcadium/Rio Tinto (U.S./Australia), SQM (Chile), Tianqi Lithium (China), and Ganfeng Lithium (China).

In 2024, Albemarle produced 277,000 tons of LCE for 16% of total world production. Net sales were $5.3 billion, down 44% from the year before ($9.6 billion) due to a continuing drop in refined lithium prices. This caused gross profits to collapse from $1.1 billion in 2023 to just $62 million in 2024. Conse-

313 U.S. Geological Survey.

quently, net income went from $1.5 billion in 2023 to a net loss of $1.1 billion in 2024. This cratering of profits led its stock to do the same, which kept the company's stock price relatively flat from 2020-2025.

Albemarle had an aggressive mindset from its creation, leading it to try to dominate the space it operated in. The company continued to expand during the COVID-19 pandemic of 2020 and the rupture of the BEV bubble in 2022/2023. Lithium prices reached unsustainable heights in 2022, enabling the company to achieve record profits while encouraging its continued growth. However, as the global lithium extraction enterprise expanded to capture this value, there was resulting overproduction which caused prices to decline rapidly. As a result of these dynamics, Albemarle was caught with a large footprint but a shrinking share of the market. Although it didn't help Albemarle stockholders, the company's peers in the industry suffered similar fates with SQM retaining the most of its previous value.

South32 - Manganese

S32 is a large international Australian company employing over 9,900 people, dealing in alumina, aluminum, copper, zinc, lead, silver, nickel, and manganese. S32 produced 4.5 million tons of manganese in 2024 with operations in Australia, South Africa, and one under development in southern Arizona. The manganese production was split almost evenly between their Australian operations (2.3 million tons) and their South Africa operations (2.2 million).

Significant manganese deposits are distributed among seven countries with South Africa, Australia, China, and Brazil holding 94% of global reserves. In 2024, the world produced 20 million tons of manganese with four countries dominating the industry: South Africa producing 7 million tons (35%), Gabon 4.6 million tons (23%), and Australia 2.8 million tons (14%). The U.S., Canada, and Mexico produced no manganese and only Brazil produced any of significance in the Western Hemisphere (770,000 tons). This puts the U.S. in a vulnerable supply chain situation because they must import 100% of their needs.[314]

The U.S. used to mine manganese in Arizona and New Mexico but has had no active domestic operations since 1970. While the U.S. has maintained a manganese stockpile in Wenden, AZ since the 1950s, DOD is in the process of selling it off and with no plans to replace it. From 2020-2023, the U.S. imported most of its manganese ore and concentrate needs from Gabon (63%), South Africa (23%) and then Mexico (13%). The U.S. gets its ferromanganese from intermediaries like Malaysia (24%), Australia (16%), Norway (15%), and South Africa (14%) because it is cheaper to do this than making it in the U.S.

Because manganese is predominately used as an additive to steel, the price of manganese tracks global steel production. This means manganese supply chains have evolved to serve the steel industry because metals flow to where they are used. Although the industry is very small compared to steel, manganese is increasingly used in EV batteries to improve the chemistry of NMC and LMFP products.[315] Since China dominates the EV battery space, 17 of the 19 HPMS (High-Purity Manganese Sulphate) manufacturing plants in the world (89%) are located there with the other two being in Mexico and Belgium.

S32 received a $20 million grant from DOD and a $166 million grant from DOE in 2024 to support their manganese operations in Arizona which includes a HPMSM (High-Purity Manganese Sulfate Monohydrate) production plant. It is not obvious where S32 is getting its HPMSM technology considering they have never operated in the space before and have filed no related patents. S32 believes the U.S. is the only location that their HPMSM operation might be successful based on their grants and Inflation Reduction Act 45X tax credits.

The company earned revenue of $5.4 billion in 2024 which was a slight 3% decline from the previous year with $5.6 billion. While these were big numbers, the company suffered a net loss of $203 million in 2024 which was moderately

314 U.S. Geological Survey.

315 LMFP batteries give increased ranges over LFP competitors by 10%-15%.

worse than the previous year's loss of $173 million. Most of this loss was attributable to the company's alumina/aluminum operations which together composed 63% of their base metals earnings followed by manganese (11%), copper and zinc (9% each) and then nickel (8%).[316]

S32's manganese operation in the U.S. will be a very small part of their overall metals operations, perhaps just 1%. Therefore, the success or failings of the company will be based on their other larger operations and not their Arizona footprint. Importantly, the company will struggle to get traction in the established HPMS/HPMSM market. For context, in China, Hunan Yuneng began building a 160,000 metric tpa LMFP cathode facility at the end of 2024 and a separate 100,000 metric tpa project in Shanxi Province is nearing completion. Other LMFP cathode projects are beginning in China (at least four), Japan, UK, and South Korea. It's hard to see S32 competing with the China/Asia market prices even with IRA 45X assistance.

ATI Incorporated – Specialty Metals

ATI is a U.S. manufacturer of specialty materials with 7,700 employees and facilities in Poland and China. ATI has a polymetallic business model using a range of critical minerals (nickel, titanium, chromium, manganese, zirconium, cobalt, niobium, vanadium, hafnium, tungsten) addressing the aerospace, defense, medical, energy, and electronics sectors.[317] The company's business is

316 S32's annual report ran from June 2023-June 2024.
317 ATI changed its name from Allegheny Technologies Incorporated in 2022.

weighted towards the aerospace and defense industry, which accounts for 62% of sales, specifically jet engines and airframes. Since ATI is not in the mining business, it must trade for all its metals needs.

Due to their varied metals use, with all identified as critical minerals, ATI necessarily has complex and vulnerable supply chains. For example, they source much of their zirconium, hafnium, molybdenum, and titanium sponge from China. This is problematic considering the ongoing trade and tariff wars and Beijing's willingness to enforce export restrictions to limit U.S. access to critical minerals. The company also sources nickel, cobalt, and titanium sponge from Japan who only acts as the middleman for these resources. The relative security of these supply chains depends on where the minerals ultimately originate from. At the end of 2024, the company had $1 billion committed to raw materials purchasing contracts. ATI could insure their position by hedging with long-term contracts, from geographically varied sources, and stockpiling.

ATI is particularly sensitive to its nickel supply chain, using 35,000 tons of it in 2024. They have intelligently varied their nickel sources, bringing it in from five countries: Canada, Norway, Japan, Finland, and South Africa. It is interesting to note that ATI's customers have asked them to hedge their nickel volatility exposure, pushing them to secure nickel futures contracts through the London Metals Exchange (LME). We must understand that futures are just one hedging mechanism and not an airtight guarantee, with ATI losing $4.2 million in 2024 on their LME contracts.[318]

We can see why this happened with nickel reaching a high in 2022 of $25,800 a metric ton, declining to almost $21,500 a ton in 2023, to a low of $17,000 a ton in 2024. Since ATI hedged against nickel prices going higher, and they did the opposite, they lost on their hedge. But a futures hedge is like paying homeowner's insurance, you pay it hoping your house never burns down. While the commodities industry is focused on data analytics, they can get trends wrong by overlooking qualitative analysis. It was known that Chinese companies invested heavily in nickel operations in Indonesia which raised world production from 3.2 million tons in 2022 to 3.7 million tons in 2024, with the corresponding drop in prices.

Part of any assessment of a company's viability is if their business model brings in continuing clients or if they are starved for contracts. A backlog of

318 ATI Annual Report 2024.

business indicates a company has desirable product lines which are in demand, ensuring a reliable income stream. In 2023, ATI had $3.8 billion in backorders which increased to $3.9 billion for 2024. The company anticipated 70% of the 2024 orders would be fulfilled in 2025, meaning the remainder would be pushed to 2026 along with any new orders. Most of these orders were from their High Performance Materials & Components (HPMC) division, $3.3 billion worth, and much less for the Advanced Alloys & Solutions (AAS) division which was only $600 million.[319]

ATI is a profitable company with sales of $4.3 billion in 2024, up from $4.1 billion in 2023. Gross profits also increased to $898 million in 2024 as compared to $802 million in 2023. However, net income decreased to $367 million in 2024 for an 8.4% margin as compared to $410 million in 2023 for a margin of 9.8%. ATI received Advanced Manufacturing Production Credit from the Inflation Reduction Act in the amount of $10.1 million in 2023 and $22.7 million in 2024.

Moving forward, the company needed to expertly manage its supply chain risks to avoid delayed acquisitions and higher prices. The ongoing tariff war orchestrated by the Trump administration, which already resulted in critical minerals export controls by Beijing, was a chief concern. One inflation mitigation strategy not discussed was buying into an established mining operations to ensure access to preferential long-term contracts with competitively priced products.

319 ATI Annual Report 2024.

Lynas Rare Earths

As we mentioned in the previous chapter on REE, Lynas is an Australian company with 1,100 employees that owns their Mount Weld mine and a processing plant in Malaysia. The company has their Kalgoorlie processing facility in Western Australia that produces mixed rare earth carbonate (MREC). Their Malaysian operation with solvent extraction circuits made two Heavy REE (HREE) products for the first time in 2024, dysprosium and terbium. The company has plans to increase its HREE separation capability to include SEGH (samarium, europium, gadolinium, holmium) The company's operational flow is to mine REO at Mt. Weld, ship it to and process it at Kalgoorlie, and then ship it to and refine it into saleable products in Malaysia.

It makes no obvious sense why Lynas built their REE processing plant in Malaysia and not Australia until we understand that the government gave them a 12-year tax exemption. Clearly, Australia missed the opportunity to onshore REE critical minerals, the same mistake the U.S. made. A previous REE plant run by Mitsubishi Chemical in Malaysia at Bukit Merah was determined to have leaked dangerous pollutants resulting in birth defects and leukemia. The plant was closed in 1994 and Mitsubishi has paid $100 million in clean-up costs.[320] With a new government in power and continuing opposition by residents and environmentalists, Lynas must satisfy their concerns and live with the possibility of losing public support and being shut down.

This possibility has a direct impact on the company's operations and decisions. For example, Lynas recently renewed its operating license through March 2026 which doesn't provide much long-range certainty. Part of the agreement with the Malaysian government in securing the license was increasing their R&D investment in the country from 0.5% to 1% of gross sales. Malaysia's Atomic Energy Licensing Board will oversee the R&D program focused on the removal of naturally occurring radioactive material (NORM) from their products. If Lynas fails to comply with this oversight mechanism, their operating license can be revoked.

In 2023, Malaysia announced that they would ban the export of unprocessed REE to retain more of the value chain in the country. This put pressure on Lynas to fast track their separation circuits. This also impacted China who

320 Looi, Florence. "Controversial rare earth plant in fight for survival in Malaysia." Al Jazeera, November 26, 2018.

imports 8% of their unprocessed REE from Malaysia to include from illegal mining operations.[321] To attract more downstream REE operations, the Malaysian Investment Development Authority (MIDA) announced incentives for foreign REE businesses in 2022. The country is caught between differing local and national pressures to develop its own REE industry, to retain more REE value in the country, and mitigating environmental and health damages. If China was denied access to its unprocessed REE, we can expect Chinese companies to establish domestic facilities, something they haven't had to do.

Lynas signed a contract with the DOD in 2020 to build a HREE separation facility in the U.S. In 2021, Lynas received $30 million through the Defense Production Act (DPA) to build a Light REE (LREE) separation facility as well. In 2022, the company received a $120 million grant to build its HREE facility which would be collocated with the LREE facility in Seadrift, Texas on the Gulf of Mexico. In 2023, DOD increased its support to Lynas' U.S. projects with a $258 million total grant. Presently, the Seadrift project is most likely behind schedule as Lynas has stopped promoting it and didn't mention it in their H1 2025 report.

In 2024, Lynas produced 10,900 tons of REO of which 5,650 tons were NdPr. They had sales revenue of $282 million, down greatly from $450 million in 2023. Net profit was $51 million for a robust 18% margin, a big drop from $189 million and a 42% margin in 2023. This drop in sales was due primarily to the price of NdPr which went from $60,400 a metric ton in 2023 to $44,000 a ton in 2024. Also, the price of lanthanum and cerium products dropped so far due to Chinese overproduction that Lynas couldn't sell them at a profit.[322]

The company's Malaysia location continues to look like a mistake that increased its supply chain insecurity and put its future REE production in doubt. Based on the uncertain environment in Malaysia, Lynas will need its U.S. location for strategic redundancy and the company should consider building a refinement plant and a REE permanent magnet facility in Australia. The decision to prioritize short-term tax breaks over long-term geographic logic and operational control fundamentals may not work out.

321 "Malaysia: Export of Rare Earths Minerals to be Banned." HKTDC Research, October 24, 2023.
322 Lynas' annual report runs from June 2023-June 2024.

ALCOA Corporation - Aluminum

ALCOA is the U.S.' largest aluminum producer with 13,900 employees, an international footprint, and operations in the three relevant market segments: bauxite, alumina, and aluminum.[323] ALCOA owns six bauxite mines (two in Brazil, one in Africa, one in Saudi Arabia, two in Australia) and buys bauxite from third-parties. The company has seven alumina refineries: two in Brazil, one in Europe, one in Saudi Arabia, and three in Australia. The company has thirteen aluminum smelters: three in Canada, two in the U.S., two In Brazil, four in Europe (Iceland, Spain, Norway x 2), one in Saudi Arabia, and one in Australia.

World bauxite reserves are widely distributed with thirteen different countries producing it to include Guinea (130 million tons), Australia (100 million tons), and China (93 million tons) which are responsible for 72% of all production. The U.S. produces only limited amounts of non-metallurgic bauxite. Alumina is even more widely dispersed among nineteen major producers with China (84 million tons), Australia (18 million tons), and Brazil (11 million tons) accounting for 79% of world production. The U.S. produced 720,000 tons, much less than 1% of global production in 2024.

323 Bauxite is mined and then processed for alumina which is then smelted to make aluminum.

The U.S. imports 75% of its bauxite needs, sourcing most of it from Jamaica (67%), Turkey (9%), and Guyana (8%). The U.S. is also import dependent for 59% of its alumina needs, sourcing most from Brazil (89%), Jamaica (10%), and Australia (7%). From a supply chain perspective, the U.S. is fortunate to be so close to Jamaica and Brazil which produces more than enough to meet its import needs. Having said that, the U.S. does source most of its aluminum value-chain needs from foreign countries which makes this mineral relatively insecure.

In 2024, the U.S. made 670,000 tons of aluminum which was less than 1% of world production and down 33% from 2020 when it made 1 million tons. The U.S. has increasingly imported more of its aluminum needs, going from 38% in 2020 to a much higher 47% in 2024. Overall. Aluminum production is widely distributed with twelve countries being major players and many other countries operating at a much smaller scale. China was by far the biggest producer at 43 million tons which was 60% of world production at 72 million tons. There was no one even close after China.

ALCOA produced 38 million tons of bauxite in 2024, with 71% of this capacity residing in Australia, which was more than fifteen times U.S. consumption. It is interesting to note that although ALCOA has a 14.3 million tons annual alumina production capacity, seven times more than annual U.S. consumption, none of this structure resides inside the U.S. This is because bauxite mines and alumina refiners generally are collocated and the company prefers selling to regional customers. ALCOA has a 2.6 million ton annual aluminum capacity with 345,000 tons of this residing in the U.S. from two smelters. While the company could supply four times the U.S.' aluminum needs, they produce only 50% of it. However, the company produces 960,000 tons in neighboring Quebec which could cover all U.S. importation needs.

The two most significant influences on ALCOA's aluminum smelter positioning are energy prices and associated carbon emissions. The company has two smelters in Norway and three in Quebec because they receive competitively priced hydropower. ALCOA has another smelter in Iceland because of its access to low-carbon, cheap geothermal power. A salient reason why energy intensive metal industries have left the U.S. is because of its expensive, high-carbon energy sources. This is part of the wealth-inflation trap which hangs over the entire country.

ALCOA returned to profitability in 2024 with $11.9 billion in sales and cost of goods sold at $10 billion. This was improved from the previous year with $10.5 billion in sales and $9.8 billion in cost of goods sold. Although the company's net profit was a mere $60 million for a 0.5% margin, this was better than the previous year's loss of $651 million. While third-party bauxite sales dropped by $100 million in 2024, alumina sales were up $1.1 billion, and aluminum up $314 million. This was based on the price of alumina going from $358 a ton to $472 a ton and aluminum up a mere $13 per ton. The company expects challenges in 2025 with lower bauxite production, flat alumina sales, a slight increase in aluminum production, and increased global inflation.

Because most of ALCOA's business structure resides in foreign countries, the company has a high sensitivity to global pricing of its three products, impacted most by the China market. Beyond this, increased tariffs and other trade barriers would raise ALCOA's cost of doing business and would be necessarily inflationary. Importantly, the company has constructed an ex-China supply chain, although its position in Australia is exposed to the Asia market. ALCOA requires open and secure global sea lanes for its business model to prosper with its bauxite most at risk in Australia. The company's alumina/aluminum center of gravity resides in the Western Hemisphere and Western Europe where it is easier for the U.S. to secure.

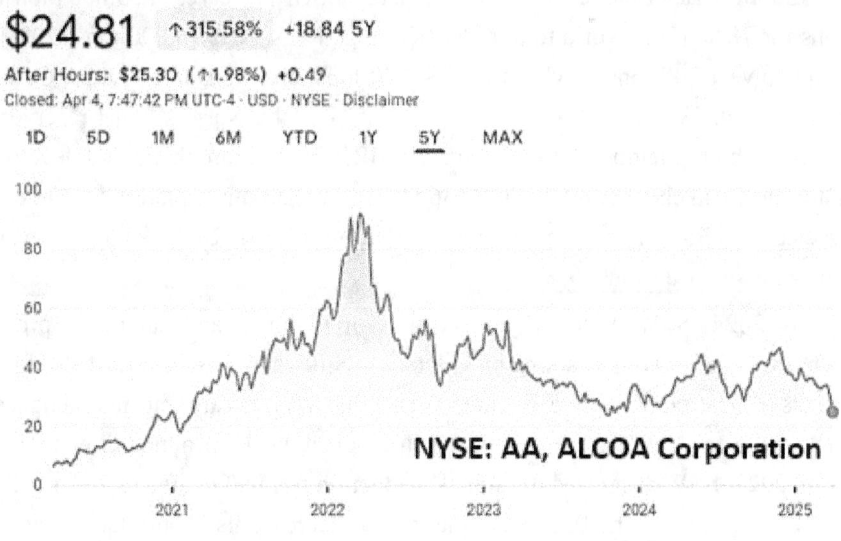

Sibanye Stillwater – Platinum Group Metals (PGM)

Sibanye Stillwater (SSW) is a South African company with an international footprint and operations in Australia, India, Finland, France, Zimbabwe, South Africa, Argentina, Mexico, the U.S. and Canada. The company's U.S. footprint includes two urban mining operations (aka recycling), a future lithium-boron JV, and PGM extraction. The company extracts gold, nickel, zinc, and PGM. PGM consist of platinum, palladium, iridium, rhodium, ruthenium, and osmium. While SSW has traditionally been a gold and PGM focused company, they have been transitioning to recycling and battery mineral operations.

In 2024, the U.S. produced an estimated 8 metric tons of palladium and 2 metric tons of platinum.[324] The country further imported 69 tons of palladium, 72 tons of platinum, 36 tons of PGM waste & scrap, 1.4 tons of iridium, 1 kilogram of osmium, 15 tons of rhodium, and 10 tons of ruthenium. Palladium prices dropped dramatically from $2,200 a troy ounce in 2020 to just $980 a troy ounce in 2024, meaning many existing operations became uneconomic. The U.S. imported 36% of its palladium needs with most coming from Russia (32%) and South Africa (32%) and then Belgium (8%). The U.S. imported 85% of its platinum needs with most coming from South Africa (42%), Belgium (12%), and Germany (10%).

South Africa is believed to have the largest PGM reserves at 63,000 metric tons for 78% of the world total of 81,000 tons. Russia has 16,000 tons (20%), Zimbabwe 1,200 tons (1.4%), the U.S. 820 tons, and Canada 310 tons. Combined, South Africa and Russia control 97.5% of the world's PGM reserves. Since both are members of the China-led BRICS coalition, this could develop into a political chokepoint. In 2024, 360 tons of palladium & platinum were extracted with South Africa accounting for 192 tons (53%), Russia 93 tons (26%), and Zimbabwe 34 tons (9%).

In 2024, SSW mined 12 metric tons of platinum and palladium products from their two operations in Montana – Stillwater East and East Boulder mines.[325] The company's Stillwater West mine was in care and maintenance status due to declining 2E prices which reached $988 an ounce, down 21% from 2023. SSW decreased its annual production from 600k ounces 2E in 2020 to 425k ounces 2E in 2025. SSW planned to decrease its 2E production even

324 These are U.S. Geological survey estimates that differ from SSW 2025 reporting.

325 SSW recovered 425,842 ounces of 2E products from their two active mines. 2E = platinum & palladium. 35.274 ounces = 1 kilogram. 1,000 kgs = 1 metric ton.

lower in 2025, to just 225k -270k 2E ounces based on costs of $1,420 to $1,460 per ounce.

SSW's U.S. PGM recycling operations for the year were 316k 3E ounces, down significantly from 850k 3E ounces in 2020.[326] The company observed macro pressures on new vehicle production which meant owners kept their existing vehicles longer so there were less vehicles scrapped and thus less 3E to recover. Their overall recycling operations consist of facilities in Pennsylvania, Mexico, and India. U.S. PGM recycling operations contributed $17 million for the year while recycling of other metals contributed $15 million.

SSW is under severe financial distress. Although it had revenue of $6.1 billion in 2024 and 2023, it incurred net losses of $311 million in 2024, an improvement from a net loss of $2 billion the previous year. The company anticipates receiving 45X tax credits for its PGM recycling operations for 2023 and 2024, adding a total of $91 million in revenue. SSW estimated they would receive $120 million in 45X tax credits for 2024. In January 2025, DOE provided a $996 million loan guarantee to Rhyolite Ridge (R2) LLC to extract lithium and boron and develop an onsite lithium carbonate processing facility in Nevada. The R2 project is a JV between Australian mining company Ioneer LTD and SSW.

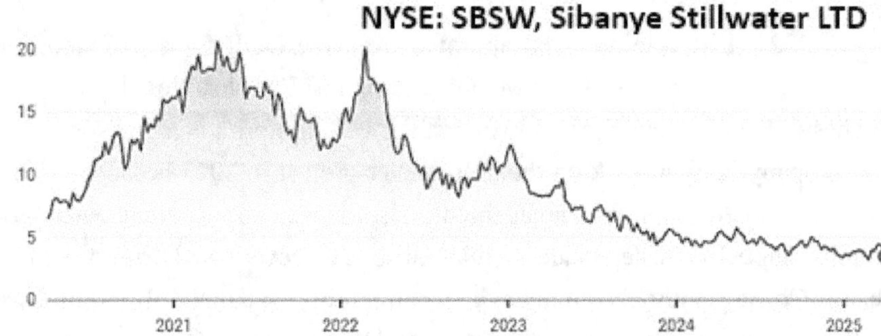

SSW's U.S. operations are under pressure because they rely primarily on the production of new ICE (Internal Combustion Engine) cars that require cat-

326 3E = platinum, palladium, & rhodium.

alytic converters and then the scrapping of older ICE vehicles to recover these same catalytic converters. If this circular process becomes disrupted, then they have interwoven demand and supply issues. However, SSW has much larger problems in that the more the world transitions from ICE vehicles to BEVs, the more their total addressable market (TAM) shrinks. When the U.S. transitions to an all-BEV fleet, it will no longer have platinum, palladium, and rhodium supply chain insecurity.

Li-Cycle - Battery Minerals

Li-Cycle Holdings Corporation is a Canadian company with 240 employees specializing in the recycling of lithium-ion batteries (LIB) and the production of shredded metals and a mixed minerals "black mass" which includes lithium, nickel sulphate, cobalt sulphate, and MHP (Mixed Hydroxide Precipitate). The company has offices in Canada (Ontario), Europe (Germany), the U.S. (Arizona, Alabama), and Asia. Li-Cycle had in place the capacity to recycle 50,000 tons of LIB per year. The company uses proprietary recycling technology that is protected by seven different patents.

The company had black mass offtake agreements with Glencore (an international mining company with HQ in Switzerland) and Traxys (a global raw materials trading company with HQ is Luxembourg). Li-Cycle had agreements to provide LG Chem and LG Energy Solutions 20,000 tons of nickel. However, in 2024, the company didn't receive enough LIB volume to recycle to cover its operational costs. This limited revenue was compounded by the reality that the company expanded too quickly, forcing the company to stop its plans for hubs in France, Norway, and Canada.

In 2024, Li-Cycle received approval from the DOE for a $475 million Advanced Technology Vehicles Manufacturing (ATVM) loan to advance their Rochester Hub in New York. However, their U.S. footprint is in question with the company halting work on their Rochester project in 2023 because of cost overruns and financial mismanagement. Also, it was not apparent what geographic sense Rochester made in relation to the recycling of battery supply chains. Consequently, the company stopped trading on the NYSE in February 2025 due to the drop in value of its stock and began trading OTC.

In 2024, Li-Cycle suffered net losses of $137.7 million, almost the same as 2023 with net losses of $138 million. The company had revenue of $28 million in 2024, almost triple what it earned in 2023, which was $9.7 million. Li-Cycle recycled 9,113 tons of battery material resulting in 5,395 tons of black mass, although they sold 5,919 tons. This meant the company sold its black mass for $4,730 per ton. The company's cost of sales was $76.6 million meaning each ton of black mass cost over $12,940 for a loss of $8,210 per ton.

Li-Cycle operates in an already very competitive market where China dominates due to their established LIB recycling industry. The end-of-life (EOL) LIB black mass reached a high of $23,000 a ton at the end of 2021 in China and then declined sharply after, to $7,200 a ton today.[327] Process LIB black mass reached slightly higher prices of $25,000 due to its superior mineral quality before also declining sharply. Since black mass competes with traditionally mined products, its price must track with virgin minerals or below to be a better option to buy. LIB recycling competitors include Redwood Materials in the U.S., Fortum Battery Recycling in Finland, and Posco in Poland.

Recycling LIB, also known as "urban mining", has many advantages over traditional extraction. Since an urban mining company deals with resources already present in the country, it has an incredibly simplified supply chain. For an urban miner, any big city with a large population of BEVs is its supply chain. Therefore, a LIB recycler is best served by setting up shop in Los Angeles, New York City, or Chicago. Also, the urban miner has virtually no environmental concerns, foreign supply chain worries or immediate tariff concerns.

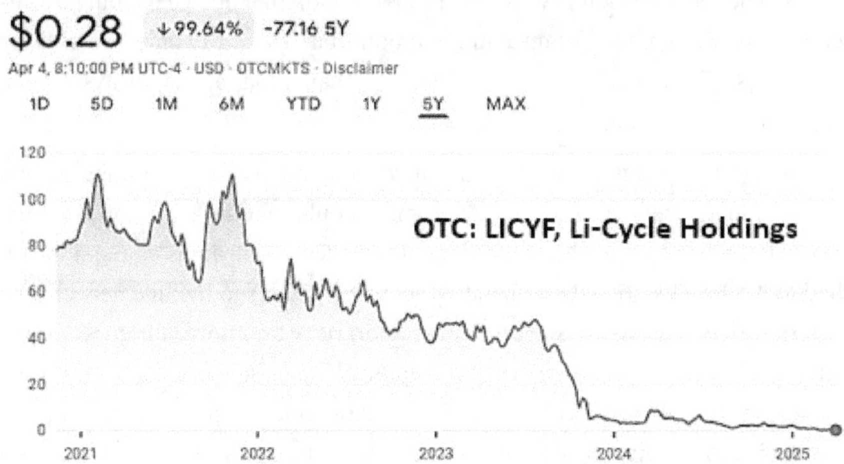

327 LCO (Lithium Cobalt Oxide) Battery Black Mass, 23%-30% cobalt content, metric ton, April 2025.

To achieve critical minerals security, it is crucial that the U.S. develop a robust, successful, and mandatory battery minerals recycling industry. Once critical minerals enter the U.S., they must not leave or be discarded, they need to stay in the country and be reused. This demands the building out of an urban mining enterprise in the U.S. and a readjustment of the country's "everything is disposable" mindset. One important way the U.S. government can help this still-fragile industry is purchasing black mass for the National Defense Stockpile. It is imperative that the U.S. provides the support, capital, and has the patience to get companies like Li-Cycle operating profitably at commercial scale.

CMI Fund

As seen from this chapter, it was hard to find successful, publicly owned, U.S. critical mineral companies. Of these ten companies, only four were U.S. owned, five operated at a loss in 2024, and three had negative returns over the last five years. If we put \$100 into this fund five years ago, \$10 into each company, we would have made a profit of \$134.70. In comparison, an S&P 500 Index Fund would have returned 24% less over the same period. It's up to the individual whether they prefer the low-risk security of the S&P 500 fund or the higher returns and sometimes dumpster fire of the CMI Fund. It's interesting to see that the three companies with the highest returns had complex supply chains. The real question is what this fund will look like one year from now after the expansion of the Trump administration's tariff war. But only two of these companies, 5N and ATI, have metal supply chains that are majority-sourced from China: germanium and tungsten.

If the U.S. wants to bolster its critical minerals security through a fund like this, there are measures the government could take to help. For example, it could commit to purchasing products from these companies as required for the Stockpile. This includes expanding its requirements to include new critical materials like black mass, something that didn't exist until we started recycling batteries. Washington could also backstop investors' risk by underwriting losses and limiting them to 10%. Because it takes time for new critical mineral companies to solidify their business, there could be an investor lock-in period of five years. However, with these government assurances come government requirements. Companies in the index would have to meet published management, financial, and operational best practices for them to be included in the fund. If they violated these best practices, as verified by annual audits, they would be removed from the fund.

Critical Minerals Index Fund (CMIF), April 2020-April 2025					
Mineral	**Company**	**Market Cap**	**P/E Ratio**	**5-Year**	**Return**
Aluminum	ALCOA	$64 billion	88	315%	$31.50
Beryllium	Materion	$1.7 billion	287	131%	$13.10
Germanium	5N+	$338 million	23	246%	$24.60
Graphite	Novonix	$158 million	0	(-61%)	($6.10)
Lithium	Albemarle	$7.8 billion	0	26%	$2.60
Manganese	South 32	$8.1 billion	0	27%	$2.70
PGM	Sibanye	$2.4 billion	0	(-47%)	($4.70)
Rare Earths	Lynas	$4.1 billion	135	373%	$37.30
Black Mass	Li-Cycle	$12.4 million	0	(-99%)	($9.90)
Spec Metals	ATI Inc.	$6 billion	17	436%	$43.60
	Total:	**$94.6 billion**		**5-Year Return:**	**$134.70**

**S&P 500 Index: 103% Five-year return on $100 investment = $103.00*

If there was more than one option for a particular mineral, the government could invite into the fund the company with the most secure supply chains. For example, if Li-Cycle produced competitively priced lithium from its domestically recycled batteries, they would get the nod as opposed to, say, Rio Tinto which only had foreign sourcing. Companies that did the most to avoid adversarial and contested mineral sourcing would be the best candidates. Also, companies that were adept at sidestepping geographic, political, technological, and production chokepoints to ensure reliable mineral flows would be ideal. Companies that did this would be rewarded with access to much larger capital as promised by this fund.

While this CMI Fund is a theoretical exercise, Interior Secretary Burgum brought up the idea of a critical minerals Sovereign Wealth Fund (SWF) in April 2025. The SWF would act as a financial backstop to those companies that invested in approved critical minerals projects to limit their losses. However, because the federal government operates at a deficit, the SWF would incur more debt spending. If the SWF was used to invest directly in critical minerals projects, our CMI Fund exercise shows that it could be done profitably. The

SWF managers would have to do their homework, choose carefully, and include foreign companies.

Because the U.S. has the largest economy in the world, it can access and unlock capital to move the critical minerals enterprise forward. This should be done in a manner that encourages public investment, minimizes investor risk, and rewards economically viable companies. However, we cannot escape the reality that China thinks in terms of its Geopolitical Return on Investment when securing its minerals and this means Beijing will subsidize uneconomic operations. The U.S. may end up doing everything it can in the minerals space and still come up short in comparison to China's raw materials machine. In this environment we should remember a quote from Sean Connery in *The Untouchables.* After recognizing that everything they were doing to put away Chicago mobster Al Capone wasn't enough, he asked Elliot Ness: And then what are you willing to do?

Conclusion

Ten Minerals Truths

The Planetary Minerals System

Our Earth has a singular metals and minerals system that doesn't recognize humanity's contrived boundaries or exclusive economic zones. A country's inherent minerals wealth is based on happenstance and where the lines on a map coincide with randomly placed mineral deposits. However, human knowledge combined with technology can improve a nation's access to these minerals or develop substitutes. For instance, any nation can develop synthetic graphite manufacturing which obviates the need for natural flake graphite reserves. Or a country may develop the ability to extract metals like lithium and magnesium from the ocean. Therefore, it is possible for a country to access minerals previously denied them through technological innovation.

Countries have tried at various times in history to secure more of the planetary minerals system by expanding their borders. The Roman Empire did this two millennia ago with their conquest of the Mediterranean to secure the metals essential for their Iron Age society. Europe colonized the Western Hemisphere, Africa, and parts of Asia from the 1400s-1800s, resulting in the most concentrated control of metals and minerals ever seen in human history. The U.S. also embraced this idea as illustrated by moving its borders further westward through the Louisiana, Southwest, and Alaska Purchases.

However, beginning with the Napoleonic Wars and ending with World War II, the great European countries consumed themselves in a series of wars of annihilation. These conflicts destroyed Europe's ability to project power globally, resulting directly in the loss of their colonies and accompanying resources. With worldwide decolonization came the idea of resource nationalism, where the minerals of the former colonies now belonged to each of the newly independent states. This decentralization of minerals control resulted in a complex international minerals regime characterized by political fragmentation.

The idea of expanding geographic boundaries to secure more of the planetary minerals system largely went out of vogue until only recently. With Russia's invasion of Ukraine in 2022, Moscow subsequently offered a minerals deal with the U.S. based on the parts of Ukraine that they conquered. While Russia didn't invade Ukraine to exploit its metals and minerals, it became a target of opportunity for them. In 2019 and again in 2025, the Trump administration expressed its interest in "buying" Greenland from Denmark based on the desire to secure its minerals resources. If this were to happen, it would be the first time since 1941 that a country expanded its borders to acquire new territory for the express purpose of securing its minerals.

Ubiquitous Minerals Insecurity

As discussed, no country inherently has the minerals within its boundaries to satisfy its everyday industrial needs and thus every country lives with a certain level of minerals insecurity. Where a country falls on the scale of insecurity can change over time, depending on what it does to address this problem and the dynamics of the international environment. Importantly, we often find a country's minerals security improving or declining based on how threatened they feel in the international system.

For example, the U.S. had a high level of minerals security through the 1930s due to its abundant minerals reserves and relatively simple economy. But, as the U.S. entered WWII and relied on increasingly complex technology, requiring a growing variety of minerals, it became increasingly minerals insecure. During the war and through the 1950s, the U.S. enacted robust measures which temporarily increased its overall minerals security. After the Soviet Union collapsed, the U.S. lost interest in its own minerals security as it felt confident and unthreatened in the world. Thirty years later, the U.S. again became interested in minerals security based on the perceived threat to its standing in the international system by China.

We also see that countries can take a different approach, as China has. Instead of being reactive and practicing crisis management as policy like the U.S., Beijing took proactive measures to improve its own minerals security, beginning in the late 1980s. In one example, China built the world's largest natural and synthetic graphite industry to support established industrial needs like refractories and their growing battery industry. Today, China dominates the graphite space, creating a global production chokepoint which the U.S. now relies on.

Beyond this example, Beijing invested in its metals and minerals supply chains to such a degree that the U.S. found itself majority-sourcing twenty-five of its identified critical minerals from China. Beijing did this by providing the U.S. continuing access to these minerals, creating a sense of security, and not triggering a defensive response. The U.S. eventually realized that it lost control of its supply chains with the minerals security provided by China just a temporary illusion. Beijing was always prepared to use its control of the U.S.' critical minerals supply chains as geopolitical leverage.

Cellphone Syndrome

Nothing has contributed more to the U.S.' ongoing minerals insecurity than Cellphone Syndrome where increasingly sophisticated technology needs have created equally complex metals and minerals supply chains. For perspective, the Roman Empire, which controlled a quarter of the globe's population, ran on just seven metals. In contrast, the modern cellphone requires at least thirty-five minerals, making it impossible for any one country to source them. The next best option is to control as much of the midstream processing as possible.

Every cellphone requires a lithium-ion battery (LIB) which most likely consists of lithium-nickel-manganese-cobalt chemistry for the cathode and then a mixture of synthetic and natural flake graphite for the anode. For the cathode, the U.S. has both brine and hard rock lithium deposits but extracts little to date. The U.S. also mines low volumes of nickel and cobalt but no manganese. For the anode, the U.S. has no active natural flake graphite mines or synthetic graphite operations. Not only does the U.S. have to import every one of these minerals, but it doesn't actually manufacture batteries. It assembles them using imported technology from China, South Korea, and Japan.

Another integral component of cellphones is rare earth permanent magnets (REPM) used in speakers, microphones, and micro vibration motors. Until 2023, the U.S. exported all its light rare earth elements (LREE) to China for processing and still needs to export its heavy REE (HREE) for refinement. It wasn't until 2025 that the U.S. regained a modest domestic REPM manufacturing capability, previously relying on China for 93% of its REPM needs. To put this disparity in perspective, China makes more REPM in a single day than the U.S. makes all year.

Finally, the cellphone's electronics require a host of other critical minerals like gallium, indium, tin, germanium, arsenic, tantalum, and tungsten, all of which the U.S. doesn't mine or produce for primary smelting. In just one illustration, China produces 99% of the world's gallium, used for LED displays, meaning the U.S. directly or indirectly sourced all its needs from its chief competitor. Many people may be unaware that Apple iPhones are not made in the U.S., they are made by the Taiwanese company Foxconn. Their largest facility is in Zhengzhou, Henan Province, China with over 200,000 workers. Ironically, the most "American" of all U.S. technologies is Chinese-made, facilitated by China's own critical minerals supply chains.

Mutually Assured Minerals

Over many centuries, the world developed the concept of Mutually Assured Minerals (MAM), where countries agreed to freely trade minerals with each other. MAM has become the norm and only in rare circumstances, usually during a war, would a country refuse to sell minerals to another country. After WWI, the victorious allied powers discussed the establishment of a global trading cartel administered by the League of Nations to guarantee the flow of minerals to all countries. Along with this idea of MAM, the allies also discussed shutting off this same flow of minerals to nations that started wars of aggression.

At the end of WWII, the U.S., French and British Empires controlled most of the world's minerals resources through their colonies which reinforced the idea of MAM. However, the MAM concept was confronted by an increasingly fractured world that rejected colonialism while newly independent countries embraced resource nationalism. Now, the U.S. and other major industrial powers had to trade with scores of former colonies to ensure their metals and minerals needs. While the U.S. competed with the Soviet Union for resources, notably on the African continent, the MAM concept still dominated global groupthink.

When the U.S. became disinterested in its own minerals security after the fall of the Soviet Union, the MAM concept justified its actions. As China began securing its own critical minerals supply chains while simultaneously capturing the U.S.', it intentionally supported the MAM concept which reinforced the U.S.' offshoring efforts. MAM was the overarching conceptual framework that meant the U.S. could always trade for the minerals it needed. While there were some threats to MAM like China halting its exports of REE to Japan in 2010, these were short-lived aberrations that didn't represent the norm.

The U.S. began eroding both the MAM concept and its associated reality beginning in 2018 with its trade wars directed against China which also undermined the concept of Mutually Assured Technology (MAT). Beijing retaliated by enforcing incrementally stricter export restrictions that severed the U.S.' critical minerals supply chains majority-sourced from China. MAM only works when all parties buy into the concept and can change quickly if one or more parties defect from its conceptual regime. In this case, the U.S.' shattering of MAT led to Beijing's rejection of MAM.

Denial of Disruption

The concept of Mutually Assured Minerals is underpinned by the established system of free and secure trade which itself requires a continuous Denial of Disruption (DOD). This is because the global flow of metals and minerals can only occur if their movement between continents and countries is assured. Consequently, every nation has an inherent interest in maintaining the ability to trade freely since their economies rely on it. However, there can be defectors from this free trade regime which raises complications as to who will provide the necessary DOD.

Since 90% of all trade occurs by sea, this makes the six major shipping chokepoints geostrategic terrain. These chokepoints are: 1) the Malacca Strait (between West Sumatra and Malaysia), 2) the Suez Canal and Bab el-Mandeb Strait (between Yemen and Djibouti and Eritrea), 3) the Cape of Good Hope (southern point of the African Continent), 4) the Gibraltar Strait (between Spain and Morocco), 5) the Panama Canal, and 6) the Drake Passage (between South America and Antarctica).[328] Global trade can only occur if these chokepoints are open to continuous shipping.

The Panama Canal is a 51-mile waterway cutting across the country that separates North and South America. The U.S. built the canal from 1904-1914 and managed the passageway until 1977 when it was turned over to Panama. About 5% of world shipping and 40% of U.S. container traffic passes through the canal. Of concern to the U.S., in 1988, the Hong Kong company CK Hutchinson won the contract to run the two major ports on either end of the

328 For the southern tip of South America, alternate routes include the Beagle Passage and the Straits of Magellan.

canal. In March 2025, the U.S. pressured Panama to force CK Hutchinson's divesture of the ports, selling their operations to a U.S. backed consortium for the tidy sum of $22.8 billion. The Trump administration stated that China's control of the ports was a national security threat, although they had nothing to do with the actual passage of maritime traffic. Regardless, this was a DOD effort by the U.S. to protect a critical military and economic chokepoint.

In another DOD operation, U.S. forces bombed Iranian-backed Houthi rebels in Yemen from March-May 2025. Yemen sits astride the Mandeb Straight, where the Gulf of Aden becomes the Red Sea and enters the Suez Canal. In 2024, 13,200 ships passed through the canal carrying 524 million tons of cargo.[329] Justification for the strikes included the rebels' targeting of commercial and military shipping passing through the strait. In this case, the U.S. flexed its military muscle as a global systems administrator to keep shipping lanes open that were used by all countries to include China. It is reasonable to assume that the world's most powerful countries will take action to keep global economic chokepoints open which explains China's extreme interest in the South China Sea and the Malacca Strait.

Just in Time Minerals

Hand in hand with the assumption of Mutually Assured Minerals came the idea of maximizing metals and minerals supply chain efficiencies. To the American 90-day profit driven brain it made no sense to pay an extra penny for excess minerals to just lay around in a warehouse or at a dock somewhere. Accordingly, the U.S. developed the mindset that it only needed minerals when it needed them and that its Denial of Disruption efforts would ensure that this would happen on time, every time. Like all self-serving strategic assumptions, the Just in Time Minerals (JITM) idea works until it doesn't.

For the U.S., the single greatest example of JITM thinking was its willful negligence of the National Defense Stockpile. While the U.S. previously took its critical minerals security seriously, this degraded over time as the Cold War came to a quiet end. Successive U.S. administrations saw the stockpile as something to be sold off for short-term budget balancing and saw no need to reinvest in it since it assumed it could always get the minerals it needed. Today, the U.S. has only 4% of what it would need for a one-year critical minerals reserve showing how Washington went all-in on JITM.

329 htps://www.suezcanal.gov.eg/English/Navigation/Pages/NavigationStatistics

The U.S. should have been disabused of its JITM groupthink after experiencing the COVID-19 pandemic from 2020-2022. The pandemic severely disrupted global supply chains, delaying deliveries, and increasing average shipping rates from China to the U.S. by 178% in 2020.[330] All critical minerals were impacted with prices of battery-grade lithium skyrocketing 700% by the end of 2022. However, the U.S. military had no chokepoint to bomb for a Denial of Disruption operation because an unseen virus isn't intimidated by an aircraft carrier. Because JITM thinking meant there was no need to store mineral reserves as a form of insurance against emergencies, when raw material prices exploded, the U.S. was unable to mitigate the soaring inflation.

In 2024, the U.S.' growing trade war with China resulted in Beijing responding with retaliatory export restrictions on critical minerals which the U.S. depended. This meant the U.S. would face increased lead times and much higher prices on a wide range of minerals from Heavy REE to gallium and tungsten. Since Beijing rejected the concept of MAM, this necessarily meant JITM was no longer viable because China controlled half of the U.S.' critical mineral supply chains. JITM only works if the far-flung global supply chain runs like a Swiss watch, and because the U.S. was unprepared for this self-induced disruption, time had run out.

Be Like Water

Many economic strategists don't initially realize that minerals flow to where they are used. This means minerals almost always go from where they are extracted to where they are refined, from the seller to the buyer. For example, the majority of the global supply of battery minerals flow to Asia and China because that is where EV battery manufacturing takes place. It is most efficient from a cost and supply chain perspective for sellers and buyers to do business directly with each other to eliminate third-party intermediaries. Thus, production acts as a powerful magnet, drawing metals and minerals supply chains to it.

While this direct sales model is most desirable, it doesn't always happen due to free trade disruptions such as export controls. For example, in April 2025, Beijing put export restrictions on the direct sales of seven different REE to the U.S. It made sense that the U.S.' Asian allies (Japan, Taiwan, and South Korea) would subsequently act as go-betweens to purchase REE from China and then resell it to the U.S. at a premium. That same month, Beijing contacted

330 U.S. International Trade Commission.

numerous South Korean businesses warning them not to do this with the implication that China would cut off its REE exports to Seoul in retaliation.

Once there is a buyer and a seller, pressure is placed on the market to complete the transaction, even if this means operating outside of established norms. As mentioned in a previous chapter, as much as one-third of China's REE production is done illegally and sold on the black market. In this way, extra-legal sellers perform intermediary functions to get minerals to a buyer, a process that can include passage through a third country to "wash" the transaction. Also, the smuggling of cobalt from the Congo is well documented where the minerals often pass through several other African countries before export to hide their origins.

While it can be difficult for a country to manage and control the flow of its own minerals, it is even more challenging for a third-party country to try and restrict the same. In WWII, the U.S. put great effort into restricting Germany's access to tungsten which was still able to secure this metal from black-market sellers in China through 1944 via U-boats. And during the Cold War, the U.S. tried to restrict the Soviet Union from acquiring lithium for its hydrogen bomb program. Moscow was able to secure the lithium from a variety of sources both domestic (Trans-Baikal, Urals) and external (East Germany, Czechoslovakia, North Korea, Rhodesia). Minerals find a way.

Endless Resource Fallacy

The U.S. political leadership has long succumbed to the Endless Resource Fallacy (ERF) which is the idea that the U.S., and other countries, can mine forever to get the resources its society and economy need. This is clearly not true since the Earth's planetary minerals system is finite and humanity must work within these limits. In other words, we got what we got. The world's various mining associations probably won't tell you that the logical conclusion to continuing resource consumption over time is inevitable minerals extinction.

As early as the 1920s, the U.S. debated the role of mining as part of an overarching critical minerals strategy. Domestic companies wanted to fill the U.S.' minerals needs to include the National Defense Stockpile. The godfather of the U.S.' critical minerals strategy, Dr. Charles Kenneth Leith, argued the opposite. Since the U.S.' mineral deposits were obviously finite, the country should use imported minerals as much as possible to preserve the U.S.' own limited resources. Continuous domestic mining would put the U.S.' economic mineral reserves on a trajectory to zero.

With this in mind, let's take a look at the Canadian company Lundin Mining Incorporated which owns and operates the Eagle Mine in Michigan and produces copper and nickel. Nickel is an identified critical mineral by U.S. Geological Survey and copper will likely be in the next several years. The mine began operations in 2014 and is forecasted to be depleted by 2030. From a critical minerals strategy perspective, once these metals have been completely mined out, how did this make the U.S. any more secure? If these metals went to the national stockpile, one could argue that this did enhance U.S. minerals security, but they didn't.

Since operations like the Eagle Mine will eventually exhaust the U.S.' finite minerals reserves, the only viable long-term solution is the recycling of all metals and minerals. This requires the U.S. to change its disposable mindset where it has developed the destructive habit of throwing everything in a landfill when they are done with it. Many metals are infinitely recyclable which means Urban Mining is the only answer to our terminal minerals depletion dilemma. However, this requires societies to make products from the start with the idea of recycling baked into their design. Over a long enough timeline, the nations with the most robust Urban Mining enterprises will enjoy the most critical minerals security.

Crisis Management is Bad Policy

Because the U.S. became disinterested in its own minerals security and no longer had a conceptually viable strategy, it resorted to what it did best – crisis management. With no credible National Defense Stockpile, half of its critical minerals majority-sourced from China, and most technology supporting supply chains flowing to Asia/China, the U.S. thought it would "just figure it out" when push came to shove. From 2023-2025, China emplaced increasingly strict retaliatory export restrictions on its critical minerals trade with the U.S., putting Washington's default "parts of a strategy" to the test.

In one example of many, Tesla announced in April 2025 that its Optimus humanoid robot project was on hold because it could no longer source rare-earth permanent magnets (REPM) from China. This was a stunning admission by a tech company who had a BEV manufacturing plant in Shanghai and should have understood the REPM supply chain because they used them in their electric motors. Even more perplexing was the fact that Elon Musk personally participated in the Trump administration's chaotic tariff war with China. How did Musk not forecast and then prepare for REPM supply chain disruption that he helped to orchestrate? Musk realized too late that his company's assumption-based strategy based on Mutually Assured Minerals and Just in Time Minerals worked until it didn't.

The salient lesson from this experience is that a country needs secure critical mineral supply chains before they need secure critical minerals supply chains. It takes many years to develop resilient pathways for just a single mineral. A country can't just press the easy button and have a lithium hard rock mine magically appear seconds later. What ensures resilient minerals supply chains is consistent, coherent policy executed over time and space. The U.S.' lack of critical minerals planning resulted in an emergency of its own doing.

The U.S.' non-existent graphite industry is the perfect illustration of the long time-horizon required for a secure minerals supply chain. The Australian company NOVONIX began its synthetic graphite anode division in 2017, with the advantages of a 100% domestically sourced supply chain and IP ownership. However, eight years later, they still didn't have a product. Most likely, it won't be until 2030 that they can produce graphite anode material (GAM) at commercial scale which will be at the tail end of a fourteen-year process. Secure minerals supply chains cannot be created quickly in times of emergency.

Geologists Don't Make Policy

It should be clear to the reader that domestic politics, defined by competition between self-interested stakeholders, have largely driven the U.S.' critical minerals policy since the 1950s. I recently mentioned to an acquaintance that "geologists don't make policy." And by that I meant experts in the field aren't the ones who make critical minerals policy decisions for the U.S. government. To be sure, experts are questioned by politicians during specific events like periodic congressional hearings, but there is no critical minerals expert sitting as the Metals and Minerals Czar driving intelligent policy. My friend was mildly insulted by my observation that he, as a career geologist, did not drive our national minerals strategy and never would.

Perhaps the most influential geologist in U.S. history was Professor Charles K. Leith, referenced several times in this book. He sat on every important critical minerals board for the U.S. government from the 1920s through the 1950s, and it took him at least a decade to convince the Roosevelt administration that it should have a National Defense Stockpile. While Leith swung a big minerals stick, what really drove the U.S. strategy was confrontation with the wartime reality that it had insecure supply chains and it needed to do something other than business as usual if it wanted to win the war. In other words, crisis management as a default policy.

To reinforce this idea, what mineralogist advised the many successive administrations from Nixon to Trump to sell off the National Defense Stockpile until it was whittled down to virtually nothing? What geologist told the Clinton and Bush administrations that it was a smart to sell off Magnequench so that the country no longer had a domestic rare earth permanent magnet manufacturing capability? Who was the educated academic who insisted that the U.S. should close its only Rare Earth research institute in 1998? And what global minerals supply chain expert made the argument that the U.S. didn't need to pair manufacturing with battery minerals to ensure its access to these raw materials?

If the U.S. wants to change its critical minerals security trajectory, it requires a strategy based on consistent policy across administrations that is continuously advised by experienced experts. There is no issue more bipartisan than this. The existing system doesn't work where the country's geological experts, U.S. Geological Survey, are buried so deep under the Department of the Interior that the executive branch acts like they don't exist. A dedicated group of mineral experts should be positioned at the highest level of government to advise both the President and Congress. But this also means that these same political entities need to actually listen to the experts and take their advice. While geologists don't make critical minerals policy, they should.

Epilogue

Iron and Steel

Kurakhove - December 2024

The Elektrostal steel plant sat like a tired metal giant, anchoring the west end of Kurakhove, a small gritty town whose identity was part industrial, part agricultural. Next to the Elektrostal was the equally imposing Kurakhove Power Station, a dirty coal-fueled plant built during Stalin's first Five-Year Plan. The eastern part of town was residential, a combination of ugly concrete Soviet apartment buildings and modest individual homes. The town was built next to a reservoir on its northern side. Everything else was open farmland as far as the eye could see, broken up by lines of trees that served as windbreaks to protect the crops.

Even though Kurakhove was less than thirty miles west of Donetsk, the Russians still hadn't captured it. When they started their offensive in early 2022, the Russians advanced to the north and south of the town, hoping to flank it and cut it off. However, they got bogged down in the open fields, lost momentum, and dug in. Static warfare ensured for almost three years as the Russians couldn't muster enough forces to get past Ukraine's trench system outside Donetsk. Moscow had expended their strength early on while taking Mariupol and their failed attempt to capture Kyiv. The Donetsk-Kurakhove front became a backwater on the FLOT, military speak for the Forward Line of Troops.

Although the opposing forces in Kurakhove didn't know it, the town sat at the nexus of the country's untapped mineral deposits. Under their feet, reserves of titanium, lithium, uranium, and rare earths all came together. Although Ukraine was mainly known for its iron ore and manganese deposits, in fact Hitler directed their capture in 1941, it was also blessed with a variety of minerals deemed "critical" by the U.S. and Europe. When Trump returned to office in January 2025, these critical minerals became a political bargaining chip between Washington, Kyiv, Moscow, and the European Union. But that didn't matter right now. Those were vague topics that out of touch politicians talked about - it didn't concern the business of soldiers.

The Russians started grinding westward from Donetsk in the summer of 2024, finally forcing the Ukrainian defenders to fall back from their established positions. By August, the Russians were directing airstrikes against Kurakhove proper, hitting the power plant several times with glide bombs. This was part of the Russian strategy to take out the Ukrainian power grid, making it harder to fight while wrecking their economy. At the end of October, Russian forces were pressuring the eastern end of the town, finally gaining a foothold while taking heavy casualties from drones and minefields. Then, they blew up the reservoir's dam, flooding the surrounding terrain, hoping to block Ukrainian troop movements. In November, the Russians were fighting house to house as they moved forward to capture the Elektrostal. It would take three months and thousands of dead and wounded before they got there.

WARNING: The reader is advised to go back to the safety of earlier chapters.

Dusk settled in as Vitali moved his squad up to the west side of the Elektrostal. He waited on one knee until he saw three red lights flash from a blown-out window stacked with sandbags. That was the signal that he was observed by the unit inside and it was okay to move forward. They only went in and out of the defunct steel factory under the cover of darkness because of pervasive drone surveillance by the *katsaps*. That was old-school derogatory slang for the Russians referring to their goatees. The Ukrainians also called them "orcs" from the movie *The Hobbit* because they resembled the mindless hordes from Mordor, dying in droves as they carried out their evil mission.

As soon as Vitali stepped through the doorway, he moved to the side so his squad could file past him. His men knew to go to the second floor and get into positions for the night, replacing the crew that had just finished a 24-hour shift. Vitali fist-bumped the other squad leader who had flashed the "okay" with his light.

"We didn't think you and your girlfriends would show up tonight," the squad leader said mockingly.

"Well, we were at your Mom's house for dinner, she's a really good cook," Vitali responded.

"Fuck you, bitch," said the squad leader, smiling. He then gave Vitali a quick summary, "It's been relatively quiet besides the usual bullshit. I think they're bringing up reinforcements. The orcs will probably do another push tonight. We reinforced the entrances some more and fixed the window netting. The mines are still in place between us and the power plant but they can get around them."

The ground floor entrances and windows were all blocked with machinery so the orcs couldn't get in and the netting kept drones from flying inside the building. The mines would slow down but not stop the orcs who would send "meat waves" to clear the way. Vitali's squad had rotated through the steel plant several times over the last few weeks and knew the drill. The other squad filed down the stairs and out the door, back to friendly lines. The squad leader counted six of them out, which made him the seventh.

"Don't let the orcs catch you jerking off on your guard shift, bro," the squad leader gave Vitali a final fist-bump as the last soldier exited the steel plant.

"Have fun with your boyfriend tonight, sailor," Vitali said with a straight face. The other squad leader gave him the middle finger, then disappeared into the night. Shit-talking each other was both tradition and a finely honed art among soldiers, it was how they kept each other mentally tough. It also served to check each other's sanity and morale. If a soldier couldn't take rough humor, then they couldn't take the horrors of the battlefield. If you couldn't handle someone talking about fucking your mother, then how the fuck were you supposed to handle your best friend getting their fucking head blown off right next to you? Most civilians never understood this.

Vitali went upstairs to check on his men. He knew Fedor, the assistant squad leader, would already have them in place. "Fedor" was really just a nickname but they called him that because he looked like the Russian MMA fighter Fedor Emelianenko. He was thirty years old, big and blocky, with thinning, short-cropped hair. He had a tattoo of the unit crest on his neck, an emerald blue shield with a white anchor. Fedor used to live in Donetsk but left in 2014 when the Russian-backed separatists took it over. The squad routinely referred to him as "the Russian spy."

Inside the Elektrostal steel plant.

"How we doing?" Vitali asked.

"Pavlo is set up on the south side with a good loophole." Fedor pointed to the outline of a figure laying on a mattress on the concrete floor. Pavlo was from the capital, Kyiv, and joined the army two years ago. Although he used to work part-time in a bakery while going to college to become an accountant, he was a good shot. Pavlo was armed with an M110 SASS (Semi-Automatic Sniper Rifle) which was painted flat-earth and fired the standard NATO 7.62 mm round. The SASS had a Knights Armament suppressor and Leupold 3.5-10x40 mm scope with illuminated reticle. He would use the moonlight and any mistakes to find targets, like an orc lighting a cigarette. While he was not a skilled sniper, he was competent at his job and had ten kills already.

"I put Vladimir in the slot," Fedor said, nodding his head toward the center position. Vladimir had a Heckler & Koch MG5 7.62 mm belt-fed machine-gun with a Hensoldt ZO 4x30 optic aka "the pig". The Germans still made the best weapons. He was sitting in a metal folding chair with his MG on a wooden table in front of him. The gun was back two feet from an opening made from concrete blocks and a 2" x 6" with sandbags on top. He had two-hundred rounds of ammo belted together to feed the pig. Every fifth round was a tracer. Vladimir was twenty-eight, tall with a slight build and black hair. He had been in the army for a year and worked on his parents' farm near Melitopol before the war. He had a generally quiet disposition.

"The brothers are on the north platform in the prepared positions." Fedor poked the first two fingers on his right hand across his body towards their direction. Each position consisted of stacked sandbags over a waist- high wall of concrete blocks. The idea was to build fortified positions within the massive building while assuming the two-foot thick rebar reinforced concrete walls could eventually be breached.

Ihor and Denis grew up in Kharkiv and had been in the Army only six months. Ihor was twenty-five and of average height and build. His brother, Denis, was two years younger with a short, stockier build. Both had Polish MSBS Grot 5.56 x 45 mm rifles with Eotech Holographic Hybrid Sights which the unit bought on www.gunbroker.com. Ihor also had an AT-4 anti-tank rocket launcher. Denis was the team medic, having taken a two-week combat trauma management training course offered by Alex Vindman's non-profit military training company.[331] They spent much of their time busting each other's balls as many brothers do.

Fedor went over to Vladimir's position and sat in a cheap plastic chair so he could help spot targets and get more ammo when required. Each man, including him, carried a 100-round belt of ammo to feed the pig. He would take turns looking out towards the power plant with a pair of Steiner binoculars and his PVS18 night vision device the unit had crowd-funded and ordered on www.amazon.com. Because a 24-hour shift was a long time, everyone had to get into a relaxed state of alertness. Staring into a scope for too long would fatigue your eyes and fry the brain. Defending urban terrain was a marathon, not a sprint. That is until the shit hit the fan.

Vitali, satisfied with the arrangements, sat on a crude metal bench near the brothers. He pulled out a plastic bottle of water and a protein bar. They might have a long night ahead. Vitali was in charge of a reconnaissance squad in the 35th Marine Brigade (Separate) and his mission was to warn of any Russian

331 Alex Vindman worked on the National Security Council from 2018-2020 and testified during President Trump's impeachment trial.

advance towards the Elektrostal, inflict as many casualties as possible, and pull out if they were going to be overrun. At least that was the theory. The Russians had already taken most of the town and this was the Ukrainians' last stand before they got ejected altogether.

The recon squad used to have nine people but they had taken three casualties and hadn't received replacements. Three months ago, Valerii stepped on a land mine and lost his right leg below the knee and was now working in a drone manufacturing plant with a black prosthetic limb. Two weeks after that, Oleksandr was hit by a lucky shot from a TOS-1A which obliterated the building he was in.[332] They only found parts of his charred body. And then they lost Mykyta last month in a drone attack when they were retreating from the power plant. He took shrapnel in both legs and was in a military hospital in the rear with no word on how he was doing. They were all stuck in a meatgrinder and there was no getting out of it.

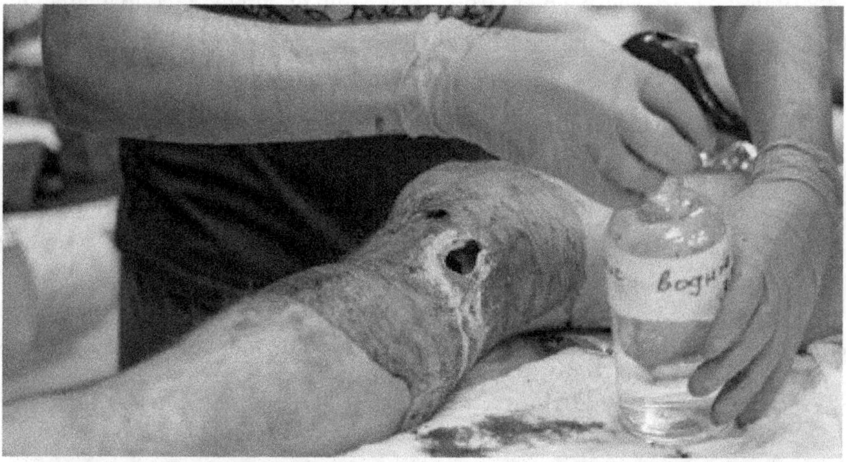

A surgeon removes shrapnel from Mykyta's legs. (M. Shandyba)

Ihor stood up from his position and took a piss on the floor. He looked over at Vitali and walked towards the metal stairs, "I'm going to find a chair downstairs, I'm not sitting on this bucket again all night."

"Okay, but if you turn your cellphone on, I'm going to throat punch you." Vitali enforced a strict no-phone policy because the Russians could target them by social media posts and cellular geolocation. It didn't matter that the Russians knew they were defending the building.

332 The TOS-1A by Russian nomenclature is a Heavy Flamethrower System that fires twenty-four 220 mm rockets with thermobaric warheads.

Ihor made an exaggerated scared look on his face, started to say a smartass comment, thought better of it, and merely said, “Yes, Sergeant.”

Ihor’s younger brother turned his head towards the stairs and said matter of factly, “Dipshit.”

After finishing his snack, Vitali turned on his handheld high-powered radio and went to the frequency the Russians were using. Time to do some PSYOPS.

“This is headquarters, report your status ASAP,” Vitali demanded in his best authoritarian voice.

“Our headquarters doesn’t give a shit about us, *khokhol,*”a voice said through the radio. Khokhol was a derogatory term the Russians used for the Ukrainians which literally meant tufts of cereal stalks.

“Wut Yevgeny doing, bro? Did his family get the flowers we sent?” Vitali was referring to Yevgeny Prigozhin, the former commander of the Russian mercenary unit called The Wagner Group. Prigozhin attempted a coup against the Russian military leadership in 2023 and later died in a plane crash that August. Although Wagner had since been disbanded, its former unit members were absorbed by the regular Russian army and fighting in Kurakhove.

“They were just cheap sunflowers, bitch. Send your monthly salary to our Paypal account and we’ll buy some better ones,” the voice over the radio teased.

“I guess he got tired of sucking Putin’s dick.”

“Sure, because I heard his dick is even smaller than Zelensky’s,” laughter erupted over the radio. The Russians sounded young, maybe in their late teens and early twenties, with one foot in their graves, and they knew it.

“When are you St. Petersburg pussies going to get off your asses and do your jobs? We’re bored.” St. Petersburg was where Wagner’s headquarters was located.

“We’ll come over if we can fuck your sister again,” the laughter was even louder.

“You can have her, she looks like a cow.” Vitali was laughing too. “Well, I gotta go and call in an airstrike on you bitches. Make sure you wear your body armor tonight.”

“Go ahead, khokhol, our dumbfuck leaders call in airstrikes on us all the time!” More laughter. Even though they were killing each other, they were both just doing what their countries told them to do, locked in the same senseless game of death.

Vitali smirked, turned off the radio, and looked through the nearest gun-port. It was a cold crisp night with a three-quarter moon. It was approaching midnight and, except for some muffled explosions in the distance, it was quiet. He got off the bench, stretched his arms, and walked over to check on the brothers. He squeezed Ihor on the shoulder and then Denis. They each nodded their heads, confirming they were alert. Denis was eating an apple. Vitali went over to the MG, saw that Fedor and Vladimir were having a whispered conversation, so he walked over to the sniper position. Vitali kneeled on the mattress, being careful not to upset Pavlo's rifle which was resting on two sandbags covered by a folded towel. It was his job to make sure his men didn't zone out or accidentally fall asleep.

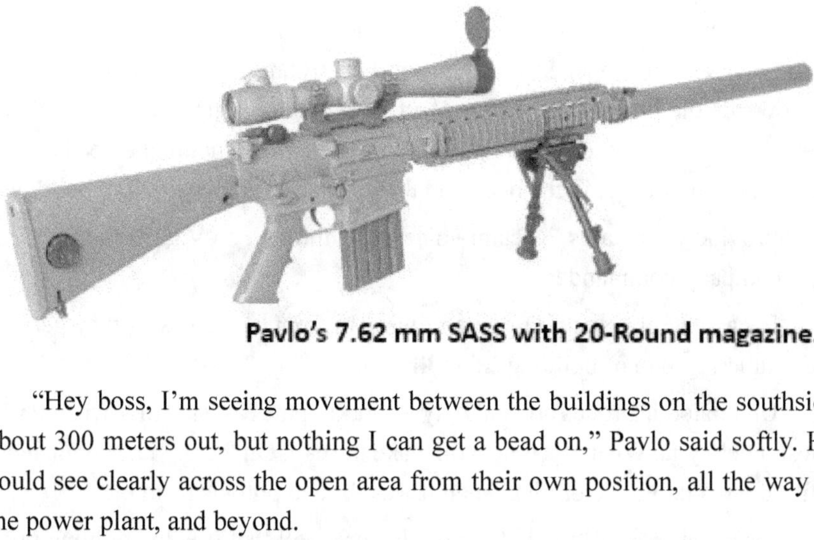

Pavlo's 7.62 mm SASS with 20-Round magazine.

"Hey boss, I'm seeing movement between the buildings on the southside about 300 meters out, but nothing I can get a bead on," Pavlo said softly. He could see clearly across the open area from their own position, all the way to the power plant, and beyond.

The sound was muted first, then much louder, like something ripping through the air. Artillery. The first rounds were off target, but they would get adjusted. These were big shells coming in, probably from a 152 mm self-propelled gun battery way behind the FLOT. Even though the Russians no longer had artillery superiority, the Ukrainians had been knocking out a thousand month, the orcs could still put together a concentrated barrage when needed. The shells were now coming in faster and closer to their position, some of them were smoke rounds. There was nothing they could do except hope a round didn't make a direct hit on the building, and if it did, hope it wouldn't penetrate the roof.

"Keep a look out for movement," Vitali yelled. If the orcs were making a push on them, they would use the artillery for cover.

Pfffft! Pfffft! Pfffft! Pavlo's gun hissed as his bullets left the rifle and streaked through the long suppressor. "They're working their way south through the buildings," he explained.

BOOM! A 152 mm high-explosive round made a direct hit on the roof, showering the interior with dust and concrete shards, but it was on the west end of the building which was fifty yards away. The outside of the building began to receive incoming fire which made sharp smacking sounds on the exterior concrete. Green tracers reached out to them from the power plant as Russian machine-gun teams opened up.

"I got movement!" Fedor yelled in his deep voice as he crouched low next to the pig. Vladimir opened fire with short 5-7 round bursts, sending red tracers towards the base of the power plant, targeting a group of orcs who raced towards the next row of buildings. The brothers were shooting selectively as Russian infantry came in the open and then disappeared into random buildings.

"Provide your status," a calm voice came through on Vitali's radio. It was their company commander.

"It's a general assault. Orcs are moving in from both sides. If they get into the southern group of buildings, they'll flank us."

"Understood. Drones are out. Arty is working the east side of town, but that doesn't help you. When it's time, you make the call. Out here." The commander left it up to Vitali to determine when it was time to pull his team out.

Ihor leaned toward the hole in the factory wall that was his fighting position and fired the AT4 down and into the one-story building directly in front of him. The round hit the roof, blowing a hole in it and showering the inside with shrapnel. Simultaneously, an incoming explosion struck the wall of their building, knocking him backwards and onto the cement floor. Vitali ran over, turned on the miniature light attached to his cut-down kevlar helmet, and assessed his injuries.

"Medic!" he yelled. Denis fired off two more rounds, dropped his magazine, inserted a fresh one, and hurried over to his older brother. He saw that Ihor had a shrapnel wound in his thigh with bright red blood oozing out, indicating an arterial bleed. He quickly took a rubber and velcro tourniquet from his brother's side cargo pocket and emplaced it above the wound. Ihor was still in shock – the extreme pain would come later.

"Oh my god, it blew your dick off!" Denis exclaimed, looking intently into his brother's eyes.

"Oh, fuck," Ihor sat up, looked down at his crotch in horror, and then realized his brother was lying.

"Just kidding, bro," Denis laughed as Ihor laid back down on the floor with a groan, a look of relief on his face.

"Stop talking about your dicks you two idiots and move him to the CCP!" Vitali barked. The casualty collection point was the entrance on the west side of the building that they came through earlier. Vitali grabbed a 100-round belt of 7.62 ammo from Ihor's daypack, walked over to the pig, and threw it over Fedor's shoulder.

"Ihor is wounded and needs CASEVAC. We can't hold this fucker much longer," Vitali advised. Fedor nodded his head and attached the 100-round belt as Vladimir kept firing in controlled bursts.

"They are in the southern group of buildings, boss. They ain't stopping for shit," Pavlo warned as he looked through the scope of his SASS. Pffft! Pffft! More suppressed bullets sought their targets.

"Pavlo, you go downstairs and provide cover for the brothers. Go!" Vitali watched him pick up the sniper rifle and head down to the ground floor. He then turned and faced the MG team.

"You two cover us while we prepare to move. In one minute, you displace downstairs for exfil. Got it?" Fedor gave a thumbs up while Vitali threw his own 100-round belt of ammo over Fedor's shoulder. Vitali ran down the stairs, tripped on the last one, and fell face first onto the rubble strewn floor. Fuck me, he thought. His body armor, helmet, and adrenaline ensured it didn't hurt. He got up and moved to the CCP.

A Russian 2S3 Akatsiya 152 mm self-propelled howitzer fires at the Elektrostal.

“How is Ihor?” Vitali asked.

“He’s in shock and still bleeding. He needs higher care ASAP.” Ihor was his brother and it was his responsibility to get him out, whatever it took. He owed it to their parents. Vitali understood and nodded his head. Fedor and Vladimir made it down the stairs and took a knee near the door.

“You’re face is bleeding, you get hit?” Fedor asked.

“Nah, I tripped on the stairs and face-planted. You two move out first down the trench. Make sure you signal our guys when you get close so they don’t light you up.” Vitali said, pointing to the MG team. He looked over at Denis, “Then, you take your brother while Pavlo and I provide cover. Move.”

The MG team moved off into the night and down the trench that led to friendly lines. Outside was a cacophony of death and violence. Russian artillery rounds were landing farther west as their infantry moved in. Machine-guns hammered away from nearby buildings as the orcs pounded the Elektrostal. Intermixed with this ugly orchestra was the high-pitched whirring of Ukrainian drones with thermal cameras as they dropped 40 mm bomblets on Russian soldiers caught in the open.

“Go!” Vitali tapped the back of Denis’ helmet who had draped his brother’s arm around his shoulders. The two stumbled away, down the trench. Vitali and Pavlo took positions in the rubble and searched for targets, occasionally firing their weapons when one appeared. After sixty seconds, Vitali slapped Pavlo on the back of the helmet.

"Go!" Pavlo peeled off and jogged down the trench. Vitali saw a group of orcs crawling for cover, slid a frag grenade from his chest harness, pulled the pin, waited two seconds, and threw it. CRUMP! He couldn't tell if he got them or not. He waited another thirty seconds before moving out, bullets and shrapnel whizzing through the air like angry bees. He made it fifty yards when an explosion lifted him off his feet and dumped him in the bottom of the trench.

Vitali couldn't move his arms or legs and his hearing was gone. However, he did manage to uncontrollably piss and shit all over himself. He stared up into the cold dark sky, the stars shining back at him. Well, time was up, death was never graceful. He had a wife he would never see again and a son who would grow up without a father. It was just as well, he'd be joining the tens of thousands of Ukrainian soldiers who already gave the ultimate sacrifice. He was just a statistic now.

The Russians were assaulting the Elektrostal, realizing that it was undefended. They would soon probe the trench to see if there was a general collapse in the lines. Vitali still couldn't move as he tried to will his right hand into grabbing another hand grenade from the front of his vest. He wasn't going to be taken prisoner. He tried again with supreme effort, but his arm barely moved and his glove got stuck on the velcro of his ammo pouch. The grenade was still out of reach. Imagine being so fucked you couldn't even kill yourself, he thought. Vitali wondered if Ihor was okay and if the rest of the team got out alive. Bullets skipped off the side of the trench wall – the orcs were pushing forward. This was it.

A big round face suddently appeared several inches in front of his. The bulky figure grabbed the radio from his vest as he saw its mouth move in slow motion. He could sort of make out what he was saying as his hearing started to return but it still sounded like the garbled words of a monster.

"Blue Sky! Blue Sky! Blue Sky!" the figure yelled into the radio.

"Roger. Be advised to unass your location ASAP," a voice responded.

"Get your fucking ass up, you lazy khokhol bitch!" The soldier put Vitali's arm over his shoulder and picked him up by the crotch with the other arm in a fireman's carry. Only Fedor was big and strong enough to do this. Bright red tracer rounds arced over their heads, covering their movement as the bullets reached out towards unseen Russian infantry. Vladimir's cheek was pressed firmly against the stock of the pig, his right eye looking directly through the sight as he burned through his last belt of ammo. Fedor looked back over his shoulder into Vitali's bloody and bearded face, "It's HIMARS o'clock, motherfucker."

The Blue Sky HIMARS mission launches towards Kurakhove.

Blue Sky was code for a pre-planned volley of HIMARS (High Mobility Artillery Rocket System) directed at their positions if they were overrun. The first and second M31A2 227 mm rockets with 200-pound Unitary Warheads struck the power plant, thirty feet apart, blowing holes in the roof and spreading shrapnel inside the building, killing everyone within the blast radius. The third and fourth rockets hit the steel plant, doing the same. Several seconds later, rockets five and six with M30A1 Alternative Warheads exploded over the group of buildings south of the steel plant where the Russians were swarming. Each warhead blew 180,000 pieces of tungsten steel shrapnel earthward, shredding all humans and thin-skinned vehicles. Anyone and anything not under hard cover was well and truly fucked.

Vitali looked back towards Kurakhove as he bounced on Fedor's broad shoulders. Explosions and bright colors filled the night sky as the town burned and tracers crisscrossed in the dark. The carnage looked both surreal and beautiful. He watched the outline of the Elektrostal, backlit by the flames, get smaller and smaller as Fedor carried him away from the battle. And that was the last time he ever saw the steel plant.

(As of publication, the Zelensky administration had signed a limited critical minerals deal with the U.S. on April 30, 2025. Invading Russian forces had sustained an estimated 1 million casualties, both dead and wounded. Kurakhove was still under enemy control and the 35th Marine Brigade continued to fight to regain control of its country.)

Top Row, Left to Right: Denis, Ihor, Pavlo, Mykyta, Valerii.
Bottom Row, Left to Right: Fedor, Vladimir, Oleksandr, Vitali.

In the fields the bodies burning, as the war machine keeps turning.

Index

Aluminum (Al)

Background

Aluminum is made from alumina which in turn comes from bauxite, a sedimentary rock with high contents of both aluminum oxide and gallium. An estimated 70% of Bauxite worldwide is refined into alumina using the hydrometallurgical Bayer process which is thermal energy intensive.[333] Alumina is further refined into aluminum by the Hall-Herold smelting process, requiring copious amounts of electrical energy. Energy accounts for as much as 25% of the total cost of the final aluminum product. Bauxite is classified as either metallurgic (processed into aluminum) or non-metallurgic (abrasives, refractory products). Aluminum has many manufacturing uses, including the transportation industry, military aircraft, and semiconductors. Historically, 21% of aluminum consumption has been in the construction industry, 20% in transportation, 10% in the electrical sector, and 10% in machinery & equipment.[334]

Bauxite

In 2024, the world produced 450 million tons of bauxite led by Guinea with 130 million tons (29%), Australia with 100 million tons (22%), and China with 93 million tons (21%). The U.S. extracted no metallurgic bauxite and only small amounts of non-metallurgic bauxite. In 2024, the U.S. imported 2.8 million metric tons of bauxite and consumed 1.8 million tons of which 76% was refined into alumina or aluminum hydroxide.[335] Imported bauxite prices remained low at just $30.00 per ton. The U.S. imported more than 75% of its overall bauxite needs and all its metallurgic needs. U.S. industry held 250,000 tons of bauxite in stock which would last under two months based on annual consumption.

Guinea, Vietnam, Australia, Brazil, Jamaica, and Indonesia hold two-thirds (20 billion tons) of the world's bauxite reserves (30 billion tons). Generally, the countries with the most bauxite reserves are its largest producers, except for China who extracts bauxite at rates disproportionate to its reserves. While the U.S. has insignificant bauxite reserves, they could extract alumina from other sources such as clays which is uneconomic and would have to be subsidized.

333 https://www.aluminum.org/bauxite-101

334 CRU Consulting. "Opportunities for aluminum in a post-Covid economy." 2022.

335 Aluminum hydroxide has a variety uses such as a fire retardant in polymers.

Alumina (Aluminum Oxide)

In 2024, the U.S. produced 810,000 tons of alumina and imported an additional 1.3 million tons. Of the produced tonnage, 69% went to primary aluminum smelters and the rest for non-metallurgic uses. The U.S. industry held yearend stocks of 180,000 tons, a three-month supply based on average consumption rates of 2 million tons annually. Imported aluminum averaged $570.00 USD a ton, much higher than bauxite, reflecting the additional processing costs. The U.S. imported 59% of its alumina needs.

China, Australia, and Brazil accounted for 79% of world alumina production (140 million tons) with the remainder widely distributed geographically. China is the single largest annual producer at 84 million (59%) of total production which gives it pricing power, moving it towards monopoly status. In contrast, the U.S. is a minor player in the alumina space, producing just 0.005% of the world total. The privately owned Atlantic Alumina Company (ATALCO) owns and operates the only remaining U.S. alumina processing plant in Gramercy, LA.[336]

Aluminum

Aluminum is used for primary production (from alumina), secondary production (from scrap, recycling), and military grade (high-purity) products. In 2024, the U.S. produced 670,000 tons of primary aluminum and 3.6 million tons of secondary aluminum. The U.S. imported 5.4 million tons of aluminum with apparent consumption being 4.3 million tons. Year-end stocks held by industry were 1.6 million tons which would last four months, based on annual consumption. Annual U.S. spot prices averaged $2,600.00 per ton. From 2020-2024, the U.S. imported on average 44% of its aluminum needs.

The world produced 72 million tons of aluminum in 2024 with China leading with 43 million tons (60%), followed by India with 4.2 million tons (6%) and Russia with 3.8 million (5%). The U.S. imported most of its aluminum needs from Canada (56%), then the UAE (8%) and Bahrain (4%). A country's aluminum capability is determined by the number of smelters it has and the corresponding annual production capacity. The U.S. was down to only four operational smelters in 2024.

336 ATALCO is a subsidiary of the U.K. based Concord Resources LTD.

ALCOA - Financially Distressed

The U.S.' largest aluminum manufacturer is ALCOA, founded in 1886 with headquarters in Pittsburgh. ALCOA is the owner of seven bauxite mines in Australia, Brazil, Guinea, and Saudi Arabia. The company has alumina operations in each of these countries plus a fifth one in Spain. ALCOA has a total of twelve smelter operations with three in Canada and two in the U.S. ALCOA purchased Australian company Alumina Limited in 2024 with a combined production (in 2023) of 41 million tons of bauxite, 11 million tons of alumina, and 2 million tons of aluminum.

The company produced 2.6 million metric tons of aluminum in 2024 and has one smelter in New York with a 130,000 tpa capacity and one in Indiana with a 270,000 tpa capacity. ALCOA relies on high-carbon emitting coal and natural gas to power its two U.S. smelters despite energy being its most expensive input. Although the company had a modest net income of $60 million in 2024, it lost $651 million in 2023 and lost $123 million in 2022.

Century Aluminum – Financially Distressed

Century Aluminum, with headquarters in Chicago, is the second largest U.S. aluminum producing company. The company has three U.S. smelters: one in South Carolina with a 230,000 tpa capacity, and two in Kentucky - one with a 220,000 tpa capacity and the other with 250,000 tpa. Century idled its Hawesville, KY plant in 2022 which produced high-purity military-grade aluminum. The company's largest aluminum smelter is in Iceland with a 317,000 tpa capacity. Century produced 381,000 tons of aluminum in 2024.

In 2023, Century became the majority owner of the Jamalco 55/45 JV in Jamaica consisting of both bauxite mining and a 1.4 million tpa alumina operation. Century ships 770,000 tpa of alumina to their Iceland smelter with follow on sales to Europe.[337] With their current business model, Century does not import alumina from their JV to their U.S. smelters, they buy it from Glencore (which is the majority owner of Century) and Concord (which owns ALCOA). Century's financial outlook improved greatly in 2024 with a net profit of $318 million, which was much better than previous years with net losses of $43 million in 2023 and losses of $14 million in 2022. In Q1 2024, the DOE threw the

337 Century paid $1.00 for the JV in a literal fire sale. The JV incurred $41 million in losses for 2023.

company a lifeline, granting the company $500 million for a new low-carbon aluminum smelter.

Magnitude 7 Metals (M7M) - Bankrupt

As an example of the U.S.' aluminum decline, M7M closed its high-purity military-grade Missouri smelter with a 263,000 tpa capacity in early 2024. The smelter was previously owned by Noranda Aluminum which went bankrupt in 2016. M7M spent an estimated $55 million annually on energy costs, primarily sourced from a nearby coal-fueled power generation facility. In 2020, M7M predicted their imminent closure as their operational costs per ton were likely $2,000.00 per ton while selling their product at $1,680.00 per ton.[338]

Actions Taken

According to the DARS (Defense Acquisition Regulations System) 48 CFR 252.225-7009 Restriction on Acquisition of Specialty Meals, any steel alloy product with more than 25% aluminum content acquired by the DOD must be melted or produced in the U.S.

The Bipartisan Infrastructure Law and Inflation Reduction Act provided the Department of Energy (DOE) with $6.3 billion to fund their Industrial Demonstrations Program. Of this, $930 million went to new metal operations, with $664 million going specifically to four separate aluminum operations. Century's green aluminum smelter received $500 million, Constellium took $75 million for a zero-carbon aluminum casting plant, Golden Aluminum got $22 million to upgrade their existing facility with Nexcast technology, and Real Alloy Recycling received $67 million for a zero-waste secondary aluminum waste project.[339]

Incentives & Tariffs

Under the Inflation Reduction Act, an aluminum company would receive a 10% tax credit under the Section 45X Advanced Manufacturing Production Credit if they "converted from bauxite to a minimum purity of 99% alumina by mass or purified to a minimum purity of 99.9% aluminum by mass." In 2024, ALCOA received $71 million and Century $90 million in tax credits.

338 Decena, Karl. "Report: Mo. Aluminum smelter on brink of closure after racking up losses." S&P Global, February 28, 2020.

339 https://www.energy.gov/oced/industrial-demonstrations-program-update

Domestic bauxite mining companies receive a 22% depletion allowance (there are several small companies) while foreign companies receive a 14% rate (there are none).

In February 2025, the Trump administration established a 10% tariff on aluminum imported from Canada and 25% tariffs with no exceptions for others. Some countries were subject to additional Section 232 25% import tariffs.

U.S. Supply Chain Security Strategy Moving Forward

The U.S. has chosen to acquire tariff-free aluminum from its allies and has managed to build a surprisingly ex-China value chain. Newly instituted 25% tariffs in 2025 will not help the U.S. aluminum industry unless this is paired with additional smelter capacity. An important reason for this decline is the inability of the U.S. to provide cost-competitive low-carbon energy. One solution is to use funding through the DPA to provide ALCOA and Century with solar powered electricity with battery back-up at scale to reduce the cost of and decarbonize their electricity inputs. Unless the U.S. develops new cost-effective manufacturing, technology and supporting ecosystems, America is likely to lose its remaining primary smelter capacity.

Multiprong Approach

- In 2022, the Defense National Stockpile held no bauxite or aluminum products. In 2024, the Defense Logistics Agency (DLA) acquired 17,000 metric tons of high-purity aluminum and 1,500 tons of aluminum alloys and intends to acquire 3,200 tons of aluminum products in 2025. A one-year supply of bauxite and aluminum based on annual consumption would be 3.8 million tons.
- According to the International Aluminum Institute, global recycling rates of aluminum are around 32% and in the U.S. 37% of aluminum production was from recycled scrap. Secondary aluminum requires 95% less energy than using primary production smelters.
- While aluminum has the benefit of being infinitely recyclable, it can be substituted by other materials. Composites can replace it in aerospace applications and glass, paper, and steel can be used in the packaging sector. In the auto industry, aluminum can be substituted with composites, steel, and titanium.

2024 U.S. Bauxite Imports (metric tons)			
Country	Volume	Value	Price/Ton
Jamaica	2 million	$51 million	$25.50
Turkey	363,000	$22 million	$60.60
Australia	246,000	$17 million	$69.10
Guyana	192,800	$41.6 million	$215.70
China	78,400	$37 million	$471.90
Brazil	6,300	$2.2 million	$349.20
Netherlands	1,280	$876,000.00	$684.00
Total	2.88 million	$171.6 million	$59.46

2024 Aluminum Oxide Imports (metric tons)

The U.S. imported 1.07 million tons valued at $639 million for an average of $595.00 a ton. Most of this came from Brazil with 824,300 tons (82%) valued at $374 million for an average of $453.00 a ton.

2024 Aluminum Hydroxide Imports (metric tons)

The U.S. imported 434,700 tons valued at $267 million for an average of $615.90 per ton. Most of this came from Brazil with 223,200 tons (51%) valued at $128 million for an average of $573.00 per ton.

**Data from UN Comtrade HS Codes 2606, 2818.20, 2818.30*

Antimony (Sb)

Background

Antimony is found mainly in stibnite and is used in alloys, flame retardants, lead-acid batteries, bullets, night vision goggles, and semiconductors. The U.S. does not mine antimony and all ores and other semi-finished and finished products are imported. In 2024, the world produced 100,000 metric tons of antimony with China accounting for 60%, then Tajikistan with 17%, and Russia with 13%. The world has an estimated 2 million tons of antimony reserves with China holding 33.5%, Russia 17.5%, and Bolivia 15.5%. The U.S. imported 85% of its overall antimony needs with antimony oxides being the highest volume import by far. Of this, the U.S. imported 76% of its needs from China, 11% from Belgium, and 6% from Bolivia.

Antimony is a globalized commodity with a complex supply chain, passing through many countries, depending on what form it is in (ore, concentrates, refined products). China is both the single largest producer and importer of antimony ore, with the neighboring countries of Australia, Russia, Myanmar, and Tajikistan shipping in significant portions of their ore and concentrates to China.[340] Consequently, China has become the central midstream antimony processing hub, exporting refined antimony oxide worldwide. While China is the top exporter of antimony oxides, the U.S. is the top importer, making the U.S. antimony supply chain dependent on its chief competitor in the international system.

U.S. Antimony Corporation – Financially Distressed

The U.S. Antimony Corporation (USAC), located in Montana, is the only company in the U.S. with a smelter that makes antimony products (oxide, metal, trisulfide). They own one smelter in Mexico. USAC began mining antimony in 1968 but ceased these operations in 1983 because it was cheaper to import foreign sources. The company claims that it gets most of its antimony ore from a Canadian supplier. In 2024, the company sold 729 tons of antimony for sales of $11 million and a net loss of $1.7 million which was an improvement from 2023 with a net loss of $6.3 million.

340 U.S. company Comsup Commodities Inc owns Tajikistan's Anzob LLC antimony mining complex.

China

Chinese antimony production declined noticeably beginning in 2010 with the shutdown of approximately 100 smelters as the government cracked down on illegal mining operations and environmental degradation.[341] In 2011, China produced 150,000 tons of antimony which dropped to 60,000 tons in 2024. China's antimony industry is concentrated mainly in Lengshuijiang City, Hunan Province and is divided between private and state-owned companies. In Lengshuijiang there are seven private sector companies with an estimated total capacity of 40,000 tpa. In 2023, China imported 18,000 metric tons of antimony ore/concentrate from over twenty countries and just 87 tons of trioxides from seven countries. A Chinese CEO stated during a 2024 interview that he expects reduced inventories to continue, overall antimony production to decline, for global demand to increase and prices to rise.[342]

As Chinese extraction continues to decline, antimony will be increasingly difficult to secure for the U.S. Beijing will likely act in the future to protect this diminishing resource by enacting export controls such as quotas, duties, and bans. Equally likely, Chinese refining companies will increase their importation of antimony ore and concentrate from allies like Bolivia, Russia, and Tajikistan. While China has and actively manages a national stockpile that includes metals commodities, it is unknown how much antimony supplies it stores.

Actions Taken

In 1991, the Coalition for Fair Trade in Refined Antimony Trioxide (consisting of four U.S. manufacturers) filed a petition with the ITC (International Trade Commission) alleging unfair dumping of refined antimony trioxide by China.[343] China National Nonferrous Metals Import and Export Corporation (CNIEC) and Minmetals International Nonferrous Metals Trading Company provided information for the inquiry. The ITC determined that the U.S. antimony industry was threatened by China's sale of antimony at "less than fair value." However, at present, there are no antidumping or countervailing duties in place.

In 2016, the U.S. requested consultations with China through the WTO's Dispute Settlement Body alleging that China had violated standing protocol by

341 U.S. Geological Survey, Mineral Commodity Summaries, January 2011.
342 www.asianmetal.com, Executive Interviews.
343 This was the first anti-dumping petition filed against China in this sector.

adding export duties and quotas to several minerals including antimony.[344] For example, in 2014, China's Ministry of Commerce granted antimony oxide quotas at 41,477 metric tons.[345] China responded that it emplaced quotas to protect its limited natural resources and protect the environment through sustainable development measures. This could also signal that China is taking measures to stockpile antimony and has less for export which may result in increasing prices.[346]

Canadian company Perpetua Resources intends to restart their Stibnite Gold Project in Idaho, a formerly active antimony operation with operations planned for 2028. However, estimated reserves are 100,000 tons which would only provide the U.S. with a five-year supply based on average consumption rates. Perpetua requested a $1.8 billion loan from the U.S. Export-Import Bank and received $59 million through the Defense Production Act and $15 million from the Defense Ordnance Technology Consortium. Currently, Perpetua does not sell a product and is under financial distress, losing $14.4 million in 2024 and $18.7 million in 2023.

Australian mining company Felix Gold is pursuing gold extraction operations in Alaska where they intend to produce antimony as a byproduct. Samples taken reveal high grades of antimony up to 28%. Felix does not know how much total contained antimony there is nor do they know if they can extract it in an economic manner. Felix has no active operations, has $1.3 million cash on hand, and operated at a loss of over $2 million in both 2023 and 2022.[347]

Incentives & Tariffs

Under the Inflation Reduction Act a company would qualify for a 10% tax credit under the Section 45X Advanced Manufacturing Production Credit if their antimony product is "converted to antimony trisulfide concentrate with a minimum purity of 90% antimony trisulfide by mass or purified to a minimum purity of 99.65% antimony by mass."

Domestic antimony mining companies receive a 22% depletion allowance (U.S. Antimony) while foreign companies receive a 14% rate (there are none).

344 Case #DS508.

345 Shair, Wendy. "China issues first batch of 2014 export quotas for antimony, tin, silver." S&P Global, December 13, 2023.

346 China began enforcing antimony export quotas starting in 2000.

347 Felix Gold annual report 2023.

The tariff schedule encourages the import of all antimony products. As of April 2025, antimony is exempt from Trump's tariffs to include China. However, this is irrelevant based on China's antimony ban.

Beginning on September 15, 2024, China will commence restricting antimony exports to "safeguard national security and interests and fulfill international obligations such as non-proliferation." Chinese exporters will have to apply for an export license for antimony products as well as for dual-use antimony technology that could have military applications. In December 2024, China banned the export of antimony products to the U.S. Antimony metal prices nearly doubled from $8.91 to $17.50 a pound.

U.S Supply Chain Security Strategy Moving Forward

China has achieved an antimony monopoly, mining or processing an estimated 80% of the world's annual production and supplies the U.S. with three-quarters of its own refined antimony needs. This makes the U.S. highly vulnerable to supply chain disruption or economic coercion by Beijing. There are no economic antimony operations in North America with Canada's and Mexico's domestic mining industries both largely defunct except for insignificant volumes.

A Multiprong Approach

- The Defense Logistics Agency held 99 tons of antimony in the national stockpile as of 2022 and announced the purchase of 1,100 tons of antimony in both 2023 & 2024 and 700 tons in 2025. A one-year stockpile of antimony based on U.S. annual consumption would be 22,000 metric tons. The U.S. waited far too long to begin stockpiling antimony and is now paying premium prices with all products suffering from inflation.
- The U.S. meets an estimated 15% of its antimony needs from secondary lead smelter recovery (lead-acid batteries). A mandatory national recycling, recovery, and reuse program would maximize access to this resource.
- The Department of Defense should add antimony to the DARS (Defense Acquisition Regulations System) *48 CFR 252.225-7009 Restriction on Acquisition of Specialty Meals*, mandating that any specialty metal composed of antimony must be melted or produced in the U.S. DOD should also add antimony to the existing DFARS

(Defense Federal Acquisition Regulation Supplement) that prohibits the federal government from acquiring certain metals and alloys from China, Russia, Iran, and North Korea.

- Barring any new discoveries, the U.S. must accept that the North American antimony value chain is dead and plan accordingly. Section 45X tax credits and government grants to companies pursuing potential mining operations will likely fail unless they develop new technology to make their operations economic. The U.S. should immediately begin stockpiling at scale and shift their reliance from China's antimony supply chain onto other primary producers which most likely means Australia.
- Every effort should be made to find substitutes such as the Army replacing its M855 lead/antimony 5.56 bullets with the new M855A1 Enhanced Performance Round steel/copper slugs. Also, the legacy lead-acid batteries containing antimony and used in the auto industry should be engineered out of modern vehicles.

2024 U.S. Antimony Ore Imports (metric tons)			
Country	**Volume**	**Value**	**Price/Ton**
Mexico	482.0	$1.9 million	$3,940.00
India	10.0	$253,800.00	$25,380.00
Austria	2.1	$386,600.00	$184,000.00
Total	494.1	$2.54 million	$5,140.00
2024 Antimony Oxides Imports			
China	13,700	$131 million	$9,500.00
Belgium	7,400	$47 million	$6,300.00
France	2,600	$14.7 million	$5,600.00
Bolivia	2,280	$17.2 million	$7,500.00
Thailand	1,800	$5.4 million	$3,000.00
Others	1,120	$7.5 million	$6,700.00
Total	28,900	$222.8 million	$7,700.00
2024 Unwrought Antimony; Powders, Scrap			
Thailand	1,780	$30.1 million	$16,900.00
India	873	$13.8 million	$15,800.00
China	493	$10.6 million	$21,500.00
U.K.	488	$8.3 million	$17,000.00
Vietnam	719	$14.6 million	$20,300.00
Others	887	$18.9 million	$21,300.00
Total	5,240	$96.3 million	$18,370.00
**UN Comtrade data HS code 2617.10, 2825.80, 8110*			

Arsenic (As)

Background

Arsenic is a toxic heavy metal commonly found in sulfur-containing minerals such as arsenopyrite and pyrite and is frequently recovered secondary to other minerals like gold, silver, lead, and copper. Arsenic metal is combined with other metals to make alloys such as bronze, copper, and lead (bullets). Arsenic acid is commonly used in herbicides, wood preservatives, and treating glass. Arsenic trioxide is used to make arsenic acid and in the pharmaceutical industry to treat cancer. Arsenic sulfide is used in semiconductors, explosives, and pigments.

The U.S. does not mine arsenic and neither does Canada or Mexico, highlighting North America's supply chain vulnerability. Global arsenic production is highly concentrated with Peru (27,000 tons), China (24,000 tons) and Morocco (6,000 tons) accounting for 98% of extraction in 2024 which was 58,000 tons. Although the exact size of total reserves are unknown, they are estimated to be 1.2 million contained tons. In 2024, the U.S. relied 100% on imports with 52% of arsenic products coming from China, 26% from Morocco, and 16% from Malaysia.[348]

At one point, the U.S. had fourteen different active arsenic smelter operations with production beginning in 1910 and peaking in 1944 before the last smelter in Washington State closed in 1985. Most production was arsenic trioxide, recovered as flue dust and sludge from silver, copper, gold, and lead smelting operations. By 1960, all arsenic production in the U.S. was the byproduct of copper operations.[349]

The end of the industry accelerated when the Occupational Safety and Health Administration (OSHA) determined in 1978 that inorganic arsenic was a carcinogen. Soon after, the Environmental Protection Agency (EPA) began regulating all sources of arsenic pollution. The arsenic industry, faced with increasingly strict emission requirements at the local, state, and national levels, chose to close their operations rather than pay to upgrade and bring their smelters into compliance.[350]

348 U.S. Geological Survey 2024 Arsenic Report.

349 Loebenstein, J. "The Materials Flow of Arsenic in the United States." Bureau of Mines, 1994.

350 Ibid.

Gallium Arsenide (GaAs) Wafers

The most critical use of arsenic for the U.S. economy is the high-tech manufacturing of semiconductors which every modern society requires to function. More than one trillion semiconductors were sold in 2023 for $515 billion, with China being the single largest market, accounting for 36% of U.S. semiconductor company sales. The U.S. employs 345,000 people in the semiconductor industry and the recent CHIPS Act, providing a 25% advanced manufacturing investment tax credit, will increase the number of related industry jobs.[351]

While most wafers sold are made from silicon, GaAs substrates are superior for use in microwave components for cellphones, satellite communications and television broadcasting. Other uses include opto-electronic products such as industrial lasers, LEDs, night vision goggles, and facial recognition applications. The material used in these GaAs wafers is high-purity arsenic metal (99.9999%). U.S. manufacturer AXT Inc., with headquarters in Fremont, CA operates in this strategic technology space, building specialized non-silicon wafers.

AXT has 1,400 employees and makes all of its GaAs wafers in China due to lower labor and property costs relative to the U.S. The company has partial ownership of and a board seat on a high-purity arsenic supply company and recently created their own subsidiary to produce and sell arsenic. Although only 10% of their sales are to North America, the U.S. imposition of 25% tariffs on wafers imported from China has significant impact. For example, AXT paid import tariffs of $1 million in 2023, $3.3 million in 2022, and $1.3 million in 2021 on its various wafers manufactured in China. ATX is under financial stress, with net losses of $11.6 million in 2024 and $17.8 million in 2023.

China

China mainly extracts its arsenic secondary to zinc, lead, copper, and tin mining and a lesser amount through arsenic ore operations (historically 3% by volume).[352] Because China has such a robust domestic arsenic byproduct industry with low prices, they import very little of it – just four metric tons in 2023. In contrast, China exported 41,000 metric tons of arsenic byproducts.[353]

351 "State of the U.S. Semiconductor Industry, 2023." Semiconductor Industry Association.

352 Shi, Ya-Lan, et. al. "Anthropogenic Cycles of Arsenic in Mainland China: 1990-2010." Environmental Science & Technology, 2017.

353 UN Comtrade HS 2620.

For other arsenic products, China exported only 2,600 metric tons led by India (31%), the U.S. (25%), and Turkey (5%). China's arsenic supply chain is inherently secure as they are a primary producer with no import needs.

Action Taken

The U.S. government has taken no significant action to secure its arsenic supply chain.

Incentives & Tariffs

Under the Inflation Reduction Act a company would qualify for a 10% tax credit under the Section 45X Advanced Manufacturing Production Credit if their arsenic is "purified to a minimum of 99% purity by mass."

The domestic arsenic mining companies receive a 14% depletion allowance (there are none) while foreign companies receive a 14% rate (there are none).

Arsenic was not mentioned in April 2025 as being exempt from tariffs which was a mistake because the U.S. is 100% import dependent.

U.S Supply Chain Security Strategy Moving Forward

From a strategic technology perspective, the U.S. is most concerned with the production of GaAs wafers although these can be substituted in many cases with gallium nitride. To develop a more secure ex-China high-purity arsenic metal supply chain, the U.S. can add tariffs on Chinese GaAs products so their German and Japanese competitors become the obvious choice. The U.S. government could provide financial incentives (grants, tax credits) for private industry to build a dedicated wafer-grade high-purity arsenic metal production facility. Regardless of the way ahead, due to the global arsenic metal enterprise dominated by China, any change to a more secure supply chain involves subsidizing the U.S.' own industry.

Multiprong Approach

- The Department of Defense should enact a DFARS (Defense Federal Acquisition Regulation Supplement) that prohibits the federal government from acquiring arsenic products from China, Russia, Iran, and North Korea.
- It is unknown how much arsenic is recovered from electronic scrap or semiconductor manufacturing but it is most likely very low.

- In 2022, the Defense National Stockpile held no arsenic products and the Defense Logistics Agency (DLA) published no intentions to acquire any through 2025. A one-year stockpile of arsenic products based on U.S. annual consumption would be 9,100 metric tons.
- Even though the U.S. imports all its arsenic needs, this supply chain vulnerability can be mitigated through substitution. For example, U.S. industry uses most arsenic imports (80%) for herbicides, pesticides, and wood treatment, all which can be substituted by other existing products.

2024 Arsenic Trioxide Production (metric tons)

Country	Extraction	% of Total	Source
United States	none	none	
Peru	27,000	46%	Copper
China	24,000	41%	Zinc, Tin
Morocco	6,000	10%	Cobalt
Belgium	1,000	1.7%	
Other	240		
Total	58,200		

2024 U.S. Imports of Arsenic Products

Arsenic Acid: 9,700 tons from Malaysia valued at $11.1 million

Arsenic Trioxide: 5,550 tons valued at $3.3 million, with 72% from China, 18% from South Korea, and 10%, from Belgium.

Arsenic Metal: 533 tons valued at $1.5 million, averaging $2,900.00 a ton with 498 tons from China (93%).

**UN Comtrade and USITC Data*

Barite/Baryte (Ba)

Background

The mineral barite consists of barium sulfate, with the U.S. recovering most of its needs from bedded-sedimentary deposits. Barium sulfate has several uses, including as a radiocontrast for x-ray imagery, light reflecting applications, and as an ingredient for plastics and rubber. In the U.S, it is used mainly (90%) in the oil drilling industry as a weighting agent to increase the density of drilling mud. Since barium sulfate is used predominately in the extraction of fossil fuels (oil and natural gas), the number of active drilling rigs in a market can be an accurate indicator of its demand. In 2010, the American Petroleum Institute (API) specified the use of barite 4.1-specific-gravity as opposed to 4.2-sg which extended production life in the U.S.[354]

In 2024, the U.S. extracted relatively small volumes of barite, an estimated 425,000 metric tons, with Canada producing none and Mexico 330,000 tons; the U.S. typically imports 75% of its needs annually. Global barite production is highly concentrated with India (2.6 million tons), China (2.1 million tons) and Morocco (1 million tons) accounting for 69% of extraction. Although the exact amount of total world reserves is unknown, it is estimated to be 2 billion tons with the U.S. having 150 million tons. From 2020-2023, the U.S. imported 40% of its barite from India, 25% from China, and 17% from Morocco.

The U.S. Barite Industry

Historically, U.S. barite production was enough to meet national demands until 1950 when growing consumption was increasingly satisfied with imports. Until the mid-1980s, the U.S. held the line by still meeting three-quarters of its barite needs with domestic production. After that, even though U.S. demand grew, domestic production remained suppressed as lower priced imports were a preferred option. The gap between domestic production and imports would be even larger today if the Nevada barite enterprise had not lobbied the API to introduce the 4.1-sg specification.

In 2024, all domestic barite production came from three active mines in Nevada. The dynamics of the industry have evolved such that Nevada mines barite and then processes it at various crushing facilities for use in western and

354 Beginning in the 2000s, U.S. barite-4.2 specific-gravity reserves were running low and Chinese products were becoming increasingly cheaper to import.

central oil drilling operations. Imported barite is shipped to gulf coast states and then used primarily in offshore drilling operations in the Gulf of Mexico. This domestic/foreign division is explained by ocean shipping rates that are much lower than ground rates, resulting in barite products being used in proximity to the cheapest mode of delivery.

India

The majority of India's barite resources (92%) are located in the state of Andhra Pradesh with its most productive operation being the Mangampet mine. State-owned Andhra Pradesh Mineral Development Corporation (AP-MDC) runs a massive open pit operation (1,800 meters across) located in the southeastern part of the country, 55 miles from the coast on the Bay of Bengal. APMDC contracts the private company Thriveni Earthmovers to extract up to 3 million tpa which is 95% of total annual Indian barite production. APMDC has already extracted 40 million tons of barite ore from estimated reserves of 74 million tons, meaning the mine will reach its end of life in 2034.[355] From 2019-2022, APMDC sold its 4.2-sg barite products for $70.00-$75.00 per ton and its 4.1-sg products for $50.00-$55.00 per ton.[356]

China

China has a robust barite extraction industry, producing 2.1 million tons in 2024, sending 540,000 tons (28%) to its single biggest customer, the United States. The industry is focused on Guizhou, an inland province that requires 400 miles of overland travel to reach the coast, adding to overall costs. China's total sale of barite exports in 2023 averaged $162.42 USD per ton while world sales averaged $185.26 per ton.[357] If the U.S. added a 25% tariff to Chinese barite imports which averaged $141.51 in 2023, this would raise their price to $176.88. While this is still below the world average, U.S. gulf coast buyers would look to source their barite elsewhere as Chinese imports were already priced higher than their peers like India and Mexico.

Actions Taken

In 2018 and 2019, the Trump administration considered placing a 25% Section 301 tariff on barite imports from China. The API opposed these tariffs

355 "Andhra Pradesh govt earns Rs 1,000 crore from baryes exports." The Times of India, February 8, 2023.

356 Trade Lane Analytics, before additional costs like shipping.

357 UN Comtrade data, world average based on 94% of reported exports.

during U.S. Trade Representative (USTR) hearings in 2019, arguing that the U.S. oil industry had no suitable replacement ready for barite drilling mud. If Chinese barite imports ceased, the U.S. would have to import more from India and Morocco to compensate which were of inadequate quality and did not consistently meet API specifications. To make these products usable, they would have to be mixed with Chinese barite which met API specifications. That same year, the oil industry doubled down on its own barite supply chain vulnerability by getting 11 congressional representatives to sign a letter addressed to the USTR, opposing barite tariffs.[358]

Furthermore, six different drilling companies petitioned the USTR against the imposition of tariffs, citing several reasons. A primary one was that alternative weighting agents, while available, were more expensive than barite. Second, China would not be negatively impacted as they would just sell their barite product to other markets at higher prices which would improve their profitability. Finally, the overall increase in drilling costs would make the U.S. oil and gas industry less competitive and would drive buyers to OPEC and Russia. Consequently, the barite tariff proposals were never implemented. This is a great example of U.S. special interest groups driving critical minerals security decisions to maximize their own profits.

Incentives & Tariffs

Under the Inflation Reduction Act, a company would qualify for a 10% tax credit under the Section 45X Advanced Manufacturing Production Credit if the barite "which is barium sulfate purified to a minimum purity of 80% barite by mass."

- The domestic barite mining industry receives a 14% depletion allowance (3 x Nevada companies) while foreign companies receive a 14% rate (there are none).

Barium compounds were exempted from tariffs in April 2025 by the Trump administration. The normal tariff schedule encourages the import of barite while taxing other products at overall low rates.

U.S Supply Chain Security Strategy Moving Forward

Because the U.S. is unable to produce barite at volume in an economic manner, it is dependent on imports which is unlikely to change. Specifically,

358 Seven from Texas, two from Louisiana, one from Ohio, one from W. Virginia.

cheap Indian imports are the U.S.' barite center of gravity, a better alternative than Chinese dependence. However, this supply chain extending to Asia ensures it remains vulnerable to disruption. The oil industry is the central culprit for continuing barite vulnerability to Chinese suppliers.

There are several substitutes for barite as a weighting agent in drilling mud to include celestite, hematite, ilmenite, manganese tetraoxide, calcium carbonate, galena, and others. An estimated 85% of all drilling muds used worldwide employ barite as their primary weighting agent with the remaining 15% using a variety of products. Barite is the preferred agent in most drilling operations because of its low cost, ideal qualities (specific gravity), and established supply chain. The U.S. oil industry has fought the transition to different drilling mud ingredients and has opposed the imposition of tariffs that would shift U.S. away from Chinese barite imports.

Multi-pronged Approach

- The U.S. can provide incentives to the Mexican barite industry to increase production and continue exempting them from barite tariffs.
- Graduated tariff increases should be instituted on Chinese imports to shape supply chains to other partners like Morocco.
- Focus R&D on alternative weighting agents like hematite-barite.
- In 2022, the Defense National Stockpile held no barite and the Defense Logistics Agency (DLA) announced no plans to acquire any through 2025. A one-year stockpile of barite based on U.S. annual consumption would be 2.4 million tons.
- To remove the need for barite altogether, the U.S. can transition off fossil fuels and pursue renewable energy generation which does not require drilling mud.

2024 Barite Production (metric tons)			
Country	**2020**	**2024**	**Reserves**
United States	348,000	425,000	150 million
China	2.8 million	2.1 million	110 million
Iran	202,000	310,000	100 million
Kazakhstan	445,000	650,000	85 million
India	1.6 million	2.6 million	51 million
Turkey	180,000	220,000	34 million
Russia	287,000	250,000	12 million
Morocco	410,000	1 million	NA
Laos	180,000	300,000	NA
Mexico	323,000	330,000	NA
Pakistan		130,000	NA
Rest of World	329,000	320,000	NA
Total	6.8 million	8.2 million	

2024 U.S. Imports - 1.9 million metric tons

India: 654,000 tons (34%) - Mangampet Mine

Morocco: 338,000 tons (18%) - tariff exempted

China: 321,000 tons (17%)

Mexico: 296,000 (16%)

Vietnam: 167,000 (9%)

Laos: 164,000 tons (8%)

**USGS & UN Comtrade data*

Beryllium (Be)

Background

Beryllium is acquired mainly through the mining of bertrandite, beryl or phenakite ores which are then processed through crushing, grinding and leaching with sulfuric acid, resulting in a sulfate. This sulfate is further processed to remove impurities and contaminants, creating beryllium hydroxide. The beryllium hydroxide is then used in any number of applications such as metal alloys. Beryllium products have a score of applications to include sub-sea telecommunications, nuclear reactors and warheads, Forward Looking Infrared Radar – FLIR sensors, and advanced memory high-performance logic applications.

In 2024, the U.S. led the world in beryllium production with 180 contained tons, followed by Brazil with 80 tons, China with 77 tons, and Mozambique with 24 tons. Combined, these four countries accounted for 99% of world beryllium extraction estimated at 360 tons. Although exact beryllium reserves are unknown, they are likely more than 100,000 tons. The U.S. is believed to hold 60% of world beryllium reserves to include locations in Nevada, South Dakota, Texas, and Alaska. Beryllium-copper master alloy averaged $1.5 million per ton.[359]

The U.S. imported 546 tons of beryllium copper plate with almost all this coming from Japan (93%).[360] The U.S. imported much lower volumes of beryllium copper master alloys at 17 tons with most coming from Kazakhstan (99%). Just 14 tons of beryllium powders and scrap imports were dominated by Kazakhstan (43%) and the remainer from Europe. Finally, 9 tons of beryllium oxides were imported with almost half from Estonia.[361]

Materion Corporation, NYSE: MTRN

The history of the U.S. beryllium industry is a history of the Materion Corporation which was known as Brush Wellman Inc. until they changed names in 2011. Materion is an Ohio based company with 3,400 employees specializing in the manufacturing of high-performance materials and the only one with domestic bertrandite extraction operations. The company has been in business

359 From U.S. Geological Survey data. Contained beryllium content.

360 These were most likely refined products from U.S. imports and then re-exported to the U.S.

361 USITC database.

since 1931 with offices in Asia, Europe, and North America. Materion extracts bertrandite at their Spor Mountain open pit mine in Utah, ninety miles southwest of Salt Lake City, which has been active since 1968.

The company extracted 253 tons of beryllium ore in 2024, 202 tons in 2023, and 191 tons in 2022. The mine has an estimated 18,500 tons of beryllium reserves remaining which should last another 92 years, based on current rates of extraction. The company makes beryllium hydroxide at their Utah milling site which they subsequently ship to their Ohio site. Materion is under financial stress with a net loss of $8.2 million in 2024, balanced by net income of $90 million (5% margin) in 2023, and $84 million (5% margin) in 2022. The company received $9 million from the 45X Advanced Manufacturing Production Credit.

China – Second Largest Player

In 2023, China imported 19.2 metric tons of beryllium products with 99% of this coming from Kazakhstan.[362] Combined with China's own annual production, this provided Beijing with 117 tons of beryllium; their own exports of the product were insignificant. The Ningxia Non-ferrous Metal Research Institute is China's principal beryllium research and production site, making China one of only three countries in the world with this capability which includes the U.S. and Kazakhstan. SOE Shuikoushan Nonferrous Metals in Hunan Province and Fuyun Hengsheng Beryllium Industry Company in XUAR also have finished beryllium product capabilities.

In 2020, the Chinese beryllium industry started a strategic alliance of concerned members to better coordinate and improve the national beryllium value chain.[363] The participating companies were China Color (Ningxia) Oriental Group, Ningxia Company, and the Northwest Rare Metal Research Institute. The Laboratory of Rare Metal Special Materials hosted the conference in Yinchuan. There were over 100 representatives from various state entities and mining companies who recognized beryllium as a strategic material for national defense, the military industrial base, and the national economy.[364]

362 UN Comtrade database HS Code 811212.

363 Formally the "Association of the China Beryllium Industry Technological Innovation Strategic Alliance."

364 "China's first rare metal beryllium industry strategic alliance established." Shanghai Metals Market, October 13, 2020.

Kazakhstan: A Declining Industry

Historically, the U.S. sourced low-grade beryllium from the state-owned Ulba Metallurgical plant who used bertrandite ore supplied from Russia since Kazakhstan does not have its own beryllium reserves. This was a continuation of the supply chain relationship from when Ulba provided finished beryllium products to the former Soviet Union. Materion signed a ten-year agreement with Ulba for 25,000 pounds of beryllium ingots a year, from 2003-2013. U.S. Geological Survey estimated that Ulba would run out of stockpiled beryllium around the year 2022. Ulba has a variety of product lines like low-enriched uranium, tantalum, niobium (magnets), and REE with sales offices in several countries, including Moscow and Shanghai.

Actions Taken

Materion closed the U.S.' only primary beryllium manufacturing facility in 2000 for a variety of reasons including outdated equipment, health risks and related lawsuits, and lack of demand.[365] In 2003, Congress requested that DOD conduct a study to determine the adequacy of the U.S. beryllium industrial base to meet their requirements. DOD's subsequent report revealed that the U.S. beryllium supply chain was no longer secure due to Materion's plant closing, the lack of adequate supply from dwindling national stockpile reserves, and the inability of foreign partners to meet their metal purity requirements (Kazakhstan).

DOD estimated that as of the date of the report (2004), they would run out of high-purity beryllium by 2015. They considered three options: transfer U.S. beryllium manufacturing technology to their Kazakh partners, pursue an accelerated R&D program for alternatives, or authorize a cost sharing program with Materion through the Defense Production Act (DPA). DOD recommended subsidizing Materion's operations and Congress agreed. Congress authorized $74 million from 2005-2011 to update the Materion facility and then another $11.8 million from 2021-2024. Materion's updated facility in Elmore, Ohio was completed in 2011.

This is a success story in that the U.S. identified the criticality of beryllium to the national defense industry and created a plan to modernize the U.S.' only beryllium manufacturing plant. This is also a failure in that the U.S. was unable

365 Beryllium is highly toxic with exposure leading to lung cancer and immunocompromise called Beryllium Sensitization.

to get ahead of the problem and identify that action was required before the plant actually closed. Thus, the U.S. suffered an eleven-year gap in its primary beryllium production capability. It must be noted that Materion didn't have the capital to upgrade its own manufacturing capability and could only do so through subsidies.

Utah Governor Cox signed SCR003 in 2022 recognizing Utah as a significant producer of 28 critical minerals to include beryllium and that state public land should be open to extracting these critical minerals. Other than putting a statement on the public record, this resolution has no actual impact on critical mineral operations. Highlighting this fact, Utah offers no incentives for beryllium mining which is charged a tax rate of 2.6% (based on 125% value of mining costs) and a 4% royalty rate.

Incentives & Tariffs

Under the Inflation Reduction Act, a company would qualify for a 10% tax credit under the Section 45X Advanced Manufacturing Production Credit if their beryllium is "converted to copper-beryllium master alloy or purified to a minimum purity of 99% beryllium by mass."

The domestic beryllium mining industry receives a 22% depletion allowance (Materion) while foreign companies receive a 14% rate (there are none).

Beryllium was not included on the Trump administration's April 2025 critical mineral tariff exemptions which is problematic because the U.S. imports significant quantities of finished beryllium products.

U.S Supply Chain Security Strategy Moving Forward

The U.S. has an enviable position as the world's largest producer of beryllium with a vertically integrated domestic beryllium value chain and being a net exporter of finished beryllium products. The likely long-term threats to this position include Materion depleting its bertrandite mine and the company becoming unprofitable due to superior competition from Chinese manufacturers. Countries like Russia and Brazil have the beryllium reserves but not the manufacturing capability. Countries that have the technological sophistication to develop their own advanced processing capability are either G7 members or U.S. allies like South Korea.

Multi-pronged Approach

- The U.S. should monitor the domestic beryllium value chain and determine when and if additional government assistance is needed.
- In 2022, the National Defense Stockpile held 69.3 tons of beryllium products with the Defense Logistics Agency (DLA) disposing 8 tons in 2023, 2024, and 2025, leaving 45.3 tons. A one-year stockpile based on average consumption would be 150 tons, so the current amount would last four months. For background, a company placing a bid on the beryllium for sale from the stockpile must be incorporated either in Canada or the U.S. and have sold beryllium to U.S. customers within the last ten years. This narrowed the number of qualified buyers considerably and Materion likely used this as an opportunity to buy back its own beryllium - which it previously sold to DLA - at discounted prices.
- While Materion recovers upwards of 40% of beryllium scrap, it is unknown how much the overall industry recovers this product and it may be 20%. Mandatory recovery of all excess material should be instituted for a rare metal costing $1.5 million a ton.
- Beryllium is difficult to replace because of its combination of qualities such as stiffness, light weight, and resistance to extreme temperatures . Regardless, R&D efforts should continue to find replacements whenever possible such as copper-nickel-tin spinodal alloys.

2024 Beryllium Production (metric tons)			
Country	**2020**	**2024**	**Exports**
United States	165	180	70
China	70	77	200 kg
Brazil	3	80	
Mozambique	3	24	24 (China)
Madagascar	1	1	
Rwanda	1	1	
Uganda	7	1	
Kazakhstan			19 (China)
Nigeria			153 (China)
Total	250	364	

*The U.S. imported 360 tons of beryllium copper plates valued at $9 million, with 79% coming from Germany. (5 mm thickness)

*The U.S. imported 17.7 tons of beryllium copper master alloys valued at $1 million with 96% from Kazakhstan.

*The U.S. imported 225 tons beryllium copper plates valued at $5.1 million, with 95% coming from Japan. (Less than 5 mm thickness, 500 mm width)

*The U.S. imported 2.3 tons of beryllium oxide & hyrdroxide valued at $73,000.00, CIF with 48% from India.

**Data from USGS, USITC*

Bismuth (Bi)

Background

While Bismuth can be found as an ore in bismuthinite and bismite, it is most commonly recovered as a byproduct of refining other metals like lead (primarily), tin, tungsten, copper, gold, and silver. Bismuth is a non-toxic brittle metal with a low melting point and is used in alloys, electronics, jewelry, pigments, pharmaceuticals, and cosmetics. Bismuth-tellurium-oxide is a paste used as a semiconductor for thermoelectric applications. The military and hunting sectors have used bismuth to replace toxic lead bullets with varying degrees of success.[366]

The U.S. lost its ability to produce primary refined bismuth material in 1997 when ASARCO (American Smelting and Refining Company) closed its Omaha lead smelting facility due to continuing unmitigated pollution concerns. ASARCO subsequently filed for bankruptcy in 2005 based on the need to pay for the clean-up of 80 different contaminated sites that it owned. In 2009, ASARCO and its parent company Grupo Mexico agreed to pay $1.79 billion to the EPA, Department of Justice, and Departments of the Interior and Agriculture for environmental pollution remediation.

While primary bismuth recovery operations ended in 1997, the U.S. still maintained a lead smelter capability, and thus the potential to recover bismuth, until 2013. That year, the Doe Run Company closed the U.S.' last primary lead smelter facility in Herculaneum, Missouri because of its inability to meet EPA clean air requirements and could not afford to build a new, cleaner plant using an electrowinning process.[367]

In 2024, China led the world in bismuth production with 13,000 tons, followed by Laos (1,100 tons), South Korea (1,000 tons), and Japan (500 tons). China controlled 81% of the market giving it monopoly status while China and Laos together accounted for 90% of the world market. Exact Bismuth reserves are unknown. High purity bismuth averaged $10,600.00 per ton.[368]

The U.S. imported 1,846 metric tons or 94% of its estimated bismuth needs with the remainder coming from secondary production (scraps, recycling, re-

366 Bismuth is more expensive than lead with less density. Test rounds fired through rifles have proven to be less stable and thus less accurate.

367 Doe Run is the largest lead manufacturer in the U.S.

368 U.S. Geological Survey 2024.

use). The U.S. relied on China for 962 tons of its bismuth needs (52%) and 638 tons from South Korea (35%). In turn, the U.S. exported almost 500 tons of bismuth products with most going to Canada (168 tons), then Mexico (137 tons), and China (51 tons).[369] From 2020-2024, the U.S. imported 93% of its bismuth needs with 67% coming from China.

Actions Taken

The U.S. has done little to secure its Bismuth needs other than to import as much as possible from its partner South Korea. China has steadily increased its own production of bismuth over the last decade.

Incentives & Tariffs

Under the Inflation Reduction Act, a company would qualify for a 10% tax credit under the Section 45X Advanced Manufacturing Production Credit if their bismuth is "purified to a minimum of 99% purity by mass."

Domestic bismuth mining companies receive a 22% depletion allowance (there are none) while foreign companies receive a 14% rate (there are none).

China instituted bismuth export licensing controls in February 2025. Bismuth products were exempted from tariffs in April 2025 by the Trump administration.

U.S. Supply Chain Security Strategy Moving Forward

The U.S. has an insecure bismuth position because of its own lack of production and reliance on China for the majority of its imports. There is no stronger case for the need to stockpile a critical mineral than bismuth.

Multi-pronged Approach

- In 2022, the U.S. National Defense Stockpile held no bismuth products, having sold its entire bismuth stocks in 1997. The Defense Logistics Agency announced no plans to acquire bismuth products through 2025. A one-year stockpile based on average consumption would be 1,400 tons.
- Another obvious move is mandating a national recycling program as very little bismuth is recycled in the U.S., perhaps as low as 3%.
- To address the fundamental problem of domestic production, the USG should work with private industry to develop a clean process

369 UN Comtrade data HS 8106.

for extracting bismuth from lead and employ the Defense Production Act to provide the funding for this capability.

- The U.S. should provide incentives for private industry in Canada and Mexico to develop an ex-China midstream bismuth production capability.

2024 Bismuth Production (metric tons)

Country	2010	2024	% of Total
United States	None	None	
China	6,500	13,000	81%
Laos	None	1,100	7%
South Korea	None	1,000	6%
Japan	None	500	3%
Kazakhstan	150	180	
Bolivia	90	70	
Bulgaria	None	50	
World Total	8,900	16,000	

2024 U.S. Bismuth Imports

The U.S. imported 1,796 tons of bismuth products valued at $20.5 million for an average of $11,400.00 a ton.

South Korea: 787 tons (44%) valued at $8.4 million

China: 758 tons (43%) valued at $7.4 million

Japan: 107 tons (6%) valued at $1.19 million

**UN Comtrade data HS code 8106*

Cerium (Ce)

Background

Cerium is one of the seventeen REE (Rare Earth Elements) designated as critical minerals and is part of the light REE (LREE) lanthanide series. REE are commonly found together and are thus usually collectively mined and processed. REE are commonly found in bastnaesite, a fluorocarbonate mineral, and monazite, a phosphate mineral. Cerium has many uses, including the manufacturing of magnets, catalytic converters, alloys, electrodes, ignition devices, and glass. Production volumes of REE are reported as REO (Rare Earth Oxides) and as an overall group total, not as specific elements.

In 2024, China led the world in REO production with 270,000 metric tons, which was 69% of total world production of 390,000 tons. China was followed by the U.S. with 45,000 tons (12%), Burma 31,000 tons (8%), and Australia 13,000 tons (3%). World REO reserves are estimated at 90 million tons with China holding 44 million tons (49%), Vietnam 3.5 million tons (4%), Brazil 5.7 million tons (6%) and Russia 3.8 million tons (4%). The U.S. holds an estimated 1.9 million tons and Canada 830,000 tons. Cerium oxide is relatively inexpensive, selling at just $1,000.00 per metric ton.[370]

Historically, Burma has exported 100% of its REO products to China, meaning 77% of total REO production cycles through China with just these two alone, giving Beijing an REO monopoly. In 2023, China imported 2,875 metric tons of cerium compounds, with 2,128 (74%) coming from Malaysia, 573 tons from India, 83 tons from Japan, and 5 tons from the U.S. For exports, China shipped out 9,455 tons with Japan receiving 2,589 tons (27%), Taiwan 1,797 tons (19%) and the U.S. 892 tons (9%). It is interesting to note that more than half of China's cerium exports went to its primary regional and global competitors.[371]

The U.S. imported 2,350 metric tons of cerium compounds in 2024 with 1,300 tons from China (55%), 338 tons from Japan, 352 tons from Malaysia, and 270 tons from Estonia. The vast majority was from Asia making it a geographic chokepoint. The U.S. in turn exported just 353 metric tons with most

370 U.S. Geological Survey 2024. Canada and Mexico produce no REO.
371 UN Comtrade database HS 284610.

going to Japan (94 tons), Canada (61 tons) and China (50 tons). The U.S. also exported 49 tons to Beijing's rival, Taiwan.[372]

MP Materials (MPM)

MP Materials (NYSE: MP) is a U.S. company with 680 employees that runs the country's only active REE mine in Mountain Pass, California. Their bastnaesite mineral operation is located 50 miles southwest of Las Vegas, just across from the California/Nevada state line, adjacent to Highway 15, connecting Las Vegas to Los Angeles. MP produced 45,400 tons of REO in 2024, up from 41,500 tons the year previously. The company is a vertically integrated example of the "mine to magnet" value chain that the U.S. would like to build to break China's REE dominance.

MP Materials had a net loss of $65 million in 2024, which was a reversal of net profits of $24 million in 2023 (9.5% margin) and $289 million in 2022 (55% margin). At the end of 2024, the company had almost $851 million in cash balanced by $1.2 billion in liabilities. The extreme change in margins was due to the change in pricing of NdPr per ton, meaning China increased production which lowered prices and impacted profitability. MPM seeks to increase revenue moving forward based on increasing REO processing volume and future magnet production.

China – REE Monopoly

Although China extracts only two-thirds of REEs, upwards of 90% passes through there for processing and refinement. The REE industry in China is diversified with at least thirty separate companies involved although Beijing has moved to consolidate the sector. In 2021, Beijing consolidated three of the largest SOE REE firms into the singular SOE China Rare Earth Group which now controls 62% of China's HREE market.[373] Importantly, China's Negative List for Foreign Investment Access prohibits foreign mining companies from participating in its domestic REE sector. In 2024, a new silicate mineral called Nipeiite was discovered at an active REE mine in Henan Province with the highest known cerium content.

China exported 9,455 metric tons of cerium compounds (HS 284610) in 2023 with most going to the advanced economies of Japan (27%), Taiwan

372 Ibid.

373 Zhou, Qian and Sofia Brooke, "China Merges Three Rare Earths State-Owned Entities to Increase Pricing Power and Efficiency." China Briefing, January 12, 2022.

(19%), the U.S. (9%), and the Netherlands (9%). Japan paid the most for these products at $1.49 per kg, Taiwan got bargain basement prices at just $00.72 per kg, the U.S. paid $1.40 per kg, and the Netherlands $1.26 per kg. China exported another 9,000 tons of ferrocerium products (HS 3606) which were much more widely distributed with the largest volume going to the U.S. (45%) followed by the Dominican Republic (6%), and Japan (4%).[374]

Actions Taken

In 2020, MP Materials was awarded a $9.6 million Defense Production Act (DPA) Technology Investment Agreement (TIA) grant to construct a LREE processing and separation capability.

In 2022, MP Materials was awarded a $35 million contract by DOD's Office of Industrial Base Policy, Industrial Base Analysis and Sustainment program, to build a heavy REE (HREE) processing facility at Mountain Passs.

MPM was awarded $58.5 million in 2022 through the Department of Energy's Section 48C Advanced Energy Project tax credit program to build their Fort Worth, TX magnet facility. The City of Fort Worth provided MP with a seven-year tax break on up to 60% of its property taxes.

For 2023, MPM qualified for a 10% tax credit, estimated at $38.4 million, for production costs under Section 45X Advanced Manufacturing Production Credit if its products are "converted to cerium oxide which is purified to a minimum purity of 99.9% cerium oxide by mass or purified to a minimum purity of 99% cerium by mass."

MPM received a $14.79 million tax credit in 2021 through the state's California Competes Tax Credit program which was spread over 2021-2025 if the company met agreed to milestones such as hiring and investments.

Incentives & Tariffs

Domestic REE mining companies receive a 14% depletion allowance (MP Materials) while foreign companies receive a 14% rate (there are none) for monazite, bastnaesite, and xenotime extraction operations.

The Trump administration exempted cerium from its April 2025 tariffs schedule. In 2023, China banned the export of cerium magnets technology, adding them to its "Catalogue of Technologies Prohibited and Restricted from

374 UN Comtrade data.

Export." In 2026, the U.S. will impose a 25% tariff on imported Chinese permanent magnets.

U.S Supply Chain Security Strategy Moving Forward

The U.S. has a vulnerable cerium position because it imports most of its needs directly from China. Although the U.S. produces cerium domestically, it historically sent it to China for refinement and follow-on sales. The likely long-term threats to this position include MP Materials depleting its Mountain Pass mine or the company becoming unprofitable due to continuing lower price competition from Chinese manufacturers. Countries like Vietnam, Brazil and Russia have large REE/cerium reserves but not the manufacturing capability. To date, only China, the U.S., and Malaysia (Australia) have the technological sophistication to develop their own advanced processing capability.[375]

Multi-pronged Approach

- The U.S. should monitor the domestic cerium value chain and determine when and if additional government assistance is needed. MP Materials has received sufficient government subsidies to date although they must continue to lower costs.
- In 2022, the U.S. held no cerium products in its National Defense Stockpile. The Defense Logistics Agency (DLA) announced that they were purchasing upwards of 550 tons of cerium products each in 2023 and 2024 but none in 2025. Based on the U.S.' probable annual consumption of 1,650 metric tons, this supply would last eight months. Most likely, DLA purchased this cerium from MP Materials which would have cost $5.5 million based on average export prices.
- It is unknown how much cerium is recycled or reused, but it is likely very small volumes. A mandatory national cerium recycling, recovery, and reuse program would maximize access to this resource.
- Cerium oxide can be replaced by other materials such as tin oxide, zirconium oxide and aluminum oxide, depending on the use. However, cerium is hard to replace for its primary uses as alternatives do not perform as well.

375 Vietnam has a limited REE processing capability.

2024 REO Production (metric tons)		
Country	**Extraction**	**Reserves**
United States	43,000	1.9 million
China	270,000	44 million
Burma	31,000	Unknown
Australia	13,000	5.7 million
Thailand	13,000	4,500
Nigeria	13,000	Unknown
Total	**390,000**	**90 million**

World Cerium Production: 156,000 tons (based on 40% of REO production)

Cerium Compounds

U.S. Imports: 2,350 tons, $19.3 million value (2024)

China: 1,300 tons, $3.5 million value

Malaysia: 352 tons, $344,000.00 value

Japan: 338 tons, $13.8 million value

Estonia: 270 tons, $361,000.00 value

**UN Comtrade data HS Code 2846.10*

Cesium (Cs)

Background

Cesium is commonly recovered from pollucite and is primarily used as an additive for drilling fluids in the oil extraction industry (75% of global cesium use), for atomic clocks, semiconductor etching, infrared technology applications, 5G communications, and the medical industry (cesium-137). Historically, there have only been three productive cesium mines, one each in Canada, Australia, and Zimbabwe. Presently, the only active mine is owned by the Chinese mining company Sinomine Resources Group.

Although exact data is not available, there may be global reserves of just 200,000 contained tons of cesium concentrated mainly in Canada (two-thirds of all reserves), Australia, Zimbabwe, Namibia, and China.[376] While the U.S. does have limited cesium occurrences, it is uneconomic to mine and the U.S. primarily imported cesium through the Cabot Corporation until 2019. Presently, the U.S. imports 100% of its cesium needs. Historically, U.S. demand has been relatively low – just 25 metric tons per year.[377]

Because cesium products are sold in low non-commercial volumes, there is no indexed or known average market price. Companies requiring regular and relatively large volumes of cesium buy directly from cesium specialty manufacturers through negotiated sales agreements. In 2024, high-purity cesium metal 99.99% purity sold as low as $10.00 a gram and as high as $100.00 a gram on the spot market. This reveals a wide range of pricing from just $10,000.00 a kilogram to $100,000.00 per kilogram. As just one example, Thermofisher advertised its high-purity cesium metal for $41.00 a gram or $41,000.00 a kilogram.

China – Cesium Monopoly

Chinese mining company Sinomine Resources Group bought the Tantalum Mining Corporation of Canada (Tanco) from U.S. company Cabot Corporation in 2019.[378] Tanco claims that their underground mine at Bernic Lake in Manitoba, Canada holds 82% of the world's known reserves of pollucite. Sinomine reopened their Tanco mine in 2021, which had been closed since 2015, to produce lithium, tantalum, and cesium which they ship to China for refinement. In

376 Sinomine Annual Report 2023.
377 U.S. Geological Survey, 2005.
378 Shenzhen Stock Exchange SHE: 002738.

2023, Sinomine committed $130 million to build an ore concentrator plant to further refine its lithium and cesium products in North America.[379]

Sinomine has two cesium specialty production centers, one in Winnipeg, Canada and the other in Jiangxi Province, China. The company is a full-spectrum cesium manufacturer, producing cesium salts, carbonates, sulfates, nitrates, hydroxides, iodides, and acids. Sinomine also has two cesium formate centers for its drilling fluid operations, one in Aberdeen, Scotland and the other in Bergen, Norway. They sold 2,946 barrels of cesium formate in 2023, up from 2,597 barrels the previous year.

In 2022, Sinomine bought the Bikita Mine in Zimbabwe where it modernized the facility to increase both lithium and cesium production from its pegmatite reserves. While Sinomine advertises the Bikita mine as a cesium resource, it is most likely depleted and presently does not produce any cesium – it is primarily a lithium operation.

Sinomine is a profitable company with no signs of financial distress. In 2023, the company brought in $150 million of operating revenue and $124 million from other investments for a gross income of $274 million. Net income after total costs was $137 million for a very high 50% margin. Sinomine ended 2023 with $605 million in cash and equivalents on hand, up from $308 million the previous year.

Canada

Canadian mining company Power Metals Corporation (PMC) is developing three critical mineral lines of effort: tantalum, lithium, and cesium.[380] Specifically, PMC is developing their Case Lake lithium/cesium project in Ontario with no projected date for extraction operations to commence. Sinomine purchased 5.7% of PMC shares in 2021 where PMC agreed to sell all its products to Sinomine which would then process them at Sinomine's Winnipeg facility. In 2022, the Canadian government ordered Sinomine to exit PMC in a move to secure Canada's critical mineral supply chain. Australian mining company Winsome Resources Limited subsequently bought Sinomine's shares and later purchased 19% of PMC.[381] Winsome also picked up Sinomine's previous

379 https://en.imsilkroad.com/p/332908.html

380 TSXV: PWM.V. PMC has no active operations and is unprofitable.

381 ASX: WR1. Winsome has no active operations and is unprofitable.

offtake agreements and would be responsible for finding buyers for their three product lines.

Actions Taken

Canada had several laws in place to prevent the purchase of Tanco by Sinomine yet did not use them. These laws included the *Foreign Invest Review Act* (1973) where Sinomine's purchase should have triggered a review by the Foreign Investment Review Board (FIRB), the *Canadian Ownership and Control Determination Act* (1985), and the *Investment Canada Act* (1985) which was amended in 2021.

Cesium Incentives & Tariffs

Under the Inflation Reduction Act, a company would qualify for a 10% tax credit under the Section 45X Advanced Manufacturing Production Credit of their cesium is "Converted to cesium formate or cesium carbonate or purified to a minimum purity of 99% cesium by mass."

Domestic REE mining companies receive a 14% depletion allowance (there are none) while foreign companies receive a 14% rate (there are none) for monazite and, bastnaesite and xenotime extraction operations.

Cesium was not included in the Trump administration's April 2025 tariff exemptions.

U.S Supply Chain Security Strategy Moving Forward

The U.S. has extreme cesium supply chain insecurity as it imports 100% of all cesium needs and the only known active cesium mine is Chinese-owned.

Multi-pronged Approach

- The U.S. and Canada should work together to identify an acceptable buyer from a critical minerals security perspective for the Tanco cesium business and develop the incentives to maintain ownership. Then, Canada should use the *Investment Canada Act* to order Sinomine's divestment with one option being Sinomine's restriction to being a minority owner (49%).
- The U.S. should work with Canada to identify ways to incentivize Power Metal's cesium extraction operations if they prove to be viable.

- The U.S. has failed to develop cesium market surveillance tools that effectively track the production and movement of cesium. In order to acquire the necessary data to make intelligent critical mineral decisions, the U.S. International Trade Commission (USITC) should create a dedicated HTS code for cesium.
- In 2022, the U.S. National Defense Stockpile did not hold any cesium reserves and the Defense Logistics Agency had no plans to purchase any through 2025. The U.S. may consume 25 tons of cesium annually.
- It is believed that cesium brines are reused at an 85% rate.[382] It is unknown how much other products such as cesium metal is recycled or reused, but it is likely to be in very small volumes. A mandatory national recycling, recovery, and reuse program would maximize access to this resource.
- Cesium can possibly be replaced in certain circumstances by rubidium, potassium, and sodium, depending on the use.
- The U.S. should identify and track cesium mining operations globally and consider using the Defense Production Act to support their activity when feasible.

382 U.S. Geological Survey 2024. Customers rent Tanco's cesium formate brine and return the majority for reuse.

Chromium (Cr)

Background

Chromium is primarily extracted from chromite, which is a mineral composed mostly of chromium oxide and iron oxide.[383] Chromium is used mainly as a minority element in ferrochromium alloy to make steel which increases hardness, heat, and wear resistance. Because chromium is a hard and brilliant metal that resists corrosion, it is commonly used in electroplating applications (i.e., chrome plating). Upwards of 95% of mined chromite is used in ferrochrome applications.[384] Smelting ferrochromium is energy intensive that is done largely with electric-arc furnaces, requiring an average of 4 MWh per ton.[385]

In 2024, the world produced 47 million metric tons of chromium with South Africa producing 21 million tons (45%), Turkey 8 million (17%) and Kazakhstan 6.5 million (14%). In 2023, China imported 18.2 million tons of chromium ores and 3.2 million tons of ferrochromium with most coming from South Africa, Kazakhstan, and Turkey. Japan imported 42,000 tons of ores and 526,000 tons of ferrochromium with most also coming from South Africa and Kazakhstan. Germany imported 117,000 tons of ore and 105,000 tons of ferrochromium with most coming from Kazakhstan, Turkey, the Netherlands, and Finland.[386]

The U.S. has no economic chromium mineral resources, extracts no chromium domestically, and imported 77% of its needs. In 2024, the U.S. consumed less than 1% of total world chromium production, importing 97,700 tons of ores and concentrates, 433,000 tons of ferrochromium, and 17,200 tons of chromium metals. The U.S. produced 100,000 tons of secondary chromium products from recovered scrap metal which was 23% of apparent total consumption of 440,000 tons of all chromium products.[387]

---

383 While chromium is found in scores of minerals, only chromite is economically viable for extraction.

384 Du Preez, Stephanus, et al. "An Overview of Currently Applied Ferrochrome Production Processes and Their Waste Management Practices." Minerals, June 2023.

385 Patel-Campbell, Claire. "Energy prices remain dominant in ferro-chrome markets." Fastmarkets, January 24, 2022.

386 U.S. Geological Survey and UN Comtrade data.

387 USGS Data; UN Comtrade data HS Codes 2610, 720241, 720249, 811221, 811222.

Yildirim

In 2023, the U.K. based company Elementis Global sold its U.S. chrome and chemicals business for $170 million to Turkish company Yildirim which renamed its new acquisition American Chrome and Chemicals Inc. (ACC). Elementis sold its chrome business for a variety of reasons including a lack of continuity with its business strategy, high greenhouse gas emissions, and market volatility impacting its margins. In 2022, Elementis' U.S. Chromium operations brought in $185 million in revenues with operating profits of $23 million for a 12% margin. Because Elementis' chromium business used carbon emitting natural gas as opposed to renewable energy, it was responsible for 63% of the company's overall energy costs.

ACC headquarters is in Texas and is a division within the Yilmaden Holding Metals and Mining Group. They are the only U.S. based company that consumes imported chromium ores and concentrates for primary production and are the largest producer of chromium chemical products in the country. ACC produced 105,000 tons of products in 2023, underwent several minor energy-saving factory upgrades, and renegotiated future chromium ore offtake agreements.[388] In 2024, Yilmaden intended to start chromium metal production at their Bear Metallurgical Company located in Pennsylvania.

Actions Taken

According to the DARS (Defense Acquisition Regulations System) 48 CFR 252.225-7009 *Restriction on Acquisition of Specialty Meals*, any steel alloy product with more than 25% chromium content acquired by the DOD must be melted or produced in the U.S.

Incentives & Tariffs

Under the Inflation Reduction Act, a company would qualify for a 10% tax credit under the Section 45X Advanced Manufacturing Production Credit if their products are "converted to ferrochromium consisting of not less than 60% chromium by mass or purified to a minimum purity off 99% chromium by mass." Even though ACC is foreign owned, it would still qualify for the 45X tax credits since its products are made in the U.S.

388 As of 2024, ACC's website was not active and Yilmaden did not recognize that they owned ACC in their company presentations.

- Domestic chromium mining companies receive a 22% depletion allowance (there are none) while foreign companies would receive a 14% rate (there are none).

Chromium was excluded from the Trump administration's April 2025 tariff schedule. The normal schedule encourages the import of ores and concentrates while taxing other products at overall low rates.

U.S Supply Chain Security Strategy Moving Forward

While the U.S. imports three-quarters of its chromium needs, it has developed reliable supply chains from suppliers who are not its chief competitors in the international system. It should maintain the security of these existing supply chains. The U.S. should maintain surveillance of its one remaining chromium production facility to ensure it remains economic and in friendly hands. Since ferrochromium smelting operations are energy intensive, an obvious move would be supplying utility-scale solar power with accompanying battery storage through the Defense Production Act if necessary.

Multi-pronged Approach

- In 2022, the U.S. National Defense Stockpile held 52,044 tons of chromium products. The Defense Logistics Agency (DLA) announced the offloading of 24,000 tons of ferrochromium and 500 tons of chromium metal from the strategic stockpile in 2023, 2024, and 2025 that would effectively offload its holdings. A one-year supply based on annual consumption would be 440,000 metric tons.
- Since chromium cannot be replaced by other materials in steel production, a mandatory national recycling, recovery, and reuse program would maximize access to this resource.

2024 Chromium Production (metric tons)		
Country	**Extraction**	**Reserves**
United States	none	630,000
Zimbabwe	1.1 million	540 million
Kazakhstan	6.5 million	320 million
South Africa	21 million	200 million
India	4.1 million	79 million
Turkey	8 million	27 million
Finland	1.9 million	8.3 million
Others	2.9 million	Unknown
Total	47 million	1.2 billion

2024 U.S. Imports: (ores & concentrates)

South Africa: 95,800 tons (98%), $41.8 million value, with an average price of $436.00 per ton.

2024 U.S. Imports: (ferrochromium) 395,800 tons

South Africa: 177,000 tons (45%), $200 million

Finland: 107,000 tons (27%), $135 million

Kazakhstan: 44,000 tons (11%), $98 million

Average price of $1,424.00 per metric ton

**USGS & UN Comtrade Data HS 2610, 7202.41*

Cobalt (Co)

Background

Cobalt is rarely extracted as a primary element (as in Morocco) and is mostly acquired secondary to nickel and copper mining (as in the Congo). Cobalt has a variety of uses to include in high-strength metal alloys, as a blue pigment in glass and pottery, magnets, and as a radioactive element in cancer treatments. Today, cobalt is primarily used, in the positive cathode of lithium-ion ternary batteries for the electric vehicle industry. The continuing pressure for increased cobalt extraction comes from the battery sector.

In 2024, the Democratic Republic of the Congo (DRC) led the world in cobalt production with 220,000 contained metric tons which was 76% of total world production of 290,000 tons. The DRC was followed by Indonesia with 28,000 tons (10%), and then Russia 8,700 tons (3%). World cobalt reserves are estimated at 11 million tons with the DRC holding 6 million tons (55%), Australia 1.7 million tons (15%), and Indonesia each 640,000 (6% combined). The U.S. holds an estimated 70,000 tons of cobalt reserves and Canada 220,000 tons. The London Metal Exchange assessed the average price of cobalt at $24,000.00 a metric ton.[389]

In 2024, the U.S. imported just 13.7 metric tons of cobalt ores and concentrates while paying $13,800.00 a ton with 44% coming from China.

The U.S. imported 3,775 tons of cobalt chemical products, mostly from Europe, for an average price of $14,800.00 a ton. Finally, the U.S. imported 11,600 tons of unwrought metals, powders, and scrap from a variety of ex-China sources for an average price of almost $32,000.00 a ton. The U.S. imported negligible amounts of finished cobalt products from China.[390]

Lundin Mining

Canadian company Lundin Mining owns their Eagle Mine located in Michigan which produced 300 tons of cobalt in 2024, which was exported for processing. The mine is primarily a nickel and copper operation, producing 16,000 tons of nickel, 14,000 tons of copper, and low volumes of cobalt in 2023. The Eagle Mine, in production since 2014, is not a future source of cobalt since its nickel and copper reserves will be depleted by 2029.

389 U.S. Geological Survey. Mexico does not produce cobalt.
390 USITC data.

Missouri Cobalt

U.S. Strategic Metals (USSM), formerly Missouri Cobalt Holdings, is a battery minerals start-up that estimates their Madison mine holds 17,500 tons of cobalt, 25,500 tons of nickel, and 32,500 tons of copper. The mine and nearby areas had been mined for lead and other metals since the 1700s, thus has a history of pollution, and was declared an EPA superfund site in 2011. The company's Phase I construction will enable them to process 87,600 tons of ore annually.

Idaho Cobalt Operations – Financial Distress

Australian company Jervois Mining USA operates their Idaho Cobalt Operations (ICO) which will produce gold, copper, and cobalt, with estimated reserves of 33,000 tons of cobalt. In 2023, Jervois received $15 million in funding by the Department of Defense under the Defense Production Act to develop a cobalt refinery. In Q2 2024, the company stopped exploration activity pending environmental regulatory reviews. Jervois also stopped its extraction operations because their costs were higher than average cobalt concentrate prices.

China's Cobalt Monopoly

In 2023, China imported 16,700 tons of cobalt ores/concentrates, with 99% of this coming from the DRC, for an average price of $2,300.00 a ton. China also imported over 400,000 tons of intermediate cobalt products, with 97% coming from the DRC, for an average price of $6,190.00 a ton. For exports, China shipped out just 4,300 tons of cobalt ore, with almost 2,400 tons going to South Korea for an average price of $24,500.00 a ton. Beijing also exported almost 5,200 tons of intermediate products with 2,100 tons going to the Netherlands for an average price of close to $37,400.00 a ton.[391]

This data shows several things to include Beijing's close mineral trade relations with the DRC where they get cobalt products at very low prices and in turn resell them at high margins. As seen here, China sold their cobalt products to South Korea and the Netherlands for six times their cost. Importantly, China uses most of its imports to make finished products with the majority being NCM (nickel cobalt manganese) lithium-ion batteries for their electric vehicle industry. That is why we see China re-exporting only 2% of its cobalt products as the other 98% is used in (mostly) battery manufacturing.

391 UN Comtrade data HS 2605, HS 8105.

Actions Taken

While new mining projects in Michigan could qualify for funding from the state through the Strategic Site Readiness Program and Strategic Outreach and Attraction Reserve (SOAR), the Eagle mine has not received any such grant. Companies extracting non-ferrous minerals in Michigan pay a 2.75% severance tax based on the value of the minerals sold and are exempt from provisions of the General Property Tax Act 206 of 1893.

Missouri presented two separate critical mineral bills in 2024, the Missouri Defense and Energy Independence Act, SB 1360 and the Grants for Independence from Foreign Influence Fund which would provide up to $6 million in tax credits for mining companies like U.S. Strategic Metals. The state awarded $16 million in grants to the Missouri University of Science & Technology to establish a program dedicated to critical minerals research.

In Idaho, the purchase of minerals used in manufacturing to make a finished product are exempt from taxation as is the purchase of other mining items and equipment used to extract minerals. The state has a mine license tax of 1% of the value of the ores mined and extracted.

The DOD provided Canadian company Fortune Minerals a $6.4 million grant in 2024 through the Defense Production Act in support of the U.S.-Canadian Joint Acton Plan on Critical Minerals. Canada's Department of Natural Resources provided the company a $5.6 million grant.

According to the DARS (Defense Acquisition Regulations System) 48 CFR 252.225-7009 *Restriction on Acquisition of Specialty Metals*, any steel alloy product with more than 25% cobalt content acquired by the DOD must be melted or produced in the U.S.

The DFARS (Defense Federal Acquisition Regulation Supplement) to the 2019 NDAA (National Defense Authorization Act) Section 871 prohibits the acquisition of samarium-cobalt magnets produced in China, Russia, North Korea or Iran.

Incentives & Tariffs

Under the Inflation Reduction Act, U.S. based mining operations qualify for 10% production cost tax credit under Section 45X Advanced Manufacturing Production Credit if the extracted cobalt "is converted to cobalt sulfate or purified to a minimum purity of 99.6 percent cobalt by mass."

The domestic cobalt mining industry receives a 22% depletion allowance (U.S. Strategic Metals) while foreign companies receive a 14% rate (Eagle Mine, Jervois Mining).

Cobalt is exempted from the Trump administration's April 2025 tariff schedule. The tariff schedule encourages the import of ores and unwrought cobalt products while taxing chemical compounds at overall low rates. In 2021, China emplaced a 4% tariff on the imports of cobalt metal, lowered it to 2% in 2022, and then removed it in 2023 due to low domestic demand which was primarily for the magnet sector.[392] In 2023, China banned the export of the technology to make samarium-cobalt magnets, adding them to its "Catalogue of Technologies Prohibited and Restricted from Export." In 2026, the U.S. will impose a 25% tariff on imported Chinese permanent magnets.

U.S Supply Chain Security Strategy Moving Forward

The U.S. has a vulnerable cobalt position as it relies on imports for two-thirds of its needs, with 95% coming from ex-China sources. If the U.S. developed a domestic NMC (Nickel Manganese Cobalt) ternary lithium-ion battery industry, it would be mostly import-dependent.

Multi-pronged Approach

- The U.S. should continue to monitor viable U.S. and North American cobalt projects and provide financial support when feasible. While the U.S. has provided support to two cobalt projects through the DPA, this does not make them fundamentally economic.
- In 2022, the U.S. National Defense Stockpile held 348 tons of cobalt products with the Defense Logistics Agency having no plans to acquire any more through 2025. A one-year stockpile of cobalt based on U.S. annual consumption would be 8,500 metric tons. U.S. private industry held an estimated 900 tons of cobalt in stock, with London Metal Exchange warehouses holding only 34 tons – a supply of just five weeks.
- The U.S. meets an estimated 25% of its cobalt needs through scrap metal. A mandatory national recycling, recovery, and reuse program would maximize access to this resource.

392 Li, Zihao. "China's removal of cobalt tariff from 2023 unlikely to affect market amid thin domestic demand." Fastmarkets, January 5, 2023.

- Chinese battery manufacturers have substituted cobalt use in their batteries with less expensive LFP (Lithium Iron Phosphate) batteries. Cobalt can also be replaced by a variety of other metals, depending on the application, although with a loss of performance.

2024 U.S. Imports (metric tons)

Ores & Concentrates: 13.7 tons valued at $189,000.00 (China 44%, Canada 28%, Germany 27%).

Average Cost: $13,800.00 per ton

Cobalt oxide: 1.8 tons valued at $36.5 million (Finland 56%, Belgium 17%, China 3%)

Average Cost: $20,280.00 per ton

Cobalt metals: 11,600 tons valued at $388 million (Norway 21%, Canada 17%, Japan, 16%, Madagascar 15%)

Average Cost: $32,400.00 per ton

**USGS & UN Comtrade data HS Code 2605, 2822, 8105*

Dysprosium (Dy)

Background

Dysprosium is one of the seventeen REE (Rare Earth Elements) and is part of the heavy REE (HREE) lanthanide series. Dysprosium is not found as a free element and is commonly found in xenotime, bastnaesite, and monazite. It is used in nuclear reactor control rods, magnets (it has the highest magnetic strength along with holmium), and specialty alloys for sonar applications (Terfenol-D). Dysprosium is increasingly used for its magnetic qualities in electric motors for the BEV industry and windmills for renewable energy generation. The U.S. defense industry uses dysprosium in a wide variety of applications such as Hellfire missiles, JDAM guided bomb systems, AH-64 Apache helicopters, MQ-1B Predator drones, M109 Paladin artillery systems, and nuclear-powered attack submarines.

The U.S. imports almost 100% of its dysprosium needs with U.S. mining company MP Materials extracting negligible amounts and sending most of their product to China for processing. Prices for dysprosium oxide (minimum 99.5% purity) in the U.S. and Europe closely track one another, increasing 116% and 122% respectively in early 2022 as compared to 2019. However, prices dropped steadily to mid-2024 with prices just 13% and 18% respectively of the 2019 benchmark. In mid-2024, dysprosium oxide (minimum 99.5% purity) was selling in the China market for $260,000.00 a metric ton.[393]

China has established a dysprosium monopoly with an estimated 98% of world production coming from their REE operations. Their mining takes place in the southern part of the country from clay and sand deposits. In 2013, most dysprosium was extracted through illegal operations, which Beijing subsequently cracked down on. By 2018, an estimated 80% of dysprosium extraction was now conducted by legitimate mining operations which reduced the global dysprosium supply. Upwards of 90% of dysprosium oxide was consumed in China, 9% in Japan, and the remaining 1% elsewhere.[394]

In a comprehensive study by D. Eheliyagoda et. al. an estimated 38,580 metric tons of dysprosium was mined globally from 1988-2021 for an average of 1,169 tons a year. Of this amount, China mined 87% of dysprosium ores.

393 Shanghai Metals Market.

394 Adamas Intelligence, 2018.

Losses during the beneficiation and separation process resulted in 25,800 tons of dysprosium with China accounting for 90% and Japan 9%. The U.S. refined and separated much less than 1%.[395]

Permanent Magnet Synchronous Motor Industry

Dysprosium is used primarily as a minority element in NdFeB (Neodymium Iron Boron) permanent magnets (PM) in traction motors for electric vehicles with its overall content depending on the grade of magnet alloy required. In 2022, an estimated 12% of worldwide NdFeB production was for the EV industry, a number that was sure to increase with accelerating EV adoption.[396] Dysprosium is used as a partial substitution for neodymium in certain magnets because it allows the motor to operate at higher temperatures. Magnet manufacturers thrift dysprosium in their products to reduce cost but the overall growth of the PM traction motor sector has ensured growing dysprosium demand which will most likely outstrip future supply, driving up prices.

The three main types of AC traction motors used in the EV industry are permanent magnet (PM) motors (82% of the market), induction motors (IM) (14%), and wound rotor synchronous motors (WRSM) (4%).[397] While PM motors cost more than induction motors due to the expense of NdFeB magnets, they require less copper material and thus weigh less and are more energy efficient. Tesla's Model Y, the #1 selling passenger car in the world for 2023, used a PM motor in the rear and an induction motor in the front on its AWD versions. The second largest BEV manufacturing in the world, BYD, also makes their own PM motors and is the largest buyer of NdFeB magnets in the China NEV (New Energy Vehicle) market.

In 2023, Tesla announced that its next generation PMSM (Permanent Magnet Synchronous Motor) would be REE-free, presumedly using a ferrite magnet design. Ferrite is magnetic ceramic containing iron-oxide with material inputs much cheaper and easier to obtain than their REE competitors. While ferrite magnet PMSM perform as well or better than REE containing NdFeB magnets, they weigh up to 30% more and are prone to demagnetization. Ferrite magnets

395 Eheliyagoda, Disna et al. "Tracing the multiregional evolution of the global dysprosium demand-supply chain." Resources, Conservation & Recycling, 2023.
396 "Implications: Tesla Announces Next Generation Rare-Earth-Free PMSM." Adamas Intelligence, March 2, 2023.
397 Gobbi, Massimiliano et al. " Traction motors for electric vehicles: Maximization of mechanical efficiency – A review." Elsevier, 2023.

could also be used to thrift both neodymium and dysprosium to reduce costs and improve supply chain access.

Actions Taken

The DFARS (Defense Regulation Acquisition Regulation Supplement) to the 2019 NDAA (National Defense Authorization Act) Section 871 prohibits the acquisition of NdFeB magnets produced in China, Russia, North Korea or Iran. This also effectively prohibits the use of China produced dysprosium if used to thrift neodymium in this use case.

The USG has provided grants to two companies to secure increased REE productions (MP Materials, Lynas Rare Earths).

Incentives & Tariffs

MP Materials would receive a 10% production cost tax credit under Section 45X Advanced Manufacturing Production Credit if their extracted dysprosium is "converted to not less than 99% pure dysprosium iron alloy by mass or purified to a minimum purity of 99% dysprosium by mass."

Domestic REE mining companies receive a 14% depletion allowance (MP Materials) while foreign companies receive a 14% rate (there are none) for monazite, bastnaesite, and xenotime extraction operations.

REE were exempted from the Trump administration's April 2025 tariff schedule. The same month, China sellers were required to obtain an export license from the Ministry of Commerce. In 2023, China banned the export of the technology to make NdFeB magnets, adding them to its "Catalogue of Technologies Prohibited and Restricted from Export." This will affect dysprosium used to thrift NdFeB magnets. In 2026, the U.S. will impose a 25% tariff on imported Chinese permanent magnets.

U.S Supply Chain Security Strategy Moving Forward

The U.S. has a vulnerable dysprosium position as it relies mostly on imports from China like it does for all its REE needs. The U.S. should monitor new ex-China REE extraction operations worldwide, assist them when feasible, and secure long-term offtake agreements for stockpiling purposes.

Multi-pronged Approach

- The U.S. should invest in magnet R&D programs and find ways to thrift or replace dysprosium needs such as Tesla's announced shift to ferrite magnet PMSM to minimize dysprosium use and shift to more reliable supply chains not dominated by China. Research has been conducted into a variety of synthetic magnets and alternatives using materials such as cobalt with no obvious solution gaining traction to date.

- In 2022, the U.S. National Defense Stockpile held a paltry 203 kgs of dysprosium products with the Defense Logistics Agency having no plans to acquire any through 2025. Annual consumption is an estimated 14 tons.
- The U.S. should invest in R&D to improve manufacturing systems and implement a mandatory dysprosium recycling program since an estimated 40% of dysprosium is lost during the manufacturing process.[398] Less than 3% of dysprosium is recycled from end-of-life products.[399]
- The U.S. has failed to develop dysprosium market surveillance tools that effectively track its production and movement. To acquire the necessary data to make intelligent critical mineral decisions, the U.S. International Trade Commission (USITC) should create a dedicated HTS code for dysprosium.
- The U.S. should consider supporting other domestic REE operations like the company USA Rare Earth to create strategic redundancy.

398 Adamas Intelligence, 2018.

399 Eheliyagoda, Disna et al. "Tracing the multiregional evolution of the global dysprosium demand-supply chain." Resources, Conservation & Recycling, 2023.

Dysprosium Production 1988-2021 (metric tons)

World: 38,580 tons of ore, 1,677 tons per year

China: 33,679 tons (87%), 1,169 tons per year

Refining & Separation (25,793 tons)

China: 23,119 tons (90%)

Japan: 2,407 tons (9%), EU: 134 tons, U.S.: 48 tons

Intermediate Products (22,413 tons)

China: 15,126 tons (67%)

Japan: 2,074 tons (9%) , EU: 1,369 tons (6%), U.S.: 457 tons

Manufacturing & Final Products (22,009 tons)

ICE Vehicles: 3,390 tons (15%)

Air Conditioners: 2,521 tons (11%)

MRIs: 2,493 tons (11%)

Wind Turbines: 2,377 tons (11%)

Electric Bikes: 2,293 (10%)

Electric Vehicles: 2,257 tons (10%)

Industrial Robots: 1,743 tons (8%)

Washing Machines: 1,330 tons (6%)

Production Stream Losses (16,572 tons , 43%)

Mining & Beneficiation: 11,355 tons (68%)

Refining & Separation: 2,444 tons (15%)

Intermediate production: 2,368 tons (14%)

Manufacturing: 404 tons (2%)

**Data from D.Eheliyagoda et al. (October 4, 2023)*

Erbium (Er)

Background

Erbium is one of the seventeen REE (Rare Earth Elements) and is part of the heavy REE (HREE) lanthanide series. To extract this critical mineral, erbium containing minerals are crushed and then treated with sulfuric acid, followed by sodium hydroxide, ammonium oxalate, nitric acid, magnesium nitrate, resin absorption, washed with complexion agents, and finally heated at high temperatures. Erbium is used in the medical sector to include laser surgery applications and dental procedures. It is also used in optical communications, nuclear control rods, alloys, and as a colorant in glass, jewelry, and porcelain. Erbium oxide (minimum 99.5% purity) in the China market sold for $25,000.00 a metric ton in early 2021, peaked at a high of $52,500.00 a ton in April 2022, and dropped to $42,300.00 a ton by June 2024.[400]

Based on available customs import records which are incomplete, the U.S. doesn't understand how much erbium it imports and consumes annually. We do know that for the five years from 2019-2023 the U.S. accepted fourteen shipments with erbium products. Six shipments arrived from China, five from Italy, two from the Netherlands, and one from South Korea. An estimated 37 tons of erbium oxide was imported with 70% coming directly from Italy and 25% from China. Not included in this number were 4.2 tons of erbium-doped fiber optic network cable and an unknown amount of Tris(methylcyclopentadienyl)erbium, a metal that is used in semiconductor materials. Possibly 70% of imported erbium oxide was for the glass manufacturing industry.[401]

Erbium Doped Fiber Amplifier's (EDFA) were invented in 1987 and subsequently used to simplify fiber optic transmission lines which previously relied on optical-to-electric converters. Erbium demand will continue to grow as fiber optic cable use accelerates in support of 5G telecommunications acceleration worldwide. Companies like AT&T, Verizon, Charter Communications, and CenturyLink are the largest fiber optic cable providers in the U.S. while Huawei, ZTE, and Fiberhome are major Chinese providers. China has devel-

400 Shanghai Metals Market.

401 Because of the omissions and incomplete data provided in bills of lading, U.S. Customs and Border Patrol is unable to conduct effective import surveillance of erbium products.

oped the largest fiber optics communications network in the world to support its internet and 5G technology applications.

Actions Taken

The U.S. has done nothing specifically to secure its erbium supply chain other than what it has done for the larger group of REE.

Incentives & Tariffs

MP Materials receives a 10% production cost tax credit under Section 45X Advanced Manufacturing Production Credit if their extracted erbium is "purified to a minimum purity of 99 percent by mass."

Domestic REE mining companies receive a 14% depletion allowance (MP Materials) while foreign companies receive a 14% rate (there are none) for monazite, bastnaesite, and xenotime extraction operations.

All REE were exempted from the Trump administration's April 2025 import tariff schedule. The regular tariff schedule encourages the import of erbium oxide while taxing other products at overall low rates.

In 2023, the EU doubled its anti-dumping duties on imports of Chinese fiber optic cables, ranging from 39% to 88%. In 2024, China continued its countervailing duties on U.S. optical fiber preforms ranging from 17% to 41%.

U.S. Supply Chain Security Strategy Moving Forward

The U.S. has a vulnerable erbium position as it relies on imports from China like it does for most of its REE needs. The U.S. should continue to monitor new ex-China REE extraction operations worldwide, assist them when feasible, and secure long-term offtake agreements for stockpiling purposes.

Multi-pronged Approach

- In 2022, the U.S. National Defense Stockpile held no erbium products and the Defense Logistics Agency announced no acquisitions of it through 2025. A one-year stockpile of erbium oxide based on possible consumption is just six tons.
- The U.S. should explore establishing domestic REE/erbium extraction other than Mountain Pass and Lynas Rare Earths.
- The U.S. lacks effective erbium market surveillance and should improve its knowledge of its own national erbium needs and consumption by enforcing accurate import data. Specifically, the U.S.

International Trade Commission (USITC) should establish a dedicated HTS code for erbium products.

National Telecommunications Network

Argentinian company Domus Network imports its erbium-doped fiber optic cable from Shenzhen, China for distribution in the U.S. and Latin America.

Europium (Eu)

Background

Europium is one of the seventeen REE (Rare Earth Elements) and is part of the Light REE (LREE) lanthanide series. Europium is commonly found with other rare earth elements in occurrences of bastnaesite, loparite, xenotime, and monazite. Europium is used to dope glass in lasers and optoelectronic devices while europium oxide is used as a red phosphor in fluorescent lamps, televisions, and computer screens. Europium was previously used in Nuclear Magnetic Resonance (NMR) machines before being substituted largely by modern superconducting magnets.

Europium oxide (minimum 99.95% purity) in the China market was $26,850.00 a metric ton in June 2024.[402] However, this depends on which distributor it is purchased from and in what quantity as other prices range from $45,000.00 to $80,000.00 a ton. As with all REE, China dominates the production and processing of europium and the China market controls the pricing. However, the U.S. does produce europium and is working to develop a domestic value chain that does not require Chinese processing.

The Color Television Boom

The discovery in the early 1960's of europium-doped yttrium orthovanadate red phosphor revolutionized the color TV industry. Molybdenum Corporation of America (MCA) owned the Mountain Pass REE mine at the time which had bastnaesite deposits with high europium contents of 0.1%. Due to the demand from the TV industry, MCA built a europium oxide processing plant in 1965 and increased their production six-fold to 6.1 million lbs. of TREO (Total Rare Earth Oxide) or just over 3,000 tons. In 1964, MCA produced just 1,845 lbs. of europium oxide which increased to over 11,000 lbs. in 1965 before leveling off to an average of 7,000 lbs. annually through 1970. Today, MP Materials sells a SEG+ (samarium, europium, gadolinium) concentrate with other lesser amounts of REE included.

One study calculated that 7,561 metric tons of europium concentrates (285 tons were imported or 3.7%) entered the Chinese production chain from 1990-2018. Of this amount, 4,383 tons (58%) were processed into primary products while 866 tons (11%) were exported, 681 tons (9%) were lost as waste, and

402 Shanghai Metals Market.

1,631 tons (21.5%) remained as surplus. Of 4,779 tons processed into intermediate products, 396 tons were imported (8%), 877 tons were lost (18%), and 3,903 tons became manufactured products (81%). Of this, most was used in fluorescent lamps (91%). In 2018, the U.S. shipped an estimated 11 tons of europium to China for refinement where the U.S. then re-imported 11 tons of finished europium products.[403]

Actions Taken

The U.S. has done nothing specifically to secure its europium supply chain other than what it has done for the larger group of REE.

Incentives & Tariffs

MP Materials receives a 10% production cost tax credit under Section 45X Advanced Manufacturing Production Credit if their product is "converted to europium oxide which is purified to a minimum purity of 99.9% europium oxide by mass or purified to a minimum purity of 99% by mass."

Domestic REE mining companies receive a 14% depletion allowance (MP Materials) while foreign companies receive a 14% rate (there are none) for monazite, bastnaesite, and xenotime extraction operations.

All REE were exempted from the Trump administration's April 2205 tariff schedule. The normal tariff schedule encourages the import of europium oxide while taxing other products at overall low rates.

U.S. Supply Chain Security Strategy Moving Forward

The U.S. has a vulnerable europium position as it relies on imports of processed material from China like it does for most of its REE needs.

Multi-pronged Approach

- The U.S. should explore establishing domestic REE/europium extraction other than Mountain Pass. Of note, MP Materials believe that the world will be in a state of europium oversupply through 2040.
- In 2022, the U.S. National Defense Stockpile held 35.7 tons of europium products while the Defense Logistics Agency published no plans to purchase any more through 2025. Annual consumption

403 Wang, Qiao-Chu, et al. "Byproduct Surplus: Lighting the Depreciative Europium in China's Rare Earth Boom." Environmental Science & technology, September 28, 2020.

may be 11 tons. Therefore, the U.S. may have a three-year supply which is unusual for the country's mostly unfilled stockpile.

- The U.S. has not developed effective europium market surveillance and should improve its knowledge of its national europium needs and consumption. Specifically, the U.S should enforce accurate import data with the U.S. International Trade Commission (USITC) establishing a dedicated HTS code for europium products.
- A Chinese study indicated that most europium is not recycled when the products it is used in reach their end-of-life, with 89% by volume lost as waste.[404]

From a 1965 ad for a Sylvania General Telephone & Electronics Color TV.

404 Ibid.

Fluorspar/Fluorite (Flr)

Background

Fluorspar is the mineral form of calcium fluoride (CaF_2) where the intermediate product is hydrofluoric acid. Fluorspar products are used in the smelting, glass, ceramics, optics, cement, uranium, aluminum, and refrigerant industries. Acidspar, a high-grade fluorspar concentrate, is increasingly used in the manufacturing of lithium-ion batteries for electric vehicles with applications for cathodes, anodes, lithium electrolytes, and battery cell separators. Acidspar demand already outstripped supply starting in 2024 and total annual demand by the battery sector will be 1.6 million tons by 2030 which would be 18% of 2024 production.[405]

In 2024, China led the world in fluorspar production with 5.9 million metric tons which was 62% of total world production of 9.5 million tons. China was followed by Mexico with 1.2 million tons (13%), and Mongolia with 1.2 million tons (13%). World fluorspar reserves were estimated at 320 million tons with Mexico holding 68 million tons (21%), China 86 million tons (27%), and South Africa 41 million tons (13%). The U.S. has low volume fluorspar reserves and thus looks to its North American neighbor, Mexico, for most of its fluorspar products. The U.S. is 100% import dependent.[406]

In 2024, the U.S. imported 370,000 metric tons of fluorspar products worth $170 million for an average cost of $460.00 a ton. The most came from Mexico at 270,000 tons (73%), then South Africa with 48,000 tons (13%), and China with 38,000 tons (10%). Imports from China were 14% above the average import cost at $526.00 a ton. This was one of the rare instances where Chinese mineral products weren't the most competitively priced.[407]

China's Fluorspar Monopoly

In 2023, although China was the largest producer, they imported another 1 million metric tons of metallurgical grade products for a total of 6.7 million tons or 77% of world production. Most of imports came from Mongolia (912,000 tons), meaning it shipped 98% of its fluorspar production to China for

405 Benchmark Mineral Intelligence, February 2024.
406 U.S. Geological Survey. Canada produces low volumes of fluorspar products.
407 UN Comtrade data, HS Codes 252921, 252922.

an average cost of $138.00 a ton. In contrast, China imported very little acid grade products (16,000 tons) and hydrofluoric acid (10,800 tons).

China exported 195,000 tons of metallurgical grade products for an average of $411.00 a ton, almost three times what it cost to import from Mongolia. Beijing exported 182,000 tons of acid grade products which it sold for an average of $467.00 a ton. For the largest segment, China exported almost 274,000 tons of hydrofluoric acid for an average cost of $1,507.00 a ton with the largest amounts going to South Korea (75,000 tons), Japan, (69,000 tons), and Taiwan (38,000 tons) which combined were two-thirds of all exports.

In March 2024, China's Mine Safety Administration (MSA) began a nationwide fluorspar mining safety inspection schedule to target illegal fluorspar operations; close, consolidate, and upgrade select mines as necessary; and improve overall safety caused from recent deadly mining accidents. From March to May 2024, companies would conduct self-inspections; from June to July provincial level inspections would be conducted; in August the MSA and emergency management departments would conduct a final overview and assessment at the provincial level. These actions might temporarily raise prices due to decreased production, which could be alleviated by increasing imports from neighboring Mongolia.[408]

Illinois – Fluorspar

While the state of Illinois has no active fluorspar mining operations, the Hastie Mining and Trucking Company located in Cave-in-Rock produces low volumes of fluorspar secondary to limestone extraction. The Illinois-Kentucky Fluorspar District hosted at least 125 different fluorspar mining companies over the period of 1925-1995, producing more than 21 million tons of raw ore. Production spiked during WWI at 150,000 tons and then again during WWII at 200,000 tons and remained elevated until 1968 when production steadily dropped off as imports increased. The last recorded U.S. production at volume (eight tons) was in 1996.[409]

Fluorosilicic Acid (FSA)

Approximately 40,000 tons of FSA were recovered in the U.S., secondary to phosphoric acid production from phosphate rock. This production came in

408 "China to carry out special rectification of fluorite safety production." CCM, March 26, 2024.

409 https://ilmineswiki.web.illinois.edu/wiki/Circular_604/Production_History

part from Nutrien, which is the largest phosphoric acid producer in the U.S., and Mosaic, the largest phosphate rock and fertilizer manufacturer in the country. FSA is considered a waste byproduct by the phosphate industry with many environmental concerns. Hydrofluorosilicic acid has been used in the U.S. primarily to treat public drinking water supplies although it has been targeted by the EPA for containing dangerous levels of arsenic.

Department of Energy (DOE)

The DOE used hydrofluoric acid as part of the process to enrich uranium for military and civilian uses since the early 1940's. In 2010, DOE began the process of decommissioning depleted uranium hexafluoride (DUF6) and converting it to depleted uranium oxide. At the start, DOE had 67,000 cylinders containing 800,000 metric tons of DUF6 which it converted at its facilities in Kentucky and Ohio. As a result of this conversion process, DOE produces and sells aqueous hydrofluoric acid (HF) to an undisclosed private U.S. company. From 2011-2021, DOE sold 13,673,000 gallons (56,000 tons) of HF acid for $8.67 million or $154.00 per ton. Obviously, this gives the company an HF product below market rates that it then uses to make higher margin finished products.[410]

Ares Strategic Mining – Financial Distress

Canadian company Ares Strategic Mining (TSXV: ARS) owns their Lost Sheep Fluorspar Project in Utah. They received a $4.4 million loan from the Department of Agriculture in 2022 to advance its operations to include a metallurgical lumps processing plant. The company also received $10 million in loans from the State of Utah which will help fund an acidspar production plant in Delta, UT. Ares will have to produce fluorspar at much less than the costs of imports to be competitive. Ares does not yet sell a product and is unprofitable, losing $2.9 million in 2024.

Mexico

Koura, a subsidiary of Orbia Advance Corporation, owns and operates their Las Cuevas fluorspar mine in San Luis Potosi in central Mexico which is described as the most productive fluorspar mine in the world.[411] Koura is the world's single largest exporter of acidspar while the U.S. is its largest importer, highlighting this important mutual relationship. The San Luis Potosi operation

410 Nuclear Waste Cleanup, GAO, July 2022.
411 Formerly Mexichem Fluor until 2019.

has an adjacent rail line running north/south, connecting to the U.S. port of Laredo after 400 miles of twists and turns, providing a secure land link to its U.S. customers.

In 2022, Orbia received a $100 million grant from DOE to build a LiPF6 (lithium hexafluorophosphate) facility – the first in North America - at their existing site in St. Gabriel, Louisiana. Of note, Orbia will pay to use the LiPF6 technology license from Japanese company Kanto Denka Kogyo. Orbia's plant will have a 10,000 tpa battery-grade electrolyte salts capacity and will come online by 2026. Orbia is also partnered with Belgian chemicals company SYENSQO[412] to build another plant on site to produce polyvinylidene fluoride (PVDF) binding agent, also used in the production of lithium-ion batteries.[413]

Actions Taken

In 2024, the Department of Defense provided an $8.4 million contract to Orbia Fluor & Energy Materials located in Wisconsin to supply specialized electrolytes. In 2023, Orbia's Wisconsin facility began electrolyte production which was formerly Silatronix until bought by Orbia in 2021. Customers buying these electrolytic products included Navitas Systems, Lithion Battery, and Forge Battery.

Incentives & Tariffs

A domestic fluorspar mining operation (Ares) would qualify for a 10% tax credit under Section 45X Advanced Manufacturing Production Credit if the extracted fluorspar is "purified to a minimum purity of 97% calcium fluoride by mass or purified to a minimum purity of 99% fluorspar by mass."

The domestic fluorspar mining industry receives a 22% depletion allowance (Hastie Mining) while foreign companies receive a 14% rate (Ares).

Fluorspar was exempted from the Trump administration's April 2025 tariff schedule. The regular schedule encourages the import of all fluorspar products.

U.S. Supply Chain Security Strategy Moving Forward

While the U.S. imports almost a 100% of its fluorspar needs, the U.S. has a relatively secure supply chain based on Orbia's operations in neighboring Mexico. The U.S. strategy should involve strengthening this existing relationship and supporting domestic operations if they prove viable.

412 SYENSQO spun off from Solvay in 2024 to focus on specialty chemicals.
413 Orbia news release, November 21, 2023.

Multi-pronged Approach

- In 2022, the National Defense Stockpile held no fluorspar products while the Defense Logistics Agency published no intentions to purchase any through 2025. A one-year stockpile of fluorspar products based on U.S. annual consumption would be 430,000 metric tons.
- As discussed, HF acid is recovered from depleted uranium while primary aluminum producers recycle fluorspar products from their smelting operations. A mandatory national recycling, recovery, and reuse program would maximize access to this resource.
- The U.S. should continue to recognize the importance of LiPF6 and other related products in the EV battery sector and provide necessary support to competitive projects as illustrated by DOE awarding a grant to Orbia's new production facility.
- A variety of products can replace fluorspar fluxes depending on the use. The American Innovation and Manufacturing Act authorizes the EPA to phase down the production of hydrofluorocarbons by 85% by 2036 which will force substitution.

Above, the Koura fluorspar plant in Mexico from which the U.S. imports the majority of its products.

2024 U.S. Fluorspar Imports (metric tons):

Metallurgical grade: 31,300 tons, $10.5 million

Mexico: 16,500 tons (53%), $2.2 million

China: 13,100 tons (42%), $7.2 million

Total imports average cost: $335.00 per ton

Acid grade: 339,000 tons, $159 million

Mexico: 253,000 tons (75%), $116.8 million

South Africa: 47,000 tons (14%), $23.5 million

Total imports average Cost: $470.00 per ton

**UN Comtrade data HS 2529.21, 2529.22*

Gadolinium (Gd)

Background

Gadolinium is one of the seventeen REE (Rare Earth Elements) and is part of the Light REE lanthanide series. Gadolinium is commonly found with other REE in occurrences of bastnaesite, loparite, xenotime, monazite, and gadolinite (although only in trace amounts). Gadolinium has many uses to include neutron radiography, nuclear reactors, alloys, MRIs, phosphors in x-rays, optical devices, and superconductors. Gadolinium's biggest use is thrifting neodymium in NdFeB magnets. Due to the continuing use of gadolinium-based contrast agents (GBCAs) in MRIs, they have increasingly entered our drinking water systems as pollutants and is associated with nephrogenic systemic fibrosis.

In June 2024, gadolinium oxide (minimum 99.99% purity) traded in the China market at $27,000.00 a metric ton.[414] Lower grade gadolinium (minimum 99.95% purity) traded 15% less at $22,900.00 a ton. In 2023, the U.S. imported an estimated 34 tons of gadolinium products at an overall cost of approximately $900,000.00. Of this, 28 tons (82%) came from six Chinese companies and one South Korean business (their products originated from China) while the remaining six tons (18%) were imported by the Belgian company Solvay Group.[415] While Belgium imported two-thirds of its gadolinium products from the Netherlands, the Dutch in turn imported 91% of their products from China.[416] Most likely, 95% or more of the U.S.' imported gadolinium products originated from China.

China Gadolinium Production History

As with other REE, China has been the single largest producer of gadolinium, extracting an estimated 34,000 tons from 1990-2018. At its height in 2006, 78% of gadolinium was extracted from ionic clays with the rest coming from bastnaesite ores and the Bayan Obo mining district. Today, most domestic extraction comes from Bayan Obo (50%), bastnaesite (30%), and then ionic clays (20%). The lower production from ionic clays will likely remain suppressed due to increasingly stringent regulation by Chinese mining officials

414 Shanghai Metals Market.
415 U.S. Customs & Border Protection, Bills of Lading, January – December 2023.
416 UN Comtrade code HS 2846.90.

intent on closing illegal mining operations and enforcing safety and environmental laws.[417]

Historically, China exported most of its gadolinium products and imported little. More than 95% of exports went to Japan (75%) and South Korea (20%), with the remainder largely going to the U.S. and Europe. This changed with increased domestic consumption and China becoming a net importer of gadolinium by 2017, shipping in products from Myanmar (88%) and Malaysia (12%). In 2018, China imported over 2,200 tons of gadolinium while producing 965 tons domestically.[418]

In 2006, thrifting NdFeB (Neodymium Iron Boron) magnets became the biggest source of domestic gadolinium consumption, surpassing use in the glass/optics industry for the first time. By 2018, the permanent magnet sector absorbed 57% of annual gadolinium use with the second largest being gadolinium oxide used in the manufacturing of cell phones. Even though neodymium prices declined greatly from their peak in 2011 ($500,000.00 per ton in the China market) and stabilized at much lower prices ($49,000.00 per ton in 2024), magnet manufacturers continued thrifting with gadolinium.

Actions Taken

The DFARS (Defense Regulation Acquisition Regulation Supplement) to the 2019 NDAA (National Defense Authorization Act) Section 871 prohibits the acquisition of NdFeB magnets produced in China, Russia, North Korea or Iran. This also effectively prohibits the use of China produced gadolinium if used to thrift neodymium in this use case.

The U.S. has taken no specific action to secure its gadolinium supply chain other than what it has done overall for all LREE.

Incentives & Tariffs

MP Materials receives a 10% production cost tax credit under Section 45X Advanced Manufacturing Production Credit if their product is "converted to gadolinium oxide which is purified to a minimum purity of 99.9% gadolinium oxide by mass or purified to a minimum purity of 99% gadolinium by mass." MP Materials SEG+ (samarium, europium, gadolinium) oxide concentrate qualifies for the credit.

417 Zhao, Shen, et al. "Supply and demand conflicts of critical heavy rare earth element: Lessons from gadolinium." Elsevier, 2023.
418 Ibid.

Domestic REE mining companies receive a 14% depletion allowance (MP Materials) while foreign companies receive a 14% rate (there are none) for monazite, bastnaesite, and xenotime extraction operations.

All REE are exempted from the Trump administration's April 2025 tariff schedule. That same month, Chinese sellers were required to obtain an export license from the Ministry of Commerce. In 2023, China banned the export of the technology to make neodymium-iron-boron magnets, adding them to its "Catalogue of Technologies Prohibited and Restricted from Export." This will affect gadolinium used to thrift NdFeB magnets. In 2026, the U.S. will impose a 25% tariff on imported Chinese permanent magnets.

U.S. Supply Chain Security Strategy Moving Forward

The U.S. has a vulnerable gadolinium position as it relies on imports of processed material from China like it does for most of its REE needs, possibly 95% in this case.

Multi-pronged Approach

- The U.S. could explore establishing domestic REE extraction other than Mountain Pass.
- Typically, 10%-11% of gadolinium is lost during the finished manufacturing process, showing the need for a nationally mandated recycling, reuse, and recovery program to ensure maximum access to this material.[419]
- In 2022, the National Defense Stockpile held no reserves of gadolinium while the Defense Logistics Agency announced no intent to secure any through 2025. Based on annual consumption, a one-year stockpile of gadolinium would be 34 tons.
- The U.S. has failed to develop gadolinium market surveillance tools that effectively track its production and movement. In order to acquire the necessary data to make intelligent critical mineral decisions, the U.S. International Trade Commission (USITC) should create a dedicated HTS code for gadolinium.
- Manganese has been studied for years as a possible replacement to gadolinium as a contrast dye used in MRIs.

419 Zhao, Shen, et al.

China Gadolinium Production 2000-2018				
Year	**Production**	**Exports**	**Imports**	**Shortage**
2000	1,109 tons	846 tons	2 tons	84 tons
Domestic Use: Oxides - 144 tons, Metals - 95 tons				
2006	2,342 tons	789 tons	None	(+715 tons)
Domestic Use: Metals - 312 tons, Oxides - 308 tons, GdFe Alloys ***(magnets) - 195 tons***				
2011	1,435 tons	1,042 tons	None	667 tons
Domestic Use: Metals - 581 tons, Oxides - 325 tons, GdFe Alloys ***(magnets) - 459 tons***				
2018	965 tons	225 tons	2,219 tons	(+2,041 tons)
Domestic Use: Metals - 687 tons, Oxides - 432 tons, GdFe Alloys ***(magnets) - 592 tons***				

* Gadolinium oxide (99.5%), China market, $22,900.00 ton

* Gadolinium loss during manufacturing in 2018: 625 tons

* China: 833-ton domestic shortage expected by 2030

* 11% loss of material during the manufacturing process

*U.S. imported 82% of gadolinium directly from China in 2023

***Data from Shen Zhao et al.*

Gallium (Ga)

Background

Gallium is mainly produced secondary to bauxite, zinc, and copper ore extraction. About 95% of the world's gallium is extracted from the aluminum process where less than half of the available gallium is recovered.[420] Gallium is used to make gadolinium gallium-garnet jewelry, alloys, to dope NdFeB magnets, and in the electronics industry. Specifically, gallium arsenide (GaAs) is used in circuit applications; gallium nitride (GaN) is used in semiconductors, transistors, and radar systems; gallium phosphide and indium gallium nitride is used in LEDs, photovoltaics, and quantum heterostructures in substrates.

In 2024, China led the world in gallium production with 750 metric tons which was 98.6% of total world production of 760 tons. China was followed by Russia with six tons, Japan three tons, and South Korea three tons. There is an estimated 500,000 tons of gallium in existing bauxite reserves. Because gallium is primarily an aluminum byproduct, more can be produced depending on associated aluminum operations. The Chinese government sets annual gallium quotas for their aluminum industry and thus regulates the global supply and pricing.[421]

The U.S. produces no gallium and is thus 100% reliant on imported products. From 2020-2023, the U.S. imported most of its gallium metal from Japan (24%), then China (19%), Germany 19%), and Canada (17%). Total U.S. gallium metal imports dropped slightly from 11.4 tons in 2023 to 10.8 tons in 2024, indicating that Chinese export restrictions had not taken effect yet. China didn't introduce a dual-use ban on gallium exports to the U.S. until December 2024. Doped and undoped GaAs wafers are the U.S.' primary gallium products for import. It is important to note that while most of these products did not come directly from China, their upstream value chain originated there.

Indium Corporation

Indium Corp. is the only U.S. company that refines high-purity gallium from imported low-purity gallium metal and scrap metal. Founded in 1934, Indium is a private U.S. company with 1,400 employees and headquarters in

420 Jia, Hongxiang, et al. "Evolution of the Anthropogenic Gallium Cycle in China from 2005 to 2020. Frontiers, July 11, 2022.
421 U.S. Geological Survey 2024.

Clinton, NY that specializes in precision electronics soldering and advanced materials manufacturing involving indium, tin, germanium, and gallium. Beyond the U.S., the company has facilities in Europe, India, Singapore, South Korea, Malaysia, and China.

China's Dominant Gallium Enterprise

In 2000, China was just a minor player in the gallium market dominated by Australia, Germany, Japan, and Russia. However, as China's economy expanded and became more sophisticated, Beijing made a concerted effort to become a major player in the semiconductor space. From 2005-2020, an estimated 745 million tons of bauxite were mined in China with 36,500 tons of gallium available for secondary recovery. However, due to limited extraction capabilities, only 12,600 tons of gallium were recovered (35%). Just over 3,000 tons of gallium entered the refining process while 3,500 tons were lost as waste. During this period, an estimated 984 tons of excess gallium were stockpiled.[422]

From 2020 to 2023, Chinese gallium production exploded from 317 metric tons (2020) to 423 tons (2021), and then to 600 tons a year (2022 & 2023) as required by Beijing production quotas. Combined, this was 1,940 tons of gallium, with another 3,800 tons lost in the overall manufacturing cycle (950 tons a year), meaning China loses more gallium to inefficient processes than the entire world consumes annually. If their historic 17% recycling rate remained steady, Chinese companies recovered 646 tons of gallium or an average of 161.5 tons annually.

From 2005-2020, China consumed 51% of its own gallium production while exporting the rest. However, this has changed where Beijing now refines the majority of its gallium into 99.99% high-purity products which it then exports to the advanced economies for manufacturing of GaAs wafers. Since China does not produce large volumes of its own GaAs wafers, it reimports these from other countries like Japan, Germany, and South Korea. As mentioned, the U.S. imported just 4% of its GaAs doped wafers from China in 2023, although the gallium originates in China.

Russian Gallium Production

Publicly traded company Rusal is the second largest producer of aluminum in the world and recovers gallium secondary to aluminum red mud waste which it then refines at their Nikolaev Alumina Plant (NGZ) into 99.99% -99.999%

422 Evolution of the Anthropogenic Gallium Cycle, 2022.

purity products. While Russia has a modest gallium production capability provided by Ruslan and a historic consumption rate of five tons per annum, the country produces only low volumes of GaAs wafers and imports most of their GaAs needs (90%). While Russia can produce its own gallium, it has been unable to develop a robust semiconductor industry to consume it.

Japan's Gallium Production

The Akita Zinc Company LTD is a wholly owned subsidiary of Dowa Metals and Mining with 200 employees. Akita owns Japan's largest zinc smelting and refining operation where their Iijima smelter has a 220,000 tpa capacity and recovers gallium secondary to its primary operations. Dowa Electronics Materials further refines this product into high-purity gallium oxide 99.9999% and produces gallium arsenide wafers, infrared LEDs, and gallium nitride (GaN) HEMT (high-electron mobility transistor) epiwafers. Dowa actively recovers gallium from its GaAs scrap for subsequent reuse.

Korea Zinc Company LTD

Korea Zinc (KZ), founded in 1974, employs over 1,800 people, producing 640,000 tons of zinc, 412,000 tons of lead, and 26,400 tons of copper annually. KZ, with subsidiaries in Australia, Vietnam, and the U.S., produces a variety of smaller volume products such as gold, silver, bismuth, indium, and gallium. With South Korea's production of just two tons of gallium annually, it is a minor line of effort for KZ compared to its main products.

Actions Taken

The DFARS (Defense Regulation Acquisition Regulation Supplement) to the 2019 NDAA (National Defense Authorization Act) Section 871 prohibits the acquisition of NdFeB magnets produced in China, Russia, North Korea or Iran. Accordingly, the defense contracting industry cannot acquire NdFeB magnets with a supply chain connected to China or Russia starting in 2027. This indirectly impacts gallium as it is also used to dope NdFeB magnets.

Incentives & Tariffs

A company would qualify for a 10% production cost tax credit under Section 45X of the Advanced Manufacturing Production Credit if the extracted gallium "is purified to a minimum purity of 99% by mass."

Domestic and foreign gallium mining companies (there are none) receive the same 14% depletion allowance.

Gallium was exempted from the Trump administration's April 2025 tariff schedule. The normal tariff schedule encourages the import of doped GaAs wafers while taxing other products at overall low rates, except for China who incurred a 25% rate. In 2023, China banned the export of the technology to make NdFeB magnets, adding them to its "Catalogue of Technologies Prohibited and Restricted from Export." This indirectly impacts gallium as it is also used to dope NdFeB magnets. In 2026, the U.S. will impose a 25% tariff on imported Chinese permanent magnets.

In 2023, China announced that companies exporting gallium products would require an export license through their provincial Ministry of Commerce (MOFCOM) office. MOFCOM has the authority to deny the license and violators of the licensing guidelines are subject to civil and criminal penalties. In December 2024, China banned the export of dual military use gallium products to the U.S. The grey market and third-party resellers could still get gallium into the U.S., so imports will depend on how effectively China can enforce their export ban.

U.S Supply Chain Security Strategy Moving Forward

The U.S. has a vulnerable gallium position since it imports 100% of its primary needs while 98.6% of the world's unrefined gallium products originate in China. The U.S.'s gallium insecurity is tied directly to its bauxite insecurity as one begets the other. The U.S. could increase its gallium supply chain security by increasing long-term offtake agreements with Japan and South Korea to spur increased primary production (at greater costs).

Multi-pronged Approach

- The U.S. should monitor future viable U.S. and North American gallium projects and provide financial incentives if viable.
- The administration could use the Defense Production Act to support new lines of gallium extraction from existing U.S. owned bauxite operations such as those already run by ALCOA and ATALCO.
- In 2022, the National Defense Stockpile held no gallium products while the Defense Logistics Agency (DLA) published no intent to purchase any through 2025. A one-year supply of gallium metal based on annual consumption would be 11 metric tons and 180 tons for GaAs wafers. Private industry held an estimated 2.7 tons of gallium products in stock.

- It is unknown how much gallium scrap is processed, but a mandatory national recycling, recovery, and reuse program would maximize access to this resource.
- Gallium can be replaced by silicon or indium in certain wafers depending on the application and performance required. For years, gallium has been replacing silicon since it performs better in certain functions.

U.S. Gallium Imports 2024

Product	Value	Volume	Price
GaAs Wafers (Doped)	$62,300.00	194 kg	$321.00/kg
GaAs wafers (Undoped)	$141 million	683 tons	$206k/ton
Gallium Metal	$4.8 million	10.8 tons	$444k/ton

**USITC data HTS code 2853.90.9010, 3818.00.0010, 8112.92.1000*

Germanium (Ge)

Background

Germanium is mainly recovered secondary to lead, zinc (U.S., Canada), and coal ash (China) operations and is increasingly sourced from e-waste recycling operations with some estimates as high as 30% of total annual global consumption. Germanium is used in many high-tech applications such as polymer catalysts, infrared technology (IR), fiber optics for 5G networks, semiconductors, and solar cells. For the national defense base, germanium IR applications are used in night vision devices (NVDs), armored vehicles, drones, and aircraft. Germanium solar cell applications are used for both commercial and defense, terrestrial and space use.

In 2022, China produced an estimated 180 tons of germanium which was 86% of the world's production of 210 tons. Canada produced 20 tons (9.5%), Russia six tons (3%), and Belgium four tons (2%).[423] There are an estimated 8,600 tons of germanium reserves worldwide although accurate amounts are impossible to know due to germanium's status as a byproduct.[424] Annually, only a relatively small percentage of available germanium is recovered because most companies do not conduct extraction operations, preferring to focus only on their primary product. The two largest producers of germanium are Yunnan Chihong Zinc & Germanium Company (66 tons produced in 2023) and Yunnan Lincang Xinyuan Germanium Industrial Company.

In the U.S., a Canadian company extracts zinc in Alaska and then ships it to their refining facility in British Columbia to extract germanium for re-import. In Tennessee, a Belgian company extracts zinc and germanium concentrate but then exports it for refinement and re-importation. The Defense Logistics Agency (DLA) has a dedicated germanium recycling program as does Belgian company Umicore. The U.S. consumes an estimated 30 tons a year of germanium and imports more than 75% of its germanium needs.

In 2024, the U.S. imported 20 metric tons of germanium metal products worth $42 million for an average of $2.1 million a ton. From 2020-2023, most came from China (51%), then Belgium (27%), and Germany (15%). The U.S.

423 USGS Gallium & Germanium Report 2024.

424 "Di Juqing: germanium 40 years from now, global stock depletion is expected to be 120 tons in the next few years." SMM, May 25, 2018.

also imported 13 tons of germanium dioxide (GeO2) worth $18.2 million or $1.4 million a ton. Almost all this GeO2 came from just two countries, Belgium (53%) and Canada (41%). While the U.S. has minimized direct importation from China, its other trading partners most likely used products originating from there.

Teck Resources Limited (TRL), NYSE: TECK

TRL is a diversified Canadian company with headquarters in Vancouver that runs a variety of oil, coal, copper, zinc, and lead operations, including secondary products like molybdenum, indium, and germanium. They have operations in the U.S. (zinc, lead, copper), Canada (zinc, copper, coal), Australia (zinc), and Latin America (zinc, copper). TRL is a profitable company with net profits of $203 million in 2024. TRL runs the Red Dog zinc-lead mine in Alaska but ships its zinc-lead concentrates to its smelter in Trail, British Columbia where it makes a variety of specialty products like germanium dioxide (GeO2), germanium tetrachloride (GeCl4), and fiber optic grade GeO2.

Red Dog produced 556,000 tons of zinc concentrate in 2024. However, TRL has issued guidance to draw down operations 20%-25% to 365,000-400,000 tons by 2027. Since the company produces germanium secondary to its zinc operations, germanium production will also drop proportionally. The lowered production guidance is most likely because Trek pays increasing royalty rates to the NANA Regional Corporation, an Alaska Native Regional Corporation. In 2027, the royalty rate goes up from the current 40% to 45% and then up to 50% in 2032 where it remains flat.

Nyrstar NV, EBR: NYR – Financial Distress

Nyrstar is an international Belgian mining company with 4,000 employees that owns their Middle Tennessee zinc complex with two underground mines at Cumberland and Gordonsville with an onsite concentrate processing plant (50,000 tpa capacity) located at Gordonsville.[425] Nyrstar also has their East Tennessee zinc complex consisting of three underground zinc mines with the zinc concentrate processed onsite at their Young operation. Zinc concentrate from both operations is sent to their smelter in Clarkesville for further processing. The Gordonsville products contain germanium and gallium which is extracted in Clarkesville.

425 Nyrstar is majority-owned by Singapore based Trafigura Group.

The Clarkesville facility is the only primary zinc smelter in the U.S. capable of producing germanium concentrate. In Q4 2023, Nyrstar halted operations at its Middle complex due to low zinc prices, which halted its germanium and gallium operations. Nyrstar wants to construct a $150 million advanced germanium and gallium refinery at the Clarkesville site which would meet 80% of U.S. domestic demand which is roughly 24 metric tons. Currently, Nyrstar ships these concentrates overseas for processing.

As indicated by the company's temporary pause in zinc operations, Nyrstar is in a state of financial distress, losing $4.5 million in 2024. While the company would like its proposed germanium/gallium facility to come online in 2026, Nyrstar has not gained any financial support from the U.S. federal government. This lack of support is tied directly to Nyrstar's history where it bought debt-distressed mining companies and then declared bankruptcy itself in the U.S. in 2019. The same year, Singapore-based Trafigura Group became a majority shareholder, providing Nyrstar with critically needed capital infusion. However, minority shareholders subsequently sued Nyrstar for $1.2 billion alleging the company provided Trafigura with unreasonably favorable zinc offtake agreements leading to its bankruptcy. Litigation is ongoing.

5N+ Semiconductors, TSX: VNP

Canadian company 5N Plus with headquarters in Montreal is an international company with 800 employees and facilities in Canada, the U.S., Germany, China, and Laos. They manufacture semiconductors, solar cells, chemicals, high-purity metals and other specialty alloys including mixtures of bismuth and indium. 5N produces their germanium wafers for use in terrestrial and space solar cells at their St. George, Utah facility.

5N was profitable in 2024 with net earnings of $14.6 million which was a drop from $15.4 million in 2023. Cost of sales also increased to $211 million from $184 million the year before. Part of the earnings decrease was due to currency translation which cost them $4.9 million. 5N held $51 million in raw materials, which was up from $36 million the previous year, which indicates they might be stocking germanium. Since $202 million of revenue was from their semiconductor sales, 5N is highly exposed and sensitive to the germanium market.

In 2024, DOD awarded 5N $14.4 million through the Defense Production Act (DPA) to expand their production capability of germanium substrates for use in solar cells for defense and commercial satellites. The money will be spent over the course of four years to upgrade 5N's St. George manufacturing facility. In Q1 2024, 5N signed a $135 million contract with AZUR SPACE Solar Power GmbH to produce solar cells.

Umicore in Oklahoma

Umicore SA is an established Belgian multinational advanced materials and recycling company that originally got its start in the Belgian Congo in the early 1900s as the copper mining company Union Miniere. In 2003, the company bought EaglePicher's germanium operations in Quapaw, Oklahoma for $15 million. The renamed Umicore Optical Materials USA produces and distributes optical-grade germanium IR material, germanium metal, germanium tetrachloride, and germanium dioxide. The company also produces germanium products from scrap metal.

Actions Taken

DLA began an optical-grade germanium recycling program in 2022 where it recovers the mineral from decommissioned military equipment such as night vision goggles. The program is expected to recover upwards of three tons of usable germanium a year. It is unknown how much germanium scrap is processed in the U.S., but a mandatory national recycling, recovery, and reuse program would maximize access to this resource.

Incentives & Tariffs

A company would qualify for a 10% production cost tax credit under Section 45X of the Advanced Manufacturing Production Credit if the extracted germanium is "converted to germanium tetrachloride or purified to a minimum purity of 99.99% germanium by mass." Neither Teck nor Nyrstar qualify for this provision

Both domestic (there are none) and foreign germanium mining companies (Teck, Nyrstar) receive the same 14% depletion allowance.

Germanium was excluded from the Trump administration's April 2025 tariff schedule. The normal schedule taxes all germanium products at overall low rates, including China.

In 2023, China announced that germanium sellers required an export license through their provincial Ministry of Commerce (MOFCOM) office. MOFCOM has the authority to deny the license and violators of the licensing guidelines are subject to civil and criminal penalties. In 2024, China banned the export of dual-use germanium products to the U.S.

U.S Supply Chain Security Strategy Moving Forward

The U.S. has a vulnerable germanium position since it imported 75% of its primary needs with some of this originating directly from China. Also, the only company that produced germanium concentrates in the country (Nyrstar) is likely headed to another bankruptcy.

Multi-pronged Approach

- The U.S. should monitor Nyrstar and see if the company recovers from its current financial and legal challenges. If the company becomes viable again or his sold as the result of bankruptcy, the U.S. should consider using the DPA to support construction of a germanium/gallium refining facility.
- In 2022, the National Defense Stockpile held 20.9 metric tons of germanium products and 68,671 individual germanium wafers. The Defense Logistics Agency (DLA) announced it was disposing of 5 metric tons of germanium products in 2024 and 2025. DLA announced no plans to acquire new germanium products through 2025. DLA previously stored its four-inch germanium wafer stockpile with Umicore and 5N before consolidating its storage of 101,939 six-inch wafers with 5N. A one-year supply based on annual consumption would be 30 metric tons.
- Germanium wafers have largely been replaced by much cheaper silicon wafers although germanium's performance is still preferable in transistors. Chalcogenide glass can substitute germanium metal in infrared applications.

Graphite (Gr)

Background

Graphite is a crystalline form of carbon which is widely distributed geographically where natural graphite is extracted through traditional open pit mining and artificial/synthetic graphite is made from petroleum coke and coal tar products. Graphite is used as a lubricant, in brake linings, refractory applications, steel production, semiconductors, and increasingly as the negative anode in EV batteries. Synthetic graphite is used in electric arc furnace electrodes; graphite, both artificial and natural, is one of the few materials other than metals that can conduct electricity. Synthetic graphite is more expensive to produce and has a higher carbon footprint as it originates from petroleum products.

In 2024, China produced 1.27 million metric tons (79%) of natural flake graphite out of total global production of 1.6 million tons. Africa's Graphite Triangle (Madagascar, Mozambique, Tanzania) produced 189,000 tons (12%) and Canada produced just 20,000 tons (1%). Natural graphite is relatively plentiful with 290 million tons of reserves identified, led by China (28%), Brazil (25%), and Africa's Graphite Triangle (23%). Synthetic graphite reserves are equally plentiful and a country can produce as much as they need to, based on associated petroleum coke reserves. For example, the U.S. produced 300 million barrels of petroleum coke products in 2023.[426] China is the largest producer of natural and synthetic graphite in the world and possibly 100% of EV battery anodes transit through China at different stages of production.

The U.S. has had no active natural graphite extraction operations since 1979, although several projects are under way, and imports all its needs. In 2024, the U.S. imported 60,000 metric tons of natural flake graphite, consuming 52,000 tons valued at $115 million for an average cost of $2,220.00 a ton. From 2020-2023, the U.S. imported on average 43% of its natural flake graphite from China, 13% from Canada, 13% from Mexico, and 13% from Mozambique. [427]

Novonix, OTC: NVNXF

Australian company Novonix is a battery technology start-up specializing in EV battery cathodes and anodes. Novonix is building a synthetic graphite factory in Chattanooga, TN and is exploring a natural graphite project in Aus-

426 U.S. Energy Information Administration.
427 U.S. Geological Survey Graphite Report 2024.

tralia. The company will build a 150,000 tpa synthetic capacity and has partnerships with South Korean battery manufacturer LG Energy Solutions (LGES), KORE Power, and Panasonic. Because Novonix doesn't yet produce graphite, they had a loss of $78 million in 2024. The company received a $100 million grant from DOE in 2023 and a $754 million loan in 2024. The company benefits from owning its own graphite anode technology.

Anovion Technologies

Anovion is a private U.S. company with headquarters in Chicago and facilities in New York, West Virginia, and North Carolina. The company began synthetic graphite anode material production in 2021 and has a 5,000 tpa capacity while developing a larger facility in Georgia with a 50,000 tpa capacity and a start date of 2025. Anovion received a $117 million grant in 2022 from the DOE under the Bipartisan Infrastructure Law to increase their production capacity with the company committed to an accompanying $294 million.

Graphite One Inc (G1), OTC: GPHOF

G1 is a Canadian company developing a natural flake graphite operation in Alaska with production beginning in 2028 with a capacity of 25,000 tpa. The company also intends to produce natural and artificial graphite anode material and start a battery recycling facility at a site in Ohio. G1 received a $37.5 million grant through the Defense Production Act (DPA) in 2023 for battery anode production. The company was also awarded $4.7 million from the Defense Logistics Agency (DLA) to develop a graphite-based foam fire suppressant rather than PFAS chemical-based suppressants. Importantly, G1 does not have the intellectual property to execute their plan and is under negotiations with an undisclosed Chinese company for a technology licensing agreement. The company lost $6.7 million in 2024.

Westwater Resources Inc, NYSE: WWR

U.S. company Westwater Resources Inc. (WWR) is developing a natural flake graphite mine in Alabama and a battery grade graphite anode plant that will use their own proprietary purification technology. WWR's graphite processing plant is under construction and will have an initial capacity of 12,500 tpa, most of which will go to South Korean battery manufacturer SK On. While the company had $10 million in cash on hand to start 2024, is still required $152 million to finish its processing facility.

Syrah Resources, OTC: SYAAF

Syrah Resources is an Australian company with an active natural flake graphite mine in Mozambique and an unfinished processing facility in Louisiana. Their plan is to ship their unprocessed graphite concentrate from Africa to their facility in the U.S for processing. Syrah produced 35,000 tons of graphite in 2024 and sold it to buyers in South Korea and Indonesia. In 2022, the company received a $220 million grant from DOE to advance their Louisiana facility. In 2023, Syrah received a $150 million conditional loan from the U.S. International Development Finance Corporation to support its Mozambique operations. Syrah lost $125 million in 2024.

Actions Taken

DOE has provided substantial grants to Novonix, Anovion, and Syrah - $437 million combined. In 2018, the U.S. applied 10% tariffs on Chinese graphite products which were subsequently raised to 25%. Several companies applied for tariff exclusions including Tesla and Sk Innovation since 100% of graphite anodes for EV batteries are imported from China. The Biden administration eventually waived the 25% tariffs on Chinese graphite products although these waivers are set to expire in January 2026.

Incentives & Tariffs

A company would qualify for a 10% production cost tax credit under Section 45X of the Advanced Manufacturing Production Credit if the extracted graphite is "is purified to a minimum purity of 99.9% graphitic carbon." This includes both natural and synthetic graphite products.

Domestic graphite mining companies (there are none) receive a 22% depletion allowance for natural lump and amorphous products while foreign companies (none are active) receive a 14% rate. Both domestic and foreign mining companies (none are active) receive a 14% depletion allowance for natural flake graphite production.

Graphite was excluded from the Trump administration's April 2025 tariff schedule. The regular tariff schedule taxes all graphite products at overall low rates, including China.

On December 17, 2024, the American Active Anode Material Producers (AAAMP) submitted a petition to the U.S. International Trade Commission (USITC) for antidumping and countervailing duties on Chinese graphite imports. The petition argued that tariffs of 828% - 921% would be required to compensate for China's unfair practices. On February 3, 2025, USITC made a preliminary determination that China exported artificially cheap graphite to the U.S. to suppress development of a domestic graphite industry.

In 2023, Beijing required Chinese graphite producers to apply for an export license (renewed every six months) at the provincial MOFCOM (Ministry of Commerce) office for both natural and synthetic graphite products. Violations of the regulation can result in civil and criminal penalties. In 2024, China banned dual-use graphite export to the U.S.

U.S Supply Chain Security Strategy Moving Forward

The U.S. has a vulnerable natural graphite position since it imports 100% of its primary needs with 43% originating directly from China. Canada and Mexico produce little graphite which cannot meet U.S. needs. The U.S. can extract natural graphite and produce synthetic graphite with the understanding they are not competitive with the Chinese enterprise and must be subsidized by the federal government.

Multi-pronged Approach

- Most graphite waste products are discarded and a mandatory national reuse, recycle, and recovery program would maximize continuing access to this resource. However, most graphite is expended during its application (like electrodes) and is released into our environment.
- In 2022, the U.S. National Defense Stockpile held no graphite while the Defense Logistics Agency (DLA) announced no plans to acquire any through 2025. A one-year supply of natural graphite based on annual consumption would be 52,000 metric tons and synthetic graphite would be 96,000 tons.
- Natural and synthetic graphite compete with one another as substitution possibilities. Natural flake graphite has a lower carbon footprint while synthetic graphite has superior properties for batteries, although more expensive. Silicon is being tested as a possible graphite replacement in battery anodes as it conducts electricity and stores more lithium ions.

U.S. Artificial Graphite Imports 2024 (metric tons)

The U.S. imported 115,700 metric tons valued at $430.8 million for an average price of $3,700.00 a ton.

China: 85,900 tons, $283 million. 74% of total imports.

Spain: 5,600 tons, $9.5 million.

Mexico: 5,400 tons, $25.8 million.

France: 5,000 tons, $11.9 million.

South Korea: 3,800, $33.7 million.

U.S. Natural Flake Graphite Imports 2024 (metric tons)

The U.S. imported 74,000 tons valued at $148.8 million for an average price $2,010.00 a ton.

China: 35,700 tons, $100 million. 48% of total imports.

Canada: 10,400 tons, $14.6 million.

Madagascar: 8,400 tons, $8.5 million.

Mozambique: 7,800 tons, $6.1 million.

Mexico: 7,500 tons, $5.9 million.

Overall, the U.S. imported 189,700 tons of graphite products with China directly accounting for 121,600 tons (64%).

**UN Comtrade Data HTS Code 3801.10, 2504*

Hafnium (Hf)

Background

Hafnium does not exist as a free element and is most commonly found with zirconium and is extracted from heavy mineral sands deposits. Hafnium is extremely resistant to corrosion and is used in optical coatings, plasma cutting, electrodes, semiconductors, superalloys in space applications, and neutron absorbing control rods in nuclear power plants. Because hafnium and zirconium frequently occur together, their production data is generally reported together. Zirconium and hafnium generally occur in zircon at a ratio of 50:1 so hafnium extraction volumes are much lower. Since hafnium is a byproduct of zirconium extraction operations, most reporting covers zirconium but not hafnium production. As 90% of zirconium products are used in the nuclear industry, most hafnium is extracted as part of this process.

Because Australia produced 33% of the world's zirconium in 2024, they are most likely the largest producer of hafnium. They were followed by South Africa (20%), Mozambique (11%), and the U.S. (6%).[428] In 2024, the U.S imported 61.2 metric tons of unwrought hafnium products with most coming from Germany (63%), the U.K. (14%), and China (13%). The U.S. imported much less wrought hafnium products, just 13.2 tons, with Germany providing the most (86%) and then China (23%).[429]

The U.S. produces undisclosed amounts of hafnium as a byproduct of zirconium mining operations in Georgia and Florida (Chemours Company, spun-off from DuPont). Two companies in the U.S. made hafnium metal products from intermediate zirconium chemicals. The private company Zirconium Research Corporation in Oregon provides a variety of zirconium, niobium, and hafnium products, mainly serving the alloy industry. Stone & Webster, a subsidiary of Westinghouse, produces hafnium products for the nuclear power industry at their western zirconium facility in Ogden, Utah. Several other companies make refined hafnium products to include American Elements in Los Angeles, Fine Metals Corporation in Virginia, and Thermo Fisher Scientific. The U.S. hafnium enterprise is set up to import unrefined products and then to produce and export more refined products.

428 U.S. Geological Data.

429 UN Comtrade data HS codes 811231, 811239.

ATI, NYSE: ATI

ATI is a publicly traded specialty metals company with headquarters in Texas that primarily serves the defense and aerospace industries (65% of overall sales). The company specializes in nickel, titanium, zirconium, niobium, and hafnium metals – all of which are designated critical minerals by the U.S. government. In the 1970s, an ATI subsidiary in Albany, OR developed a high-purity hafnium production process.[430] ATI uses hafnium to make high-temperature, high-performance specialty alloy products for nuclear power plants as well as hafnium metal precursors for the electronics industry. The company was profitable with a net income of $367 million in 2024.[431]

Actions Taken

There has been no U.S government support specific to the hafnium industry. There has likely been no support to Chemours because of their ongoing legal liability.

Incentives & Tariffs

- Domestic hafnium mining companies (Chemours Company) receive a 22% depletion allowance while foreign companies (there are none) receive a 14% rate.

Under the Inflation Reduction Act, a company would qualify for a 10% production cost tax credit under Section 45X of the Advanced Manufacturing Production Credit if the extracted hafnium is "purified to a minimum purity of 99.9% by mass."

Hafnium wasn't excluded from the Trump administration's April 2025 tariff schedule. The normal tariff schedule taxes hafnium products at overall low rates, including China.

U.S Supply Chain Security Strategy Moving Forward

The U.S. has a vulnerable hafnium position because of its reliance on Chemours who had net profit of $86 million in 2024 for a margin of just 1.4% which improved from a net loss of $238 million in 2023. In 2023, Chemours, DuPont, and Corteva Inc. reached a $1.19 billion settlement with the EPA

430 This location was later designed as an EPA superfund site to clean up ground soil pollution from Teledyne Wah Chang Albany (TWCA) operations. TWCA at one time produced 40 tpa of hafnium.

431 Previously Allegheny Technologies Incorporated,

over their role in polluting water sources with cancer causing polyfluoroalkyl substances (PFAS).[432] Chemours agreed to pay $595 million which does not address claims by individuals, water suppliers, States, or the U.S. government.

Additional litigation is ongoing and more damages are likely in the future and could be substantial. Various countries are taking actions to limit or ban PFAS and hydrofluorocarbons (HFCs) which will negatively impact Chemours' business model. In 2023, the Netherlands found Chemours liable for pollution from its Dordrecht facility from 1984 to 1998 with penalties yet to be determined. Still other litigation is pending and damages could be substantial. In 2024, the Chemours board fired its CEO and CFO for illegal financial manipulation.

Multi-pronged Approach

- It Is unknown how much hafnium is recycled or recovered, but it is most likely low. A mandatory national reuse, recycling, and recovery program would maximize continuing access to this resource.
- In 2022, the U.S. National Defense Stockpile held no hafnium reserves while the Defense Logistics Agency (DLA) is authorized to acquire a very large quantity of hafnium - 2,300 metric tons in 2025. A one-year supply based on annual consumption would be 11 metric tons. It is unknown why DLA purchased a 209-year supply of hafnium while neglecting other more pressing minerals like HREE.
- The U.S. requires better domestic hafnium surveillance mechanisms. For instance, Chemours does not mention its hafnium production data in its annual reports.
- Hafnium can be replaced by zirconium in certain alloy applications. Control rods in nuclear plants can be replaced with silver-indium-cadmium rods, although hafnium was used to replace those.

432 Corteva is also a spin-off of DuPont.

U.S. Hafnium Imports 2024 (metric tons)			
<u>Product</u>	<u>Value</u>	<u>Volume</u>	<u>Price</u>
Unwrought powder,	$133.9 million	61.3 tons	$2.18 mil a ton
waste & scrap	Germany: 36.5 tons, $82.6 million		
HS 8112.31	U.K.: 8.7 tons, $16.2 million		
	China: 8.4 tons, $18.3 million		
	France: 4.5 tons, $9.5 million		
	Canada: 2.5 tons, $7 million		
Other articles	$42.3 million	13.2 tons	$3.2 mil a ton
HS 8112.39	Germany: 11.3 tons, $37.8 million		
	China: 1.7 tons, $4.3 million		
Total	**$176.2 million**	**74.5 tons**	**$2.3 million**

*China accounted for 10.1 tons of U.S. hafnium imports by volume (13%) and $22.6 million by value (13%). For "other hafnium articles", this was a huge shift from 2023, where the U.S. sourced 74% of its needs directly from China. The shift was smaller for powders where China previously provided 14%.

**UN Comtrade Data*

Holmium (Ho)

Background

Holmium is one of the seventeen REE (Rare Earth Elements) and is part of the heavy REE (HREE) lanthanide series. Holmium is commonly found with other rare earth elements such as yttrium, terbium, and dysprosium in occurrences of monazite, and gadolinite (although only in trace amounts). Holmium is used in medical laser applications, glass, ceramics, magnets, and nuclear control rods since it absorbs neutrons. Holmium arsenide is used in semiconductor and photo optic applications. Manufacturers have explored using holmium to thrift neodymium in NdFeB magnets.

There is little publicly available data on the global production and flow of holmium. The U.S. company MP Materials produces mainly light REE (LREE) as opposed to HREE which includes holmium thus it is believed the U.S. imports 100% of its holmium needs from China. Germany, Korea, and Japan also produce and export refined holmium products. Chinese entrepreneur Wei Wu founded the Michigan based REE trading firm Pacific Industrial Development Corporation in 1992 which imports holmium oxide from China. In summer of 2024, holmium oxide (at least 99.5 % purity) sold for $68,000.00 a metric ton in the China market.

Actions Taken

The U.S. has done nothing specifically to secure its holmium supply chain other than what it has done for the larger REE space such as providing grants to Australian company Lynas Rare Earths and MP Materials to develop a HREE capability in the U.S.

Companies receives a 10% production cost tax credit under Section 45X Advanced Manufacturing Production Credit if their holmium products are "converted to a purity of 99% by mass."

Incentives & Tariffs

- Domestic REE mining companies receive a 14% depletion allowance (MP Materials) while foreign companies receive a 14% rate (there are none) for monazite, bastnaesite, and xenotime extraction operations.

Holmium was excluded from the Trump administration's April 2025 tariff schedule. The regular schedule encourages the import of holmium oxide while taxing other products at overall low rates.

U.S. Supply Chain Security Strategy Moving Forward

The U.S. has a vulnerable holmium position as it relies on 100% of its imports like it does for most of its HREE needs. The U.S. should continue to monitor new ex-China HREE extraction operations worldwide, assist them when feasible, and secure offtake agreements for stockpiling purposes.

Multi-pronged Approach

- The U.S. should continue its support to Lynas Rare Earths and MP Materials to build a HREE processing capability in the U.S.
- In 2022, the U.S. National Defense Stockpile held no holmium reserves and the Defense Logistics Agency published no intentions to purchase any through 2025. The U.S.'s annual holmium consumption is unknown and may be 10 metric tons.
- The U.S. should develop effective critical mineral surveillance tools to understand the global production and flow of holmium products to include the U.S. International Trade Commission developing a holmium specific HTS code to collect accurate date on its importation.
- In some laser uses, holmium can be replaced with thulium, also a designated critical mineral and REE.

Indium (In)

Background

Indium is chemically similar to gallium and thallium and is most commonly recovered as a byproduct from sphalerite mining, a zinc-sulfide ore, and less frequently from chalcopyrite, a copper-iron sulfide mineral. Indium was previously used to coat bearings in aircraft engines to prevent corrosion and is now mostly used as indium tin oxide (ITO) to coat glass such as flat panel displays. It is also used in the electronics industry for solders, as an element in semiconductors, usually as trimethylindium (TMI), and in 5G fiber-optics telecommunications.

Because the U.S. does not recover indium secondary to any ores, it imports 100% of its needs. In 2024, China extracted 760 metric tons of indium which was 76% of the world total of 1,080 tons. South Korea was the next major producer with 180 tons, then Japan with 60 tons, and Canada 35 tons. The U.S. imported 250 tons of refined indium products with most coming from South Korea (29%), Japan (18%), and Canada (14%) averaged from the years 2020-2023.[433]

Teck Resources Limited (TRL), NYSE: TECK

As mentioned in the section on germanium, TRL is a diversified Canadian company with headquarters in Vancouver that runs zinc and copper operations in the U.S., Canada, Peru, and Australia, producing indium as a secondary product. In the U.S., the company operates the Red Dog zinc-lead mine in Alaska, transporting the ore to its smelter in Trail, British Columbia where it makes a variety of specialty metal products. This creates the dynamics of the company extracting indium from the U.S., processing it across the border in Canada, and then selling its products back to American businesses. Because TRL plans to decrease its zinc production by 30%, indium production will also drop proportionally. For perspective, indium plays such a small part of TRL's overall business model, it isn't mentioned in their annual reports.

Nyrstar NV, EBR: NYR – Financially Distressed

Also mentioned in the germanium chapter, Nyrstar is an international Belgian mining company that owns their Middle Tennessee zinc complex com-

433 U.S. Geological Survey Indium Report 2024.

posed of two underground mines.[434] While the company extracts zinc in the U.S., indium products are made at their smelter in Auby, France, using a RLE (Roast, Leach, Electrolysis) process where they began producing refined Indium products in 2012. France produces just 1% of the world's total indium production. Nyrstar did not build an indium manufacturing capability in the U.S. because it was uneconomic and with the company's ongoing financial distress, it isn't feasible without a large cash infusion such as a grant from the DOE or through the DPA.[435]

Indium Corporation (IC)

IC is a private specialty metals company based out of New York State with operations in Asia (Singapore, Malaysia, India, Korea, China) and Europe (Germany, UK). The company has a smelter capability and produces a variety of silver, gold, bismuth, germanium, gallium and indium products specializing in liquid and solid-state alloys and solders for the electronics industry. IC runs an established metals recycling program which includes indium products and specifically ITO (indium tin oxide) recovery.

Korea Zinc Company, KRX: 010130

KZC is a publicly trade South Korean company that produced 827,000 tons of zinc concentrate in 2024, along with 445,000 tons of lead and 32,000 tons of copper.[436] KZC has subsidiaries in Australia, Vietnam, and the U.S. KZC produces high-purity indium (minimum 99.998%) for bonding, soldering, and ITO targets for LCD panels.[437] South Korea produces only small quantities of zinc, importing more than 99% of its needs with most coming from North America, Australia, and then South America - surprisingly little comes from China. Thus, Korea has the same zinc/indium supply chain insecurity as the U.S., although having the world's second largest indium production capability after China.

Actions Taken

The U.S. government has taken no specific measures to enhance their domestic indium industry or supply chain security.

434 Nyrstar is majority-owned by Singapore based Trafigura Group.

435 UN Comtrade and U.S. Geological Survey data.

436 KZC is the single largest producer of zinc in the world.

437 South Korea has designated indium as a critical mineral.

Incentives & Tariffs

A company would qualify for a 10% production cost tax credit under Section 45X of the Advanced Manufacturing Production Credit if the extracted indium is "converted to indium tin oxide or indium oxide which is purified to a minimum purity of 99.9% by mass or purified to a minimum purity of 99% indium by mass."

Domestic mining companies receive a 14% depletion allowance (there are none) while foreign companies receive a 14% rate (Teck Resources).

Indium was excluded from the Trump administration's April 2025 tariff schedule.

In 2023, China announced that companies exporting gallium products – including indium gallium arsenic - would require an export license through their provincial Ministry of Commerce (MOFCOM) office. MOFCOM has the authority to deny the license and violators of the licensing guidelines are subject to civil and criminal liability.

U.S Supply Chain Security Strategy Moving Forward

The U.S. has a vulnerable indium position since it imports 100% of its primary needs with less than 5% originating directly from China and only 7% coming from Canada. Presently, the only economic extraction of indium in the U.S. is done by a Canadian mining company which actually processes it in British Columbia.

Multi-pronged Approach

- The U.S. should monitor Teck Resources and consider providing it government resources to expand its indium production. Because Teck produces its indium on the border with Washington State, there is no advantage of building an indium production facility in the U.S.
- In 2022, the U.S. National Defense Stockpile held no indium reserves while the Defense Logistics Agency (DLA) announced no plans to purchase any through 2025. A one-year supply based on annual consumption of refined indium products would be 300 metric tons.
- Although Indium Corporation has a recognized, established recycling program, the U.S. at the national level does not have a com-

prehensive reuse and recycling program which should be mandatory.

- Aluminum Zinc Oxide (AZO) has been looked at to replace indium in ITO although more research needs to be done.

U.S. Indium Imports 2024			
Product	**Value**	**Volume**	**Price**
Unwrought & powders	$66.5 million	239 metric tons	$278,200.00 per ton
	Japan: 63.3 tons, $17.3 million		
	China: 52 tons, $14.9 million		
	South Korea: 36.8 tons, $11.6 million		
	Taiwan: 34.8 tons, $11.3 million		
	Bolivia: 20.5 tons, $697,000.00		
	Canada: 20.3 tons, $6.7 million		
*China accounted for 22% of imports by volume and 22% by value. The U.S. Asian allies accounted for 56% by volume while the Western Hemisphere accounted for17% by volume.			
**Data from USITC, HTS code 8112.9230.00*			

Iridium (Ir)

Background

Iridium is classified as a PGM (Platinum Group Metals) consisting of palladium, platinum, iridium, osmium, rhodium, and ruthenium. Iridium is found in higher concentrations in asteroids and the distribution of iridium in our Earth's crust is most likely due to the previous impact by asteroids and the ensuing fallout.[438] Iridium is generally produced as a byproduct of platinum and palladium mining and is found in countries with those reserves. Iridium is an extremely hard, dense metal with extraordinary thermal and corrosion resistance qualities. It is used as a metal, in alloys for the aerospace industry, spark plugs, crucibles, and electrodes. Iridium is used in the medical imaging sector and for cancer treatment.

Because PGM are dominated by palladium and platinum production and use, iridium production is largely overlooked as a much smaller volume co-product. In 2024, South Africa was the largest producer of PGM (53%), followed by Russia (26%), and Zimbabwe (9%). The world consumed an estimated 8.1 tons of iridium in 2023 with most used in the electrochemical sector (36%), then electrical (25%), and automotive (7%).[439] In 2024, the U.S. imported 1.4 tons of iridium valued at $214 million for an average of $153,000.00 per kg. The U.S. imported most of its iridium from South Africa followed by fellow G7 countries of UK, Germany, Japan, and Italy.

The most significant PGM production comes from the Bushveld Igneous Complex in South Africa, then Russia (Nornickel, as a byproduct of nickel production), Zimbabwe, the Sudbury Complex in Canada (the site of an asteroid strike), and the Stillwater Complex in the U.S. The Stillwater Complex is in Montana which is mined by South African company Sibanye Stillwater. In Canada, the South African holding company Impala Platinum Holdings PTD (Implats) owns the subsidiary Impala Canada Limited.

Actions Taken

The U.S. government has taken no specific measures to enhance the iridium supply chain other than apply zero tariffs.

438 Becker, Luann. "Repeated Blows." Scientific American, 2002.
439 SFA (Oxford), Sibanye Stillwater presentation.

Incentives & Tariffs

A company would qualify for a 10% production cost tax credit under Section 45X of the Advanced Manufacturing Production Credit if the extracted iridium is "purified to a minimum purity of 99% by mass."

Domestic mining companies receive a 22% depletion allowance (there are none) while foreign companies receive a 14% rate (Sibanye Stillwater).

Iridium was exempted from the Trump administration's April 2025 tariff schedule. The regular tariff schedule doesn't tax PGM or iridium.

U.S Supply Chain Security Strategy Moving Forward

The U.S. has a vulnerable iridium position since it imports 100% of its primary needs with Sibanye Stillwater producing no iridium in the U.S. in 2024. The U.S.' PGM center gravity is maintaining good ongoing bilateral trade relations with South Africa and guaranteeing open and secure shipping routes between the two countries. While the U.S. imports no iridium from China or Russia, it must be concerned with South Africa's status as a member of BRICS.

Multi-pronged Approach

- In 2022, the U.S. National Defense Stockpile did not disclose holding any iridium products. However, the Defense Logistics Agency announced it was disposing of 489 troy ounces (15 kg) of iridium in 2023, 2024, and 2025. A one-year supply based on annual consumption would be 1.4 metric tons.
- Although PGM recycling is widespread and is driven by PGM pricing, it is mainly focused on the recovery of platinum.[440] There are many private companies that have established PGM and iridium recycling programs such as Specialty Metals in Connecticut. At the national level, the U.S. does not have a comprehensive reuse, recovery, and recycling program which should be mandatory.
- Iridium can be replaced in some circumstances with platinum, ruthenium, and osmium (both designated critical minerals). Due to its unique characteristics, substitutions can result in a loss of performance.

440 Worldwide, there are tens of thousands of companies involved in PGM recovery, recycling, and resale.

U.S. Iridium Imports 2024			
Product	**Value**	**Volume**	**Price**
Unwrought & powders	$173 million	1.16 metric tons	$149,000.00 per kg
HTS 7110.41.0010	South Africa: 821 kg, $124.6 million		
	U.K.: 193 kg, $28.9 million		
	Germany: 89 kg, $13.1 million		
	Japan: 53 kg, $6 million		
Semi-manufactured	$31.7 million	198 kg	$160,100.00 per kg
HTS 7110.49.0010	U.K.: 147 kg, $23.5 million		
	Japan: 8.5 kg, $1.28 million		
	Germany: 41 kg, $6.8 million		
*While the U.S. imports all its iridium needs, 100% comes from ex-China countries with the understanding South Africa is a member of the China-led BRICS coalition.			
**Data from USITC data base*			

Lanthanum (La)

Background

Lanthanum is one of the seventeen REE (Rare Earth Elements) designated as critical minerals and is part of the light REE (LREE) lanthanide series. Lanthanum is commonly found with fellow REE cerium and is a relatively common mineral and is more abundant than lead. Lanthanum uses include the medical industry as a phosphate-binder in the treatment of kidney failure, as a component of NiMH (Nickel Metal Hydride) batteries used in hybrid vehicles, in alloys for hydrogen absorption, and mixed with steel and molybdenum for specific use cases to improve performance. A major use of lanthanum in the U.S. is for refining fossil fuel products.

As mentioned in previous sections on other REE, production volumes are reported as REO (Rare Earth Oxides) and as an overall group total, not as specific elements. The U.S. has one REO operation at Mountain Pass in California and the U.S. mining company MP Materials (MPM) estimates that 32.3% of the REO it extracts consists of lanthanum. MPM completed its new REO processing plant in 2023 where it can now produce and sell lanthanum carbonate as an individual product. In 2024, lanthanum carbonate averaged $850.00 a metric ton with predictions that it would rise to $1,550.00 a ton in 2030 and then plateau there. In 2024, less than 1% of MP's sales were from its lanthanum carbonate product.[441]

In 2024, the U.S. imported 63.1 metric tons of lanthanum carbonate valued at $553,000.00 for an average of a $8,760.00 a ton. Two-thirds of this came from China (42 tons) with Estonia being the next largest provider (20 tons). The U.S. imported 20 tons of other lanthanum products with all of it coming from China. In total, the U.S. relied on 75% of these lanthanum products from China. This was in line with MPM historically sending its REO to China for processing which then required the refined products to be imported back to the U.S. for consumption.[442]

Separately, the U.S. has been the single largest importer of lanthanum carbonate as it is used for fuel cracking catalysts and along with cerium in catalytic converters for ICE vehicles. Accordingly, there is increasing downward pres-

441 MP Annual Report 2024.
442 USITC data HTS Codes 2846.90.8070, 2805.30.0005.

sure on production and pricing as the expansion of the BEV industry means less gasoline and emission controls are required. Going forward, the lanthanum carbonate market will most likely be in a state of oversupply and prices will remain flat or even decrease, depending on market dynamics.

Actions Taken

As discussed previously, MPM received grants through the Defense Production Act and from the Department of Energy to construct an REE processing facility at their Mountain Passs location and to build their Fort Worth, TX magnet facility.

Incentives & Tariffs

MPM qualifies for a 10% tax credit under the Section 45X Advanced Manufacturing Production Credit if its lanthanum products are "purified to a minimum purity of 99% by mass."

Domestic REE mining companies receive a 14% depletion allowance (MP Materials) while foreign companies receive a 14% rate (there are none) for monazite, bastnaesite, and xenotime extraction operations.

All REE products are exempted from the Trump Administration's April 2025 tariff schedule. The regular schedule encourages the import of lanthanum products with overall low rates.

U.S Supply Chain Security Strategy Moving Forward

The U.S. has an insecure lanthanum position since it relies on China for 93% of its imports, although this will change as MPM's processing capability comes online. The likely long-term threats to this position include MP Materials depleting its Mountain Pass mine or the company becoming unprofitable due to continuing superior competition from Chinese manufacturers. To date, only China, the U.S., and Malaysia (Australia) have the technological sophistication to develop their own advanced processing capability.[443]

Multi-pronged Approach

- The U.S. should monitor the domestic lanthanum value chain and determine when and if additional government assistance is needed. MP Materials has received sufficient government subsidies to date although they must continue to lower costs and product prices.

443 Vietnam has a limited processing capability.

- In 2022, the U.S. National Defense Stockpile did not reveal any lanthanum holdings. The Defense Logistics Agency (DLA) announced they were purchasing upwards of 1,300 metric tons of lanthanum each in 2023 and 2024 and then 1,100 tons in 2025. If DLA purchases the lanthanum from China, it will cost them about $82 million (3,700 x $22,300.00). A one-year supply may be 264 metric tons meaning the above purchased amounts would last 14 years.
- It is unknown how much lanthanum is recycled or reused, but it is likely around 1% which is the overall rate for REE. Recycling is difficult because the REE are mixed with other elements, are used in such low volumes that very little is recovered and usually involves hydrochloric acid. Research has shown that lanthanum oxide can be recovered from fluid catalytic cracking (FCC) catalysts although widespread implementation has not occurred. A mandatory national, recovery, recycling, and reuse program would maximize access to this resource. However, due to relatively low lanthanum product pricing, economic recycling measures are unlikely.
- Lanthanum can be replaced in medical usage for renal failure but with reported reduced effectiveness. A transition off fossil fuels for energy generation will reduce lanthanum needs in this use case.

U.S. Lanthanum Imports 2024			
Country	**Volume**	**Value**	**Price/kg**
China	42.3 tons	$385,000.00	$9.10
Estonia	20 tons	$109,000.00	$5.45
Austria	500 kg	$4,270.00	$8.54
Germany	320 kg	$38,100.00	$119.00
South Korea	40 kg	$4,300.00	$107.50
India	10 kg	$11,100.00	$1,110.00
Total	63.1 tons	$553,000.00	$8.76

(HTS 2846.90.8070: REE carbonate mixtures containing lanthanum as the predominant metal.)

Lanthanum, not intermixed or interalloyed

*The U.S. imported 20 tons of lanthanum products from China valued at $404,000.00, averaging $20,200.00. (HTS 2805.30.0005)

*The U.S. imported a total of 83.1 metric tons of lanthanum products valued at $957,000.00 with 75% coming from China.

**Data from USITC*

Lithium (Li)

Background

Lithium is a soft alkali metal and is the least dense of the metals. Although it is commonly found in pegmatites, it is also present in underground brines and in low concentrations in the ocean. Historically, lithium was used for medicine, ceramics, lubricants, industrial dehumidifiers, and the hydrogen bomb program until its use more recently became dominated by EV batteries. Specifically, lithium is used in the cathode (positive terminal) of lithium-ion batteries (LIB) due to its relatively high energy density compared to alternatives. Lithium is relatively abundant and is found in large quantities in Australia (hard rock mining) and South America's Lithium Triangle composed of Chile, Argentina, and Bolivia (brine extraction).

In 2024, the world produced an estimated 1.2million metric tons of LCE (lithium carbonate equivalent).[444] Australia led with 468,000 tons (34%), followed by Chile with 260,000 tons (20%), and then China with 218,000 tons (17%). The U.S. and Canada were minor producers with both contributing a combined total of 31,400 tons (2%). Chile is believed to hold 9.3 million contained tons in reserves, Australia 7 million tons, Argentina 4 million tons, and the U.S. 1.8 million tons out of an estimated total world reserve of 30 million tons. The Lithium Triangle may hold 303 million ton of LCE resources in the form of underground brine lakes.[445]

Since an estimated 87% of lithium is used in LIBs, they have become intertwined. LIB manufacturing is dominated by Asia with 67% being produced by Chinese companies, 18% by South Korea, and just 3% by Japan.[446] This means Western car manufacturers most likely buy batteries from one of these three countries for their EVs. China led the world by exporting 2.3 million metric tons of LIB with the most going to the U.S. (27%), then Germany (14%), and South Korea (10%).[447] From a supply chain perspective, the largest lithium producers ship their products to the various battery manufacturers which are located predominately in Asia, although LIB manufacturing is slowly shifting to Europe and North America.

444 The lithium industry refers to lithium volume in terms of LCE.
445 U.S. Geological Survey.
446 Data by SNE Research.
447 UN Comtrade database 2023.

Albemarle Corporation, NYSE: ALB

Albemarle is a U.S. lithium mining and processing company with active extraction operations in the U.S. (Nevada), Chile, and Australia with midstream refinement operations in Australia, China, and the U.S. (North Carolina). The company has other chemical production operations such as bromine, catalysts, and aluminum products. Albemarle produced 207,000 tons of LCE in 2024 with 133,000 tons coming from hard rock mining in Australia, 69,000 tons from brine operations in Chile, and 5,300 tons LCE from brine operations in Nevada. This meant Albemarle was responsible for 16% of world LCE production.

Although the Silver Peak, Nevada lithium brine operation has been running since the 1960s, none of its owners have increased its production. Albemarle believes the Silver Peak lithium reserves are 477,000 tons of LCE which means they will exhaust their Nevada site in the year 2114. Albemarle's predecessor, Foote Mineral Company, opened the Silver Peak brine operation in 1966 because it was cheaper than their hard rock lithium operation in North Carolina which they closed in 1986. Foote Mineral began their brine operation in Chile in 1984 also because it was cheaper than their North Carolina hard rock operations.[448]

Albemarle's profits collapsed in 2024 with a net loss of $1.1 billion due to a global lithium oversupply and corresponding lower prices. With losses this big, it was little help that the company received $9.4 million in 45X tax credits. This was because Argentina increased production by almost 50,000 tons of LCE, Chile increased production by 40,000 tons, Zimbabwe by almost 38,000 tons, China by 28,000 tons, and Brazil 25,000 tons. Overall, the world produced an additional 191,000 tons LCE from the previous year although Albemarle didn't contribute to this as their production remained flat as compared to 2023.

Arcadium Lithium/Rio Tinto

American lithium company Livent merged with Australian mining company Allkem in 2024 to form Arcadium Lithium which was subsequently bought in March 2025 by the British-Australian mining giant Rio Tinto. Arcadium had lithium hard rock mining operations in North Carolina until closing them in 1998. Arcadium has lithium brine operations in Argentina, a hard rock operation in Australia, and processing facilities in the U.S., Europe, China, and Ja-

448 Lyon, Eric. "The Lithium Economy." 2023.

pan. The company also makes specialty lithium metals and butyllithium for the pharmaceutical, agriculture, and polymer sectors. The company's U.S. headquarters is in Philadelphia.

In 2024, Arcadium produced 42,300 tons of LCE from their various operations, 140,000 tons of spodumene concentrate, and 1,860 tons of other lithium products. The company's net income was $131 million for a 13% margin which dropped from $330 million and a 38% margin in 2023. This drop was due to the global overproduction resulting in softer LCE prices. However, since the company was much smaller than Albemarle, they had less exposure to the market and less overreach. Arcadium is in the process of acquiring two undeveloped hard rock projects in Canada, the James Bay and Whabouchi mines.

U.S. Magnesium (USM) – Financially Distressed

USM is a private U.S. company in Rowley, Utah that runs magnesium and lithium production operations. In 2018, the company constructed a plant to process waste-magnesium salts into LCE using evaporation ponds to create a rich lithium feedstock. In 2024, Canadian company International Battery Metals LTD (IBAT) inked a partnership with USM to provide their proprietary DLE (direct lithium extraction) plant. The plant will process brine recovered from USM's waste-magnesium salts to produce 5,000 tpa of lithium chloride as feed for USM's ongoing LCE production. USM produced no lithium in 2024. (We'll discuss USM's financial problems in the magnesium chapter.)

Lilac Solutions

Lilac is a U.S. company located in Oakland, CA specializing in Direct Lithium Extraction (DLE) technology. The company has developed a proprietary Ion Exchange (IX) process using ceramic beads to extract lithium from brine in a closed-loop method with much less environmental impact than established methods currently in use. Lilac's technology was tested at Lake Resources' Kachi brine project which is currently stalled due to lack of funding. The company received a $50 million grant from the Department of Energy in 2022 to advance their DLE IX technology, indicating DOE sees viability in their process. Lilac published a white paper in 2024 showcasing their Gen 4 IX technology, although they still have not produced any product at commercial scale in an economic manner.

Actions Taken

Albemarle received a $90 million grant in 2023 through the Office of Industrial Base Policy as authorized by the Defense Production Act with money appropriated through the Inflation Reduction Act. The grant will fund the reopening of Albemarle's NC hard rock lithium mine (which will most likely be put on hold). Additionally, in 2022, the Department of Energy provided $1.6 billion in grants from the Bipartisan Infrastructure Law to 12 different projects in support of the lithium battery value chain.

Under the Inflation Reduction Act, Albemarle qualifies for a 10% tax credit under the Section 45X Advanced Manufacturing Production Credit if they refine their products into LCE or lithium hydroxide or "purified to a minimum purity of 99.9% by mass."

Incentives & Tariffs

Domestic lithium mining companies receive a 22% depletion allowance (Albemarle) while foreign companies receive a 14% rate (there are none) for both hard rock and brine extraction operations.

The general tariff schedule taxes all lithium products at overall low rates. Chinese imports have an additional Section 301 tariffs of 7% which increased to 25% starting August 1, 2024, for an overall rate of 28.4%. Lithium was excluded from the Trump administration's April 2025 tariff schedule.

U.S Supply Chain Security Strategy Moving Forward

The U.S. has a relatively insecure lithium position because its only active domestic lithium brine operations in Nevada produced 5,300 tons of LCE. While the U.S. has historically used relatively low volumes of lithium, domestic demand will grow as more battery companies come online that in turn create greater supply chain insecurity. Having said that, Albemarle and Arcadium/Rio Tinto are two of the largest lithium companies in the world and have built the global architecture to import all the U.S.' lithium needs.

Multi-pronged Approach

- While the U.S. has several hard rock lithium mines being developed domestically, there is no indication they can be mined economically with costs competitive with Australia and the Lithium Triangle. The U.S.' most effective long-term approach to ensure a competitive domestic lithium enterprise would be the develop of economic DLE

(Direct Lithium Extraction) technology to exploit the Smackover Formation, the Great Salt Lake, other lithium brines near the Salton Sea, and our oceans.

- In 2022, the U.S. National Defense Stockpile held 5.6 tons of lithium products. The Defense Logistics Agency (DLA) did not announce any lithium acquisitions or disposals through 2025. Based on estimated annual consumption, the U.S. should maintain reserves of 7,000 tons of LCE which they could purchase from Albemarle. In the 1950s, the U.S. government stockpiled large amounts of lithium for its hydrogen weapons program and was the single largest driving of demand in the global lithium market. The Foote Mineral Company, which later evolved into Albemarle, provided much of this lithium.
- Historically, lithium used outside of the battery sector had low recycling rates. Countries are increasingly aware that they must recycle their end-of-life lithium-ion batteries to retain critical minerals. The majority of recycled lithium is from EV batteries, a trend that will accelerate. Many car and battery manufacturers have established their own battery recycling programs such as Tesla and Chinese company CATL. In the U.S., major EV battery recyclers include the private company Redwood Materials and Canadian company Li-Cycle. A mandatory national, recovery, recycling, and reuse program would maximize access to this resource.
- Battery companies are looking to replace lithium with other materials like sodium, although current chemistry suffers from reduced energy density. Improvements like solid-state batteries could reduce the volume of lithium required.

U.S. Lithium Carbonate Imports 2024 (metric tons)			
Country	Volume	Value	Price/ton
Chile	8,480	$120.7 million	$14,200.00
Argentina	6,780	$78.5 million	$11,600.00
Others	200	$3.1 million	$15,500.00
Total	15,460	$202.3 million	$13,085.00

*This data shows that 99% of U.S. imports are from the Lithium Triangle and reflects imports from Abemarle, Rio Tinto, and SQM.

***UN Comtrade data HS Code 2836.91*

U.S. Lithium-Ion Battery (LIB) Imports 2024 (metric tons)			
Country	Volume	Value	Price
China	325,900	$16.4 billion	$50,300.00
Japan	34,900	$1.7 billion	$48,700.00
South Korea	26,500	$1.3 billion	$49,000.00
Hungary	19,700	$996 million	$50,500.00
Canada	14,900	$753 million	$50,500.00
Poland	12,700	$644 million	$52,280.00
Others	37,700	$2 billion	$53,000.00
Total	472,300	$23.8 billion	$50,390.00

*China accounted for 69% of all LIB imports while Asia accounted for 82%. If we include production by Hungary and Poland, which are Asian-owned, the number goes to 89%.

***UN Comtrade Data, HT Code 8507.60*

Lutetium (Lu)

Background

Lutetium is a heavy REE (Rare Earth Element) which is more abundant than silver, is very dense, with low toxicity to humans. The metal can be recovered from monazite with other REE but is only found in low concentrations and takes many processing steps to extract it. The metal is commonly found along with fellow HREE yttrium. Lutetium metal is expensive, starting at $3,600.00 a kg in the U.S. or $3.6 million per metric ton. The isotope lutetium-177 was approved in 2022 to treat prostate cancer (as was gallium-68).[449] REE, like lanthanum, cerium, and lutetium are most commonly used in the petroleum industry as fluid catalytic cracking (FCC) catalysts.

The only REE company in the U.S., MP Materials, does not sell lutetium.[450] As China is the world's largest producer of REE, they are also the largest producer of lutetium. Historically, MP Materials shipped its REE to China for refinement, allowing Beijing to extract lutetium from products that originated in the U.S. Today, 82% of imported lutetium oxide comes from China and another 14% from Malaysia, combining for 96% of total imports. In total, the U.S. relies on China for 75% of the different REE used in the petroleum FCC space.

Actions Taken

As discussed in previous REE sections, MP Materials has received grants through the Defense Production Act and from the Department of Energy to construct an REE processing facility at their Mountain Passs location and to build their Fort Worth, TX magnet facility.

Incentives & Tariffs

MPM qualifies for a 10% tax credit under the Section 45X Advanced Manufacturing Production Credit if its lutetium products are "purified to a minimum purity of 99% by mass."

Domestic REE mining companies receive a 14% depletion allowance (MP Materials) while foreign companies also receive a 14% rate (there are none) monazite, bastnaesite, and xenotime extraction operations.

449 https://www.uchicagomedicine.org/cancer/types-treatments/prostate-cancer/treatment/lutetium-177-psma-therapy-for-prostate-cancer

450 MP Materials includes lutetium in their SEG+ product line but they did not record any sales of it for 2024.

REE were excluded from the Trump administration's April 2025 tariffs schedule. The same month, Chinese sellers were required to obtain an export license from the Ministry of Commerce. Also, American REE imports arriving in China received a 125% retaliatory tariff.

U.S Supply Chain Security Strategy Moving Forward

The U.S. has an insecure lutetium position since it has a 100% import reliance with 82% coming from China, although this might change as MPM's processing capability comes online. The likely long-term threats to this position include MP Materials depleting its Mountain Pass mine or the company becoming unprofitable due to continuing superior competition from Chinese manufacturers. To date, only China, the U.S., and Malaysia (Australia) have the technological sophistication to develop their own advanced processing capability.[451]

Multi-pronged Approach

- The U.S. should monitor the domestic lutetium value chain and determine when and if additional government assistance is needed. MP Materials has received sufficient government subsidies to date although they must continue to lower costs and product prices.
- In 2022, the U.S. National Defense Stockpile held no lutetium reserves. The Defense Logistics Agency (DLA) made no announcements about either disposing of or acquiring lutetium through 2025. A one-year reserve of lutetium oxide would be 11,000 tons and cost approximately $110 million.
- It is unknown how much lutetium is recycled or reused, but it is likely around 1% which is the overall rate for REE. Recycling is difficult because REE are mixed with other elements, are used in such low volumes that very little is recovered and usually involves hydrochloric acid. To recover lutetium from fluid catalytic cracking (FCC) catalysts, more R&D should be conducted. A mandatory national, recovery, recycling, and reuse program would maximize access to this resource.

451 Vietnam has a limited processing capability.

- REE used in FCC could possibly be reduced by introducing the use of phosphorous although more research is required. Also, replacing fuel usage with renewable energy reduces the need for lutetium.

U.S. Lutetium Imports 2024 (metric tons)

Country	Volume	Value	Price/Ton
China	8,250	$98.6 million	$11,950.00
Malaysia	840	$1 million	$1,190.00
South Africa	214	$4.3 million	$20,000.00
Estonia	94.1	$587,000.00	$6,200.00
Austria	79.8	$6.5 million	$81,400.00
Others	55.4	$10.3 million	$185,900.00
Total	9,533.3	$121.3 million	$12,700.00

* 86% of imports came from China and 95% came from both China and Malaysia. This is a clear geographic chokepoint.

***USITC data, HTS Code 2846.90.80*

Magnesium (Mg)

Background - Metals

Magnesium is an alkaline metal that only occurs naturally with other minerals and is commonly recovered by the electrolysis (using a direct electric current) of magnesium salt brines. In fact, magnesium is the only structural metal found in brine and thus does not require open pit mining. However, magnesium can also be recovered from the mineral magnesite (magnesium carbonate MgCO3) which is found in veins of serpentinite and ultramafic rocks. Magnesium metal is mainly used as an alloy with other metals like aluminum and titanium because it is lighter than both steel and aluminum. Its predominant use is in the auto industry but also in aluminum alloy cans, aerospace applications, steel, and pyrotechnics.

In 2024, the world produced an estimated 1 million metric tons of magnesium metal (primary production through smelters). China led with 950,000 tons (95%), followed by Brazil with 20,000 tons, Israel with 20,000 tons, and Kazakhstan with 20,000 tons. The U.S. has no active magnesium metal smelter and must import all its primary magnesium metal products. The U.S. did produce 113,000 of tons secondary magnesium from old and new scrap. From 2020-2023, the U.S. imported the majority of its magnesium metal products from Israel (17%), followed by Canada (15%), Turkey (12%), and Czechia (9%).

Despite China being the single largest producer of magnesium metal in the world, the U.S. imports low volumes of it from Beijing, just 10%. The world has a 2.1 million ton annual primary smelter capacity with China having 1.8 million tons (86%). The world is believed to hold several billion tons of magnesium with most being in our oceans. Thus, the chokepoint for magnesium metal production is smelter capacity.

U.S. Magnesium (USM)

USM is a private U.S. company in Rowley, Utah that closed the country's only primary magnesium operation in 2022. The company is located adjacent to the Great Salt Lake with a capacity of 63,500 metric tons a year of primary magnesium and 9,000 metric tons of lithium carbonate. The company has suffered from long-term environmental law violations. In 2021, the Department of Justice (DOJ) and the EPA settled with USM over violations of the Resource

Conservation and Recovery Act (RCRA) where the company agreed to spend $37 million to address continuing pollution concerns.

For background, Magnesium has been extracted from this location since 1972. Magnesium Corporation of America (MagCorp) was formed in 1993 and was wholly owned by Renco Metals. MagCorp and Renco Metals filed for bankruptcy protection in 2001 and then sold MagCorp back to themselves (the Parent Entities) under the name of USM. The court appointed Chapter 7 trustee subsequently sued the Parent Entities for fraudulent conveyance, winning a $214 million judgement in 2015. In 2018, the EPA entered into a bankruptcy settlement with MagCorp and Renco metals, recovering $23 million.

In 2009, the USM production facility in Utah was added to the list of EPA Superfund cleanup sites. Currently, the EPA continues to monitor USM's activities regarding air, water, and soil contamination that also endangers wildlife and USM employees. Some of USM's waste is disposed on federal land overseen by the Bureau of Land Management. Unsurprisingly, with this continued environmental liability and management problems, the Department of Energy has not provided any grants to USM as they have identified them as a poor investment.

In 2021, USM's smelter suffered a failure, interrupting planned production secured through existing offtake agreements. This caused magnesium prices in the U.S. to go from $4,960.00 a ton in 2020, to $7,460.00 a ton in 2021, and then $15,000.00 a ton in 2022. Prices recovered slightly in 2023, down to "just" $10,000.00 a ton. This shutdown may indicate that USM was running old equipment that has not been updated and is prone to mechanical failure. Due to their lawsuit pay-outs, they may not have the capital to modernize their smelter.

Magrathea Metals (M2)

Magrathea is a private U.S. company with headquarters in Oakland, CA. For context, Magrathea is the name of a fictional planet from the *Hitchhiker's Guide to the Galaxy* whose society specialized in building luxury planets – their business model eventually bankrupted the rest of the Galaxy. In today's galaxy, M2's model is the recovery of carbon neutral magnesium metal from seawater in the San Francisco Bay area. They have already produced a test product and are constructing a two-ton per year pilot plant. M2 has also partnered with American multinational food company Cargill to provide brine for magnesium extraction. Although it remains to be seen if M2 can produce economic magnesium at scale, they provide the possibility of domestic production with a secure supply chain and an endless resource (the ocean). M2 received a $28 million grant from the DOD to build a full-scale demonstration plant. Alex Grant is the company's CEO who is also a co-founder of the previously discussed DLE technology company Lilac Solutions.

Magnesium Compounds

Magnesium compounds have many uses such as insulation, as a water softener, deicing, refractory materials, in medicine as an antacid, treating low magnesium levels in humans, fire retardants, fertilizers, and as a component of cement. In the U.S., magnesium oxide (MgO) was mostly recovered from seawater and brines although a company in Nevada (Premier Magnesia LLC) mined magnesite and a company in Washington State mined olivine (Millbank Materials Group).[452] Because seven different companies extract MgO in the country, the U.S. is in a far better position than it is with magnesium metal production.

In 2024, the world produced 22 million tons of MgO from magnesite mining with China leading with 13 million tons (59%), Russia 2.5 million tons (11%), and Brazil 1.8 million tons (8%). The U.S. produced about 130,000 tons of MgO from magnesite mining and Canada 150,000 tons. The U.S. produced 430,000 tons of MgO compounds, imported 520,000 tons and averaged 53% import reliance from 2020-2023. Averaged over this period, the U.S. imported 61% of its MgO from China, 9% from Israel, 8% from Brazil, and 8% from Canada.

One of the largest MgO producers is the publicly traded company Compass Minerals with a 750,000 tpa Mg chloride capacity from its Great Salt Lake operations in Utah.[453] Publicly traded Martin Marietta Materials Inc. extracts MgO and hydroxide from brines and produce Mg products at their Texas and Ohio facilities – they sold $320 million of Mg products in 2024. Also, publicly traded Intrepid Potash runs Mg operations at the Great Salt Lake as well and sold $5.3 million of Mg chloride products in 2024, largely for road deicing purposes.

452 MgO is used to represent content in magnesite, magnesium chloride, magnesium hydroxide, and magnesium sulfate.

453 750,000 tons x 47.8% = 358,500 tons of MgO. This would be 83% of the U.S.' annual production.

Actions Taken

Magrathea Metals has received financial support from DOD to advance their magnesium electrolysis project as this provides a different approach than USM's established process with aging equipment. The Department of Commerce has placed high level tariffs on imported Chinese magnesium products.

Incentives & Tariffs

U.S. Magnesium and Magrathea qualify for a 10% tax credit under the Section 45X Advanced Manufacturing Production Credit if they refine their magnesium products "to a minimum purity of 99% by mass."

Domestic and foreign magnesium mining companies receive a 14% depletion allowance from dolomite mining (there are none) and both receive a 5% allowance for brine extraction operations.

Magnesium products imported from China have received additional duties under the Tariff Act of 1930 beginning in 2000 after an anti-dumping investigation initiated by USM. These duties were renewed again in 2023 at a rate of 111.73%. Magnesium was excluded from the Trump administrations April 2025 tariffs.

U.S Supply Chain Security Strategy Moving Forward

The U.S. has an insecure magnesium metal position because it has no active domestic operations and its only former producer is U.S. Magnesium who previously declared bankruptcy and faces ongoing legal liability and equipment modernization issues. The U.S. has a stronger MgO position because of its redundant domestic extraction base.

Multi-pronged Approach

- The most effective long-term approach is developing new magnesium extraction technology for brine and seawater which is cost-competitive (Magrathea). The U.S. could look at expanding and supporting Canada's MgO industry and increase its supply chain pathways with Brazil. However, the U.S. buys most of its Mg products from China because they have the lowest prices. U.S. buyers can choose to go elsewhere, but at a higher cost.
- In 2022, the U.S. National Defense Stockpile did not report any magnesium reserves. The Defense Logistics Agency (DLA) announced acquisitions of 3,500 metric tons of magnesium in 2024

and 2025. Based on annual consumption, a one-year supply of magnesium metal products would be 200,000 tons and magnesium compounds 890,000 tons. Current reserves would last a single day. After WWII, the U.S. government stockpiled magnesium but periodically sold off its stores until they were completely depleted in 1975.[454]

- The U.S. recovers large amounts of magnesium scrap which has averaged around 100,000 tons annually.
- Magnesium can be substituted by aluminum and zinc in alloys and castings although performance suffers due to weight considerations.

An aerial view of U.S. Magnesium's now defunct operations in Utah. As of 2025, USM was run by a court-ordered receiver after the company refused to pay for environmental pollution mitigation as agreed to in a previous settlement with the EPA.

454 Lieberman, Marvin B. "The Magnesium Industry in Transition." UCLA, 2000.

U.S. Magnesium Metal Imports 2024 (metric tons)

Country	Volume	Value	Price/Ton
Israel	28,900	$91.8 million	$3,170.00
Turkiye	13,900	$44.7 million	$3,200.00
South Korea	10,400	$43.4 million	$4,170.00
Canada	8,900	$39.2 million	$4,400.00
China	5,700	$23.8 million	$4,170.00
Mexico	5,600	$33.4 million	$5,900.00
Others	16,600	$86.7 million	$5,200.00
Total	90,000	$363 million	$4,030.00

While the U.S. only imported 10% of its magnesium metal directly from China, 95% of primary magnesium production in the world was by China. (UN Comtrade HS Code 8104)

U.S. Magnesium Compound Imports 2024 (metric tons)

The U.S. imported 440,900 tons of sintered magnesia valued at $230 million for an average cost of $522.00 a ton. Most came from China (63%), Canada (11%), and Brazil (8%). (UN Comtrade HS Code 2519.90)

The U.S. imported 73,900 tons of sulphates valued at $18.7 million for an average of $253.00. Most came from China (53%), India (17%), and Mexico (10%). (UN Comtrade HS Code 2833.21)

The U.S. imported 66,700 tons of chlorides valued at $29.4 million for an average cost of $440.00 a ton. Most came from Israel (62%) and the Netherlands (21%). (UN Comtrade HS Code 2827.31)

Manganese (Mn)

Background

Manganese is commonly found with iron and has many uses to include dietary supplements, water treatment, glass and ceramic manufacturing, fertilizers, in EV battery chemistry, and making alloys in the steel industry. Because manganese is primarily used in the iron and steel industry (90%), its supply and price follow these two much higher volume metals. Although only 2% of manganese is used in the battery industry, there is a growing need for High-Purity Manganese Sulfate (HPMS) to supply NMC (Nickel Manganese Cobalt) and LMFP (Lithium Manganese Iron Phosphate) batteries. In 2024, 17 of the 19 HPMS refining plants were in China.

In 2024, the world produced an estimated 20 million metric tons of manganese. South Africa led with 7.4 million tons (37%), followed by Gabon with 4.6 million tons (23%), and then Australia with 2.8 million tons (14%). The U.S. and Canada did not produce any at all while Brazil produced 590,000 tons, meaning the Western hemisphere accounted for just 3% of overall production. The world holds an estimated 1.7 billion tons in manganese reserves with South Africa having 560 million tons, Australia 500 million tons, China 280 million tons, Brazil 270 million tons, and Ukraine 140 million tons.[455]

Accordingly, the U.S. imports 100% of its manganese needs. For raw ore and concentrates, it imported 328,000 tons with the vast majority coming from Gabon (61%), South Africa (24%), and Mexico (13%). Very little came from China – far less than even one percent.[456] The U.S. consumed 680,000 metric tons of manganese (content) in 2024 which is more than the Western hemisphere (i.e. Brazil) produced that year.[457]

RecycLiCo Battery Materials Inc, OTC: AMYZF

RBM is a publicly traded Canadian company focused on the recycling of battery cathode material (formerly American Manganese). The company's subsidiary Rocher Manganese Inc. was created to mine manganese in Arizona using a proprietary hydrometallurgical process. However, RBD no longer actively explores or mines its Artillery Peak project in Arizona and has written

455 U.S. Geological Survey.

456 UN Comtrade data HS Code 2602.

457 U.S. geological Survey data.

off its expenses there. In 2020, the Defense Logistics Agency provided RBM a grant to process its stockpiled manganese into electrolytic manganese metal (EMM). This was called the Wenden Stockpile Reclamation and Advanced Material Processing project with the goal of testing RBM's technology. While the company successfully produced EMM, the project never progressed past this initial phase.

South32 (S32), OTC: SOUHY

South32 is developing an open pit mining operation in Arizona called the Hermosa Project. Their Taylor deposit extracts zinc, silver, and lead. The company is also looking to pursue nearby Peake copper and Clark manganese deposits. In 2024, S32 received a $20 million grant through the Defense Production Act to help fund their manganese operation.

Actions Taken

According to the DARS (Defense Acquisition Regulations System) 48 CFR 252.225-7009 Restriction on Acquisition of Specialty Meals, any steel alloy product with more than 1.65% manganese content acquired by the DOD must be melted or produced in the U.S.

While RecycLiCo received support from DLA, this was for a limited project with no longevity. Also, it remains to be seen if S32 can extract manganese in an economic manner after assistance through the DPA.

Incentives & Tariffs

S32 qualifies for a 10% tax credit under the Section 45X Advanced Manufacturing Production Credit if they refine their products to manganese sulfate or "purified to a minimum purity of 99.9% by mass."

Domestic manganese mining companies receive a 22% depletion allowance (there are none) while foreign companies receive a 14% rate (S32) for hard rock extraction operations.

Manganese was exempted from the Trump administration's April 2025 tariff schedule. In 2024, the Biden Administration proposed placing a 25% tariff on manganese products with over 20% content coming from China. China is stockpiling manganese alloys and has a 20% export tariff on manganese products.

U.S Supply Chain Security Strategy Moving Forward

The U.S. has an insecure manganese position because it produces no manganese and North America and the Western hemisphere do not produce enough to fulfill its consumption needs. The U.S. should enforce mandatory recycling, secure a one-year stockpile, survey for deposits in the U.S., and support operations in both Canada and Mexico. It also needs to maintain positive relations with countries like Gabon and South Africa while ensuring it has secure shipping lanes.

Multi-pronged Approach

- In the 1950s, GSA (General Services Administration) planned to purchase 37 million tons of manganese with 6 million tons stored in Wenden, AZ. The Manganese Purchase Depot in Wenden was opened in 1953. The U.S. subsequently sold off most of the stockpile which, today, contains just 322,000 tons of low-grade manganese ore. The DLA intends to sell off 372,000 tons of manganese products (50,000 tons of ferromanganese) in 2024 which they reposted in 2025. A one-year stockpile based on present consumption is 680,000 tons.
- If the U.S. cannot secure the manganese ore it needs domestically, it can still build the midstream capability for specific sectors of its economy. For example, General Motors (GM) is working with Australian company Element 25 (E25) to build a battery-grade HPMS plant in Louisiana which will process manganese sourced from Australia. GM provided E25 an $85 million loan where E25 will provide GM 32,500 tons of HPMS annually through a seven-year offtake agreement.
- A mandatory national recovery, recycling, and reuse program would maximize access to this resource. Very little manganese is recycled and is mainly done along with the recovery of scrap iron and steel.
- There is no adequate substitute for manganese in the iron and steel industry. More manganese will be required for HPMS in EV batteries with NMC and LMFP chemistries.

U.S. Manganese Ore Imports 2024 (metric tons)			
Country	Volume	Value	Price/ton
Gabon	201,100	$64.9 million	$322.00
South Africa	79,500	$18.3 million	$230.00
Mexico	42,200	$9.9 million	$234.00
Other	6,100	$1.9 million	$311.00
Total	**328,900**	**$95 million**	**$288.00**
**UN Comtrade Data HS Code 2602*			

Ferromanganese Imports 2024 (metric tons)			
Country	**Volume**	**Value**	**Price/Ton**
Malaysia	96,800	$111 million	$1,140.00
Norway	60,000	96.8 million	$1,600.00
Australia	53,100	$58 milliion	$1,090.00
India	39,900	$52.3 million	$1,310.00
South Africa	43,400	$59.5 million	$1,370.00
Other	10,600	$15.4 million	$1,450.00
Total	**303,800**	**$393 million**	**$1,290.00**
**UN Comtrade Data HS Code 7202.11, 7202.19*			

Ferrosilicon Manganese Imports 2024 (metric tons)			
Country	**Volume**	**Value**	**Price/Ton**
Georgia	78,700	$110.9 million	$1,400.00
Malaysia	71,800	$70.7 million	$980.00
Australia	64,700	$76.7 million	$1,180.00
South Africa	50,600	$49.7 million	$980.00
Other	92,300	$109 million	$1,180.00
Total	358,100	$417 million	$1,160.00
**UN Comtrade Data HS Code 7202.30*			

Neodymium (Nd)

Background

Neodymium is one of the seventeen REE (Rare Earth Elements) designated as critical minerals and is part of the light REE (LREE) lanthanide series. Neodymium is found with fellow REE in monazite and bastnaesite deposits and is as common as other high-volume metals like nickel and copper. Neodymium is used to color glass, in laser applications, MRI machines, in small magnets (headphones, loudspeakers, computer hard discs, high-performance aircraft, guided missile systems) and large permanent magnets (cranes, commercial scale windmills, EV motors). The largest single use of neodymium today is as an alloy in NdFeB magnets (Neodymium Iron Boron). The U.S., like all modern industrial economies, is a magnet-dependent society. By 2030, the majority of NdFeB magnets in the U.S. will used for windmills and EVs.

As mentioned in previous sections, Nd production volumes are reported as REO (Rare Earth Oxides) and as an overall group total, not as specific elements. The U.S. has one REO operation at Mountain Pass in California and the U.S. mining company MP Materials (MPM) estimates that 15.7% of the REO it extracts consists of neodymium-praseodymium (NdPr). MPM completed its new REO processing plant in 2023 where it can produce and sell NdPr oxide as an individual product. Going into 2024, MP predicts their NdPr product will sell for $131,600.00 a metric ton.

In 2024, the U.S. imported 6,075 metric tons of NdFeB magnet products worth $242 million at an average of $39,800.00 a metric ton. Although it is not reflected in the amount of NdFeB products imported, Japan is the second largest producer of these magnets after China, holding about 7% of the global market. Importantly, Japan must import the inputs required for magnet production, with much of their supply chain originating in China. For context, NdFeB magnets are composed of 69% iron, 30% are rare earths (like Nd) and just 1% is boron.[458] The ferroboron material used is American Iron and Steel Institute (AISI) 1001 low-carbon steel which the U.S. mostly imports from foreign producers. Potential domestic magnet producers are further hindered from producing competitive NdFeB products due to a lack of proprietary intellectual property (IP).

458 Federal Register, Volume 88, Number 30, February 14, 2023.

Energy Fuels Inc, NYSE: UUUU

Energy Fuels Inc (EFI) is an American company focused on the production or uranium, vanadium, REE, processing heavy mineral sands, and recycling uranium and vanadium. EFI receives monazite at their Utah facility from Chemours' operations in Georgia which EFI processes into RE carbonate. EFI then ships the product to Estonia where the Canadian company Neo Performance Materials processes it into separate REE. Currently, EFI can separate lanthanum and cerium from the RE carbonate, meaning it has higher concentrations of NdPr. The company developed a Stage I REE separation facility in 2024, producing 38 tons of NdPr with a future goal of reaching 1,000 tpa. EFI depends on inputs from Chemours and future supplies from Brazil, Australia, and Africa.

Actions Taken

As discussed in previous REE sections, MP Materials has received grants through the Defense Production Act and from the Department of Energy to construct an REE processing facility at their Mountain Passs location and to build their Fort Worth, TX magnet facility.

As of 2023, Australian company Lynas Rare Earths received a total of $258 million in grants through the Defense Production Act to construct a HREE processing facility in Texas. (Neodymium is a Light REE).

The DFARS (Defense Regulation Acquisition Regulation Supplement) to the 2019 NDAA (National Defense Authorization Act) Section 871 prohibits the acquisition of NdFeB magnets produced in China, Russia, North Korea or Iran. Accordingly, the defense contracting industry cannot acquire NdFeB magnets with a supply chain connected to China or Russia starting in 2027.

Incentives & Tariffs

MPM and EFI qualify for a 10% tax credit under the Section 45X Advanced Manufacturing Production Credit if their products are "converted to neodymium-praseodymium oxide which is purified to a minimum purity of 99% neodymium-praseodymium oxide by mass or converted to neodymium oxide which is purified to a minimum purity of 99.5% neodymium oxide by mass or purified to a minimum purity of 99.9% neodymium by mass."

Domestic REE mining companies receive a 14% depletion allowance (MP Materials) while foreign companies receive a 14% rate (there are none) for monazite, bastnaesite, and xenotime extraction operations.

REE were excluded from the Trump administration's April 2025 tariff schedule. In 2023, China banned the export of the technology to make neodymium-iron-boron magnets, adding them to its "Catalogue of Technologies Prohibited and Restricted from Export." In 2026, the U.S. will impose a 25% tariff on imported Chinese permanent magnets.

The Department of Commerce of commenced a Section 232 investigation to determine if sintered NdFeB magnets undermined U.S. national economic and security interests. The investigation concluded in 2023 that U.S. dependence on foreign imports did constitute a national security threat. The Biden administration raised tariffs on Chinese NdFeB magnets through Section 301 tariffs in September 2024.

U.S Supply Chain Security Strategy Moving Forward

The U.S. has an insecure neodymium position since MPM and EFI produced just 1,332 tons of NdPr in 2024 with 91% of NdFeB magnets coming from China, although this will start to shift when MPM's magnet facility, and others, come online. The likely long-term threats to this position include MP Materials depleting its Mountain Pass mine or the company becoming unprofitable due to continuing superior competition from Chinese manufacturers. To date, only China, the U.S., and Malaysia (Australia) have the technological sophistication to develop their own advanced REE processing capability.[459]

Multi-pronged Approach

- The U.S. should monitor the domestic and North American neodymium and NdFeB value chain and determine when and if additional government assistance is needed. The U.S. needs to focus on building a domestic magnets industry which must be paired to manufactured end-products like EV motors and wind turbines. MP Materials has received sufficient government subsidies to date although they must continue to lower costs and product prices.
- The U.S. should develop effective market surveillance tools to accurately determine how much neodymium is produced, traded, and

459 Vietnam has a limited REE processing capability.

imported which requires the U.S. International Trade Commission developing a neodymium specific import code.

- In 2022, the U.S. National Defense Stockpile did not hold any neodymium reserves. In 2023, the Defense Logistics Agency (DLA) announced that they were purchasing 600 metric tons of Neodymium and 100 tons of rare earth magnetic block (i.e. neodymium magnets). In 2024, DLA announced their intent to acquire 300 metric tons of neodymium-praseodymium (NdPr) oxide and 286 metric tons of NdFeB block magnets. In 2025, DLA announced plans to buy 300 metric tons of NdPr oxide and 450 metric tons of NdFeB block magnets. One can assume DLA is purchasing these products through Chinese suppliers. 6,000 metric tons of NdFeB would be a one-year supply based on annual consumption.
- It is unknown how much neodymium is recycled or reused, but it is likely around 1% which is the overall rate for REE. Recycling is difficult because the REE are mixed with other elements, are used in such low volumes that very little is recovered and usually involves hydrochloric acid. In 2018, DLA provided funding to private U.S. company Noveon Magnetics Inc (formerly the Urban Mining Company) to produce NdFeB products with recycled magnets recovered from end-of-life products. In 2020, the company received a $28.8 million grant from DOD through the DPA to build their NdFeB magnet recycling plant.
- Other competing magnets include hard ferrite and samarium cobalt (for higher temperature applications). Several companies have developed experimental electric traction motors for EV using no REE.

U.S Permanent Magnet Imports 2024 (metric tons)			
Country	**Volume**	**Value**	**Price/ton**
China	7,080	$359.8 million	$50,820.00
Japan	404	$20.5 million	$50,740.00
Germany	302	$15.3 million	$50,660.00
South Korea	202	$10.2 million	$50,500.00
Philippines	180	$9.1 million	$50,550.00
Taiwan	156	$7.9 million	$50,640.00
Finland	141	$7.2 million	$51,060.00
Indonesia	129	$6.5 million	$50,390.00
Switzerland	128	$6.5 million	$50,780.00
Netherlands	108	$5.5 million	$50,920.00
Other	570	$29.5 million	$51,750.00
Total	9,400	$478 million	$50,850.00

The U.S. imported a 75% of its REPM needs directly from China and 87% from Asia. The data shows that European countries can produce cost competitive products but not at the volume that China can.

**UN Comtrade Data HS Code 8505.11*

NdFeB Magnet Imports 2024

The U.S. imported 6,075 tons of NdFeB magnet products valued at $242.4 million with 5,550 tons (91%) coming from China. *(USITC HTS Code 8505.11.0070)*

Nickel (Ni)

Background

Nickel is a metal which is the fifth most common element in our Earth's crust and is used primarily as an alloy with chromium to make stainless steel. Because nickel has such high corrosion resistant qualities at extremely high temperatures, it is used as plating to protect other metals. Nickel is used in the U.S. monetary system, although a five-cent value nickel consists of only 25% nickel and 75% copper. Small amounts of nickel are found in the human diet such as baked beans. Nickel is the primary element in the cathode of NMC (Nickel Manganese Cobalt) and NCA (Nickel Cobalt Aluminum) lithium-ion ternary batteries used in EVs. Nickel is effective as a cathode material because of its high energy density but can suffer from cycle longevity issues if its accompanying lithium is exposed to air.

However, only an estimated 10% of all nickel production was for the EV battery industry in 2023.[460] Battery makers are concerned with battery-grade nickel sulfate of which 314,000 tons was made worldwide in 2023. Minerals commodities pricing agency Fastmarkets predicts annual nickel sulfate production will explode to almost 1.4 million tons by 2030. About 60% of the global nickel sulfate supply is produced in China with Japan, South Korea, and Taiwan also contributing with the Asia market accounting for an estimated 75% of total production. In the fall of 2023, battery-grade nickel sulfate hit $1,400.00 USD a ton in the China market.[461]

In 2024, the world produced an estimated 3.7 million contained metric tons of nickel. Indonesia by far produced the most with 2.2 million tons (59%) followed by the Philippines with 330,000 tons (9%), and Russia 210,000 tons (6%). China produced a modest 120,000 tons with Canada producing 190,000 tons. The world holds an estimated 130 million tons of nickel reserves to include Indonesia with 55 million tons (42%), Australia 24 million tons (18%), Brazil 16 million tons (12%) and Russia 8 million tons (6%). An estimated 300 million tons of nickel may be present in polymetallic modules on our oceans' floors.

460 Perry, Callum. "Growth expectations put more attention on European nickel sulfate market." Fastmarkets, September 2, 2023.
461 Ibid.

The U.S. produced just 8,000 tons of nickel in 2024 which was from a single mining operation. However, this nickel was exported overseas for processing, illustrating the U.S.' lack of midstream refinement capacity. From 2020-2024, the U.S. averaged a 50% annual import rate with primary nickel imports coming from, Canada (46%), Norway (11%), Australia (8%), and Brazil (6%). The London Metal Exchange assessed average nickel prices at $17,000.00 a metric ton.[462]

Eagle Mine, Michigan

The Eagle Mine, owned by the publicly traded Canadian company Lundin Mining, contains an estimated 220,000 tons of nickel and 214,000 tons of copper. However, Eagle Mine produced 192,000 tons of nickel through 2023 and at current rates of production will exhaust its limited resources by 2029. Lundin invested $275 million in updating its Humboldt Mill to process its mined ore into separate nickel and copper concentrates before shipping them outside of the U.S. for refinement. Obviously, this mine provides a limited supply that will soon run out, making the U.S. even more dependent on nickel imports when it is exhausted.

Actions Taken

The private owned Doe Run Company in Missouri received a $7 million grant through the Defense Production Act (DPA) in 2024 to construct a demonstration plant that separates nickel and cobalt from a variety of feedstocks such as the tailings from already depleted mines.

Publicly traded Canadian company Talon Metals Corporation was awarded $20 million through the DPA in 2023 to advance nickel exploration and mineral resource definition at the Tamarack Intrusive Complex in Minnesota and Michigan using its proprietary Advanced Exploration System.[463] Mining production is estimated to begin in 2027 with a lifespan of only ten years. In 2022, Talon was also awarded $114 million from the DOE to build a battery minerals processing facility in North Dakota.

In 2023, the Department of Defense awarded 6K Additive, LLC a $23.4 million grant to convert scrap material into high-grade metals and alloys including titanium, niobium, nickel, and tungsten.

462 U.S. Geological Survey Nickel Report 2025.

463 Talon is a JV with Kennecott, a division of Rio Tinto, a British-Australian international mining conglomerate.

According to the DARS (Defense Acquisition Regulations System) 48 CFR 252.225-7009 Restriction on Acquisition of Specialty Meals, any steel alloy product with more than 25% nickel content acquired by the DOD must be melted or produced in the U.S.

Incentives & Tariffs

Doe Run, Lundin, and Talon qualify for a 10% tax credit under the Section 45X Advanced Manufacturing Production Credit if their products are "converted to nickel sulphate" or "purified to a minimum purity of 99% nickel by mass."

Domestic mining companies receive a 22% depletion allowance (Doe Run) while foreign companies receive a 14% rate (Lundin, Talon) for their nickel extraction operations.

Nickel was excluded from the Trump administration's April 2025 tariff schedule.

In 2020, Indonesia banned the export of raw nickel ores which resulted in several Chinese companies establishing large midstream nickel refinement operations in the country.

U.S Supply Chain Security Strategy Moving Forward

The U.S. has an insecure nickel position since more than half is imported (57%), although most of this comes from the Western Hemisphere and established allies. Beginning in 2026, the U.S. will experience higher importation rates after its only productive mine closes. Importantly, the other proposed nickels projects are of limited duration and the increased production will be temporary.

Multi-pronged Approach

- The U.S. should focus on domestic nickel exploration and improving their long-term supply from its neighbor Canada.
- In 2022, the U.S. National Defense Stockpile held 800 tons of nickel alloys and the Defense Logistics Agency (DLA) published no intent to purchase any more through 2025. Based on annual consumption, a one-year supply would be 190,000 metric tons.
- In the U.S., 57% of nickel consumption was from recycled products which is a relatively high rate.

- Nickel can be thrifted in some applications such as alloys by using more chromium or titanium with end uses not requiring its corrosion resistance qualities.

2024 U.S. Nickel Imports

*The U.S. imported negligible amounts of unprocessed nickel ores and concentrates, just 91 metric tons with a value of $459,000.00. *(UN Comtrade Data HS Code 2604)*

The U.S. imported 50,000 tons of ferronickel valued at $189 million led by Brazil (69%), New Caledonia (21%), and Colombia (9%). *(UN Comtrade Data HS Code 7202.60)*

The U.S. imported 84,800 tons of unwrought nickel valued at $1.5 billion led by Canada (50%), Norway, (15%) and Australia (9%). *(UN Comtrade Data HS Code 7502)*

The U.S. imported 47,300 tons of nickel scrap valued at $400 million led by Canada (38%), Mexico (11%), and France (6%). *(UN Comtrade Data HS Code 7503)*

Niobium (Nb)

Background

Niobium is often recovered in the minerals of columbite and pyrochlore and has similar qualities to another critical mineral, tantalum. The two minerals are commonly found together in coltan aka columbite-tantalites aka tantalite. Niobium was formerly known as columbium until the name was permanently changed in 1949. Niobium is primarily used in specialty metals as an alloy with steel and iron (90% of its use) and in superconducting magnets in MRIs. Niobium is used in the INCONEL brand of superalloys owned by the Special Metals Corporation. Their INCONEL alloy 625 is composed primarily of nickel (58%), chromium (20%), molybdenum (8%), iron (5%), and a small amount of niobium (3%). Alloy 625 is used in high-performance aerospace, maritime, chemical process, and nuclear environment applications due to its excellent anti-corrosive, heat resisting and the stiffening/hardening qualities provided by niobium.

Niobium is not traded on metal markets like the London Metal Exchange and transfer agreements are made directly between seller and buyer who determine the price. The three major producers of niobium include two mines in Brazil (CBBM, CMOC Brasil – an international Chinese mining company) and one in Quebec (Niobec mine) which combined extract 98% of the world's niobium.[464] These three primarily extract pyrochlore to produce ferroniobium for the automotive and construction industries. In 2024, Brazil exported by far the most ferroniobium with 92,000 tons followed by Canada at 9,800 tons and Malaysia with 4,800 tons.[465] Estimated world reserves are 17 million tons.

The U.S. has not mined nor produced any niobium or tantalum ores since 1959 as its deposits are uneconomic. In 2024, Brazil produced 100,000 tons of niobium which was 91% of total world production of 110,000 tons. Canada was the next largest producer at just 7,100 tons (7%) followed by the DRC with 700 tons, Russia 350 tons, and Rwanda 200 tons. Correspondingly, the U.S. is 100% import dependent with 66% of its needs being met by Brazil and 27% from Canada. The U.S. imported 8,900 metric tons of niobium content which were broken down by ferroniobium (71%), niobium metal (20%), and niobium

464 www.tanb.org
465 UN Comtrade HS code 720293.

oxide (8%). The average price of ferroniobium products was $26,000.00 per ton.[466]

NioCorp, NASDAQ/TSX: NB

Publicly traded Canadian mining company NioCorp is currently pursuing their Elk Creek Critical Minerals Project in Nebraska with a focus on niobium, scandium, titanium, and REE products like NdPr. The company's project has an estimated 970,000 tons of ferroniobium and they have already demonstrated their ability to successfully extract niobium from the site. NioCorp believes they will be able to sell their niobium products for $45,000.00 per metric ton based on current pricing compared to operation costs of just $200.00 per ton. The company has yet to secure the funding required to begin operations since the announcing of their project in 2010.

Actions Taken

In 2023, the Department of Defense awarded 6K Additive, LLC, a private U.S. company, a $23.4 million grant to convert scrap material into high-grade metals and alloys including titanium, niobium, nickel, and tungsten.

According to the DARS (Defense Acquisition Regulations System) 48 CFR 252.225-7009 Restriction on Acquisition of Specialty Meals, any steel alloy product with more than 25% niobium content acquired by the DOD must be melted or produced in the U.S.

Incentives & Tariffs

A company would qualify for a 10% tax credit under the Section 45X Advanced Manufacturing Production Credit if their products are "converted to ferroniobium" or "purified to a minimum purity of 99% niobium by mass."

Domestic mining companies receive a 22% depletion allowance (there are none) while foreign companies receive a 14% rate (there are none) for their niobium extraction operations.

Niobium was excluded from the Trump administration's April 2025 tariff schedule.

U.S Supply Chain Security Strategy Moving Forward

The U.S. imports 100% of its niobium products with most coming from the Western Hemisphere like Brazil and Canada. Brazil is a global niobium

466 U.S. Geological Survey Niobium Report 2024.

chokepoint which China recognizes and hence their ownership of CMOC Brazil. While Brazil is a member of the China-led BRICS coalition, the group has shown no interest in collectively restricting mineral sales to the U.S. at behest of another member.

Multi-pronged Approach

- The U.S. is pursuing what limited domestic niobium production potential it has, although DOD and DOE have yet to show interest in supporting NioCorp's project. This indicates the U.S. doesn't believe their operations will be economic. The U.S. should maximize their long-term niobium supply from neighboring Canada and securing enduring pathways with Brazil.
- As of 2022, the Defense Logistics Agency (DLA) held 600 tons of ferroniobium in the strategic stockpile with plans to acquire another 150 tons in 2024 and none in 2025. A one-year reserve based on annual consumption would be 8,400 metric tons. This stockpiled amount would last the U.S. for one month.
- While exact data is unknown, the U.S. may recycle 20% of its niobium products used in the steel industry and recovered as scraps.
- Niobium can be substituted by other materials but generally with a reduction in performance and at increased costs. Replacements in alloys include titanium, tungsten, and vanadium - also critical minerals.

Palladium (Pd)

Background

Palladium is classified as a PGM (Platinum Group Metals) which consists of palladium, platinum, iridium, osmium, rhodium, and ruthenium. Palladium is the least dense with the lowest melting point of the PGM and is mostly used in catalytic converters to reduce emissions for the ICE industry. It is also used in jewelry, electronics, and hydrogen fuel cells in the automotive industry. Palladium faces long-term declining use in the automotive industry as ICE vehicles are phased out and BEVs become the dominant form of ground transportation. While there is room for palladium growth with hydrogen fuel cells, BEVs are currently the preferred means of low-carbon transportation.

The most significant PGM production comes from the Bushveld Igneous Complex in South Africa (Anglo American is a major producer), then Russia (Nornickel, as a byproduct of nickel production), Zimbabwe, the Sudbury Complex in Canada (the site of an asteroid strike), and the Stillwater Complex in the U.S. The Stillwater Complex is located in Montana which is mined by South African company Sibanye-Stillwater. North of Montana, the South African holding company Impala Platinum Holdings PTD (Implats) owns the Canadian subsidiary Impala Canada Limited.

In 2024, Russia was the largest producer of palladium, extracting 75 tons which was 39% of total world production of 190 tons. They were followed by South Africa with 72 tons (38%), Canada with 15 tons (8%), Zimbabwe with 15 tons (8%), and the United States with 8 tons (4%). The U.S. imported 63.9 tons of palladium products valued at $2 billion. Other major importers of unwrought palladium products included Japan with 39 tons, Switzerland with 37 tons, Belgium with 32 tons, and the U.K. with 29.8 tons.[467]

Sibanye-Stillwater, NYSE: SBSW

SSW is a large South African-based international mining company which owns and operates their Stillwater and East Boulder mines in Montana and the Columbus Metallurgical Complex which has a smelter, a metal refinery, and a recycling plant. In 2017, SSW bought the U.S. owned Stillwater Mining Company which was the only PGM operator in the country. In 2024, SSW U.S. operations produced 13.4 metric tons of PGM 2E products (palladium &

467 U.S. Geological Survey and UN Comtrade data HS code 711021.

platinum) and recycled/recovered 9.8 tons of 3E products (+ rhodium). The company believes there are 745 more tons in reserves to be extracted which would satisfy U.S. palladium & platinum needs for just five years. SSW's North American PGM operations lost $5.5 million in 2024.

Impala Canada Limited (ICL)

Implats purchased North American Palladium in 2019 and owns and operates the Lac des Iles mine in Ontario Province. In 2024, the company produced 8.7 metric tons of 6E concentrate (platinum, palladium, rhodium, ruthenium, osmium & gold). ICL sold $296 million of 6E products with platinum sales accounting for $242 million, palladium accounting for $44 million, and $10 million for the remainder. Implats (the parent company) lost $909 million for 2024 due to loss of revenue from lower PGM prices. ICL is not a source of future PGM security for the U.S. since the mine will be depleted in three years.

Glencore

Swiss-based international mining conglomerate Glencore owns and operates two nickel mines in Canada and one in Norway which produce PGM as a byproduct of ongoing nickel mining. In 2024, these byproducts resulted in the extraction of 2.18 tons of palladium, 0.78 tons of platinum, and 0.09 tons of rhodium products. However, Glencore is focused primarily on its high-volume and value minerals which are coal, copper, nickel, and zinc. The company lost $1.6 billion USD in 2024.

Actions Taken

The U.S. government has taken no specific measures to enhance its PGM/palladium supply chain other than apply zero tariffs. This is not surprising as Sibanye-Stillwater and Impala were successful companies until 2024.

Incentives & Tariffs

A company would qualify for a 10% production cost tax credit under Section 45X of the Advanced Manufacturing Production Credit if the extracted palladium is "purified to a minimum purity of 99% by mass."

- Domestic mining companies receive a 22% depletion allowance (there are none) while foreign companies receive a 14% rate (Sibanye-Stillwater).

PGM are excluded from the Trump administration's April 2025 tariff schedule which placed 30% tariffs on imports from South Africa.

U.S Supply Chain Security Strategy Moving Forward

The U.S. has a vulnerable palladium position since it imports more than a third of its needs and its only domestic operation is foreign owned with limited reserves remaining. Most of its imports comes from the BRICS countries of Russia and South Africa. Hence, the U.S.' strategy should focus on maintaining good ongoing bilateral trade relations with South Africa, transitioning away from Russian supply chains, and maximizing its recycling efforts.

Multi-pronged Approach

- In 2022, the U.S. National Defense Stockpile held negligible amounts of palladium (less than a single ounce). The Defense Logistics Agency (DLA) announced no plans to acquire palladium through 2025. A one-year supply based on annual consumption would be 83 metric tons.
- There are many private companies with established PGM recycling programs. In 2024, the U.S. recovered an estimated 45 tons of palladium which was 54% of annual consumption.[468]
- There is no adequate substitution for palladium as the most effective alternative is platinum, another expensive critical mineral. Less palladium will be required worldwide as BEVs replace ICE vehicles in the global ground transportation fleet. As evidence of this, world palladium production peaked in 2018 at 220 metric tons.

468 Worldwide, there are tens of thousands of companies involved in PGM recovery, recycling, and resale.

World Palladium Production 2024 (metric tons)			
Country	2020	2024	PGM Reserves
South Africa	73.5	72.0	63,000
Russia	93.0	75.0	16,000
Zimbabwe	12.9	15.0	1,200
United States	14.6	8.0	820
Canada	20.0	15.0	310
Other countries	2.7	4.2	
Total	**216.7**	**190.0**	**81,000**

2024 U.S. Palladium Imports

The U.S. imported 63.9 metric tons of palladium (unwrought or powder) products valued at $2 billion for an average of $31.3 million per ton. Most came from Russia (43%), then South Africa (43%), and South Korea (5%). *(UN Comtrade Data HS Code 7110.21)*

The U.S. imported just 4.4 tons of semi-manufactured palladium products valued at $168 million for an average of $38.2 million per ton. With most from Canada (84%), then Switzerland (9%), and Mexico (2%). *(UN Comtrade Data HS Code 7110.29)*

Platinum (Pt)

Background

Platinum is classified as a PGM (Platinum Group Metals) which consists of palladium, platinum, iridium, osmium, rhodium, and ruthenium. Platinum is very dense, resists corrosion, is malleable, is relatively scarce, and is mostly used in catalytic converters to reduce emissions for the ICE industry. It is also used in jewelry, electronics, and the glass industry. Platinum, like fellow PGM palladium, faces long-term declining use in the automotive industry as ICE vehicles are phased out and BEVs become the dominant form of ground transportation.

The most significant PGM production comes from the Bushveld Igneous Complex in South Africa (Anglo American is the biggest producer), then Russia (Nornickel, as a byproduct of nickel production), Zimbabwe, the Sudbury Complex in Canada (the site of an asteroid strike), and the Stillwater Complex in the U.S. The Stillwater Complex is located in Montana which is mined by South African company Sibanye-Stillwater. North of Montana, the South African holding company Impala Platinum Holdings PTD (Implats) owns their Canadian subsidiary Impala Canada Limited.

In 2024, South Africa was by far the largest producer of platinum, extracting 120 tons which was 70% of total world production of 170 tons. They were followed by Russia with Zimbabwe 19 tons (11%), Russia with 18 tons (10%), Canada with 5.2 tons and the United States with just 2 tons. The U.S. imported 72 metric tons of platinum products valued at over $2.4 billion for an average of $33.5 million per ton. Other major importers included India with 201 tons, China with 121 metric tons, Japan with 111 tons, and Belgium with 78 tons.[469]

Sibanye-Stillwater, NYSE: SBSW

SSW is a large South African-based international mining company which owns and operates their Stillwater and East Boulder mines in Montana and the Columbus Metallurgical Complex which has a smelter, a metal refinery, and a recycling plant. In 2017, SSW bought the U.S. owned Stillwater Mining Company which was the only PGM operator in the country. In 2024, SSW U.S. operations produced 13.4 metric tons of PGM 2E products (palladium & platinum) and recycled/recovered 9.8 tons of 3E products (+ rhodium). The

469 U.S. Geological Survey and UN Comtrade data HS code 7110.

company believes there are 745 more tons in reserves to be extracted which would satisfy U.S. palladium & platinum needs for just five years. SSW's North American PGM operations lost $5.5 million in 2024.

Impala Canada Limited

Implats purchased North American Palladium in 2019 and owns and operates the Lac des Iles mine in Ontario Province. In 2024, the company produced 8.7 metric tons of 6E concentrate (platinum, palladium, rhodium, ruthenium, osmium & gold). ICL sold $296 million of 6E products with platinum sales accounting for $242 million, palladium accounting for $44 million, and $10 million for the remainder. Implats (the parent company) lost $909 million for 2024 due to loss of revenue from lower PGM prices. ICL is not a source of future PGM security for the U.S. since the mine will be depleted in three years.

Glencore

Swiss-based international mining conglomerate Glencore owns and operates two nickel mines in Canada and one in Norway which produce PGMs as a byproduct of ongoing nickel mining. In 2024, these byproducts resulted in the extraction of 2.18 tons of palladium, 0.78 tons of platinum, and 0.09 tons of rhodium products. However, Glencore is focused primarily on its high-volume and value minerals which are coal, copper, nickel, and zinc. The company lost $1.6 billion USD in 2024.

Actions Taken

The U.S. government has taken no specific measures to enhance its PGM/platinum supply chain other than apply zero tariffs. This is not surprising as Sibanye-Stillwater and Impala were successful companies until 2024.

Incentives & Tariffs

A company would qualify for a 10% production cost tax credit under Section 45X of the Advanced Manufacturing Production Credit if the extracted platinum is "purified to a minimum purity of 99% by mass."

- Domestic mining companies receive a 22% depletion allowance (there are none) while foreign companies receive a 14% rate (Sibanye-Stillwater).

PGM are excluded from the Trump administration's April 2025 tariff schedule which placed 30% tariffs on South Africa.

U.S Supply Chain Security Strategy Moving Forward

- The U.S. has a vulnerable platinum position since it imports an estimated 85% of its needs and its only domestic operation is foreign owned with limited reserves remaining. Most of its imports comes from South Africa, hence, the U.S.' strategy should focus on maintaining good ongoing bilateral trade relations with South Africa, increasing imports from Canada, and growing its recycling efforts.

Multi-pronged Approach

- In 2022, the U.S. National Defense Stockpile maintained a platinum reserve of just 239 kg while the Defense Logistics Agency (DLA) planned to sell all of it in 2024 and 2025. A one-year supply based on annual consumption would be 71 metric tons.
- There are many private companies that have established PGM recycling programs. In 2024, the U.S. recovered an estimated 8.5 tons of platinum which was only 12% of annual consumption.[470] The U.S. would have to enforce mandatory regulations to recycle, recover, and reuse far more of its limited platinum resources.
- There is no adequate substitution for platinum as a catalytic converter although palladium, a more expensive critical mineral, could be used. The replacement of the ICE auto industry by EV manufacturing will reduce the demand for platinum in catalytic converters. As evidence of this, world platinum production peaked in 2018 at 190 metric tons.

470 Worldwide, there are tens of thousands of companies involved in PGM recovery, recycling, and resale.

World Platinum Production 2024 (metric tons)			
Country	2020	2024	PGM Reserves
South Africa	112.0	120.0	63,000
Russia	23.0	18.0	16,000
Zimbabwe	15.0	19.0	1,200
United States	4.2	2.0	820
Canada	7.0	5.2	310
Other countries	4.3	4.6	
Total	**165.5**	**170.0**	**81,000**

U.S. Platinum Imports 2024

*The U.S. imported 163.6 metric tons of platinum products valued at $6.9 billion for an average of $42.6 million per ton. *(UN Comtrade Data HS Code 7110)*

South Africa: 85.9 tons valued at $3.7 billion.

Russia: 27.6 tons valued at $877 million.

Germany: 13.1 tons valued at $766 million.

Belgium: 9 tons valued at $457 million.

Italy: 7 tons valued at $298 million.

South Korea: 5.6 tons valued at $228 million.

Canada: 4.2 tons valued at $162 million.

Switzerland: 2.3 tons valued at $74 million.

Praseodymium (Pr)

Background

Praseodymium is one of the seventeen REE (Rare Earth Elements) designated as critical minerals and is part of the light REE (LREE) lanthanide series. Praseodymium is found with fellow REE like cerium, lanthanum, and neodymium in monazite and bastnaesite deposits. Praseodymium is used to color glass and ceramics, in arc lighting lamps, as an alloy in aircraft engines, and magnets for EVs and windmills. In China, in 2020, the single largest use of praseodymium was for the NdFeB (Neodymium Iron Boron) magnet sector where 82% of praseodymium was used, which has most likely increased even more today.[471]

The U.S., like all modern industrial economies, is a magnet-dependent society. By 2030, the majority of NdFeB magnets in the U.S. will be used for windmills and BEVs. To understand how much NdPr (Neodymium Praseodymium) is required, 1 megawatt of power in a windmill requires 200 kg of NdPr oxide and each EV motor 1-2 kg.[472] NdPr is typically sold in a 75:25 ratio with praseodymium being the smaller element by volume. Since neodymium and praseodymium have similar characteristics for magnet use, most NdFeB magnets contain Pr. Through the 1980s, NdPr mixtures were commonly called "didymium" as were Fe-Didymium-B magnets, although this naming convention is now uncommon.

As mentioned in previous sections on other REE, production volumes are reported as REO (Rare Earth Oxides) and as an overall group total, not as specific elements. The U.S. has one REO operation at Mountain Pass in California and the U.S. mining company MP Materials (MPM) estimates that 15.7% of the REO it extracts consists of neodymium-praseodymium (NdPr). If the extracted NdPr is recovered in the ratio of 75:25, then 3.9% of the material is praseodymium. MPM completed its new REO processing plant in 2023 where it can now produce and sell NdPr oxide as an individual product. In 2024, MPM produced 1,294 metric tons of NdPr and sold 1,142 tons at $57 million in 2024.

In 2024, the U.S. imported 6,075 metric tons of NdFeB magnet products worth $242 million at an average of $39,800.00 a metric ton. Although it is not reflected in the amount of NdFeB products imported, Japan is the second

471 Jianping, Ge, et al. *Quantifying the Praseodymium Recycling Supply in China and Its Improvement Strategy*, 2024.

472 Peak rare Earths presentation 2020.

largest producer of these magnets after China, holding about 7% of the global market. Importantly, Japan must import the inputs required for magnet production, with much of their supply chain originating in China. For context, NdFeB magnets are composed of 69% iron, 30% are rare earths like NdPr, and just 1% is boron.[473] The praseodymium content of each NdFeB magnet depends on the individual manufacturer and the specific chemistry they employ based on desired end use.

Because praseodymium is primarily used in NdFeB magnets, this is the chief form its importation takes. However, the U.S. did import small amounts of praseodymium with just 1.1 tons valued at $88,500.00 with most coming from the U.K. (88%) and the rest from China (12%). But the U.K. does not mine REE or praseodymium and most likely imported it from China. Similarly, the U.K. imported 85% of its permanent magnets directly from China.

Energy Fuels Inc, NYSE: UUUU

Energy Fuels Inc (EFI) is an American critical minerals company focusing on the production or uranium, vanadium, REE, processing heavy mineral sands, and recycling uranium and vanadium. EFI receives monazite at their Utah facility from Chemours' operations in Georgia which EFI processes into RE carbonate. EFI then ships the product to Estonia where the Canadian company Neo Performance Materials processes it into separate REE. Currently, EFI can separate lanthanum and cerium from the RE carbonate, meaning it has higher concentrations of NdPr. The company developed a Stage I REE separation facility in 2024, producing 38 tons of NdPr that year with a future goal of reaching 1,000 tpa. EFI depends on inputs from Chemours and then future supplies from Brazil, Australia, and Africa.

Actions Taken

As discussed in previous REE sections, MP Materials has received grants through the Defense Production Act and from the Department of Energy to construct an REE processing facility at their Mountain Passs location and to build their Fort Worth, TX magnet facility.

As of 2023, Australian company Lynas Rare Earths received a total of $258 million in grants through the Defense Production Act to construct a HREE processing facility in Texas. (Praseodymium is a light REE.)

473 Federal Register, Volume 88, Number 30, February 14, 2023.

According to DFARS (Defense Federal Acquisition Regulation Supplement), the defense contracting industry cannot acquire NdFeB magnets with a supply chain connected to China or Russia starting in 2027.

Incentives & Tariffs

MPM and EFI qualify for a 10% tax credit under the Section 45X Advanced Manufacturing Production Credit if their products are "converted to neodymium-praseodymium oxide which is purified to a minimum purity of 99% neodymium-praseodymium oxide by mass or the praseodymium is purified to a minimum purity of 99% by mass."

Domestic REE mining companies receive a 14% depletion allowance (MP Materials, Chemours) while foreign companies receive a 14% rate (there are none) for monazite, bastnaesite, and xenotime extraction operations.

REE was excluded from the Trump administration's April 2025 tariff schedule. China imposed a 125% import tariff on U.S. REE the same month.

The Department of Commerce of commenced a Section 232 investigation to determine if the import of sintered NdFeB magnets undermined U.S. national economic and security interests. In 2023, the investigation concluded that U.S. dependence on foreign magnet imports did constitute a national security threat.

In 2023, China banned the export of the technology to make neodymium-iron-boron magnets, adding them to its "Catalogue of Technologies Prohibited and Restricted from Export." In 2026, the U.S. will impose a 25% tariff on imported Chinese permanent magnets.

U.S Supply Chain Security Strategy Moving Forward

The U.S. has an insecure praseodymium position since it produced just 1,332 tons in 2024 and imported 91% of NdFeB magnets from China, although more praseodymium will be available in the U.S. ex-China as MPM, EFI, and Lynas' processing capabilities come online. The likely long-term threats to this position include MP Materials depleting its Mountain Pass mine or the company becoming unprofitable due to continuing superior competition from Chinese manufacturers. To date, only China, the U.S., and Malaysia (Australia) have the technological sophistication to develop their own advanced REE processing capability.[474]

474 Vietnam has a limited REE capability.

Multi-pronged Approach

- The U.S. should monitor the domestic and North American praseodymium and NdFeB value chain and determine when and if additional government assistance is needed. MP Materials has received sufficient government subsidies to date although they must continue to lower costs and product prices.
- In 2022, the U.S. National Defense Stockpile did not list any praseodymium holdings. The Defense Logistics Agency (DLA) announced its intent to purchase 300 metric tons of Neodymium Praseodymium (NdPr) Oxide and 286 metric tons of NdFeB block magnets for 2024. In 2025, DLA intended to acquire 300 metric tons of NdPr oxide and 450 tons of NdFeB block magnets. One can assume DLA is purchasing these products through Chinese suppliers. 6,000 metric tons of NdFeB would be a one-year supply based on annual imports for consumption.
- It is unknown how much praseodymium is recycled or reused in the U.S. for non-magnet uses, but it is likely around 1% which is the overall rate for REEs. In 2018, DLA provided funding to private U.S. company Noveon Magnetics Inc (formerly the Urban Mining Company) to produce NdFeB products with recycled magnets recovered from end-of-life products. In 2020, the company received a $28.8 million grant from DOD through the DPA to build their NdFeB magnet recycling plant. In China, 20% of praseodymium is recycled from NdFeB scrap and then is reused in subsequent magnet production.[475]
- Other competing magnets include hard ferrite and samarium cobalt used for higher temperature applications. Some companies have developed experimental electric traction motors for EV using no REEs.

475 Jianping, Ge, et al. *Quantifying the Praseodymium Recycling Supply in China and Its Improvement Strategy*, 2024.

U.S. Praseodymium Imports 2022-2024

Country	2022	2023	2024
China	44 tons	139 kg	0
Austria	1.5 tons	0	0
United Kingdom	1.39 tons	1 ton	0

USITC Code HTS 2805.3000.15, not intermixed

Rhodium (Rh)

Background

Rhodium is classified as a PGM (Platinum Group Metal) which consists of palladium, platinum, iridium, osmium, rhodium, and ruthenium. Rhodium is a hard, rare metal with strong anti-corrosive properties and is usually found with other PGM and nickel deposits. The metal is used for neutron detecting in nuclear reactors, jewelry, electronics, electroplating, glass fibers, and most commonly (80% use) as an alloy with palladium and platinum metals in catalytic converters to reduce emissions for the ICE industry (specifically nitric oxide - NOx). Rhodium faces long-term declining use in the automotive industry as ICE vehicles are phased out and BEVs become the dominant form of ground transportation.

The most significant PGM production comes from the Bushveld Igneous Complex in South Africa (Anglo American is the major producer), then Russia (Nornickel, as a byproduct of nickel production), Zimbabwe, the Sudbury Complex in Canada (the site of an asteroid strike), and the Stillwater Complex in the U.S. The Stillwater Complex is located in Montana which is mined by South African company Sibanye-Stillwater. North of Montana, the South African holding company Impala Platinum Holdings PTD (Implats) owns the Canadian subsidiary Impala Canada Limited.

In 2024, the U.S. imported 15 metric tons of rhodium, paying $161 million a ton. In 2023, the world extracted an estimated 20.4 tons of rhodium with South Africa extracting 16 metric tons which was 81% of the world total. They were followed by Russia with almost 2 tons (10%), Zimbabwe with 1.2 tons (6%), and North America with just 425 kg (2%). The world also recycled 8.7 metric tons meaning total production from this and mining was just over 29 metric tons. The U.S. imported most of its 12 tons of rhodium from South Africa (5.8 tons), then Germany (3.6 tons), and Belgium (1.3 tons). This data shows not only the U.S. reliance on imports but the complex supply chain where primary rhodium extraction is then routed through European countries before reaching the U.S.[476]

476 SFA Oxford.

Sibanye-Stillwater, NYSE: SBSW

SSW is a large South African-based international mining company which owns and operates their Stillwater and East Boulder mines in Montana and the Columbus Metallurgical Complex which has a smelter, a metal refinery, and a recycling plant. In 2017, SSW bought the U.S. owned Stillwater Mining Company which was the only PGM operator in the country. In 2024, SSW U.S. operations produced 13.4 metric tons of PGM 2E products (palladium & platinum) and recycled/recovered 9.8 tons of 3E products (+ rhodium). The company believes there are 745 more tons in reserves to be extracted which would satisfy U.S. palladium & platinum needs for just five years. SSW's North American PGM operations lost $5.5 million in 2024.

Impala Canada Limited

Implats purchased North American Palladium in 2019 and owns and operates the Lac des Iles mine in Ontario Province. In 2024, the company produced 8.7 metric tons of 6E concentrate (platinum, palladium, rhodium, ruthenium, osmium & gold). ICL sold $296 million of 6E products with platinum sales accounting for $242 million, palladium accounting for $44 million, and $10 million for the remainder. Implats (the parent company) lost $909 million for 2024 due to loss of revenue from lower PGM prices. ICL is not a source of future PGM security for the U.S. since the mine will be depleted in three years.

Glencore

Swiss-based international mining conglomerate Glencore owns and operates two nickel mines in Canada and one in Norway which produce PGMs as a byproduct of ongoing nickel mining. In 2024, these byproducts resulted in the extraction of 2.18 tons of palladium, 0.781 tons of platinum, and 0.09 tons of rhodium products. However, Glencore is focused primarily on its high-volume and value minerals which are coal, copper, nickel, and zinc. The company lost $1.6 billion USD in 2024.

Actions Taken

The U.S. government has taken no specific measures to enhance its PGM/rhodium supply chain other than apply zero tariffs. This is not surprising as both Sibanye-Stillwater and Impala were successful companies until 2024 and didn't require government grants to remain profitable.

Incentives & Tariffs

A company would qualify for a 10% production cost tax credit under Section 45X of the Advanced Manufacturing Production Credit if the extracted rhodium is "purified to a minimum purity of 99% by mass."

Domestic mining companies receive a 22% depletion allowance (there are none) while foreign companies receive a 14% rate (Sibanye-Stillwater).

PGM were excluded from the Trump administration's April 2025 tariff schedule which placed 30% tariffs on South Africa.

U.S Supply Chain Security Strategy Moving Forward

The U.S. has a vulnerable rhodium position since it imports almost all of it its needs (95%) and its only domestic operation is foreign owned with limited reserves remaining. Most of its imports comes from South Africa and Russia which is then routed through European countries. Hence, the U.S.' strategy should focus on maintaining good ongoing bilateral trade relations with South Africa, increasing imports from Canada, transitioning away from Russian supply chains, and growing its recycling efforts.

Multi-pronged Approach

- In 2022, the U.S. National Defense Stockpile held no rhodium reserves. The Defense Logistics Agency (DLA) published no plans to acquire rhodium through 2025. A one-year supply based on annual consumption would be 15 metric tons.
- There are many private companies that have established PGM recycling programs.[477] It is possible that upwards of 30% of consumed rhodium is from recycling.
- Traditional PGM catalytic converters have been increasingly replaced with selective catalytic reduction (SCR) technology that don't require expensive PGM like rhodium for NOx remediation. The best substitution is replacing ICE vehicles with BEVs which are emission free and require no PGM. Rhodium can be thrifted in other uses like jewelry and plating with other PGM like platinum, palladium, and ruthenium as these are more abundant and less expensive.

477 Worldwide, there are tens of thousands of companies involved in PGM recovery, recycling, and resale.

U.S. Rhodium Imports 2024 (metric tons)

The U.S. imported 14.5 tons of unwrought rhodium valued at $2.2 billion for an average of $151.7 million per ton. (UN Comtrade Data HS Code 7110.31)

South Africa: 8.48 tons, $1,2 billion.

Germany: 2.8 tons, $449 million.

Belgium: 1.5 tons, $219 million.

Italy: 639 kg, $95.7 million.

United Kingdom: 606 kg, $90 million.

South Korea: 457 kg, $66.3million.

The U.S. imported just 5.7 kgs of semi-finished rhodium products valued at $3 million. (USITC Data HS Code 7110.39)

Italy: 2.9 kg, $1.5 million.

United Kingdom: 2.6 kg, $1.38 million.

Germany, Canada & Japan 211 grams.

Rhodium Production 2023 (estimated)*

South Africa: 16.58 metric tons

Russia: 1.98 metric tons

Zimbabwe: 1.27 metric tons

North America: 425 kg, Other countries: 141 kg

Extraction: 20.41 metric tons worldwide.

Recyling: 8.78 metric tons worldwide.

Total Production: 29.11 metric tons.

**Data from SFA Oxford*

Rubidium (Rb)

Background

Rubidium is a soft alkali metal which is recovered primarily as a byproduct of mining pollucite (for cesium) and lepidolite (for lithium) and is as abundant as zinc, lead, and copper. However, there is no single mineral rich with rubidium which limits its production. The isotope rubidium-82 is used in positron emission tomography, in nuclear medicine applications, and to treat depression in humans. It is also used in specialty glass, photoelectric cells, atomic clocks, atomic magnetometers, night vision devices, in research, oscillators, and to assist the global navigation satellite system.

While the U.S. has designated rubidium a critical mineral, we know surprisingly little about its supply chain. The U.S. has rubidium reserves in several known locations but they are not economic to mine and thus the U.S. extracts none domestically. The U.S. used to receive rubidium from Cabot Corporation's Bernic Lake cesium operation in Canada, but they sold it to Chinese company Sinomine in 2019. Officially, there were no known instances of rubidium mining in 2024 although it was believed some extraction occurred in China. The U.S. does not track the importation of rubidium and therefore does not know how much it consumes, but it may be only two metric tons annually.[478]

Because rubidium products are sold in low non-commercial volumes, there is no indexed or known average market price. Rubidium metal is commonly sold per gram or per 100 grams. Companies requiring regular volumes of rubidium buy directly from specialty manufacturers through negotiated sales agreements. In August 2024, rubidium metal at least or greater than 99.5% purity sold at $112.00 USD per gram in the China market which was $112 million a metric ton. Rubidium carbonate equal to or greater than 99% purity sold for $1.2 million per metric ton.

Actions Taken

The U.S. has taken no known actions to improve its vulnerable rubidium position.

478 U.S. Geological Survey Rubidium Report 2024.

Incentives & Tariffs

A company would qualify for a 10% tax credit under the Section 45X Advanced Manufacturing Production Credit if their rubidium products are "purified to a minimum purity of 99% by mass."

Domestic mining companies receive a 14% depletion allowance (there are none) while foreign companies receive a 14% rate (there are none) for their extraction operations.

Rubidium was not specifically excluded from the Trump administration's April 2025 tariff schedule. However, U.S.' import volumes are so low and mixed with other alkali metal import categories it wouldn't matter. Chinese grey market companies can easily import low volumes of rubidium to avoid market surveillance.

U.S Supply Chain Security Strategy Moving Forward

The U.S. has an insecure rubidium position since it imports 100% of its rubidium products with most originating from China. While the U.S. and Canada have rubidium reserves, they are uneconomic and produced secondarily to other mineral operations.

Multi-pronged Approach

- The U.S. should create the ability to identify the movement of rubidium into and out of the U.S. as opposed to classifying it under non-related headings. This illustrates the lack of serious measures to understand and address the U.S. rubidium vulnerability by the federal bureaucracy.
- The U.S. should pursue domestic and North American geologic survey to determine new sources of rubidium with the understanding it will be secondary to another mineral like cesium or lithium. It is also necessary to pursue new extraction technology from brine and seawater. New sources of ex-China supply may be possible with unexpected discoveries such as Everest Metal Corporation's still immature critical minerals project in Western Australia.
- In 2022, the U.S. National Defense Stockpile held no rubidium reserves and the Defense Logistics Agency (DLA) announced no plans to acquire any through 2025. A one-year supply would be two metric tons.

- It is unknown how much rubidium is recycled or reused in the U.S. but it is likely low.
- In certain uses, rubidium can be replaced with potassium and cesium.

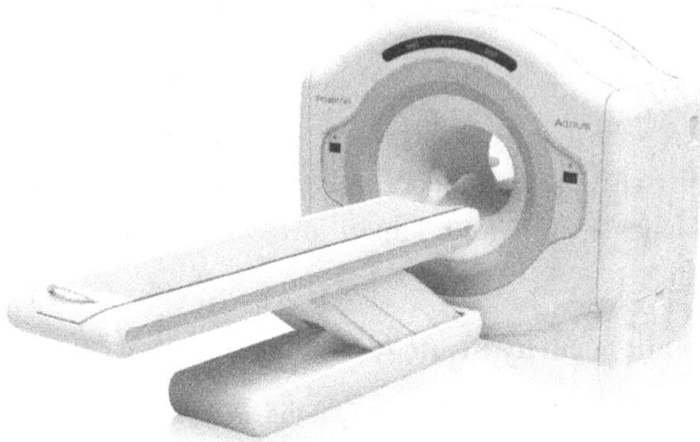

A positron emission tomography (PET) machine which uses rubidium-82 as a radiotracer to provide medical imaging.

Ruthenium (Ru)

Background

Ruthenium is classified as a PGM (Platinum Group Metal) which consists of palladium, platinum, iridium, osmium, rhodium, and ruthenium. Ruthenium is used with other PGM in alloys because of its hardening qualities, as a catalyst for making nylon, in glass fiber manufacturing, photolithography for integrated circuits manufacturing, for hard disk drives, and in the electronics industry (electric contacts). In 2024, ruthenium was used mainly in the chemical industry (46%), then in the electronics sector (33%), electrochemicals (14%), and then all other applications (15%).[479]

The most significant PGM production comes from the Bushveld Igneous Complex in South Africa (British company Anglo American is the major producer), in Russia (Nornickel, as a byproduct of nickel production), Zimbabwe (the Great Dyke), the Sudbury Complex in Canada (the site of an asteroid strike), and the Stillwater Complex in the U.S. The Stillwater Complex is located in Montana which is mined by South African company Sibanye-Stillwater. North of Montana, the South African holding company Impala Platinum Holdings PTD (Implats) owns the Canadian subsidiary Impala Canada Limited.

The U.S. imported 10 metric tons of ruthenium products in 2024, paying $15.4 million a ton. In 2023, the world extracted an estimated 28.7 tons of ruthenium which does not include secondary production from recycling. Historically, South Africa has held a monopoly on ruthenium, accounting for some 92% of extraction with Russia accounting for 3%, Zimbabwe 3%, and Canada just 2%.[480] The U.S. imported 41% of its ruthenium needs directly from South Africa, 41% from Germany and another 12% from the United Kingdom. The U.S. imported only negligible amounts directly from Russia. Much of South Africa's ruthenium production flows through European intermediaries before coming into the U.S. On average, this caused a $1 million per ton mark-up.[481] Anglo American along with South African companies Implats and Sibanye-Stillwater have established a global ruthenium monopoly.

479 *PGM Market Report*, Johnson Matthey, 2024.

480 DOE PGM Catalysts report, 2022.

481 USITC.

Actions Taken

The U.S. government has taken no specific measures to enhance its PGM/ruthenium supply chain other than apply zero tariffs.

A company would qualify for a 10% production cost tax credit under Section 45X of the Advanced Manufacturing Production Credit if the extracted ruthenium is "purified to a minimum purity of 99% by mass."

Incentives & Tariffs

- Domestic mining companies receive a 22% depletion allowance (there are none) while foreign companies receive a 14% rate (Sibanye-Stillwater).

PGM were excluded from the Trump administration's April 2025 tariff schedule while the U.S. applied 30% general import tariffs on South Africa.

U.S Supply Chain Security Strategy Moving Forward

The U.S. has a vulnerable ruthenium position since it imports 100% of it its needs and its only domestic PGM operation is foreign owned with limited reserves remaining. Most imports originate from South Africa which is then routed through European countries. Hence, the U.S.' strategy should focus on maintaining good ongoing bilateral trade relations with South Africa, increasing imports from Canada, transitioning away from Russian supply chains, and growing its recycling efforts.

Multi-pronged Approach

- In 2022, the U.S. National Defense Stockpile didn't hold any ruthenium reserves and the Defense Logistics Agency (DLA) announced no intent to purchase any through 2025. A one-year supply based on annual consumption would be 10 metric tons.
- There are many private companies that have established PGM recycling programs.[482] While there are established systems for ruthenium recycling, rates may be as low as 5% depending on the product application and industry.
- Ruthenium has similar qualities to osmium, another expensive and rare PGM. Ruthenium is considered suitable for thrifting platinum and palladium in specific uses due to its lower cost.

482 Worldwide, there are tens of thousands of companies involved in PGM recovery, recycling, and resale.

U.S. Ruthenium Imports 2024 (metric tons)
The U.S. imported 9.77 tons of ruthenium - unwrought or powder - valued at $128 million for an average cost of $13.1 million per ton. (USITC Data HTS Code 7110.41.0030)
South Africa: 5.31 tons, $65.4 million
Germany: 3.45 tons, $49.4 million
United Kingdom: 844 kg, $11.4 million
Japan: 169 kg, $2 million
Italy & Costa Rica 915 grams
*It is believed 28.7 tons of ruthenium was extracted in 2023 which does not include recycling. Most companies combine their production of ruthenium, osmium, and iridium into a single category, making it difficult to determine individual quantities.
**Data from Johnson Matthey*

Samarium (Sm)

Background

Samarium is one of the seventeen REE (Rare Earth Elements) designated as critical minerals and is part of the light REE (LREE) lanthanide series. Samarium is found with fellow REEs like cerium, lanthanum, and neodymium in monazite and bastnaesite deposits. Samarium is used in ceramics and glass, in the medical industry to fight cancers, in MRI machines, in nuclear control rods, to manufacture microwave ovens, in a variety of metal alloys, in the semiconductor space, and mostly to make magnets in electric motors requiring high temperature performance. Samarium-cobalt (SmCo) magnets were developed in the 1960s and benefit from high levels of magnet coercivity and anti-corrosive properties. Samarium composes about one-third of SmCo magnets by weight.

The U.S. produces samarium from its Mountain Pass mine where MP Materials (MPM) now sells its SEG+ product (samarium, erbium, gadolinium) although this is only 1.8% of its TREO. Until 2023, MPM sent its SEG+ products to China for refinement but can now separate and sell samarium as an individual product from its U.S. facility. Energy Fuels Inc. (EFI) intends to produce samarium products but did not sell any in 2024. For the REE industry, samarium is not a money maker because it sells relatively cheaply. In August 2024, samarium oxide at least 99.5% purity sold for $2,900.00 USD per metric ton in the China market. Samarium metal with minimum 99.9% purity sold at $11,860.00 per metric ton in the China market (including 13% VAT).

China mines the largest amount of samarium annually (and REE in general) and processes even more from what it imports. In 2020, China extracted 1,571 tons of contained samarium and imported another 310 tons for a total of 1,881 tons. Of this total, 516 tons were lost during different phases of the manufacturing process and another 708 tons of refined products were exported. Of the remaining amount, 243 tons went to magnets for EV motors, 138 tons to microwave devices, 115 tons to gearing, 77 tons for instruments, 50 tons in ceramics and glass, 30 tons for batteries, and 26 tons as catalysts in the chemical sector.[483]

483 Ge, Zewen, et al. "Assessing samarium resource efficiency in China: A dynamic material flow analysis." Resources Policy, 2022.

In China, Samarium demand rose significantly from 2010 to 2020, from an estimated 175 metric tons to 675 tons, with demand predicted to go to 1,500 tons by 2030 and possibly 1,900 tons by 2035. To make up for this increasing demand, China will have to improve its manufacturing process that loses 27% of its initial input, import more than the 16% it currently does, extract more domestically, or cut back on the 37% that is exported. If China limits exports, countries dependent on this supply will have to look elsewhere for more expensively priced products or develop their own ex-China REE mining capability.

The U.S., like all modern industrial economies, is a magnet-dependent society. While the U.S. mainly uses and imports NdFeB magnets, it also employs SmCo magnets for a variety of uses. In 2024, the U.S. imported 695 tons of SmCo magnet products valued at $11.4 million for an average of $16,400.00 per ton which is one-quarter of the average price of imported NdFeB magnets. More than two-thirds of these magnets came directly from China and the remaining balance mainly from Europe. While the U.S. imports most of its SmCo magnet needs, several domestic companies do have the ability to produce these products as well.[484] Imported SmCo products from China were by far the least expensive at only $6,800.00 per metric ton or 41% of the average SmCo magnet importation price.

Actions Taken

As discussed in previous REE sections, MP Materials has received grants through the Defense Production Act and from the Department of Energy to construct an REE processing facility at their Mountain Passs location and to build their Fort Worth, TX magnet facility.

As of 2023, Australian company Lynas Rare Earths received a total of $258 million in grants through the Defense Production Act to construct a HREE processing facility in Texas. While Lynas sells samarium products, there is no indication that they will do so at their future U.S. facility.

MPM and EFI qualify for a 10% tax credit under the Section 45X Advanced Manufacturing Production Credit if their samarium products are "purified to a minimum purity of 99% by mass."

According to DFARS (Defense Federal Acquisition Regulation Supplement), the defense contracting industry cannot acquire SmCo magnets with a supply chain connected to China or Russia starting in 2027.

484 Electron Energy Corporation & Arnold Magnetic Technologies

Incentives & Tariffs

Domestic REE mining companies receive a 14% depletion allowance (MP Materials) while foreign companies receive a 14% rate (there are none) for monazite, bastnaesite, and xenotime extraction operations. The U.S. could raise the domestic depletion rate to 22% to encourage production.

REE were excluded from the Trump administration's April 2025 tariff schedule. China put a 125% tariff on U.S. REE imports the same month which prompted MPM to stop sending its products there for processing. Samarium sellers are required to obtain an export license from the Ministry of Commerce. In 2023, China banned the export of the technology to make samarium-cobalt magnets, adding them to its "Catalogue of Technologies Prohibited and Restricted from Export."

U.S Supply Chain Security Strategy Moving Forward

The U.S. has an insecure samarium position as it historically imported 100% of its individual needs and 63% of SmCo magnets come directly from China, although more samarium will be available in the U.S. ex-China as MPM and EFI's processing capabilities come online. The likely long-term threats to this position include MP Materials depleting its Mountain Pass mine or the company becoming unprofitable due to continuing superior competition from Chinese manufacturers. To date, only China, the U.S., and Malaysia (Australia) have the technological sophistication to develop their own advanced REE processing capability.[485]

Multi-pronged Approach

- The U.S. should monitor the domestic and North American samarium and SmCo value chain and determine when and if additional government assistance is needed. MP Materials has received sufficient government subsidies to date although they must continue to lower costs and product prices.
- The U.S. does not conduct effective market surveillance of samarium and therefore does not understand is production and trade flow. Consequently, the U.S. International Trade Commission should develop its own samarium specific HTS code to track its import.

485 Vietnam has a limited processing capability.

- In 2022, the U.S. National Defense Stockpile did not hold any samarium reserves but the Defense Logistics Agency (DLA) announced they were purchasing 200 metric tons of samarium-cobalt alloy in 2024 and 60 tons in 2025. Based on imports, a one-year supply of samarium-cobalt would be an estimated 1,100 metric tons.
- It is unknown how much samarium is recycled or reused in the U.S. for non-magnet uses, but it is likely around 1% which is the overall rate for REEs. Recycling is difficult because REE are mixed with other elements, are used in such low volumes that very little is recovered and usually involves hydrochloric acid. Samarium recycling rates in China are 1%. Much can be done to improve the reuse of samarium losses during the manufacturing process and the recycling of end-of-life samarium products like magnets.
- Nissan announced a proprietary EV motor using cheaper SmCo magnets as opposed to mainstream NdFeB magnets. This is an example of SmCo magnets thrifting NdFeB magnets rather than the other way around because the SmCo prices are now significantly lower. Some companies have developed experimental electric traction motors for EV using no REE, however the problem with this has been a loss of performance.

U.S SmCo Magnet Imports 2024 (metric tons)

The U.S. imported 695 tons of SmCo magnets valued at $11.4 million, averaging $16,400.00 a ton. *(USITC Data HTS Code 8505.11.0050)*

China: 442 tons, $3 million

Germany: 195 tons, $3.3 million

Switzerland: 22 tons, $2.6 million

Japan: 17.8 tons, $910,000.00

Finland, Thailand, Malaysia & 17 tons

This was a significant drop from 2023 when the U.S. imported 1,112 tons valued at $12.2 million averaging $10,900.00 a ton. The biggest change was imports from China almost halving from 807 tons to 442 tons. Since the U.S. imported less of the cheaper Chinese magnets, the average price went up - which was a predictably inflationary result.

*63% of SmCo magnets imported came directly from China at the lowest cost per ton, down from 72% in 2023.

*An estimated 229 tons by weight (one-third) was samarium while 466 tons was cobalt.

Scandium (Sc)

Background

Although scandium is not considered a true REE (Rare Earth Elements) it is often grouped with heavy REE (HREE) due to its chemical similarities and is often found with fellow REE like lanthanum and neodymium in monazite and bastnaesite deposits but also with uranium. High concentrations of scandium are also found in thortveitite and kolbeckite, notably in Norway and Madagascar, but are uneconomic to access. Scandium is mainly recovered as a byproduct of other product streams such as titanium, aluminum, and nickel. Scandium is relatively abundant, similar to cobalt, and is used primarily in making scandium-aluminum alloys for high-performance aerospace applications. Other uses include metal-halide lamps, as a tracing agent in the oil industry, in dental lasers, electronics, lithium-ion battery applications, and in solid-oxide fuel cells (SOFC).

The U.S. hasn't extracted scandium since 1969 and is 100% reliant on imports. China is the leading producer of scandium products (Bayan Obo REE extraction) followed by Russia with global production being upwards of 40 metric tons of scandium oxide equivalent annually. Scandium is produced in such low volumes with relatively little overall value, that the U.S. and other countries typically do not track its production and movement, instead lumping it together with yttrium because they are frequently found together. Overall, scandium production capacity outpaces actual consumption with scandium oxide minimum 99.99% purity selling for $721,000.00 per metric ton in the China market in August 2024.

One assessment put annual global scandium consumption at 45 tons with 676,000 tons available for extraction and the present ability to produce 1,500 tons annually. A contributing reason for such low production and high prices is that the global scandium market is poorly structured and unorganized, resulting in noticeable inefficiency. As mentioned, the lack of effective market surveillance has resulted in the U.S. merely guessing at how much scandium is produced and imported yearly. The largest potential for increased scandium production comes from bauxite (as a byproduct), REE, and coal ash operations (as a byproduct). Byproduct operations are energy intensive, recover relatively small concentrations of scandium, and are thus expensive.[486]

NioCorp Developments LTD, NASDAQ/TSX: NB

Publicly traded Canadian mining company NioCorp is currently pursuing their Elk Creek Critical Minerals Project in Nebraska with a focus on niobium, scandium, titanium, and REE products like NdPr. The project is believed to have mineral reserves of 3,677 tons of scandium trioxide which would satisfy U.S. annual consumption needs for 183 years. The company hasn't secured the funding required to begin operations since announcing their project in 2010. Since NioCorp doesn't sell a product, they lost $11.4 million in 2024. The company has applied for a $800 million loan through the U.S. Export-Import Bank.

Rio Tinto fer et Titane

Rio Tinto's Canadian subsidiary Element North 21 (EN21) runs the RTFT operation in Quebec which began limited production in 2022 with plans to extract three tons of high-purity scandium oxide per year from titanium dioxide waste streams. The waste stream is from Rio Tinto's Iron and Titanium Technology and Critical Minerals Center in Quebec. The company intends to ramp up eventual production to 12 metric tons annually. RTFT began selling scandium-aluminum alloys for 3-D printing in 2024. Rio Tinto is also pursuing their scandium oxide Burra Project in Australia which is still early-stage and not production ready.

ScaVanger Project France

ScaVanger is a European consortium consisting of French, German, and Greek partners with headquarters in Paris and German company EIT Raw Materials Gmbh providing 70% of the funding. The project will extract scandium hydroxide from the waste streams of titanium dioxide pigment, alumina, and nickel-cobalt production. ScaVanger's goal is to produce 30 tpa of scandium trioxide to feed the European market and transition them from their current dependency on a foreign supply chain (80% from China, 20% from Kazakhstan as a byproduct of uranium mining). Initial production is planned for 2025 with commercial scale operations beginning in 2026 with an anticipated 21 tpa capacity.

486 Harald & Antoniy Sverdrup, "On the Supply Dynamics of Scandium, Global Resources, Production, Oxide and Metal price, a Prospective Modelling Study Using WORLD7." Biophysical Economics and Sustainability, April 2024.

Taganito Philippines

In 2016, the Japanese Sumitomo Metal Mining Company (SMM) moved forward with recovering scandium oxide secondary to its ongoing nickel and cobalt operations in the Philippines through its subsidiary Taganito HPAL Nickel Corporation.[487] They planned production of 7.5 tons annually of scandium oxide equivalent beginning in 2019 and have achieved this goal. In 2024, SMM recovered 11.8 metric tons of scandium oxalate which was sent to Japan for processing into scandium oxide.[488] Scandium oxalate contains sulfur which is further refined into scandium oxide.

China

Lomon Billions Group aka LB Group is a Chinese chemical manufacturing company making products for industries such as paint, plastics, rubber, paper, ceramics, and cosmetics. In 2023, the company recovered 20 tons of scandium oxide from chlorinated titanium dioxide waste acid and invested in another 10 tpa capacity increase. Based on existing waste stream flows, they can likely double or even triple existing scandium recovery volumes. This increased production could lower prices and potentially price-out competitors and condition the global scandium supply chain to acquire Chinese products.

China Minmetals, through their subsidiary Metallurgical Corporation of China, owns their Ramu nickel mine in Papua New Guinea which produced nickel sulfate and cobalt for China's EV battery industry. This operation has continuing documented pollution problems. In 2019, Minmetals began developing a scandium oxide production plant at its Tangshan, Hebei Province location which would use feedstock from its Ramu operations. In 2024, this facility produced 20 tons of scandium oxide.[489]

Russia

Russian company UC Rusal commissioned a 3 tpa pilot scandium oxide plant at their Ural Aluminum Smelter, recovering scandium oxide from red mud deposits which contain 32,500 tons of scandium oxide. The company produces small quantities of 5081 (10%) and 1581 (0.03%) scandium alloy branded as ScAlution but do not state their production levels in their annual report. In 2021, Russia exported a mere 420 kg of scandium metal with 95%

487 HPAL: High Pressure Acid Leach

488 Republic of the Philippines, Mines and Geosciences Bureau.

489 U.S. Geological Survey Scandium Report 2024.

(400 kg) going to the U.S. A 2023 report indicated California based company Bloom Energy was the single largest recipient of Russian sourced scandium for use in their SOFC technology.[490] Rusal announced in February 2025 that it was investing $5.7 million to set up another scandium extraction operation with an eventual capacity of 19 tpa.[491]

Actions Taken

In 2024, the Defense Logistics Agency (DLA) solicited DLA242-003 *Advancing Scandium Use in Metal Alloys for U.S. Weapon System Production and Sustainment* through their SBIR (Small Business Innovation Research) program. Phase I awards were $100,000.00 and Phase II $1 million.

A company would qualify for a 10% tax credit under the Section 45X Advanced Manufacturing Production Credit if their scandium products are "purified to a minimum purity of 99% by mass."

Incentives & Tariffs

- Domestic REE mining companies receive a 14% depletion allowance (there are none) while foreign companies receive a 14% rate for monazite, bastnaesite, and xenotime extraction operations. The U.S. could raise the domestic depletion rate to 22% to encourage production.

Scandium was excluded from the Trump administration's April 2025 tariff schedule. That same month, Chinese sellers were required to obtain an export license from the Ministry of Commerce. Also, China emplaced 125% retaliatory tariffs on U.S. REE imports.

U.S Supply Chain Security Strategy Moving Forward

The U.S. has an insecure scandium position as it imports 100% of its needs with most likely coming from China and Russia. The U.S. currently lacks the market understanding and technology to develop its own domestic supply chain. The one domestic scandium project has been unable to move forward and extract a product, meaning the company continues to lose money in the meantime.

490 https://en.institut-seltene-erden.de/scandium-vom-sowjet-geheimnis-zum-china-monopol/

491 "Rusal to launch production of rare-earth metal scandium this year." Reuters, February 27, 2025.

Multi-pronged Approach

- An obvious action required is the USITC providing scandium with its own unique HTS trading code (not combined with yttrium) so that its importation, overall movement, and consumption can be tracked and analyzed.
- The U.S. is pursuing what limited domestic scandium production potential it has, although DOD and DOE have yet to show interest in supporting NioCorp's project. This indicates the USG does not believe their operations will be economic or that they are production ready. The U.S. should maximize their long-term scandium supply from neighboring Canada.
- The U.S. should monitor the domestic and North American scandium value chain and determine when and if additional government assistance is needed. For example, Australian company Arizona Rare Earths plans to develop a project in La Paz, Arizona to extract praseodymium and scandium. The project is immature and not production ready as of 2025.
- In 2022, the U.S. National Defense Stockpile did not hold any scandium reserves and the Defense Logistics Agency (DLA) did not announce any intentions to purchase any through 2025. An estimated one-year supply of scandium oxide would be 20 metric tons.
- It is unknown how much scandium is recycled or reused in the U.S. but it is likely around 1% which is the overall rate for REEs. Recycling is difficult because the REEs are mixed with other elements, are used in such low volumes that very little is recovered and usually involves hydrochloric acid.
- Titanium alloys compete with scandium-aluminum for strength and weight as they are considerably less expensive.

Possible 2022 Scandium Production (metric tons)

China produced an estimated 12 tons from a variety of sources like REE and titanium waste streams.

Russia produced 10 tons from REE and as the byproduct of other mining operations.

The Philippines produced 7.5 tons as the byproduct of nickel and copper extraction operations. *(11.8 tons in 2024)*

Malaysia produced 4 tons from REE mining.

Kazakhstan produced 3 tons from REE mining.

Canada produced 3 tons as a byproduct of nickel and copper operations.

Conclusion: Because production capability far exceeds consumption, companies are either suppressing production, stockpiling, or produce and sell more volumes than we are aware of.

**Data from H. and A. Sverdrup, 2023.*

Tantalum (Ta)

Background

Tantalum is often recovered in the minerals of columbite and pyrochlore and has similar qualities to niobium. It can also be recovered from tin slag and secondary to lithium mining. The two minerals are commonly found together in coltan aka columbite-tantalites aka tantalite. Tantalum is ductile, has a high melting point and is resistant to corrosion by acids. During fabrication, it must be welded in an inert atmosphere, it cannot be soldered, and grinding tantalum is difficult. Tantalum is used to make electronic components such as capacitors and resistors for cell phones and laptops. Tantalum is used in superalloys to include jet engines, spacecraft, nuclear reactors, missiles, and the medical industry as implants.

In 2024, the world produced only 2,100 metric tons of tantalum with the Democratic Republic of the Congo extracting 880 tons (42%), Nigeria 390 tons (18%), Rwanda 350 tons (16%), and Brazil 210 tons (10%). Clearly, Africa, which accounted for three-quarters of all production, is a global production chokepoint. China produced just 76 tons while the U.S. and North America produced none at all. The U.S. hasn't produced tantalum since the late 1950s as its deposits are uneconomic to mine. Both China and Australia have large tantalum reserves, 240,000 and 110,000 tons respectively. On average from 2020-2023, the U.S. imported 22% of its tantalum needs from China, 12% from Australia, and 12% from Germany.[492]

In 2024, according to UN data HS Code 8103, the U.S. was the largest exporter of finished tantalum products with 506 metric tons, followed by South Korea with 230 tons, Japan with 188 tons, and Thailand with 121 tons. The U.S. is believed to have imported 898 tons of tantalum products valued at $226 million followed by South Korea with 290 tons, and Japan with 161 tons. There are an estimated 48 tantalum smelters in the world with half of all tantalum concentrates being processed in China.[493] Because tantalum is such a low volume and relatively inexpensive metal, it is not tracked on any index such as with the London Metal Exchange.[494]

492 U.S. Geological Survey Tantalum Report 2024.

493 Wei, Xue, et al, "A review of tantalum resources and its production." Science Press, August 2022.

494 USITC data for 2023.

Actions Taken

In 2020, DARS (Defense Acquisition Regulations System) passed a DFARS (Defense Federal Acquisition Regulation Supplement) prohibiting the federal government from acquiring tantalum metals and alloys from China, Russia, Iran, and North Korea. The effective date was August 25, 2022, and didn't affect civilian supply chains. Embedded tantalum components like capacitors in finished electronic products were exempted. In turn, China doesn't allow the importation of U.S. tantalum products.

The 2010 Dodd-Frank Wall Street Reform and Consumer Protection Act Section 1502 required the SEC to establish regulations addressing the disclosure of identified conflict minerals reference the DRC (Democratic Republic of the Congo.) Subsequently, tin, tungsten, tantalum and gold produced by the DRC were determined to be conflict minerals.

A company would qualify for a 10% tax credit under the Section 45X Advanced Manufacturing Production Credit if their tantalum products are "purified to a minimum purity of 99% by mass."

Incentives & Tariffs

- Domestic mining companies receive a 22% depletion allowance (there are none) while foreign companies receive a 14% rate (there are none) for their tantalum extraction operations.

In September, the Office of the United States Trade Representative announced final tariff modifications after completing its review of the actions imposed under section 301(b) of the Trade Act of 1974 (19 U.S.C. 2411, as amended): China's acts, policies, and practices related to technology transfer, intellectual property, and innovation. Additional categories of goods from China were subject to tariffs including a 25% ad valorem tariff on critical minerals, which included tantalum.

Tantalum was excluded from the Trump administration's April 2025 tariff schedule.

U.S Supply Chain Security Strategy Moving Forward

The U.S. has an insecure tantalum position as it imports 100% of its needs with no production from Canada and Mexico.

Multi-pronged Approach

- The U.S. should focus on Noth American tantalum exploration and secure its supply chains with Australia and African suppliers. It is preferable to secure tantalum ores and concentrates directly from Africa rather than from China after midstream processing.
- As of 2022, the National Defense Stockpile held 101 tons of tantalum columbium concentrate, 187 pounds of tantalum metal, and 3 pounds of tantalum alloy. The Defense Logistics Agency (DLA) announced their intent to dispose of 190 pounds of tantalum products and acquire 26.5 tons of tantalum for 2024. In 2025, DLA announced their intent to dispose of 190 pounds of tantalum while acquiring 32.25 tons. The U.S. consumption in 2024 was 840 tons. Thus, the U.S. likely has less than one month's supply in its stockpile.
- U.S. Geological Survey estimates that possibly 30% of tantalum production in the U.S. is from tantalum scraps recovered from the manufacturing process. The U.S. and Japan are believed to have the highest tantalum recovery rates. However, global recovery rates are likely as low as 10%.[495]
- Tantalum can be replaced with numerous materials depending on the use case such as niobium, aluminum, tungsten, nickel and so forth but with a likely loss of performance.

495 Wei, Xue, et al, "A review of tantalum resources and its production." Science Press, August 2022.

World Tantalum Production 2024 (metric tons)

Country	2020	2024	Reserves
DRC (Congo)	780	880	
Rwanda	254	350	
Nigeria	260	390	
Brazil	470	210	40,000
China	74	76	240,000
Australia	34	52	110,000
Ethiopia	69	40	
Mozambique	43	55	
Russia	49	29	
Other Countries		4	
Total	2,100	2,400	

U.S. Tantalum Imports 2024

*The U.S. imported 898 tons of tantalum products valued at $226 million, averaging $252,400.00 a ton. (UN Comtrade Data HS Code 8103)

China: 317 tons, $106 million

South Korea: 114 tons, $3 million

Indonesia: 66 tons, $3 million

Kazakhstan: 66 tons, $18 million

**U.S. Geological Survey & UN Comtrade Data*

Tellurium (Te)

Background

Tellurium is related chemically to selenium and sulfur (all three are chalcogens) and is a rare element, similar in abundance to platinum. A minority of tellurium is recovered as a primary ore from gold-tellurium deposits in China and Sweden while most is recovered from anode slimes as a byproduct of copper refining operations. Tellurium is mostly used in cadmium-tellurium (CdTe), thin-film solar panels and other thermoelectric devices (bismuth-Te) as well as specialty alloys. Tellurium is also used to increase heat resistance in rubber tires and to color glass and ceramics.

In 2024, the world produced just 980 metric tons of tellurium content with China leading the way with 750 tons (76%), both Japan and Russia with 70 tons each (7% apiece), the U.S. with 40 tons (4%), and Canada with 27 tons (3%). U.S. imports of tellurium have dropped significantly from 42 tons in 2021 to just 7 tons in 2024. This reflected a change in consumption from 42 tons in 2021 to just 12-15 tons in 2024. Two companies in the U.S. produce tellurium as the byproduct of copper production. However, these companies do not refine the tellurium, they export it or sell it to a third-party to create a refined product. The U.S. went from importing 95% of its tellurium needs in 2021 to importing just 25% in 2024. The U.S. has developed a mostly North American tellurium supply chain with less than 1% coming from China.[496]

The recovery of tellurium from copper, although the main method for acquiring the mineral, is inefficient, which makes it difficult to do so in an economic manner. Initially, 90% of potential recoverable tellurium is lost as tailings during the copper extraction and concentrate process. More tellurium is lost as the copper is refined and turned into anodes, losing another 5% of total potential recoverable Te product. After passing through the electrolytic refinery stage, only 558 tons of Te content remains in anode slimes from an original 38,600 tons of Te content. Of this, only 503 tons of tellurium is ultimately recovered or 1.3% of the theoretical total potential recoverable content.[497]

According to the USITC, the U.S. paid an average of $110,600.00 per metric ton for imported tellurium products. In September 2024, 7N high-purity

496 U.S. Geological Survey & USITC.
497 Moats, M., "Tellurium in the Copper Supply Chain." O'Keefe Institute, Missouri University of Science and Technology presentation, 2022.

tellurium 99.99999% in the China market sold for $575,000.00 a metric ton while 5N high-purity 99.999% sold for a much lower $134,000.00 a ton. The U.S. average purchase price indicates it bought 5N products which were used "as is" or refined to a higher purity. Because tellurium is such a low volume and relatively inexpensive metal, it is not tracked on an index such as the London Metal Exchange.

ASARCO (American Smelting and Refining Company)

Tucson-based ASARCO is owned by Grupo Mexico and runs a copper refining facility in Amarillo, Texas. The Amarillo refinery produces up to 260,000 tpa of 5/16 copper rod and was certified in 1996 to produce selenium and tellurium as byproducts of its copper operations. The company suspended tellurium production temporarily in 2012 while upgrading its facility. The company shut down its Amarillio operations in 2022 after the COVID pandemic disrupted global supply chains, raising transportation costs to the point where production was uneconomic. ASARCO reopened its facility in 2024. There is no information available about their tellurium production since ASARCO does not publish an annual report and Grupo Mexico does not mention it anywhere in their annual reports. However, annual production during uninterrupted operations has been estimated at 50 tons and may have been 20 tons in 2024.

Rio Tinto

Rio Tinto is an Australian international mining conglomerate which owns the giant open pit Kennecott copper mine (aka Bingham Canyon mine) in Utah, located twelve miles due south of the Great Salt Lake. Although this mine has been active since 1904, Rio Tinto did not begin extracting tellurium from it until 2022. The company pays Canadian company 5N Plus to refine the product with the majority purchased by First Solar as part of an existing supply agreement between 5N and First Solar. 5N also makes semiconductors for the security and medical imaging markets.[498] Rio Tinto produces 20 tons of tellurium annually, making a profit on their tellurium operations although it is minimal.[499]

Actions Taken

ASARCO, Rio Tinto, and 5N Plus qualify for a 10% tax credit under the Section 45X Advanced Manufacturing Production Credit if their tellurium

498 5N is a profitable company with a 6% profit margin in 2023, up from a 8.7% loss in 2022.

499 Rio Tinto news release, May 11, 2022.

products are “converted to cadmium telluride or purified to a minimum purity of 99% by mass.”

Incentives & Tariffs

- Domestic mining companies receive a 14% depletion allowance (there are none) while foreign companies receive a 14% rate (ASARCO, Rio Tinto) for their tellurium extraction operations.
- Tellurium was not excluded from the Trump administration’s April 2025 tariff schedule.

U.S Supply Chain Security Strategy Moving Forward

The U.S. tellurium position improved significantly in 2024 due to a rapid decrease in domestic consumption. The two tellurium producers in the U.S. are foreign companies, albeit from friendly and/or neighboring nations (Mexico, Australia).

Multi-pronged Approach

- The U.S. should consider providing incentives or improved technology to the two domestically located tellurium providers which could include mandating that DOD contractors only provide ex-China tellurium products.
- As of 2022, the U.S. National Defense Stockpile did not report any tellurium holdings while the Defense Logistics Agency (DLA) did not announce any acquisitions through 2025. A possible one-year stockpile would be 15 metric tons of tellurium content.
- Tellurium recovery and recycling, while feasible, is likely very low. The lack of data on the topic leaves us guessing as to exact volumes but it may be around 1%. First Solar, an American owned global solar panel manufacturer, has an established recycling program where it recycles 90% of its solar panel components to include cadmium and tellurium.
- Silicon and copper-indium-gallium selenide compete with CdTe thin-film photovoltaic solar cells. Indium and gallium are both designated critical minerals and cost more than tellurium.

U.S. Tellurium Imports 2024			
Country	Amount	Value	Price/Ton
Canada	4.5 tons	$523,800.00	$116,400.00
Belgium	910 kg	$75,500.00	$82,900.00
Philippines	454 kg	$39,800.00	$87,600.00
Japan	367 kg	$23,600.00	$64,300.00
China	93 kg	$36,200.00	$389,200.00
Total	**6.32 tons**	**$699,200.00**	**$110,600.00**

In 2022, the U.S. imported 1.8 tons of tellurium from China, which dropped to 1.2 tons in 2023. Chinese sellers must get an export license for tellurium sales to the U.S. beginning February 2025.

The U.S. sent 3.3 tons of tellurium to Canada for refinement and 284 kilograms to China.

**Data from USITC HTS code 2804.50.0020*

Terbium (Tb)

Background

Terbium is one of the seventeen REE (Rare Earth Elements) designated as critical minerals and is part of the heavy REE. Terbium is frequently found with other REE in monazite and bastnaesite deposits. Terbium is mostly used in green phosphors for lamps and televisions, in electronics, to make alloys, naval sonar systems, and as an element in Neodymium-Iron-Boron (NdFeB) magnets to increase resistance to heat.

As mentioned in previous sections on other REE, production volumes are reported as REO (Rare Earth Oxides) and as an overall group total, not as specific elements. The U.S. has one REO operation at Mountain Pass (MP) in California which consists mainly of light REE and much less heavy REE which terbium falls under. While the MP operation does have terbium, it is in such low quantities that the company does not report it and separating it is uneconomic. It remains to be seen if MP will separate and refine terbium products domestically or continue to ship them to China for processing.

Like other REE, the U.S. understands little about actual terbium production. This is because the U.S. has not established effective market surveillance tools and doesn't track its importation, lumping it together with other REE. While MP has the potential to produce terbium, the U.S. has not done so through 2024 and is completely dependent on imports, with possibly 100% of refined terbium production originating in China. In August 2024, terbium oxide minimum 99.95% purity traded in the China market for $748,000.00 USD per metric ton.

In one study analyzing the China terbium market from 2011-2020, an estimated 6,089 tons of terbium concentrate were mined for subsequent processing or just 608 tons annually. Of this total, 980 tons were imported during various phases, 2,300 tons in various products were exported, and 639 tons were lost to illegal mining and production inefficiency. As an indication of major terbium end uses, the largest amounts by far were used to make fluorescent lamps (1,914 tons), CRT - Cathode Ray Tubes (472 tons), and then Terbium-Dysprosium-Iron alloys (164 tons). During this period, China stockpiled 395 tons, which was not a significant amount compared to other REE Beijing stored.[500]

500 Gao, Cuixia, et al, "Uncovering terbium metabolism in China: A dynamic material flow analysis." Resources Policy, December 2022.

Actions Taken

As discussed in previous REE sections, MP Materials has received grants through the Defense Production Act and from the Department of Energy to construct an REE processing facility at their Mountain Passs location and to build their Fort Worth, TX magnet facility. Although the MP site historically had the capability to produce terbium oxide, there is no confirmation that the company will produce terbium at their new facility.

As of 2023, Australian company Lynas Rare Earths received a total of $258 million in grants through the Defense Production Act to construct a HREE processing facility in Texas.

MPM qualifies for a 10% tax credit under the Section 45X Advanced Manufacturing Production Credit if their terbium products are "purified to a minimum purity of 99% by mass."

Incentives & Tariffs

Domestic REE mining companies receive a 14% depletion allowance (MP Materials) while foreign companies receive a 14% rate (there are none) for monazite, bastnaesite, and xenotime extraction operations.

Terbium was excluded from the Trump administration's April 2025 tariff schedule. That same month, Chinese terbium sellers were required to obtain an export license from the Ministry of Commerce before shipping their products. China has placed a 125% tariff on U.S. REE imports.

U.S Supply Chain Security Strategy Moving Forward

The U.S. has an insecure terbium position since it most likely imports 100% of its processed needs with most (possibly 95%) originating from China. The likely long-term threats to this position include the U.S. inability to develop its own domestic terbium supply chain, including urban mining and recycling, and not developing allied/friendly terbium supply chains ex-China. To date, only China, the U.S., and Malaysia (Australia) have the technological sophistication to develop their own advanced REE processing capability.[501]

Multi-pronged Approach

- The U.S. should develop effective terbium market surveillance tools such as creating a specific USITC HTS import code so that it knows how much terbium it imports and consumes.

501 Vietnam has a limited REE processing capability.

- The U.S. can consider providing a 22% depletion allowance for MPM.
- The U.S. should monitor the domestic, North American, and allied terbium value chain and determine when and if additional government assistance is needed.
- In 2022, the U.S. National Defense Stockpile did not hold any terbium reserves while the Defense Logistics Agency announced no plans to acquire any through 2025. Although the U.S. does not know what its own terbium consumption is, 50 metric tons may be a one-year supply.
- It is unknown how much terbium is recycled or reused, but it is likely around 1% which is the overall rate for REE. Recycling is difficult because the REE are mixed with other elements, are used in such low volumes that little is recovered and usually involves hydrochloric acid. While very little recycling is done, companies have shown the ability to recycle 99% of REE products (to include terbium) from end-of-life magnets.
- Terbium use in NdFeB magnets can be thrifted as needed as itself is used already to thrift neodymium and dysprosium which are also critical minerals.

Thulium (Tm)

Background

Thulium is one of the seventeen REE (Rare Earth Elements) designated as critical minerals and is a heavy REE (HREE). Thulium is frequently found with other REE in monazite and bastnaesite deposits, in ion-adsorption clays, and in low concentrations in seawater. Thulium is used for chemical research, in solid-state lasers for surgical applications, x-ray machines, ceramic magnets for microwaves, superconductors, and counterfeiting measures in currency. The mineral is one of the rarest of the REE with global annual production estimated at only 50 tons.

As mentioned in previous sections on other REE, production volumes are reported as REO (Rare Earth Oxides) and as an overall group total, not as specific elements. The U.S. has one REO operation at Mountain Pass (MP) in California which consists mainly of light REE and much less HREE which thulium falls under. While the MP operation does have thulium, it is in such low quantities that the company does not report it and separating it is uneconomic. It remains to be seen if MP Materials will separate and refine thulium products domestically or continue to ship them to China for processing.

Like other REE, the U.S. understands little about actual thulium production. This is because the U.S. has not established effective market surveillance tools and does not track its importation, lumping it together with other REE. While MP Materials has the potential to produce thulium, the U.S. has not done so through 2024 and is completely dependent on imports, with possibly 99%-100% of refined thulium production originating from China. In August 2024, depending on the market and purity, thulium oxide minimum 99.9% purity traded at $55 million per metric ton. Thulium is not an indexed metal and sales are made directly between seller and buyer where prices can vary widely.

Actions Taken

As discussed in previous REE sections, MP Materials has received grants through the Defense Production Act and from the Department of Energy to construct an REE processing facility at their Mountain Passs location and to build their Fort Worth, TX magnet facility. There is no confirmation that the company will produce thulium at their new facility.

As of 2023, Australian company Lynas Rare Earths received a total of $258 million in grants through the Defense Production Act to construct a HREE processing facility in Texas.

MP Materials qualifies for a 10% tax credit under the Section 45X Advanced Manufacturing Production Credit if their thulium products are "purified to a minimum purity of 99% by mass."

Incentives & Tariffs

Domestic REE mining companies receive a 14% depletion allowance (MP Materials) while foreign companies receive a 14% rate (there are none) for monazite, bastnaesite, and xenotime extraction operations.

REE were excluded from the Trump Administration's April 2025 tariff schedule. That same month, China placed 125% retaliatory tariffs on the import of U.S. REE.

U.S Supply Chain Security Strategy Moving Forward

The U.S. has an insecure thulium position since it most likely imports 100% of its processed needs with most originating from China. The likely long-term threats to this position include the U.S. inability to develop its own domestic thulium supply chain, including urban mining and recycling, and not developing allied/friendly ex-China supply chains. To date, only China, the U.S., and Malaysia (Australia) have the technological sophistication to develop their own advanced REE processing capability.[502]

Multi-pronged Approach

- The U.S. should develop effective thulium market surveillance tools such as creating a specific USITC HTS import code so that it knows how much thulium it imports and consumes.
- The U.S. can consider providing MP Materials a 22% depletion allowance.
- The U.S. should monitor the domestic, North American, and allied thulium ex-China value chain and determine when and if additional government assistance is needed.
- In 2022, the U.S. National Defense Stockpile held no reserves of thulium while the Defense Logistics Agency announced no plans to

502 Vietnam has a limited REE processing capability.

acquire any through 2025. Although the U.S. does not know what its own thulium consumption is, 10 metric tons may be a one-year supply.

- It is unknown how much thulium is recycled or reused, but it is likely around 1% which is the overall rate for REE. Recycling is difficult because the REE are mixed with other elements, are used in such low volumes that little is recovered and usually involves hydrochloric acid. While very little recycling is done, companies have shown the ability to recycle 99% of REE products from end-of-life magnets.
- Thulium is used in very low volumes with little opportunity for substitution without significant loss in performance.

Above, a counterfeit Euro banknote. Thulium displays blue fluorescence under ultraviolet light. Most likely, counterfeiters do not have the technical sophistication to include thulium in their fake products thus allowing them to be detected by law enforcement authorities. (by Liis Treimann)

Tin (Sn)

Background

Tin is a soft, malleable metal which is chemically similar to germanium and lead and is mainly recovered from the mineral cassiterite (SnO2 or tin oxide). Tin is more abundant in the Earth's crust than zinc, lead, or copper. Bronze, which was made as early as 3000 BC, consists of 1/8th tin and 7/8th copper. Pewter, an alloy, is made chiefly of tin (up to 90%) and smaller quantities of bismuth, antimony and copper. Indium tin oxide is used in optoelectronic applications and tin is used to tinplate steel as a protective covering to prevent corrosion. Tin is commonly used with lead in solders for the electronics industry. In the U.S., tin is used mostly for tinplate (23%), chemicals (22%), and alloys & solder (11%).

In 2024, The world produced an estimated 300,000 metric tons of tin content with China leading the way with 69,000 tons (23%), Indonesia with 50,000 tons (17%), and Burma with 34,000 tons (11%). Overall, Asia accounted for 164,000 tons (55%) of total production, South America 81,000 tons (27%), and Africa 35,600 tons (12%).[503] The U.S. and all of North America did not produce any tin. The U.S. stopped producing tin in 1993 and stopped smelting it in 1989.

Two countries dominated the import of tin ore and concentrates which was Malaysia with 15,400 metric tons and then Thailand with 14,600 tons which combined was 97% of recorded imports. The U.S. was the largest importer of unwrought tin products with 26,200 tons followed by Japan with 18,800 tons, and South Korea with 14,700 tons. On average, the U.S. imported 75% of its tin needs from 2020-2024. The rest was produced from old and new scrap material. As with other metals, it is not surprising that the world's largest industrial economies were the biggest users of tin.[504]

According to the USITC, the U.S. paid an average of $31,000.00 per metric ton for imported unwrought (not alloys) tin products in 2024. In September 2024, tin ingots sold for $35,000.00 USD per metric ton in the China market, lead-free solder sold for $36,000.00 per metric ton, tin powder sold for $37,000.00 per metric ton, and tin concentrate (60%) out of Guangxi sold for

503 U.S. Geological Survey Tin Report 2024.

504 UN Comtrade 2024 data HS Code 2609, 8001. China's data wasn't available.

$33,000.00 per metric ton. According to the London Metal Exchange (LME), tin contracts closing in September 2024 averaged $30,975.00 per ton. That same month, LME certified warehouses held 4,625 tons of tin with 99% being stored at Port Klang, Malaysia.

International Tin Council - RIP

The International Tin Study Group (ITSG) was formed in 1947 to assess the global tin supply chain, ultimately leading to the International Tin Agreement (ITA) in 1954 and forming of the International Tin Council (ITC) in 1956. The ITC was established as a cartel consisting of the major tin producers and buyers with the intent to control the supply and thus the market price of tin. The group's intent was to benefit the member countries economically by artificially raising and sustaining tin prices. To do this, the ITC initially purchased and maintained 50,000 metric tons of tin as a buffer stock so they could acquire it when needed to raise the price of tin.

Over time, new tin producers refused to join the ITC or abide by the ITA and several members defected from the organization to sell their tin in contravention to the ITA in pursuit of higher profits. Also, cheaper alternatives became available such as plastic, aluminum, and recycled tin material. Consequently, the ITC went from controlling 71% of tin production in 1981 to just 57% in 1985. The ITC continued to purchase tin for its buffer stock, up to 64,000 tons, to manipulate its pricing to its advantage, but they never purchased enough to do so. Also, they lost large sums of money betting on tin futures, although they could no longer manipulate the global market to guarantee the desired outcome. By 1985, they were $3.4 billion in debt (in today's value).

Due to this debt caused by their decreasing control of the tin market, the ITC collapsed as a cartel in 1985. Creditors who loaned money to the organization subsequently sued the ITC to recover their losses. It was discovered that the ITC (the tin producing nations) bought tin futures using unauthorized loans which were not approved in the ITA. Because the ITC was established in England, the British government granted the organization a level of legal immunity. Ultimately, member countries refused to take legal accountability for their ITC representatives and never paid their outstanding debts to the creditors.[505]

505 Chandrasekhar, S. "Cartel in a Can: The Financial Collapse of the International Tin Council." Northwestern Journal of International Law & Business, 1989.

Today, the International Tin Association (ITA) still exists which was founded in 1932 and consists of eleven members: Belgium, Poland (both are consumer nations), Peru, Bolivia, Brazil, DRC, China, Thailand, Malaysia, Indonesia, and Australia. This is much less than the original 24 members who joined the ITC in 1954. ITA is not a price manipulating cartel but provides a forum for members to discuss tin business of mutual interest. The ITA also provides market intelligence relating to tin supply, demand, pricing, and trends to its membership. ITA offers their vision of the future tin market with TIN2030 where they see an increase in tin demand with more extracted in environmentally sustainable ways. They predict global tin needs will reach 500,000 tpa which will exhaust existing resources by the year 2033, indicating the tin industry is heading towards catastrophic disruption.

Actions Taken

The 2010 Dodd-Frank Wall Street Reform and Consumer Protection Act Section 1502 required the SEC (Securities Exchange Commission) to establish regulations addressing the disclosure of identified conflict minerals reference the DRC (Democratic Republic of the Congo.) Subsequently, tin, tungsten, tantalum, and gold produced by the DRC were determined to be conflict minerals.

A company would qualify for a 10% tax credit under the Section 45X Advanced Manufacturing Production Credit if their tin products are "purified to low alpha emitting tin which has a purity of greater than 99.99% percent by mass and possesses an alpha emission rate of not greater than 0.01 counts per hour per centimeter square." Tin with lead impurities used in solders release alpha particles which can cause errors in DRAM memory cells in electronics.

Incentives & Tariffs

- Domestic mining companies receive a 22% depletion allowance (there are none) while foreign companies receive a 14% rate (there are none) for their tin extraction operations.
- Despite its high importation rates and no primary smelter production, tin was included in the Trump administration's April 2025 tariff schedule with a minimum 10% tariff.
- In 2024, the U.S. International Trade Commission revoked a 122.5% tariff on imported Chinese tin mill products instituted in 2023 because the U.S. was not "materially injured" by them. Tin

mill products from China still retain a 25% Section 232 tariff instituted in 2018.[506]

U.S Supply Chain Security Strategy Moving Forward

The U.S. has an insecure tin position as it imported an average of more than 75% of its needs for primary production and there is no indication this will change. To date, the U.S. has ensured that it only gets negligible amounts of tin from China. At current consumption rates, the world could exhaust its tin resources by 2033.

Multi-pronged Approach

- The U.S.' primary way ahead is maintaining positive trade relationships with the major South American tin producers and consider partnering with specific companies to address high energy consumption needs by providing utility-scale solar energy with battery back-up.
- In 2022, the U.S. National Defense Stockpile reported holdings of 3,578 metric tons of tin while the Defense Logistics Agency (DLA) announced it would dispose of 688 tons in 2023, 640 tons in 2024, and 640 tons in 2025. This would leave the U.S. with 1,610 tons which would last two weeks, based on an annual consumption of 37,000 metric tons for 2024.
- The U.S. recycled an estimated 18,000 tons of tin in 2024 from old and new scrap.
- Depending on the use case, tin can be replaced by aluminum, steel, glass, plastic, and epoxy resins in solders. It is likely if global consumption continues to grow as trends show and do not discover any new major deposits, we will exhaust our limited world supplies of tin. If so, we will see in our lifetime what the forced substitution of a mass-use commodity looks like. This will obviously have a negative economic impact on the major tin producing countries and place increasing demand on aluminum, raising prices.

506 This is largely tinplated steel cans.

U.S. Tin Imports 2024 (metric tons)			
Country	Volume	Value	Price/Ton
Peru	9,100	$282 million	$31,000.00
Bolivia	8,400	$258.2 million	$30,700.00
Brazil	2,300	$71.9 million	$31,200.00
Indonesia	2,000	$55.3 million	$27,600.00
Poland	1,300	$42.1 million	$32,400.00
Canada	136	$3.9 million	$28,700.00
China	2	$46,700.00	$23,350.00
Mexico	144 kg	$8,500.00	$59,000.00
Others	1,500		
Total	**24,800**	**$769.7 million**	**$31,000.00**

*The U.S. imported about 24,800 tons of unwrought tin products valued at $769 million for an average price of $31,000.00 per metric ton.

*The U.S. imported 19,800 tons from South America or 80% of total imports. Almost nothing came from China and 9% came from BRICS countries.

**Data from USITC HTS code 8001.10.0000*

Titanium (Ti)

Background

Titanium is an abundant metal with high strength and corrosion resistance qualities and is often found in the minerals rutile and ilmenite. Because titanium has the highest corrosion resistance and strength-to-density of any metal, it is used in alloys for the aerospace industry. Titanium is also used widely in the medical field to include surgical instruments, implants, and prostheses. In the U.S., 95% of titanium dioxide (TiO2) is used in the pigment industry (like paints) with the rest distributed among welding-rod coatings, carbides, chemicals, and titanium metal (like high-performance jet engines). Titanium production is an energy intensive process where titanium ores (ilmenite & rutile) are converted to titanium sponge which is then melted into ingots and slabs.

In 2024, the world produced almost 9.4 million tons of ilmenite and rutile concentrates with China producing 3.3 million tons (35%) and African countries producing 3.8 million tons (40% - led by Mozambique and South Africa). The U.S. produced just 100,000 tons while Canada contributed 350,000 tons. The U.S. imported 600,000 tons of both concentrates which was 86% of its consumption needs. Most of these came from South Africa (32%), Madagascar (16%), and Canada (13%). Since the U.S. has an estimated 2 million tons of reserves, at current consumption rates, it would exhaust this in just three years.

In 2024, the world produced an estimated 320,000 metric tons of titanium sponge with China leading the way with 220,000 tons (69%), followed by Japan with 55,000 tons (17%), Russia 20,000 tons (6%), Saudi Arabia 15,000 tons (5%), and Kazakhstan 14,000 tons (4%). The U.S. produced less than 500 tons from a single company. The U.S.' two other remaining sponge production plants closed in 2016 and 2020 due to increasingly low prices by foreign producers and the resulting inability to compete.

The U.S. depends on imports for 95% of its needs, bringing in a total of 40,000 metric tons of titanium sponge metal products valued at $520 million for an average of $13,000.00 per ton. The U.S. imported most of their sponge from Japan (82%), Kazakhstan (9%), and Saudi Arabia (7%). The U.S. produced 850,000 metric tons titanium dioxide pigment (TiO2), imported another 250,000 tons, and were net exporters, shipping out 360,000 tons. Ti02 pigment averaged $3,200.00 a ton.

Chemours, NYSE: CC

Chemours is an international American chemical manufacturing company which is a spin-off from DuPont with operations in North America, Europe, South America, and Asia. The company owns and runs a mine in Florida and two in Georgia, extracting ilmenite, staurolite, and zircon. The company has a 1.1 million tpa TiO2 capacity. In 2024, Chemours made a net profit of $86 million for a margin of just 1.5% which was better than 2023 when they had a net loss of $237 million. The company faces up to $720 million in environmental remediation liabilities for cleaning up 109 different sites that are either currently or previously owned.

Honeywell Electronic Materials

Johnson Matthey Inc. bought the specialty metals company Alta Group in 1992 and subsequently opened a titanium sponge manufacturing plant in West Valley City, UT in 1996 (west of and adjacent to Salt Lake City). Allied Signal Inc. purchased Johnson Matthey Electronics in 1999 and merged with Honeywell that same year. Honeywell Electronic Materials in Salt Lake City makes low volumes of high-purity sodium-reduced titanium sponge, primarily for the electronics industry, with an estimated capacity of a very modest 500 tpa.

ATI Titanium LLC

ATI (Allegheny Technologies Incorporated), a subsidiary of ATI Materials, is a private U.S. specialty materials company with a titanium sponge production facility located in Rowley, UT on the western edge of the Great Salt Lake which opened in 2009. Their plant was built for a 12,000 tpa capacity and is adjacent to U.S. Magnesium's operation which makes sense as the titanium processes uses magnesium. However, ATI idled their plant in 2016 to cut costs as their products were not competitive with global titanium sponge prices. Also, they needed to update their plant, which was not possible with current prices. The plant remains closed as of 2024.

Parent company ATI Materials has a titanium melt facility in Oregon with four furnaces (closed in 2016) and another melt facility in Washington State. The company purchases titanium scrap and titanium sponge from suppliers in Japan and Kazakhstan to make its specialty titanium products. The company had sales of $4.3 billion in 2024 with a net income of $367 million for a margin of 8.4%. In 2023, they had sales of $4.1 billion with net income of $410 million for a margin of 9.8%. The company's titanium products represented 18% of overall sales in 2024.

Titanium Metals Corporation

TIMET is a private U.S. company founded in 1950 and has operated a titanium sponge production facility near Henderson, NV since 1951 with a 13,000 metric tpa capacity. TIMET has an international presence with eight separate titanium mills operating in the U.S., France, and the U.K. As early as 2018, TIMET recognized that they were being priced out of the global titanium market and it was cheaper to import titanium sponge than it was to produce it at their Henderson facility. Also, they operated equipment from the 1950s and they required a large capital investment to update their antiquated facility. In 2020, the company idled the plant and it remained closed through 2024.

Berkshire Hathaway bought TIMET in 2016 as part of their deal acquiring Precision Castparts Corporation. In 2024, TIMET began construction of a new titanium smelter in West Virginia at the site of the mothballed Century Aluminum production plant. However, the parent company Berkshire is using their BHE Renewables subsidiary to create an accompanying onsite micro grid to power the smelter. The solar array will need to supply 106 MW of power with a 50 MW LFP (Lithium Iron Phosphate) battery system.[507]

Actions Taken

In 2017, TIMET filed an anti-dumping (AD) and countervailing duty (CVD) petition with the Department of Commerce against titanium sponge imports from Kazakhstan and Japan. However, the U.S. International Trade Commission refused to pursue the claim stating that TIMET's products did not compete directly with imported sponge products. TIMET requested a variety of protectionist measures including bilateral agreements, tariffs, and quotas to artificially elevate Ti sponge prices 30% in the U.S. market.

Australian company IperionX received a $12.7 million grant from the DOD through the Defense Production Act in 2023 to construct a titanium processing plant in Virginia. The company uses a less energy intensive refining process than the existing Kroll Process, with lower emissions, and can work with titanium scrap as feedstock.[508] It remains to be seen if IperionX can produce titanium

507 Hanley, Steven. "Timet To Power Titanium Factory With Local Solar Installation in West Virginia." Clean Technica, July 29, 2024.

508 Hydrogen Assisted Metallothermic Reduction (HAMR) and Hydrogen Sintering and

products at scale with lower prices than competitors like Japan and China. The company is also exploring mineral extraction operations in Tennessee.

In 2023, the Department of Defense awarded American company 6K Additive, LLC a $23.4 million grant to convert scrap material into high-grade metals and alloys including titanium, niobium, nickel, and tungsten (all of which are designated critical minerals).

According to the DARS (Defense Acquisition Regulations System) *48 CFR 252.225-7009 Restriction on Acquisition of Specialty Meals*, any specialty metal composed of titanium acquired by the DOD must be melted or produced in the U.S.

Incentives & Tariffs

A company would qualify for a 10% tax credit under the Section 45X Advanced Manufacturing Production Credit if their titanium products are "purified to a minimum purity 99% by mass."

Domestic mining companies receive a 22% depletion allowance (Chemours) while foreign companies receive a 14% rate (there are none) for their ilmenite/rutile extraction operations.

Titanium products were excluded from the Trump administration's April 2025 tariff schedule. The regular tariff schedule encourages the import of all titanium ores and concentrates. Tariffs on titanium metal products range from low (5.5%) to moderate (15%).

U.S Supply Chain Security Strategy Moving Forward

The U.S. has an insecure titanium position since their ilmenite/rutile reserves will run out at current consumption rates in 2034, making it even more dependent on imports. Expanding its relationship with Canada and husbanding finished titanium products will be crucial.

Multi-pronged Approach

- Because the U.S. no longer manufactured titanium sponge at scale since 2020, reducing the tariff from 15% to 5% would make sense. This can change if TIMET's and IperionX's operations come online.

Phase Transformation (HSPT) processes.

- The Defense National Stockpile Center (DNSC) sold off the remainder of its titanium sponge stock in 2005 which was 2,480 tons. The Defense Logistics Agency (DLA) announced it was acquiring 1,500 metric tons of titanium products in 2023, 15,000 tons in 2024, and 15,000 tons in 2025. Based on current annual consumption (40,000 tons), current stocks would last about nine months. Because titanium sponge reacts with oxygen and can explode, it is stored in sealed drums containing argon gas.
- While true data is unknown, it is estimated that the U.S. recycles 60% of its titanium products.[509]
- Depending on the use case, titanium competes with aluminum, steel, composites and other superalloys. In the pigment sector, titanium competes with talc, kaolin, and calcium carbonate.

U.S. Titanium Ore Imports 2024 (metric tons)

Country	Volume	Value	Cost/Ton
Madagascar	180,500	$58.6 million	$324.00
Mozambique	140,400	$40.2 million	$286.00
Australia	87,695	$79.6 million	$907.00
South Africa	77,400	$91.8 million	$1,186.00
Senegal	60,000	$17.4 million	$290.00
Ukraine	32,300	$30.1 million	$932.00
Others	11,800	$44.3 million	$3,750.00
Total:	**590,000**	**$362 million**	**$613.00**

509 Thomas, D. "Cost-Effective Environmental Sustainability." NIST, October 2022.

Tungsten (W)

Background

Tungsten, also known as wolfram, is brittle yet extremely hard and dense with the highest melting point and tensile strength of all metals. Tungsten is not found in its pure form but mainly in wolframite consisting of iron-manganese tungstate. Tungsten ore is converted to tungsten oxide (WO3) and commonly used to make tungsten carbide for use in wear-resistant tools in heavy industry. Tungsten is used in superalloys where extreme strength and wear-resistance is required such as aerospace applications and for the military in high-velocity armor penetrating rounds. Tungsten carbide shot is used in shotgun shells and the military's HIMARS DPICM warheads. In electronics, tungsten is used as a connector in integrated circuits and metallic films to replace wiring.

In 2024, the world produced 81,000 metric tons of tungsten content with China producing 67,000 tons (83%), Vietnam 3,400 tons (4%), and Russia 2,000 tons (2%). The U.S. no longer extracts any tungsten ores with the last mine in Utah closing in 2016.[510] Neither Canada nor Mexico mine tungsten, meaning the North American continent must import all its needs. The U.S. imported 1,500 tons of ores and concentrates and 8,900 tons of finished products. From 2020-2023, the largest portion came from China (27%), Germany (14%), and then Bolivia (8%). The world has an estimated 4.6 million tons of tungsten reserves with China accounting for 2.4 million tons (52%).

According to the UN trade database for 2024, the U.S. imported 2,500 tons of tungsten ore and concentrates while China imported 5,800 metric tons the year before which included major producers like Russia and North Korea. (There was no data available for China in 2024).[511] This meant China processed more of the world tungsten market than just what they produced and they then exported these refined tungsten products worldwide to other customers. Most likely, more than just one-third of the U.S.' imported tungsten products originated with China and then later passed through third-party countries like Germany. In 2024, tungsten trioxide (T03) concentrate averaged a low $250.00 per ton based on Rotterdam average pricing.

510 Scheelite Metals LLC extracted 275 tons of ore after opening and then closing their mine in 2016.

511 UN Comtrade 2023 & 2024 data HS code 2611.

Actions Taken

The 2010 Dodd-Frank Wall Street Reform and Consumer Protection Act Section 1502 required the SEC (Securities Exchange Commission) to establish regulations addressing the disclosure of identified conflict minerals reference the DRC (Democratic Republic of the Congo). Subsequently, tin, tungsten, tantalum, and gold produced by the DRC were determined to be conflict minerals.

In 2020, DARS (Defense Acquisition Regulations System) passed a DFARS (Defense Federal Acquisition Regulation Supplement) that prohibited the federal government from acquiring tungsten powder and heavy alloys from China, Russia, Iran, and North Korea. The effective date of implementation was August 25, 2022, and did not affect civilian supply chains. Embedded tungsten components in a finished electronic product were exempted.

In 2023, the Department of Defense awarded U.S. company 6K Additive, LLC a $23.4 million grant to convert scrap material into high-grade metals and alloys including titanium, niobium, nickel, and tungsten (all of which are designated critical minerals).

In 2024, Tungsten Parts Wyoming, Inc. petitioned the U.S. International Trade Commission (USITC) to initiate an antidumping and countervailing duty investigation into Chinese tungsten shot. Tungsten shot is used in shotgun shells for target shooting and hunting because it is non-toxic and has good density. Lead shot was outlawed in the U.S. in 1991 to protect fowl from ingesting spent shot which is toxic. The investigation is ongoing.

According to the DARS (Defense Acquisition Regulations System) 48 CFR 252.225-7009 *Restriction on Acquisition of Specialty Meals*, any steel alloy product with more than 25% tungsten content acquired by the DOD must be melted or produced in the U.S. For the military, this impacts their HIMARS rockets that employ tungsten ball bearings as projectiles for destroying "soft" targets like infantry in the open and trucks.

Incentives & Tariffs

A company would qualify for a 10% tax credit under the Section 45X Advanced Manufacturing Production Credit if their tungsten is "converted to ammonium paratungstate or ferrotungsten".

Domestic mining companies receive a 22% depletion allowance (there are none) while foreign companies receive a 14% rate (there are none) for their tungsten extraction operations.

Tungsten was excluded from the Trump administration's April 2025 tariff schedule. The normal schedule encourages the import of all tungsten products with overall low rates. China has a 20% tariff on tungsten concentrates and restricts its export to maintain sufficient reserves. As of February 2025, Chinese sellers must obtain an export license from the Ministry of Commerce before shipping their products.

U.S Supply Chain Security Strategy Moving Forward

The U.S. has an insecure tungsten position since tungsten ores are not extracted in North America and only one country in the Western hemisphere produces modest amounts (Bolivia). Most tungsten ores and concentrates are mined in China and Beijing has recently ordered the reduction in annual quotas to protect its own reserves and raise prices. China has achieved monopoly status and is a geographic production chokepoint.

Multi-pronged Approach

- The U.S. should stockpile a one-year supply of tungsten, reinforce trade relations with existing partners like Australia, and consider providing incentives for the opening of new mines in allied countries such as Canadian mining company Almonty's ongoing Sangdong tungsten mine project in South Korea.
- In 2022, the Defense National Stockpile held 6,500 tons of tungsten ores and concentrates and 5 metric tons of tungsten rhenium ingots.[512] The Defense Logistics Agency (DLA) disposed of 1,250 tons of tungsten ores and concentrates in 2023 and another 1,000 tons in 2024, leaving just 4,250 tons in the stockpile. In 2024, DLA acquired 293 tons of tungsten (no further description). In 2025, DLA intended to dispose of 550 tons of tungsten ores & concentrates while acquiring an additional 2,250 tons. Based on estimated annual consumption, a one-year stockpile would be 8,000 metric tons. Current estimated reserves of 6,243 tons would last about nine months.
- According to the International Tungsten Association, 35% of intermediate tungsten production used recycled scrap and end-of-life tungsten products were recycled at a 30% rate.

512 Rhenium improves ductility and reduces the ductile-to-brittle transition temperature of alloys, known as the "Rhenium Effect."

- Depending on the use case, tungsten can be substituted with molybdenum, niobium, and titanium. Other replacements include lead and depleted uranium which raise their own concerns.

U.S. Refined Tungsten Imports 2024 (metric tons)

Tungsten Powders, Waste, Scrap

HTS Code	Volume	Value	Price/Ton
8101	5,990	$217 million	$36,220.00

*The U.S. imported these articles from 38 different countries with 1,140 tons coming from China (19%)

Tungsten Carbides

HTS Code	Volume	Value	Price/Ton
2849.90.3000	1,488	$69.3 million	$46,570.00

The U.S. imported these products from 11 different countries with 651 tons from China (44%).

Ammonium Tungstates

HTS Code	Volume	Value	Price/Ton
2841.80.0010	1,426	$44.3 million	$31,000.00

The U.S. imported these articles from China with 978 tons (68%) and Germany 448 tons (32%).

Tungsten Oxides

HTS Code	Volume	Value	Price/Ton
2825.90.3000	637	$20.1 million	$31,550.00

The U.S. imported these from five different countries with only 27 tons coming China (4%).

Ferrotungsten

HTS Code	Volume	Value	Price/Ton
7202.80.0000	45.4	$1.4 million	$30,800.00

The U.S. imported these low volume products from four countries with only 574 kg from China.

* Overall, of the 9,586 tons of imported tungsten products, valued at $352 million, 2,796 tons came from China (29%) which was down from 35% in 2023.

** Data from USITC*

Vanadium (V)

Background

Vanadium is a metal with unusual qualities of hardness, corrosion resistance, density, and ductility. It is found in magnetite and is often produced secondarily from heavy oils flue dust, steel slag, and uranium production. Vanadium is often alloyed with steel to increase strength while reducing weight. Vanadium is used in wind turbine towers using high-strength low-alloy steel plates. Vanadium redox flow batteries are used for grid energy storage systems with the advantages of high discharge cycle life, low cost over life of the battery, and is non-flammable. Because upwards of 90% of vanadium is used as alloys, the global steel industry drives its overall demand and thus price.

In 2024, the world produced 104,000 metric tons of vanadium content with China producing 70,000 tons (69%), Russia 21,000 tons (20%), South Africa 8,000 tons (7%), and Brazil over 5,000 tons (5%). In the U.S., vanadium was historically recovered secondary to uranium mining operations in Utah. The U.S. stopped extracting modest vanadium volumes in 2020 because it became uneconomic. The U.S. did produce 8,200 tons of vanadium from secondary products like petroleum residues and spent catalysts. The World has 18 million tons of vanadium reserves with Australia accounting for 8.5 million tons, Russia 5 million, and China 4.1 million.[513]

The U.S. imported 7,580 tons of various vanadium products which represented 40% of its needs (2,500 tons of vanadium pentoxide, 2,300 tons of ash & residues, 1,800 tons of ferrovanadium). For all vanadium products from 2020-2023, the U.S. imported the largest portion from Canada (34%), Brazil (13%), Austria (11%), and South Africa (11%). The U.S. only majority-sourced low volumes of vanadium metal & powders from China. Vanadium pentoxide averaged $10,600.00 a ton in 2024.

The private company U.S. Vanadium in Arkansas produces refined vanadium products including electrolytes for redox flow batteries. Dutch owned AMG Vanadium in Ohio produces ferrovanadium and recovers vanadium from spent catalysts using a proprietary process. AMG's Advanced Metallurgical Group also purchased International Specialty Alloys from Kennametal Inc. in 2019 with facilities in Pennsylvania which specializes in vanadium alloys.

513 U.S. Geological Survey Vanadium Report 2024.

Actions Taken

According to the DARS (Defense Acquisition Regulations System) 48 CFR 252.225-7009 *Restriction on Acquisition of Specialty Meals*, any steel alloy product with more than 25% vanadium content acquired by the DOD must be melted or produced in the U.S.

A company would qualify for a 10% tax credit under the Section 45X Advanced Manufacturing Production Credit if their vanadium is "converted to ferrovanadium or vanadium pentoxide."

Incentives & Tariffs

Domestic mining companies receive a 22% depletion allowance (there are none) while foreign companies receive a 14% rate (there are none) for their vanadium extraction operations.

Vanadium was not/not excluded from the Trump administration's April 2025 tariff schedule. The tariff schedule encourages the import of vanadium with unfinished products coming in for free and other with overall low rates.

U.S Supply Chain Security Strategy Moving Forward

The U.S. has an insecure vanadium position since primary vanadium extraction is controlled 100% by the China-led BRICS coalition with over two-thirds coming from Beijing itself. If this political block could operate as a vanadium cartel, they could make U.S. acquisition efforts difficult and raise costs. However, to date, BRICS has not shown the inclination or ability to operate as an economic cartel for any commodity.

Multi-pronged Approach

- This is an example of where the U.S. should recognize Canada as part of its national industrial and critical minerals base. In one example, Canadian company Suncor received government grants from Ottawa to advance a vanadium recovery project from fly ash. The U.S. could consider providing incentives such as DOD offtake agreements for their product as presently only 23% of fly ash-sourced vanadium comes from Canada. The rest comes from Vietnam, Kuwait, and China.
- In 2022, the U.S. National Defense Stockpile held no vanadium reserves while the Defense Logistics Agency (DLA) with no plans to

acquire any through 2025. Based on estimated annual consumption, a one-year stockpile would be 14,000 metric tons.

- It is unknown how much vanadium is recycled annually but it is done throughout the industry. USGS estimates 40% of vanadium catalysts are recycled. U.S. Vanadium can recycle 97% of vanadium used in electrolytes of redox flow batteries. Various companies continue to find improved methods to recover vanadium from steel slag.
- In the steel industry, vanadium can be substituted with manganese, molybdenum, niobium, tungsten, and titanium. Vanadium redox flow batteries compete with other technology for grid support like LFP batteries.

World Vanadium Production 2024 (metric tons)			
Country	2020	2024	Reserves
China	70,000	70,000	4.1 million
Russia	19,500	21,000	5 million
South Africa	8,500	8,000	430,000
Brazil	6,600	5,000	120,000
Australia			8.5 million
Total:	**105,000**	**104,000**	**18 million**

U.S. Imports 2024

* The U.S. imported 2,100 metric tons of vanadium ores and concentrates valued at $8.5 million, averaging $4,000.00 a ton with 99% coming from Canada.

* The U.S. imported $22.4 million value of vanadium from slag, ash & residue with 63% coming from Kuwait.

* The U.S. imported 3,800 metric tons of vanadium oxides valued at $66.5 million, averaging $17,500.00 a ton with 96% coming from Brazil & South Africa

*The U.S. imported 2,390 tons of ferrovanadium valued at $81 million, averaging $33,890.00 a ton with 63% coming from Canada.

* The U.S. imported 102 tons of vanadium scrap and powders valued at $4 million averaging $39,200.00 a ton with 93% coming from China.

*The U.S. imported 10 tons of vandium metal valued at $1.1 million, avergaing $110,000.00 a ton with 53% coming from Canada.

** Data from USGS and USITC*

Ytterbium (Yb)

Background

Ytterbium is one of the seventeen REE (Rare Earth Elements) designated as critical minerals and is part of the heavy REE (HREE). Ytterbium is frequently found with other fellow REE in monazite and bastnaesite deposits and ion-adsorption clays. Ytterbium has few commercial applications which include for research, atomic clocks, to improve the strength of steel alloys, as a dopant in yttrium garnet lasers, in the dental sector for filling teeth, and as an x-ray contrast agent. Like thulium, ytterbium is one of the rarest of the REE and only about 50 tons a year are produced.

As mentioned in previous sections on other REE, production volumes are reported as REO (Rare Earth Oxides) and as an overall group total, not as specific elements. The U.S. has one REO operation at Mountain Pass in California which consists mainly of light REE and much less HREE. While the MP operation does produce ytterbium, it is in such low quantities that the company does not report it and separating it is uneconomic. It remains to be seen if MP Materials will separate and refine ytterbium products domestically or continue to ship them to China for refinement.

Like several other low-volume REE, the U.S. understands little about actual ytterbium production. This is because the U.S. has not established effective market surveillance tools and doesn't track its importation, grouping it together with other REE. While MP Materials has the potential to produce ytterbium, the U.S. has not done so through 2024 and is completely dependent on imports, with possibly 100% of refined ytterbium production originating in China. In August 2024, ytterbium oxide 99.99% purity traded in the China market for just $14,000.00 USD per metric ton.

Actions Taken

As discussed in previous REE sections, MP Materials has received grants through the Defense Production Act and from the Department of Energy to construct an REE processing facility at their Mountain Passs location and to build their Fort Worth, TX magnet facility. There is no confirmation that they will produce ytterbium.

As of 2023, Australian company Lynas Rare Earths received a total of $258 million in grants through the Defense Production Act to construct a HREE processing facility in Texas.

MPM qualifies for a 10% tax credit under the Section 45X Advanced Manufacturing Production Credit if their ytterbium products are "purified to a minimum purity of 99% by mass."

Incentives & Tariffs

Domestic REE mining companies receive a 14% depletion allowance (MP Materials) while foreign companies receive a 14% rate (there are none) for monazite, bastnaesite, and xenotime extraction operations.

REE were excluded from the Trump administration's April 2025 tariff schedule. That same month, China enacted 125% retaliatory tariffs on U.S. REE imports, meaning it was uneconomic for MPM to ship their REO to China for midstream refinement.

U.S Supply Chain Security Strategy Moving Forward

The U.S. has an insecure ytterbium position since it has a 100% import reliance with most refined products originating from China. The likely long-term threats to this position include China emplacing export restrictions on the U.S. and not being able to get ytterbium through the only other major HREE producer of Malaysia which provides another likely 13% of REO. To date, only China, the U.S., and Malaysia (Australia) have the technological sophistication to develop their own advanced REE processing capability.[514]

Multi-pronged Approach

- The U.S. should monitor the domestic, North American, and allied ytterbium value chain and determine when and if additional government assistance is needed.
- In 2022, the U.S. National Defense Stockpile did not hold any ytterbium reserves and the Defense Logistics Agency (DLA) announced no new acquisitions through 2025. A one-year supply of ytterbium may be 10 metric tons.
- It is unknown how much ytterbium is recycled or reused, but it is likely around 1% which is the overall rate for REEs. Recycling is difficult because the REE are mixed with other elements, are used

514 Vietnam has a limited REE refinement capability.

in such low volumes that little is recovered and usually involves hydrochloric acid.

- Ytterbium is difficult to substitute with other materials without significantly reducing performance. Ytterbium can substitute yttrium in certain applications.

A ytterbium lattice clock that uses photons to measure time. *(by N. Phillips NIST)*

Yttrium (Y)

Background

Yttrium is one of the seventeen REE (Rare Earth Elements) designated as critical minerals but is neither part of the light nor heavy REE. Yttrium is frequently found with scandium and other fellow REE in monazite and bastnaesite deposits, uranium, and ion-adsorption clays - it is never found by itself. Yttrium is commonly used along with europium in color televisions, in synthetic garnets and infrared lasers, as a component of superalloys, radars, with other critical mineral zirconium in ceramics, in isotope form to treat cancers, superconductors, and in lithium iron phosphate (LFP) batteries where yttrium is used to dope the cathode which provides better stability and longevity to the battery.

As mentioned in previous sections on other REE, production volumes are reported as REO (Rare Earth Oxides) and as an overall group total, not as specific elements. The U.S. has one REO operation at Mountain Pass in California which consists mainly of light REE. While the MP operation does have yttrium, it is in such low quantities (just 0.12% of overall TREO) that the company does not report it and separating it is uneconomic. It remains to be seen if MP will separate and refine yttrium products domestically or continue to ship them to China for processing.

The U.S. understands little about actual yttrium production because it has not established effective market surveillance tools and does not track its importation, grouping it together with scandium. Consequently, the U.S. guessed its importation totals in 2024 were 470 metric tons. While MP has the potential to produce yttrium, the U.S. has not done so through 2024 and is completely dependent on imports, with possibly 100% of refined yttrium production originating in China. U.S. Geological Survey believes anywhere from 10,000 to 15,000 tons of yttrium oxide were produced by all countries in 2024. China exported 2,900 tons of yttrium oxide compounds and metals, with most going to Japan, then Italy, the U.S., and South Korea. World yttrium reserves are estimated at 500,000 tons. In August 2024, yttrium oxide 99.999% purity traded in the China market for an extremely low $6,000.00 USD per metric ton.

A study analyzing China's yttrium market from 2000-2019 estimated 146,000 tons of yttrium was produced and processed or 7,300 tons annually. Of this total, only 14,500 tons were imported during various phases, 69,000 tons were exported, and 25,000 tons were lost during the fabrication and manufacturing stages. As an indication of major yttrium end uses, the largest amounts of yttrium were used to make phosphors, optic glasses, and then Nickel Metal Hydride (NiMH) batteries. Although the demand for yttrium grew over this period, its supply was even greater, leaving China with a large surplus.[515]

Actions Taken

As discussed in previous REE sections, MP Materials has received grants through the Defense Production Act and from the Department of Energy to construct an REE processing facility at their Mountain Passs location and to build their Fort Worth, TX magnet facility.

As of 2023, Australian company Lynas Rare Earths received a total of $258 million in grants through the Defense Production Act to construct a HREE processing facility in Texas.

MPM qualifies for a 10% tax credit under the Section 45X Advanced Manufacturing Production Credit if their products are "converted to yttrium oxide which is purified to a minimum purity of 99.999% yttrium oxide by mass or purified to a minimum purity of 99.9% yttrium by mass."

Incentives & Tariffs

Domestic REE mining companies receive a 14% depletion allowance (MP Materials) while foreign companies receive a 14% rate (there are none) for monazite, bastnaesite, and xenotime extraction operations.

REE were excluded from the Trump administration's April 2025 tariff schedule. That same month, China enacted 125% retaliatory tariffs on U.S. REE imports, meaning it was uneconomic for MPM to ship their REO to China for midstream refinement.

U.S Supply Chain Security Strategy Moving Forward

The U.S. has an insecure yttrium position since it has a 100% import reliance with most originating from China, although this could change as MPM's and Lynas' processing capabilities come online. The likely long-term threats to this position include China emplacing export restrictions on the U.S. and not being able to get yttrium through the only other major producer of Malaysia which provides another likely 13% of yttrium imports. Only China, the U.S.,

515 Favot, Marinella and A. Massarutto, "Rare-Earth Elements in the Circular Economy: The Case of Yttrium." Journal of Environmental Management, Volume 240, June 2019.

and Malaysia (Australia) have the technological sophistication to develop their own advanced processing capability.[516]

Multi-pronged Approach

- The U.S. should monitor the domestic, North American, and allied yttrium value chain and determine when and if additional government assistance is needed.
- In 2022, the National Defense Stockpile held 7 metric tons of high-grade and 18 tons of low-grade yttrium oxide products. The Defense Logistics Agency announced no plans to acquire yttrium through 2025. 250 metric tons of yttrium would be a one-year supply based on estimated annual imports for consumption. Consequently, known volumes of stored yttrium (25 tons) would last just five weeks.
- It is unknown how much yttrium is recycled or reused, but it is likely around 1% which is the overall rate for REE. Recycling is difficult because REE are mixed with other elements, are used in such low volumes that little is recovered and usually involves hydrochloric acid. One study determined that it was only economic to recycle yttrium from fluorescent lamps if the price of yttrium was above $14,000.00 a metric ton. With the current state of oversupply, it is cheaper not to recycle, which would require government mandates or other incentives.[517]
- Yttrium may be substituted with other materials but with lower performance. In just one example, research has been conducted into replacing yttrium with thorium in yttrium iron garnet (YIG) applications.

516 Vietnam has a limited REE refinement capability.
517 Favot, Marinella.

Zinc (Zn)

Background

Zinc is chemically similar to magnesium and is most commonly found in sphalerite, a sulfide mineral composed of zinc and iron. However, it is also recovered as flue dust from electric arc furnace steel smelting operations. Zinc is a trace element essential for the growth of plants, coral, humans, and other animals. Zinc deficiency in humans contributes to a variety of deficiencies and diseases. Zinc was produced in ancient times for use in alloys with copper to create brass. Worldwide, 60% of zinc is consumed as a protective coating for steel called galvanizing. By 2030, the International Zinc Association calculates 280,000 tons of zinc will be used annually in wind and solar products and 300,000 tons in energy storage.

In 2024, the world produced 12 million metric tons of zinc content with China contributing 4 million tons (25%), Peru 1.3 million tons (11%), and Australia 1.1 million tons (9%). The U.S. produced 750,000 tons, Mexico 700,000 tons, and Canada 200,000 tons, meaning North America combined for 1.6 million tons or 13%.[518] The U.S. has five operations producing zinc concentrate but just one primary smelter and one secondary smelter. The world has 230 million tons of zinc reserves with Australia accounting for 64 million tons (28%), China 46 million tons (20%), and Russia 29 million tons (13%). The U.S. imported 615,000 tons of zinc products with 58% coming from Canada, 16% from Mexico, and 7% from South Korea (averaged over 2020-2023). The U.S. imported 73% of its zinc needs for the year.

Teck Resources Limited (TRL), NYSE: TECK

TRL is a diversified Canadian company with headquarters in Vancouver that runs a variety of oil, coal, copper, zinc, and lead operations, including secondary products like molybdenum, indium, and germanium. They have operations in the U.S. (zinc, lead, copper), Canada (zinc, copper, coal), Australia (zinc), and Latin America (zinc, copper). In 2024, TRL was profitable with revenue of $6.48 billion and net profit of $203 million for a margin of 3%.

In 2024, the company produced 616,000 tons of zinc concentrate with 555,000 tons from Alaska and 60,000 tons from Peru. Teck processed this concentrate into 256,000 tons of refined zinc. However, the company issued

518 U.S. Geological Survey Zinc Report 2024.

guidance to draw down its U.S. operations 20%-25% to 365,000-400,000 tons by 2027. The lowered production guidance is most likely because Trek pays increasing royalty rates to the NANA Regional Corporation, an Alaska Native Regional Corporation. In 2027, the royalty rate goes up from the current 40% to 45% and then up to 50% in 2032 where it remains flat.

A long-term risk for TRL's Alaska zinc operations is legal liability from associated pollution since the EPA identified the Red Dog mine as the most polluting mining operation in the U.S. since 2016. In 2004, TRL was sued by local residents for 824 violations of the Clean Water Act which was settled before the trial date. A 2008 lawsuit involving wastewater discharge was settled with TRL agreeing to pay up to $120 million for remediation.[519]

Nyrstar NV, EBR: NYR – Financially Distressed

Nyrstar is a Belgian mining company with 4,000 employees that owns their Middle Tennessee zinc complex composed of two underground mines at Cumberland and Gordonsville with an onsite concentrate processing plant (50,000 tpa concentrate capacity) located at Gordonsville.[520] Nyrstar also has their East Tennessee zinc complex consisting of three underground zinc mines with the zinc concentrate processed onsite at their Young operation. Zinc concentrate from both operations is sent to their smelter in Clarkesville for further processing. The Clarkesville smelter is the only primary zinc producer in the U.S. In 2023, Nyrstar halted operations at its Middle complex due to low zinc prices.

As indicated by the company's temporary pause in zinc operations, Nyrstar is in a state of financial distress, losing $4.5 million in 2024. As background, Nyrstar previously bought debt-distressed mining companies and then declared bankruptcy itself in the U.S. in 2019. The same year, Singapore-based Trafigura Group became a majority shareholder as it provided Nyrstar with critically needed capital infusion. However, minority shareholders subsequently sued Nyrstar for $1.2 billion alleging the company provided Trafigura unreasonably favorable zinc offtake agreements which contributed to its bankruptcy. Litigation is ongoing. Nyrstar's stock has fallen dramatically from a high of $69.00 a share when it opened in 2007 to just $0.06 a share in June 2024. Nyrstar faces bankruptcy and dissolution in 2025.

519 Rosen, Yereth. "Zinc producer settles suit over Alaskan mine waste." Reuters, September 4, 2008.
520 Nyrstar is majority-owned by Singapore based Trafigura Group.

Titan Mining Corporation: Financially Distressed

Canadian company Titan Mining Corporation, part of the Canada-based Augusta Group, was created in 2012 and operates their Empire State zinc mine in northern New York which produced almost 30,000 tons of zinc in 2024.[521] The company suspended operations in August 2024 due to flooding of their underground mine. It was estimated that repairing their crusher and control room would take up to two months. The company has existing zinc offtake agreements with Glencore at fixed prices and is also exploring natural flake graphite operations on property that they own. In 2024, Titan had revenue of $64 million and a net profit of $6.5 million for a 10% margin. However, the company had a net loss of $10 million in 2023.

Hecla Mining Company: Financially Distressed

Hecla Mining, established in 1891, is a U.S. company headquartered in Idaho which is focused on silver, gold, lead, and zinc mining with several operations in Canada and North America. In 2024, their Alaska operations produced 51,200 tons of zinc with their Idaho operations producing a much smaller 13,500 tons. Their one Canada zinc operation produced 1,500 tons resulting in a combined total across all three operations of 66,200 tons for the year. In 2011, Hecla paid out a $263 million settlement to settle claims with the U.S. government, the State of Idaho, and the Coeur d'Alene tribe for a century of pollution. In 2024, the company had sales of $930 million with a net profit of $35.2 million for a 3.7% margin. This was much improved from the previous year where they realized a loss of $84 million. Over the last ten years (2023-2013), the company had seven unprofitable years, putting them underwater by $266 million.

Doe Run Resources

Doe Run is a private U.S. company with 1,200 employees operating several mines in Missouri, extracting lead, copper, and zinc concentrates. While the company is privately owned and does not publish its financial performance or mine production, they may produce 70,000 tpa of zinc concentrate. In 2018, Doe Run made an agreement with the EPA to spend $48 million to clean up 4,100 identified residential areas that were exposed to historic pollution from its lead production.

521 Augusta Group has an established history of flipping mines where they buy underperforming operations, improve them, then sell them.

Befesa Zinc Metal LLC

In 2021, American Zinc Recycling Corporation was bought by Belgium company Befesa SA and was renamed Metal Recovery Holdings LLC. The company has a refinery in North Carolina which produces special high-grade (SHG) zinc from 100% recycled Waelz oxide (WOX) which comes from electric arc furnace flue dust from steel smelting operations. In 2024, Befesa's smelter has a 141,000 tpa WOX capacity, ran at 65% capacity, and operated at a $17 million loss. Since the company sold 400,500 tons of WOX worldwide, its North Carolina smelter contributed 23% of the total. Befesa had revenue of $1.4 billion with an adjusted EBITDA of $242 million.

Actions Taken

The U.S. has taken no meaningful action to strengthen and secure its zinc supply chain.

Incentives & Tariffs

A company would qualify for a 10% tax credit under the Section 45X Advanced Manufacturing Production Credit if their zinc is "purified to a minimum of 99% purity by mass."

Domestic mining companies receive a 22% depletion allowance (Doe Run, Hecla) while foreign companies receive a 14% rate (Teck, Nyrstar, Titan) for their zinc extraction operations.

Zinc was excluded from the Trump administration's April 2025 tariff schedule. The regular schedule encourages the import of all zinc products with low overall rates.

U.S Supply Chain Security Strategy Moving Forward

The U.S. has an insecure zinc position since four of its six zinc producing companies are foreign owned and three of the six are financially distressed and facing bankruptcy. The U.S. has only one primary zinc smelter (financially distressed) and one secondary smelter and both are foreign owned. The U.S. imports three-quarters of its zinc products.

Multi-pronged Approach

- The U.S. should develop incentives to ensure its two remaining zinc smelters remain active which could include negotiations with the owners to provide utility-scale solar power and battery back-up to cut electricity costs.

- Since the U.S. imports most of its zinc products from Canada and Mexico, it should ensure continuing positive trade relations and additional incentives if necessary to ensure this supply chain integrity.
- In 2022, Defense National Stockpile held 7,118 tons of zinc. The Defense Logistics Agency (DLA) announced plans to dispose of 2,500 tons in 2023, 2,500 tons in 2024, and 2,500 tons in 2025. Based on estimated annual consumption, a one-year stockpile would be 820,000 metric tons.
- It is unknown how much zinc is recycled annually but it is assessed that anywhere from 70%-90% of zinc is reused in the diecasting industry. Industry experts estimate that global end-of-life recycling rates are 34%, rolled zinc is 95%, and EAF dust recycling in North America and Europe has reached 95%.[522]
- Depending on the use, zinc can be substituted by aluminum, magnesium, and even plastics.

U.S. Zinc Ore Imports 2024 (metric tons)

Country	Volume	Value	Cost/Ton
Peru	12,900	$31.1 million	$2,410.00
Canada	4,900	$5.6 million	$1,140.00
Egypt	87.7	$99,000.00	$1,130.00
Mexico	1.4	$4,550.00	$2,670.00
Total:	**17,880**	**$36.8 million**	**$2,067.00**

**UN Comtrade Data HS Code 2608*

522 www.zinc.org

Zirconium (Zr)

Background

Zirconium is chiefly found in the mineral zircon and is mostly recovered secondary to titanium (ilmenite, rutile) and tin mining. The metal has similar qualities to hafnium and is malleable, ductile, with high corrosion resistance and melting point qualities. Zirconium is used as a refractory in the metals smelting industry, as an opacifier in ceramics, and as an alloy in the production of nuclear reactors. A commonly used form of the metal is zirconium dioxide (ZrO_2) aka zirconia which is used to substitute diamonds in jewelry.

In 2024, the world produced 1.5 million metric tons of zirconium mineral concentrates with Australia contributing 500,000 tons (30%), South Africa 300,000 tons (20%), and China 100,000 tons (7%). The U.S. produced just 100,000 tons, importing 20,000 tons of zirconium products. From 2020-2023, the U.S. sourced most of its unwrought zirconium metal and powder from China (88%). The world has an estimated 70 million tons of zirconium oxide content in reserves with Australia accounting for 55 million tons (78%), South Africa 5.3 million tons (7%), and Senegal 2.6 million tons (4%).[523]

The Chemours Company: NYSE: CC, Financial Distress

Chemours is an American chemical company founded in 2015 when it spun off from DuPont and is known for the Teflon brand among other products like titanium dioxide (TiO_2) pigment and refrigerants. The company has production centers in North America, Europe, and Asia (Japan & China). It produces about 100,000 tpa zirconium ore as a coproduct of its ilmenite and rutile extraction operations. In 2024, Chemours made a net profit of $86 million for a margin of just 1.5% which was better than 2023 when they had a net loss of $237 million. The company faces up to $720 million in environmental remediation liabilities for cleaning up 109 different sites either currently or previously owned.

In 2023, Chemours, DuPont, and Corteva Inc. reached a $1.19 billion settlement with the EPA over their role in polluting water sources with cancer causing polyfluoroalkyl substances (PFAS).[524] Chemours agreed to pay $595 million which does not address claims by individuals, individual water suppliers, States, or the U.S. government. Additional litigation is ongoing and addi-

523 U.S. Geological Survey Zirconium Report 2024.
524 Corteva is also a spin-off of DuPont.

tional damages are likely in the future and could be substantial. Various countries are taking actions to limit or ban PFAS and HFCs (hydrofluorocarbons), negatively impacting Chemours' business model.

Actions Taken

In 2024, the DoD, through the Defense Production Act (DPA), awarded U.S. company Powdermet Inc. a $1.9 million grant to establish domestic production of titanium and zirconium powders for use in energetics (i.e. explosives) for ignition and fuel source applications.

According to the DARS (Defense Acquisition Regulations System) *48 CFR 252.225-7009 Restriction on Acquisition of Specialty Meals*, any specialty metal composed of zirconium acquired by the DOD must be melted or produced in the U.S.

Incentives & Tariffs

Under the Inflation Reduction Act a company would qualify for a 10% tax credit under the Section 45X Advanced Manufacturing Production Credit if their zirconium is "purified to a minimum of 99% purity by mass."

Domestic mining companies receive a 22% depletion allowance (Chemours) while foreign companies receive a 14% rate (there are none) for their vanadium extraction operations.

Zinc was excluded from the Trump administration's April 2025 tariff schedule. The regular schedule encourages the import of all zirconium products with overall low rates.

U.S Supply Chain Security Strategy Moving Forward

The U.S. has an insecure zirconium position since its primary producer of zirconium ores and concentrates, Chemours, operated at a loss in 2023 due to damages from litigation as a result of historic pollution. The company faces continuing litigation and future damages that could be significant. The zirconium ores the U.S. imports are from overseas, primarily South Africa and Australia.

Multi-pronged Approach

- The U.S. should develop a more robust domestic zirconium powder production capability which is needed as it currently imports 61% of these products from China.

- In 2022, the Defense National Stockpile held no zirconium and the Defense Logistics Agency (DLA) acquired just 230 tons of zirconium in 2024 and 2,300 tons in 2025. Based on estimated annual consumption of 100,000 metric tons, this would last nine days.
- Several companies in the U.S. recycle zirconium scrap like Monico Alloys in California, Orxy Metals in Georgia, and Exotech in Florida.
- Depending on the use, zirconium can be substituted by chromite, dolomite, niobium, titanium, and stainless steel.

U.S. Zirconium Ore Imports 2024 (metric tons)

Country	Volume	Value	Cost/Ton
South Africa	13,500	$28.9 million	$2,140.00
Australia	10,300	$20 million	$1,940.00
Senegal	4,370	$9.8 million	$2,240.00
Others	930	$2.9 million	$3,120.00
Total:	**29,100**	**$61.6 million**	**$2,118.00**

**UN Comtrade Data HS Code 2615.10*

About The Author

Eric Lyon is the CEO and owner of GW Strategies LLC, a company focused on strategic economic analysis to include the critical minerals space. Prior to this, Eric spent his career as an Army officer conducting worldwide special operations and competitive intelligence. In 2023, he published *The Lithium Economy* which analyzes all aspects of the global lithium value chain. In 2024, Eric wrote *Feed the Dragon*, a detailed work on China's battery minerals enterprise on the African continent.

Eric grew up in New England and attended the University of Connecticut where he earned a B.A. in Political Science and History and an M.A. in International Relations. He later attended the Harvard National Security Fellowship where he studied catastrophic climate change as a national security threat and the transition to a global green economy. Eric also used the GI Bill to attend the Yale Global Executive Leadership Program. Eric resides in Tucson, AZ and can be reached at his business email: *admin@gwstrategies.net*

The author's books are available on amazon.com